F983 19

D1031829

Lineberger Memorial

Library

Lutheran Theological Southern Seminary   Columbia, S. C.

The Art

of the

Question

F983 19

The Art
of the
Question

A Guide to Short-Term
Question-Centered Therapy

Marilee C. Goldberg, Ph.D.

John Wiley & Sons, Inc.
New York ● Chichester ● Weinheim ● Brisbane ● Singapore ● Toronto

I gratefully dedicate this book to my parents

Selma Crockin Goldberg
and
LeRoy Bennett Goldberg

whose love, support, and faith in me
have never been in question.

This text is printed on acid-free paper.

Copyright © 1998 by John Wiley & Sons, Inc.
Published by John Wiley & Sons, Inc.

All rights reserved. Published simultaneously in Canada.

Reproduction or translation of any part of this work beyond that permitted by Section 107 or 108 of the 1976 United States Copyright Act without the permission of the copyright owner is unlawful. Requests for permission or further information should be addressed to the Permissions Department, John Wiley & Sons, Inc.

This publication is designed to provide accurate and authoritative information in regard to the subject matter covered. It is sold with the understanding that the publisher is not engaged in rendering professional services. If legal, accounting, medical, psychological, or any other advice or other expert assistance is required, the services of a competent professional person should be sought.

Library of Congress Cataloging-in-Publication Data

Goldberg, Marilee C.
    The art of the question : a guide to short-term question-
centered therapy / by Marilee C. Goldberg.
       p.   cm. — (Wiley series in couples and family dynamics
and treatment)
    Includes bibliographical references and index.
    ISBN 0-471-12387-0 (alk. paper)
    1. Neuro-linguistic programming. 2. Questioning—
Therapeutic use. 3. Psychotherapy. 4. Thinking. 5. Cognition.
6. Cognitive-behavioral therapy. I. Title. II. Series.
    RC489.N47G65 1998
    616.89'14—dc21
                                     97-14144
                                         CIP

Printed in the United States of America
10 9 8 7 6 5 4 3 2 1

Series Preface

WILEY SERIES IN COUPLES AND FAMILY
DYNAMICS AND TREATMENT

Our ability to form strong interpersonal bonds with romantic partners, children, parents, siblings, and other relations is one of the key qualities that defines our humanity. These relationships shape who we are, and what we become—they can be a source of great gratification, or tremendous pain. Yet, only in the mid-twentieth century did behavioral and social scientists really begin focusing on couples and family dynamics, and only in the last several decades has the theory and findings which emerged from those studies been used to develop effective therapeutic interventions for troubled couples and families.

We have made great progress in understanding the structure, function, and interactional patterns of couples and families—and made tremendous strides in treatment. However, as we stand poised on the beginning of a new millennium, it seems quite clear that both intimate partnerships and family relationships are in a period of tremendous flux. Economic factors are changing work patterns, parenting responsibilities, and relational dynamics. Modern medicine has helped lengthen the life-span, giving rise to the need for transgenerational caretaking. Cohabitation, divorce, and remarriage are quite commonplace, and these social changes make it necessary for us to rethink and broaden our definition of what constitutes a family.

Thus, it is no longer enough simply to embrace the concept of the family as a system. In order to understand and effectively treat the evolving family, our theoretical formulations and clinical interventions must be informed by an understanding of ethnicity, culture, religion, gender, sexual preference, family life cycle, socioeconomic status, education, physical and mental health, and values and belief systems.

The purpose of the *Wiley Series in Couples and Family Dynamics and Treatment* is to provide a forum for cutting-edge relational and family theory, practice, and research. Its scope is intended to be broad, diverse, and international, but all books published in this series share a common mission—to reflect on the past, offer state-of-the-art information on the present, and speculate on, as well as attempt to shape, the future of the field.

Florence W. Kaslow
Florida Couples and Family Institute

Preface

The poet Rilke gave me my first memory of appreciating questions for their own sake. In *Letters to a Young Poet*, he wrote:

> *Be patient toward all that is unresolved in your heart.*
> *Try to love the questions themselves.*
> *Do not now seek the answers, which cannot be given*
>   *because you would not be able to live them.*
> *And the point is to live everything.*
> *Live the questions now.*
> *Perhaps you will then gradually without noticing it,*
> *Live along some distant day into the answers.*
>   — RAINER MARIA RILKE

When I first read these lines some 30 years ago, I could have never imagined the journey they foretold, or that someday a book about questions would be an answer I would "live into." But as I look back, the path is illuminated as if it were a connect-the-dots pattern, each dot standing for a significant question, or thought about questions, that I either heard, was asked, or asked myself. Cumulatively, these represent major stepping stones leading to, or contributing to, this book. I would like to share some of them with you.

* * *

While I was growing up, my mother often told this story about her mother, Emma, and *her* mother, Berthe, my great-grandmother. Emma, then 12 years old, moved with the family to a new neighborhood, and became friends with a girl who invited her home to play. It must have been quite a fancy place, for an impressionable Emma came rushing home to tell her mother about the silver, the furniture, the wonder of it all. When she finally paused in her excitement, my great-grandmother had only one comment, a single question that said everything about what *she* thought was important:

"But Emma, did they have <u>books</u>?"

That question must have made quite an impact on Emma. She passed it on to her daughter, my mother, Selma, who made sure I also got the message. I wish my great-grandmother could know her legacy that this spontaneous question contributed to her great-granddaughter's love of books, and eventually to her writing one about questions.

* * *

Only once has a question stunned me into silence. It was 1975, and I was an extern at the Philadelphia Child Guidance Clinic, when Jay Haley was still there. I had read and loved his book, *Uncommon Therapy: The Psychiatric Techniques of Milton H. Erickson, M.D.* Erickson was generally acknowledged as the world's foremost authority on hypnotherapy and brief strategic therapy. Many of my colleagues were making the pilgrimage to Phoenix, where Erickson lived, and not wanting to miss out on anything, I resolved to go, too.

I made the fateful call one weekday afternoon. Erickson himself answered, and though a little unnerved, I pushed on with my mission. We chatted for only a few minutes before he dropped the bomb:

"Young lady, what makes you think I have anything to offer you?"

That question virtually knocked the breath out of me. I finally stammered out something that must have been good enough, as I was soon in Phoenix for my first two-week visit.

Erickson certainly got my attention; only later did I understand his strategy. Recognizing that I lacked specific, compelling goals for that visit, he set out to teach me to *reach* for a future I wanted, and to *do* whatever is necessary to get there. By the end of those two weeks with him, my vague interest in a cross-country driving vacation became a burning desire with a commitment to back it up. I made that trip, and in those three months had many wonderful adventures, but none more important than what I learned from those seeds that Milton Erickson planted: the power of setting *worthy* goals to move *toward*, and *doing* whatever is required—step by step, or mile by mile—to accomplish them. This book is among the fruits I continue to harvest.

* * *

Neuro-Linguistic Programming (NLP) is based on a detailed, explicit analysis of how language structures "reality." Many years of working with the principles and practices of NLP provided the basis of my recognition that the structure of a question can put the speaker in particular worlds of perception, experience, and possibility. This, in turn, led to a major premise of this book:

While language structures reality, questions help structure language.

Leslie Cameron-Bandler, a codeveloper of NLP, discovered what she called "the virtual question." This is an unconscious, reality-shaping, automatic internal question that can make an emotional hostage of the asker. I was privileged to study with Leslie, and based on her work, I began asking this question of and about my clients:

> *What are the unsuspected personal questions that frame your reality, the knowing of which could help you understand your limitations—and transcend them?*

I learned to elicit and transform these self-queries, and watched in fascination as people grew into new, life-affirming versions of their old thwarting questions. I observed firsthand that a question can shape one's personal world.

*   *   *

An eye-opening incident in a graduate school seminar on interviewing alerted me that questions were far more important than I had suspected. The professor asked us, "Why am I teaching you about asking questions?" One student responded confidently, "So we can find out what we need to know in order to do therapy." The professor seemed taken aback, and grew quiet. Finally he replied, "No, my friend, that's only part of the story." And then, after another long pause, he declared:

> *"Most of the time, if you do it right, therapy is asking questions."*

*   *   *

Waiting for the train one day, I gazed idly at the tracks and noticed the dirt and grime oozing over the concrete walls of the track well. *"How ugly,"* I thought. In the next moment a question popped into my mind:

> *How else could you look at it, or think about it?*

Instantly, I saw an image of those walls transformed into a beautiful piece of pottery covered with an interesting variegated glaze. Recognizing the power of this question, I made a habit of asking it, and it has since transformed many other instances in my life. Because this query *automatically* endows the speaker with more perceptual choices and possibilities, I have made it a standard part of my training with clients, supervisees, and workshop and seminar participants.

*   *   *

Experiences with questions like that one led to my giving workshops called the *Power of Questions*. I designed a problem-solving exercise aimed at demonstrating this maxim:

> *A question can alter any circumstance.*

Of course, a circumstance includes one's attitude toward it. In all these years we've never encountered one problem that couldn't be resolved, improved, or dissolved by asking one or more "right" new questions.

* * *

In many courses with Fernando Flores on communication, linguistics, and philosophy, he emphasized the power of organizing one's life around a single question. His was, "What is effective action?" I began asking this one about therapy and change:

What makes for real and <u>enduring</u> therapeutic success?

Fernando's work, and the answers elicited by my question, inspired many of the theories, models, and clinical practices in this book.

* * *

Hal Zina Bennett, a widely published author, and my first serious writing mentor, was very helpful in my early writing about questions. He asked this one often, and it continues to guide me:

"What is the question with heart?"

I've come to realize that many of the truest questions are asked not with the mind, but with the heart, not even in words, but with a spacious acceptance that some people call love.

* * *

Thrilled to have a book contract, and intimidated by fulfilling it, I petitioned Sam Kirschner, a highly respected author and marriage and family therapist, to mentor me through the process. Without Sam, and *his* questions to me, this book might never have seen the light of day. It has been said that:

A powerful question alters all thinking and behaving that occur afterward.

Sam shot a bull's eye early on. "You're *not* going to make your readers plow through all this, *are* you?" he asked in his characteristic, inimitable way. From that moment, my criteria questions for writing became, "What's essential?" and "Is this as succinct as possible?" For his editing prowess, we all have much to thank Sam for. And for his guidance, brilliance, wisdom—and patience—my gratitude is boundless.

* * *

Late one night, near the beginning of writing this book, I was startled awake by a dream of which I remember only the following sentence:

A question not asked is a door not opened.

I wrote it down in the dark, and went back to sleep with the experience of having received an important gift. This image became a powerful touchstone for much of the writing about questions that now appears in these pages.

* * *

About halfway through writing, another unexpected gift offered an affirming glimpse into the possibilities of question-centered therapy. One of the women who transcribed the clinical sessions in the book commented:

"This stuff really works!"

Puzzled, I asked "What stuff?" She answered, "You know, what you're teaching your clients. I've been listening to those sessions," she went on, "and it's really made a difference. My husband and I are doing very well." Intrigued, I persisted, "What kind of difference, and what can you tell me about that specifically?" She explained that she had figured out what questions her husband asked himself when he came home from work, and why her old way of greeting him made him grumpy, instead of happy to see her. She next asked herself, *"What can I do instead?"* and came up with a plan that worked beautifully. You'll find the session that led to her insight, *and* her new behavior, in chapter 6, which contains the first full therapy session in the book.

* * *

Naturally, while writing, I've asked myself repeatedly:

What can my readers gain from this book?

The essence is that asking the right questions helps clients think more clearly, take greater responsibility for themselves, and accomplish their goals more easily. They also communicate and engage in relationships more effectively. They consistently say they experience more happiness, freedom, and choice in their lives.

I asked some of my clients to comment on the difference that question-centered therapy had made for them. One woman, a 45-year-old accountant, put it this way: "It was a relief when I finally understood that asking the wrong questions practically programmed those problems I had, *and* stopped me from figuring out how to solve them. When I started asking more questions, and learned how to ask helpful ones, I put my hands on the steering wheel, and I knew how to go in the direction I wanted." She ended by saying that for her,

> ". . . *learning to ask the right question was like cracking the code on change.*"

Acknowledgments

The simple question, "What am I grateful for?" can exert a profound influence on one's consciousness, especially if it is asked often, and wholeheartedly. While traveling the long road from beginning idea to completed manuscript, I've been enriched with an abundance of answers in the generosity and valuable contributions of many friends along the way. At the head of the list are a few whom I single out to thank. Joan Barth, Larry Becker, Wayne Coleson, Sonia Helgesson, Rebel Holiday, Ken Hom, David Norris, and Audrey Reed each devoted endless hours to this book and tireless encouragement to me. My clients, supervisees, and workshop and seminar participants have been my finest teachers and best sources of inspiration. Ed Adams has been constant in his love, humor, patience, and support.

I am especially grateful for the team that made this book a reality: Florence Kaslow, the editor of this series, for believing in me and my ideas—and taking a chance on both; Kelly Franklin, my editor at Wiley, for being such a good friend and helpful guide; Mavis Smith, for her wonderful illustrations; Sam Kirschner, for his commitment, partnership, and brilliant guidance.

I also gratefully acknowledge: Marjory Alper, Paula Bram Amar, Beverly Amick, Steve Andreas, Richard Bandler, Bob Barth, Kathy Beaudoin, Hal Zina Bennett, Michael Berenbaum, Renee Blaker, Peter Bloom, Jim Bohannon, Tara Brach, Michael Broder, Lillian Brown, Deva Burns, Leslie Cameron-Bandler, Selena Chronister, Charlie Cicerale, Sid Clearfield, Grace Crouteau, Tom Curren, Jim de Leo, Cory de Torres, Robert Dato, Robert Dilts, Toni Dungan, Eileen East, Sandra Eliot, Alan Entin, Werner Erhard, Milton H. Erickson, Dean Everette, Fernando Flores, Bill Friedman, Maurice Friedman, Joel Fuhrman, Jeanette Gallagher, Susan Gardinor, Steve Garment, Jim Garrison, Michael Gelb, Nusa Maal Gelb, Justin Goldberg, Renee Singer Goldberg, Steve Goldberg, David Goldring, Pat Goldring, Vera Goodkin, Bert Gordon, David Gordon, John Grinder, Cheri Gurse, Isaac Harris, Inez Hayes, Luke Henderson, Naomi Henderson, Jaakko Hintikka, Hallock Hoffman, Bill Holland, Fran Holland, Charles Howard, Norie Huddle, Tom Hughes, Paul Jensen, Spencer Johnson, Frank Johnston, Brad Keeney, Sasha Kintzler, Larry King, Diana Adile Kirschner, Beth Koren, Tedd Koren, Bill Lamond, Dena Mallach, Martha Manning, Peg McGrath, Janice MacKenzie, Hyman Meyers, Lynn Turner

Mitchell, Marilyn Mohr, Terry Mollner, Sharon Drew Morgen, Susan Morris, Alexandra Mummery, Al Neuharth, Paul Osimo, Liz Plummer, Laurie Poss, Nancy Post, Brad Pressman, Dave Price, Mr. Alex Oliveras, Robert Rabbin, Gail Raymond, Brian Regnier, Robin Adams Richardson, Hildy Richelson, Stan Richelson, Grandmaster Jhoon Rhee, Joanna Roth, J. Lee Rutenberg, Eryn Paul Sackman, Bill Sanda, Doug Sauber, Roger Schank, Ken Schatz, Linda Schatz, Barbara Seidel, Dean Shapiro, Robert Shaw, Dawn Simons, Metha Singleton, Marsha Shank, Elizabeth Skrapits, Nancy Speelman, Sarah Stang, Arthur Stein, David Strohl, Susan Stuart, Lou Tenaglia, Renata Tesch, Linda Noble Topf, Michael Topf, Liz Treher, Master Chris Yu, Master Linda Yu, Leonard Waks, Walter Wehrle, Brandon Wheeler, Jack Wheeler, Tim White, Shadow Wolf, Cindy Wuthrich, and Jackie Zilbach.
    Thank you all.

For information on workshops, seminars, or presentations,

you may contact Dr. Goldberg at 1-800-250-7823.

Foreword

Every decade or so brings forth a seminal and breakthrough contribution to the field of psychotherapy. In the 70s, Minuchin's *Families and Family Therapy* (1974) pioneered the systemic viewpoint. In the 80s, Bradford Keeney's *Aesthetics of Change* (1983) elucidated the fundamentals of epistemology and cybernetics as they relate to psychotherapy. And now in the 90s, we have Marilee Goldberg's *The Art of the Question: A Guide to Short-Term Question-Centered Therapy.*

You might ask, "What is the paradigm shift inherent in asking questions? After all, questions have played a prominent role in exploring and understanding the truth since the days of the Socratic method and the Babylonian Talmud. Furthermore, every major branch of psychotherapy has used question asking as either a method for diagnosis or, more recently, as in the Milan family therapy school, as a basis for intervention."

The answer is quite simple. *The Art of the Question* focuses on questions themselves and not on the responses. While all the great philosophical traditions and psychotherapy classics have concentrated on the answers, this book focuses on the art of question development. It promotes the ability to ask the right questions at the right time. This, in and of itself, is a dramatic shift—a breakthrough of enormous proportions.

And this shift is extremely timely, since the climate of these times makes it even more difficult to appreciate the importance of questions. The emergence of new technologies, coupled with what they have made possible has resulted in more impatience with delay and disinterest in process than ever before. People want answers and they want them immediately. Whether the context is personal or professional, whether the problematic issue shows up in marriage or in business, the prevalent Zeitgeist is, "fix it and fix it now."

It is also problematic that the imperative of immediate answers and "quick fixes" has led to the seeming expediency of linear, cause-effect thinking. Yet, in most situations and in most of our cases there is usually no single cause for suffering or dysfunction. Shifting to an emphasis on the art of asking questions is a highly useful antidote to this cultural condition. Both clients and therapists who use questions skillfully become more process-driven so that deeper issues and concerns can manifest themselves and deeper healing can take place.

This book shows the reader how to develop the art of question asking in the service of change and growth. It is divided into three main sections. The first clarifies the role of questions in human functioning, psychopathology, and psychotherapy. The second unit describes the question-centered approach to individuals, with case studies and annotated transcripts. The third section explores couples' work using case studies and transcripts. The case material is fresh and exciting. The reader is privy to the internal questions of the therapist along with the interventions that emanate from those queries.

As Keeney wrote, "A question, by proposing a distinction, constructs its answers." This book helps the reader to generate the passionate questions necessary for learning and change. It is a book for therapists and clients. It is a book for executives and consultants. It is an important book for everyone who is searching for the keys to transformation.

Sam Kirschner, Ph.D.
Psychologist and Management Consultant
Gwynedd Valley, Pennsylvania

Contents

PART THREE

Question-Centered Therapy with Couples

PART FOUR

Conclusion

PART ONE

Understanding the Issues

1

What Makes Questions Important?

Everything we know has its origins in questions.
Questions, we might say, are the principal intellectual
instruments available to human beings.

— NEIL POSTMAN

To ask what makes questions important, one might just as easily wonder: "What makes language important?" or "What makes communication important?" or "What makes thinking important?" In other words, the subject of question asking is as primary and universal as any consideration about the ways that human beings perceive, think, feel, behave, relate, create, change, and evolve. In fact, none of these—language, communication, or thinking—could even be conceivable without the phenomenon called *question*.

If "Language [is] the house of Being . . . ," as Heidegger (1971, p. 135) wrote, then questions are the primary means by which doing, having, accomplishing, and growing are catalyzed—and often even made manifest—in our lives. Because questions are intrinsically related to action, they spark and direct attention, perception, energy, and effort, and so are at the heart of the evolving forms that our lives assume. We refer here to questions and question asking in the most inclusive sense, those which occur externally in speaking and communicating, as well as internally, in self-talk, internal dialogue, or thinking. However, despite the omnipresence of questions in our lives, few people appreciate the inherent power and potential in them. Perhaps this is because, somewhat like the wind, it is their effect, rather than their presence, which is usually most conspicuous.

Questions and Therapy

Among those cognizant of the importance of questions are therapists, who regularly invoke the advantages of this recognition to the benefit of their clients. This book aspires to build on that recognition, based on the premise that the whole domain of question asking, both internal and external, represents a gold mine of interventions, strategies, and ways of thinking about therapy itself that can enhance both its effectiveness and efficiency.

While effective therapists are intuitively skilled question-askers, many have not had extensive training in question asking per se. Fewer still have been exposed to the rich terrain of internal questioning or the inherent access it provides to the very ground in which grow the fears, concerns, beliefs, and hopes which impel people to seek therapy. This same landscape of internal questions is fertile with therapeutic possibilities, and we focus extensively on these. We explore the potential of question-centered therapeutic interventions with individuals and couples, although in actuality, of course, this work also applies to other client populations, including families, groups, organizations, and communities.

Ironically, clients seek *answers*—what they think is needed to remedy difficult situations—when they come to therapy. But this search means they often look in the wrong place. Not realizing that "new" answers could carry similar limitations as any old ones, they also don't understand that fundamental change often depends on first asking better questions. Furthermore, most clients don't realize that many of the questions they already ask, both consciously and unconsciously, lie at the source of their discontent. If the truth be told, most people barely notice the questions they ask others, much less the ones they pose to themselves. At the same time, the reasons for this negligence are quite understandable.

The Importance of Questions "Versus" Answers

We live in an answer-oriented, fix-it-quick world. In the clamor for answers—sometimes *any* answer—we often overlook quiet distinctions and fresh perspectives which could reveal whole new worlds of possibilities. Moreover, sometimes the conditioned hunt for answers represents a desperate attachment to "knowing," and a simultaneous avoidance of any anxiety associated with not knowing, or even appearing not to know. This is ironic as well as unfortunate, for often the most bountiful answers are born only after long periods of gestation and living with not knowing.

Most likely our greatest thinkers and innovators are able to "live the questions," as the poet Rilke enjoined us to do. It is probable that these individuals cultivate a recognition that would also serve our clients well—that questioning plays a fundamental role in problem solving, creativity, and change. For example, the theory of relativity stemmed from a question Albert Einstein asked himself as an adolescent, when he wondered, *"What would the universe look like if I were riding on the end of a light beam at the speed of light?"*[1,2] Such original thinking requires curiosity, an openly inquiring mind, courage, and ease with not knowing. In asking a genuinely novel question, along with the willingness to receive unexpected answers, Einstein flung open a new perceptual door. *This* new door opened a new world for humankind as well.

It is important for clients to learn that the solutions they seek lie behind doors which could remain forever closed unless opened by the right questions. Moreover, if people repeatedly make queries such as: *"Why am I such a failure?"* or *"Why do I have all the bad luck?"* or *"Why did I have to be born into such a troubled family?"* they condemn themselves to a linguistic prison of their own unwitting construction. To escape, the most reliable keys, for individuals and couples alike, are forged from skills of self-observation, evident, for example, in questioning one's questions, especially the internal ones. Therefore, a vital aspect of empowered change, as presented in this book, depends on learning to notice such self-inquiries, as well as how to analyze and revise them in accordance with criteria associated with solution seeking and possibility, rather than problem-focus, limitation, and negativity. Since we basically walk the paths in life prescribed by our questions, it makes sense to ask those which can take us where we want to go.

This book is filled with examples of clients who did just that. Some of these cases comprise entire chapters, while others appear in the form of short clinical anecdotes. In each instance, the individual or couple had worked with the standard psycho-educational concepts and components of question-centered therapy. Each case illustrates a variation of the transformational power inherent in questions and questioning. Question-centered therapy seeks to make question-asking skills explicit and practical so they can be utilized with effectiveness and efficiency in the beginning, middle, and ending phases of therapy.

Question-Centered Therapy

The power of the question holds an honored place in our shared cultural and religious Western background. Among the first words God addressed directly to humankind—through Adam and Eve—was the question, *"Where art thou?"* (Genesis 3:9). The power of the question also holds an esteemed place in mythology. In the quest for the Holy Grail, Parzival succeeded only when he asked the right question, having failed before when he hadn't thought to ask any at all. (Maher and Briggs 1988, p. 33) For many clients, therapy represents a quest. Their Grail may be a sense of authenticity, relief from depression, or the transformation of a troubled marriage into a fulfilling one. That quest began with questions such as: *"What's wrong?" "Is it bad enough to do something about it?" "What do I want instead?"* and *"Do I want that enough to work at it?"* Clients best walk the therapeutic path accompanied by questions like, *"Am I still on the right road?"* or *"Am I moving in a helpful direction?"* Moreover, they travel most expeditiously with their way lit by questions such as, *"How can I use this (anything that happens) to help me on my journey?"*

For clients, making this quest successfully requires being open to such inquiry. Their success is facilitated by taking a learning attitude, rather than a judgmental one, toward themselves, others, and their difficulties. In best-case scenarios, therapy results in more than resolving presenting problems or even achieving important goals. Clients strengthen their ability to keep facing life's inevitable challenges and disappointments, tempering this determination with forgiveness and compassion. They learn to strike that balance between certainty and humility that each of us needs for our lives to be filled with generous measures of grace, humor, love, and success.

Therapists are midwives to these quests, upon whatever level they are undertaken. Steeped in the recognition that language creates reality, question-centered therapists also understand how profoundly questions help structure the language that builds those realities. These therapists appreciate that clients' questions— internal and external, conscious and unconscious—exert a profound influence on confining them to the worlds they want to leave, and hold keys to help them move into the worlds they desire to inhabit.

The question-centered therapist holds the same healthy respect for questions as she[3] does for fire, knowing that both have the ability to create as well as devastate. As Nobel physicist Isaac Isador Rabi commented, "There are questions which illuminate, and there are those that destroy. I was always taught to ask the first kind"[4] Therapists with these sensibilities understand that the art of the question means to wield this linguistic instrument with consciousness, respect, and finesse. These therapists know they ask questions for much more than gathering information, for many of their finest, most leveraged interventions are question-centered ones. For these clinicians, questions are not at the periphery of therapy. Rather, like the treasure hidden in broad daylight, questions are at the heart and soul of therapy.

Question-Centered Therapy and Psycho-Education   The psycho-educational foundation of question-centered therapy is based on several assumptions about the "best of all possible therapy worlds." In such a utopian world, an active therapeutic partnership would result in *more* than success with desired changes; it would also realize an empowerment ideal of therapy. Clients would integrate skills of change itself, of thinking and problem-solving proficiencies to help them continuously generate creative solutions to the inevitable challenges of life. For optimum reliability, such skills would include a commitment to practice self-observation, an ability to recognize patterns, and an appreciation of how language itself can either hinder or facilitate the perception and fulfillment of new possibilities and choices. Such an empowerment model would also help the mental health profession fulfill an implied and appropriate mandate of managed care; that therapy not only be effective and efficient, but also that it help prevent the need for more therapy in the future. The premises and practices of question-centered therapy can help us fulfill such a mandate.

This chapter sets the stage for presenting question-centered therapy. It does so by exploring some ways in which the phenomenon of the *question component* of language, communication, and thinking relates to the theory and practice of therapy. In section 1 we explore some of the functions of questions in language. In section 2 we consider the relationship between questions and change.

SECTION ONE:
THINKING ABOUT QUESTIONS

Some questions have the potential to change one's life, while others may affect only the next 10 minutes. Consider the impact of "Will you run for President?" contrasted with "Will you get the mail?" To ask "How much does that car cost?" or "Can you come to a session on Tuesday afternoon at 3:00 o'clock?" solicits definitive, unambiguous answers. Questions such as, "What is the nature of change?" or "How is the formulation of a problem related to its resolution?" stimulate thinking. Inquiring of a client, "What are your goals in three and five years?" or of a client couple, "In what ways could you make your relationship more loving and satisfying?" are not meant to evoke facile endpoint answers; rather they invite exploration, introspection, and an expansion of possibilities.

More personal questions, sometimes thought of as existential or even spiritual, such as *"Who am I?"* and *"What is the purpose of my life?"* are often in the background of our clients' requests for help, even if these self-queries have never been articulated, or even noticed. Answers to questions such as, *"What do I want?"* and *"What do I believe is possible for me?"* are intrinsic to the ways we human beings make choices, and so are at the source of the actions we take and the resulting unfolding contours of our lives.

The Function of Questions in Language

We begin this exploration of questions by underscoring their function; that is, by focusing on what they *do*. Questions (including requests) initiate behavior or action, be it mental or physical. Questions focus and direct attention and energy, which is, of course, why we clinicians use them to orchestrate and guide therapy sessions. Therapists recognize, as do all effective interviewers, that the individual posing questions is generally in control of a given situation. On a mundane level, any parent attempting to distract a cranky baby by asking questions such as, "Did Johnny see this pretty new toy?" has intuitively attempted to take advantage of the attention-directing function of questions.

Questions imply relationship, whether between people or between different parts of ourselves. Why would anyone even bother to ask a question unless expecting a response, somehow, somewhere, sometime? Some people say they "can't *not*" answer questions, that answering is simply automatic for them. This may be because questions invoke that part of us that feels compelled to "close a gestalt." The importance of questions also lies in their intrinsic contribution to creative and critical thinking, which renders them fundamental for problem solving and decision making. Furthermore, it is through questions that we operationalize curiosity into behavior, and as such they are the foundation of any kind of learning, be it formal, informal, or personal.

Questions and Statements   Language, at its most elementary, is comprised of two classes of speech: questions and statements. In this book, we point to an *inherent relationship* between these. We come to recognize statements as answers to questions that preceded them, even though those questions are usually silent, implicit, or simply assumed as background. There such questions live, albeit in nonarticulated "form," in the context of situations. As Postman noted, ". . . all the answers we ever get are responses to questions. The questions may not be evident to us, especially in everyday affairs, but they are there nonetheless, doing their work. *Their work, of course, is to design the form that our knowledge will take and therefore to determine the direction of our actions*" (Postman 1976, p. 144; my italics).

Thus, for instance, if an adolescent client makes a statement that he feels unworthy, this comment could be an answer to prior internal questions such as: "*Am I as worthy or capable as my best friend?*" or "*Will I ever be worthy in my father's eyes?*" or "*Will I be worthy enough to get accepted at the college of my choice?*" In this example, more therapeutic mileage could be accrued by discovering and addressing the context-setting question, than merely focusing on the client's statement, or rather, his answer.

Questions and Behavior   Behavior, as well as statements, can be understood as representing answers to background questions, those prior questions that were silent or implicit. For example, how a person prepares for a major presentation represents behavioral answers to self-questions such as, "*What makes my topic important to this particular audience?*" "*What are the key points likely to inspire, motivate, and empower them?*" and "*What's the best way to organize and present my material for maximum impact?*"

Behaviors in relationships also represent responses to internal questions. When a clinician suggests to her client that it would be helpful to bring his parents to a session, her behavior was a response to internal questions, such as: "*What could I learn about my client's difficulties by observing his interactions with his parents?*" or "*Would changes in the family system facilitate my client's ability to achieve his therapeutic goals?*" When a teenager with a new driver's license asks his mother if she's going out that evening, he could be asking himself something like, "*Could I get her car tonight?*" or "*Will she say anything about my driving at night if I don't ask about it directly?*"

Even the ways we behave in different situations represent our answers to prior questions, usually unspecified or implicit ones. For example, upon entering a museum or library, our behavior reflects answers to, "*What behaviors are appropriate here?*" That same self-query, this time at the beach in hot summer weather, elicits quite a different response. When my client, Bill, decided to run for the school board, his behavior represented "No" to the question, "*Am I satisfied with the job the present Board is doing, especially for children with ADD, like my son?"* His choice also represented affirmative answers to: *"Could I make a contribution here?" "Do I have the time and energy to devote to this?"* and *"Am I willing to commit myself to such a venture at this time?"*

SECTION TWO: QUESTIONS AND CHANGE

Because questions are intrinsically related to action, they are naturally also at the fulcrum of change. It is probable that intentional change is always catalyzed by questions, be they internal or external, linguistic or nonlinguistic, or even whether they were noticed at all. Questions are also inherent to change due to the temporal assumption built into the linguistic form itself. Questions innately call for answers, and as long as we consider time as linear, answers *follow* the questions to which they respond, whether that future occurs in a second, an hour, or a year. In other words, change, whether it be incremental or sudden, occurs in the corridors of time.

Question Asking, Creativity, and Change

Creativity requires asking genuine questions, in other words, those to which an answer is not already known. Such questions function as openhanded invitations to creativity, calling forth that which doesn't yet exist. Every creative act thus begins implicitly or explicitly with a genuine question, generally to oneself. In the same way, illustrated by Einstein's question about the light beam, the springboard for every discovery can be understood as the right question, asked at the right time, in the right way, and to the right person(s). For every step forward, someone had to wonder whether a current situation could be changed or bettered, or simply asked, *"What would happen if I did this?"* or *"What would happen if I did that?"* That individual would have asked internal questions such as: *"Is there any other way to think about this?"* or *"What else could I do?"* or *"What possibilities 'exist' that I haven't thought of yet?"* —and then acted on his answers.

Columbus probably asked, *"Is there a sea route to India?"* Picasso, in moving into cubism, could have inquired of himself, *"In what other ways could I depict the human form?"* Murray Bowen's pioneering work with families leads to the speculation that he asked himself, *"Might it be worthwhile to interview the members of the patient's family?"* This sense of originality in questioning undergirds every creative act, whether it results in a painting, a poem, or the behavior of stepping past loyalty-based behaviors prescribed by one's family of origin, but incongruent with one's personal beliefs or goals.

Courage lies at the heart of creativity, for it includes the willingness to ask questions which might challenge, and even break up, current perceptions and patterns. Change also requires challenging and altering old patterns and perceptions, for this is the very condition that allows something new to emerge. In this way, creativity is accompanied by courage in every moment, whether it's daring to put a splash of color on a painting that could be ruined by it, or asking a question, of oneself or someone else, the answer to which might be disturbing or unwanted. Thus, the hallmarks of change include genuine questioning, courage, and creativity.

Question Asking and Research   Professionals in every field share an understanding of the importance of questions when it comes to research. The discipline of research *requires* its practitioners to function in an inquiring mode; that is, one in which the individual intentionally adopts a cognitive state that is open-minded, flexible, curious, and nondefensive. From such a mindset, the researcher develops theories, or constructs, about the issue under consideration. Then he goes about testing his hypotheses, weighing the experimental evidence, and objectively reporting his findings.

The purpose of research is discovery, learning, usefulness—and ultimately, change for the better. Any outcome is considered useful in some way; the task is to find out in what ways this could be the case. This includes disproving a hypothesis, bringing the researcher one step closer to finding out what he or she was looking for—or providing protection from straying down a misleading path. Therefore, whether the research intention was to test a hypothesis or explore an issue, some of the primary operating questions would be: *"What is objectively present?"* *"What can be learned from this?"* and *"What might be useful about this?"*

Researchers recognize that they must make a careful distinction between the kind of thinking required to test a hypothesis, in contrast with the kind of thinking required for interpreting the findings. The first cognitive paradigm, which seeks to discover whether something is true or false, right or wrong, or correct or incorrect, is naturally designed to yield a type of either/or, Yes/No answer. Any "No" answer, which is tantamount to a rejection, is inherent to the structure of the question itself. On the other hand, questions in the paradigm of interpretation and meaning, which are based on learning and usefulness, are generally inconsistent with Yes/No responses. Here, the intention is to remain open to all possibilities, making a careful distinction between one's findings and one's interpretation of those findings—or between "facts" and "opinions." In research thinking, no outcome or consideration is rejected out of hand. All are examined for utility and assumptions are explored.

Important scientific discoveries have been birthed out of this creative, fertile research thinking. For example, penicillin was discovered by Sir Alexander Fleming after he noticed an anomaly in one of his experiments. He sighted an unexpected bacteria-free circle around a mold growth, and must have wondered nonjudgmentally, *"What's this?"* and *"For what might it be useful?"* The eventual answer, which could not have existed prior to Fleming's observation and the questions it provoked, was the lifesaving discovery of antibiotics.

Thinking Skills and Change   The ability to think about one's thinking, which I am characterizing as research-like thinking, is fundamental to thinking clearly and effectively in general and for this reason, focusing on it must be included as a priority in therapy. For example, Yes/No thinking, so appropriate and necessary for most kinds of research, shows up as black/white thinking for many of our clients. While this is necessary for scientific considerations, as well as for most final decision making, when people unwittingly apply this same binary thinking to *themselves*, the rejection inherent in the thinking style itself can result in judgmental, moralistic overtones which sabotage a sturdy sense of self-efficacy and may paralyze effective action.

Black/white thinking also undermines people's ability to make the all-important distinction between the facts of a situation and their opinions and feelings about these facts. Almost invariably, it is not the facts of their lives that cause people to suffer, so much as the interpretations they make of these facts. In other words, their confusion between the facts and their opinions and feelings about these facts is often the very condition inhibiting clients' abilities to resolve their problems and make peace with themselves and others. At these times, it would be so helpful if people knew to ask themselves, for example:

- *Am I engaging in black/white thinking?*
- *Is black/white thinking appropriate, or helpful, for what I'm thinking about? (Sometimes it is.)*
- *What assumptions am I making that could get in the way?*
- *Am I confusing what's going on with my feelings about what's going on?*
- *Is the way I'm thinking making me feel worse, or making it harder to deal with my problems?*
- *How else could I think about this?*
- *What could I learn from what's going on?*
- *What might be valuable about this?*
- *What choices do I have here?*
- *What choice would be effective and affirming, and help me (or us) resolve and move beyond this?*

These kinds of questions are characteristic of a researcher's nonbiased, nondefensive, solution-seeking mindset.

Question Asking, Therapy, and the Researcher's Mindset

The researcher's mindset, like that of any creative individual, is open-minded, curious, flexible, and intentionally holds aside prejudgment. As we have seen, such a mindset is similar to that which best helps our clients resolve their problems. Regardless of diagnosis or presenting problem, therapeutic success is best assured when clients are able to develop an open, flexible, researcher's attitude toward themselves and their difficulties. However, it is no surprise that this is not the characteristic attitude of people when they first come to therapy. In fact, it is in reference to their presenting problems that even otherwise well-balanced individuals are most likely to be cognitively inflexible, perceptually limited, fearful, and defensive. Question-centered therapy uses a psycho-educational approach to facilitate clients to shift to a research-like mindset in support of their therapeutic success.

By the same token, the mindset that characterizes effective therapists is similarly open-minded, curious, and flexible. Such a mindset is what helps us meet each client in his or her uniqueness, refrain from placing them in Procrustean beds, and guard against pat solutions or facile therapeutic "answers." We even conduct sessions through research-like internal questions: *"How can I deepen rapport?" "I wonder if this will work?" "How hard can I push him on that?" "What would happen if I did something unexpected right now?" "How might he react if I mention his clenched fist?" "How can I use what just happened to therapeutic advantage?"* Furthermore, this research-like mindset is a major distinguishing characteristic of effective clinicians. One can imagine therapists as diverse as Whitaker, Perls, Satir, Erickson, Minuchin, and Beck engaging in such research-like internal questions while orchestrating their therapy sessions, even though their answers were decidedly and uniquely individual.

SUMMARY

This chapter set the stage for thinking and learning about questions and therapy. Questions—both internal and external—were highlighted as omnipresent and powerful. Statements and behavior were described as representing answers to prior, usually implicit, questions. The process of change was discussed in reference to question asking, creativity, and courage. The similarity of the researcher's questioning mindset with that of successful clients, as well as that of effective therapists, was explored. In the next chapter, we deepen the discussion of the potential of question-centered perspectives in therapy by examining the roles of questions in human functioning.

ENDNOTES

1. All internal dialogue, both questions and statements, will be italicized throughout the book.
2. Dilts, 1994b., p. 83, and personal communication.
3. To avoid confusion, the therapist throughout the book is referred to in the feminine. Clients are referred to in the masculine, except in specific cases when they could be either gender.
4. Penzias, A. "Questions That Illuminate," *Benchmark Magazine*, Fall 1991, p. 10.

2

What Are the Roles of Questions in Human Functioning?

*. . . answers establish an edifice of facts; but questions . . . make
the frame in which (the) picture of facts is plotted. They make more
than the frame; they give the angle of perspective, the palette,
the style in which the picture is drawn. . . .*
— SUZANNE LANGER

Rapport and relationship. Communication. Information gathering. Problem solving. These are the fundamental components of therapy. In the most reductionist sense, all of these occur in language, and are comprised of statements and questions, both internal and external, on the parts of clients and therapists alike. Internal questions can be considered more fundamental, since questions we ask our clients generally represent answers to our internal speculations about them. Furthermore, the difficulties that impel people to seek therapy will be reflected in, as well as generated by, their internal dialogue, and especially their internal questions.

In this chapter we explore the roles of internal questions in creating and maintaining problems, as well as in resolving them. We accomplish this through the lens of the four basic, though interrelated, areas of human functioning that every therapist must consider in relation to her clients, their problems, and their goals in seeking therapy. These areas are *thinking, feeling, behaving,* and *relating.* The major part of this discussion focuses on thinking, as cognition exerts such a pervasive influence on every other area of our lives.

SECTION ONE:
THE ROLES OF QUESTIONS IN THINKING

People come to therapy because they have a problem to resolve, or at least what they consider to be a problem. They may want specific help, as in making a particular decision or resolving a phobia. They may have less easily definable goals, such as a better relationship with a spouse or parent. They may also want to explore more global concerns and questions, such as: *"Do I want children?"* or *"How can I make my retirement most meaningful?"* or *"How can we restore the intimacy we used to have in our marriage?"* In each of these cases, the client's ability to think clearly plays a significant role in the effectiveness and efficiency of therapy, and therefore in the therapist's hypothesizing about an optimum course of treatment.

In operational terms, "thinking clearly" depends, in large part, on effectiveness in internal question asking. Therefore, in considering some of the connections between thinking and therapy, we explore question asking in relationship to problem formulation and problem solving, critical thinking, making distinctions, learning, and personal control. Each of these issues is central to therapy, as well as a core concern in the life of any human being.

Question Asking and Problems

It is logical to begin considering the relationship of thinking and therapy with the issue of how we think about problems. After all, this is the reason people seek out therapists—we are in the personal problem-solving business. However, the way "the problem" is articulated covertly and subtly forecasts the degree to which resolution and success are predictable. For this reason, we begin the discussion in this section with problem formulation. Then we move on to consider the usefulness of converting presenting problems into questions. This includes avoiding the trap of the unanswerable questions clients often unwittingly drag into therapy. Finally, we explore the utility of considering problem solving as a question-and-answer process.

Problem Formulation   The language which a client uses to describe his problems, including the tendency to reify these issues, casts a long shadow over the possibility of therapeutic success. Even the seemingly innocent phrase "my problem" packs a multiple whammy. It suggests that the client thinks he has only *one* unidimensional problem to investigate, that he may think he already knows all about it, and that the problem is "his," which probably implies guilt or blame, rather than ownership and responsibility. The phrase "my problem" also converts an issue into a burdensome "thing." Of course, the more "thingness" with which an issue is imbued, the more intractable it becomes and the less likely "it" can be resolved.

Moreover, consider the difference that language selection makes by contrasting the experience of "problem" and "puzzle," as de Shazer suggested (de Shazer 1991, p. 82). A person facing a problem could logically experience feelings such as desperation, fear, and high levels of frustration. However, one is more likely to experience speculation, concern, curiosity, and milder frustration in response to the challenge of solving a puzzle. As O'Hanlon and Wilk point out: "There are not certain entities floating around in the universe called 'problems.' . . . Something isn't a problem until someone defines it as such and sets about trying to solve it. . . . It is a product of the client's and therapist's talking together. It is created verbally and solved verbally. And how it is formulated will determine how (indeed whether) it will be solved" (O'Hanlon and Wilk 1987, p. 47).

Converting "Problems" into Questions   An alternative way to construe a problem is to convert it into a question, or series of questions, that haven't yet been answered. Cognitive theorist George Kelly, one of the fathers of cognitive therapy, considered a client's presenting symptom or problem to be a behavioral question waiting to be successfully addressed (Kelly 1963). For example, the behavior of my client, Donna, a woman with poor self-esteem, expressed the question, *"How can I get everyone to like and approve of me?"* Her obsequious behavior was her symbolic answer to this question. The behavior of an acting-out young adolescent could express the question, *"Will anybody give me definite limits and boundaries?"* His provocative behavior would represent his symbolic answer—to behaviorally test that question with his family. In these ways, we can describe present problems as representing inadequate answers to old questions.

Moreover, better "life questions" would likely bring with them better "life answers." Obtaining more effective answers first requires casting the problematic behavior in the form of a question that can be responded to in some helpful way. However, it is often the case that whatever a client considers to be his problem is anchored in place by internal questions that are virtually unanswerable, or which actually make the experience of the problem worse. Consider the dominant internal question of my client with poor self-esteem, *"Why am I so unworthy?"* Had I taken her lament literally, we might have wasted her investment of time, money, and hope in the therapeutic process.

On the other hand, reconstruing a problem as a well-formed question, or a series of such questions, grants therapeutic leverage, since action and change are built into its very construction. For instance, the problem of poor self-esteem could be transformed into questions, such as: *"What has inhibited my ability to respect and care for myself?"* *"What will it take for me to like, respect, and care for myself?"* and *"How can I get started?"* In the case of the adolescent boy, the therapist might inquire of the family, "Who will give Billy definite limits and boundaries?" and of herself, *"What changes need to occur in the family system so that can happen?"* The therapist's interventions would reflect her answers to this question. Therapy in both these cases could be thought of as a process of asking and experimenting with as many permutations of these questions as necessary.

Of course, it is the therapist's task to make certain the reformulated questions are helpful ones. As Postman noted, "It is characteristic of the talk of troubled people that they will resist bringing their questions down to a level of answerability. If fanaticism is falling in love with an irrefutable answer, then a neurosis is falling in love with an unanswerable question" (Postman 1976, p. 145). He offered as examples, *"Why are people always trying to cheat me?"* and *"When will the breaks start to come my way?"* (p. 145; italics added).

Problem Solving as a Question-and-Answer Process   Problem solving can be constructed and operationalized into a logical sequence of well-formed self-questions, in other words, those that naturally call for helpful answers. For this general conversation, we consider a different kind of "problem"—a physical one dealing with temporal and spatial orientation. For example, consider an ice skater in an important competition when she needs to assess whether to risk a triple jump, rather than playing it safe with her usual double. She does not, and cannot, make all the instantaneous, streamlined calculations that are part of solving her "problem" in actual linear linguistic thought.

However, if we slow down and freeze-frame her problem solving as a cognitive, linear, linguistic process, we get a series of questions, such as: *"Am I well rested and strong enough to be successful today?"* *"Have I practiced this jump often enough to risk it in a competition?"* and *"Does the ice look fresh enough to give me the surface I need?"* The skater's choice, expressed through her behavior of performing the triple jump, could be said to represent her affirmative answer to each in such a series of internal questions.

Here's a clinical case which illustrates the utility of formulating a problem as a series of questions, as well as considering thinking as a question-and-answer process. Another client, Carl, had an important therapy goal. He wanted to find his life partner, get married, and have children. His problem was that he was too shy even to ask a woman for a date. He had to make many decisions before getting to the point of solving his problem. First, he had to decide whether to get help. The old questions which impeded his reaching out for therapy included, *"Why am I such a failure?"* and *"Why doesn't any woman think of me as a potential husband?"* He obviously made an internal shift on his own, which was reflected in his behavior when he called me for an appointment.

At some point he answered his new, actionable internal question, *"Should I keep sitting here and worrying, or should I call a therapist?"* with the specific behavior of picking up the phone and making an appointment. Other decisions he made in response to well-formed internal questions included choosing to embark on a course of treatment, choosing to do his behavioral assignments, choosing women with whom to pursue a relationship, and finally choosing one woman as his potential mate. At that point he answered his internal question, *"Is she the one?"* with *"Yes."* He answered another internal question, *"Do I have the nerve to ask her?"* by asking Annie, "Will you marry me?" She accepted.

These examples of the ice skater and my client, Carl, allow us to consider the possibility that much thinking and problem solving, if brought to consciousness and constructed in a linear, linguistic manner, could be represented as a question-and-answer process. Such answers would be linguistic, emotional, and/or behavioral. Sometimes thousands of such minidecisions comprise the final solution of a problem.

Question Asking and Critical Thinking

A client's level of competence in critical and creative thinking has a fundamental impact on how much and what kind of therapeutic work will be necessary. Clearly, the more able an individual is to apply critical thinking skills to himself and his personal concerns, the more he can understand and deal with them successfully. This should be the case regardless of diagnosis or presenting problem. For this reason, question-centered therapy has a psycho-educational bias toward helping people develop or reinforce these cognitive skills early in treatment. The goal is for clients to use their strengthened cognitive skills in resolving presenting problems, which simultaneously empowers them with a strengthened "cognitive life boat"* from which to navigate the rest of their lives.

Skillfulness with internal questioning is fundamental to skillfulness in critical thinking. Consider these descriptions of successful critical thinking: ". . . (1) *an awareness of useful questions* to ask when presented with new information, (2) the *skills* to answer the questions, and (3) a set of *attitudes* and *dispositions* that encourage us to *want* to ask useful questions and to ask them in a *fair-minded* way" (Keeley 1995, p. 11; his italics). The attitudes Keeley pointed to included: *"wanting to question and being curious,"* . . . *"openness and honesty,"* . . . *"persistence and high frustration tolerance,"* . . . *"intellectual humility and flexibility,"* . . . *"desiring clarity, precision, and accuracy,"* and *"tolerance for complexity and ambiguity"* (pp. 13–14; his italics). Actually, such a list makes one wonder how often this idealized critical thinker would end up in therapy at all.

Question Asking and Distinctions: Draw a Distinction, Create a World

Making distinctions concerns the process of how we come to know anything, which is by noticing that one thing is different from something else. This most basic perceptual act of distinguishing difference is driven by internal questions, albeit usually nonlinguistic ones. Nevertheless, as Keeney pointed out, "A question, by proposing a distinction, constructs its answer . . ." (Keeney 1983, p. 20). Whether the question was conscious and articulated, it could be constructed retrospectively and logically in language. A sample of questions which promote dis-

---

*This term was adapted from "cognitive life raft," used by Middelton-Moz in *After the Tears*, 1986.

tinction making includes: *"What's this?" "Is it different from that?" "In what way?" "Does this add more subtlety, or any nuances, to the way I've been thinking?"* and *"Would drawing 'this' as a distinction allow me to understand, or do something that might not be possible otherwise?"*

As Keeney noted, drawing a distinction, "... whether obeyed consciously or unconsciously, is the starting point for any action, decision, perception, thought, description, theory, and epistemology" (p. 18). Emphasizing the "reality-creating" potency of distinctions, Keeney also wrote, "... language is a tool for imposing distinctions upon our world. Given a language system, we make choices regarding the patterns we discern" (p. 25) and "We literally create the world we distinguish by distinguishing it. If a distinction is not drawn, then that which it would have specified does not exist in our phenomenal domain" (p. 51).

Family therapy, per se, did not "exist in the phenomenal domain" until Bowen and others drew a symptom's distinguishing boundary around the family rather than the individual (Keeney, p. 20). This original distinction literally opened a new therapeutic door. As soon as therapists began stepping through this opening, the terrain revealed innovative therapeutic variations, such as working with extended family networks, interventions of a type which couldn't "exist" before. More recently, the ecopsychology movement has drawn another boundary, this time making the distinction that how we relate to our planet and her resources is a legitimate and worthy issue for psychology to address (see Winter 1996). Thus, we see that intentionally drawing distinctions provides powerful therapeutic leverage. As Keeney noted, "the therapist's questions and hypotheses help create the 'reality' of the problem being treated" (p. 21).

Here's an example from an initial interview in which I made a distinction which allowed my client to conceive of her problem in a new and more hopeful light. Barbara, a 25-year-old librarian, had suffered with depression and bulimia since she was about 14. Her history included several suicide attempts around that time, as well as years of productive therapy thereafter. Currently, she was successful in her job, and appeared slender, attractive, and athletic. However, she still experienced herself as "obsessed with food and my weight." She labeled her life up until age 14 as "the first phase," calling it "really good, kind of all-American." However, at age 14 her "world fell apart," and she described a number of exacerbating situations.

Recognizing that people who are depressed, as well as those who experience themselves as out of control, often cannot imagine the future, and certainly not a better one (Goldberg 1986), I asked Barbara, "If age 0 to 14 was the first phase of your life, do you consider 14 to the present to be the second phase?" She nodded, *"Yes,"* so I delivered the punch-line question: "Well then, would you say you've come to therapy to *end* that second phase, and *open up the third* one?"

Barbara gasped slightly and stared at me as she replied, "Yes, I guess so," in a startled voice. Later she commented that that was the first moment she experienced any real hope for herself. She said, "I never thought my life would be any better than a slightly improved version of the way it was. When you asked that question, it suddenly occurred to me that I could have a whole different future, though I'd still be myself." My intervention with Barbara was born of implicit self-questions such as these: *"What can I ask that could restructure her sense of time and reality?" "How can I encapsulate her self-image of being a 'depressed bulimic' as part of her past, so she could be liberated to envision the possibility of a positive future?"* and, of course, *"How can I phrase this possibility so it could be logical and natural for her to say 'Yes'?"*

Question Asking and Learning

At any level, education and learning depend upon curiosity and asking questions. Aristotle made an observation that any parent or teacher could confirm when he said, "All human beings, by nature, desire to know." Curiosity is the driver of attention, exploration, experimentation—and therefore of all learning. The experience of curiosity is equivalent to continuously living and operating out of a question frame as simple as *"What's this?"* or *"What's that?"* In this sense, even an infant curiously exploring her toes could be described as behaviorally responding to non-linguistic questions, such as, *"What are these?"* or *"Are they attached to me?"*

Learning is the basis for the acquisition of both information and competence in the life of any human being. But learning is more than simply acquiring information about the world, or even about people and relationships. Arguably, the most mature and successful individuals are those who have learned to habitually shine the light of inquiry upon themselves. Self-observation, or taking the meta-position required for second-order thinking, is the cognitive skill that comes to flower in adolescence if the rest of the developmental trail has been well traversed.

This cognitive achievement that Piaget called "formal operations" is what allows individuals to objectively observe their own thinking, as well as their ways of being and behaving—in general and in relationships. It allows the possibility of self-correction without self-condemnation for previous choices and behaviors, as well as setting more well formed goals. Such thinking is characterized by self-questions, such as: *"What's going on here?" "What am I feeling?" "What do I really want in this situation?"* and *"Am I being honest with myself?"*

Question Asking, Learning, and the Necessity of "Failure"   A crippling error in American thinking today is that success is "good" and failure is "bad." This assumption leads people to do practically anything to be successful, and perhaps even more, to avoid being a "failure." But this attitude and the behaviors it begets undermine the very foundation of learning, which depends on curiosity, question asking, and experimentation. Piaget considered failure that leads to puzzlement to be the driving force in development, or learning in the broadest sense (Gallagher, personal communication 1997). When faced with a puzzle, a contradiction, or a "failure," children must ask questions in order to reach a new level of understanding. As Piagetian scholars Gallagher and Wansart noted, ". . . errors in the application of a procedural system are desirable, because they can be very fruitful. . . .

Many procedural errors have led to new scientific discoveries . . ." (Gallagher and Wansart 1991, p. 36). Rather than being discouraged by errors, those scientists were challenged and motivated to observe, compare, and learn from the results of various hypotheses (p. 36). Such thinking has been the origin of numerous inventions such as penicillin, which was mentioned in the last chapter. Yet, self-condemnation for "errors" probably would have blocked the learning possibilities inherent in those situations, and possibly the invention of many other items or processes from which we benefit today.

This viewpoint that failure is a requirement for most learning has academic, if not public, support. Artificial intelligence expert Roger Schank wrote: "The process of building up and correcting knowledge structures is driven by the questions we ask ourselves. Expectation failures are a primary source of questions. Such failures force us to ask ourselves questions like *'What caused the failure?'* and *'How can I prevent the failure from occurring again?'* " (Schank 1995, p. 40; italics added). To operate in the world from the powerful position of a learner, one must develop "a questing mindset" (Gelb 1996). Such a mindset is the *opposite* of one that stands in critical and negative judgment of every so-called "failure."

Moreover, the success of therapy depends on learning in order for it to work at all. This suggests that explicitly recontextualizing clients' thinking about failure would make a significant contribution to therapeutic success. This would liberate the possibility of their responding to a "failure" with new growth-promoting questions, such as: *"What can I learn from this that would help me?"* *"What lessons should I pay attention to here?"* and *"What does this show me that I wasn't seeing before?"* Such questions are quite different from the habitual self-condemning internal queries that keep people mired in problems. In fact, questions such as *"What's wrong with me that I failed?"* typify the problem-causing and problem-reinforcing questions of new clients. These are exactly the kind of questions that Postman described as "unanswerable."

Question Asking and Genius   While question asking is essential for learning of any kind, it is also fundamental behavior for our most brilliant thinkers and innovators. Dilts studied geniuses such as Aristotle, da Vinci, Einstein, Freud, and Mozart (Dilts 1994, 1994a, 1995). In searching for commonalities and patterns from which we all might learn and grow, Dilts discovered that one of the primary characteristics of geniuses is the dedicated habit of asking basic questions. He wrote: "Geniuses tend to emphasize questions more than answers. They are typically very bold about their questions and humble about their answers. Certainly, a key characteristic of all geniuses is their high degree of curiosity and fascination. Rather than try to confirm and hold onto what they already know, they seek where their knowledge is incomplete. They also have a unique ability to perceive lack of success not as failure but as feedback for where to look next. Aristotle, for instance, defined four basic questions that he continually asked and a process by which he checked his assumptions and premises. . . . Mozart's music was a result of a constant query as to whether 'two notes loved each other' " (Dilts 1994a, p. 282).

Question Asking and Personal Control

The issue of personal control stands at the core of how people perceive, experience, and define themselves, as well as whether, when, and for what reasons they seek therapy. It is also central to conceptions of mental health and to many forms of therapy (Shapiro 1996, pp. 1213–1230). This issue of perceived personal control is also a cognitive and linguistic one, and despite its complexity may be expressed operationally through the kinds of questions people ask themselves. Of import is whether such questions are encoded with presuppositions of competence and positive possibility, or incompetence and certain failure. This is consistent with Seligman's conceptions of learned helplessness and learned optimism (Seligman 1974, 1991).

An individual's experience of being comfortably in control is directly related to his personal definitions of being "in control" and "out-of-control" (Goldberg dissertation, 1986). The experience of being out of control is also related to the number of perceived choices he has at any given moment. The fewer the number of perceived choices, the more out of control he may assess himself to be. For example, difficulties associated with addictions and compulsions are often accompanied by behaviors labeled and experienced as out of control. Regardless of an individual's history or the etiology of his problem, most people with these issues share cognitive and linguistic commonalities that compound their difficulties.

Problem-Focused Questions   Addictive and compulsive behaviors of any order may be accompanied—or perhaps driven by—beliefs expressed linguistically, such as, "I *am* out of control. This is the *only thing I can do* right now" or "I *am* out of control. I *can't stop* this, and therefore I have *no choice* but to keep doing it." Beliefs such as these are often answers to an internal question, such as, "Am I in control or out of control?" Since such individuals probably engage in "all-or-nothing thinking," perceiving themselves as even slightly out of control often leads them to conclude they are *completely* out of control. They may even label themselves "out-of-control persons." However, *this conclusion is often determined by the linguistic structure of the questions that lead to it.* For example, the question "*Is there anything I can do?*" calls for a Yes/No answer. If clients are *uncertain* they can regain *complete* control, they often conclude, "No. There's *not* one thing I can do. I have no choice. Therefore, I *am* out of control."

Only a slight change in the structure of the question, "*Is there anything I can do?*" predicts a transformation in the number of available options and potential solutions. An example of such a transformed question is, "*What can I do?*" This question, built on the presuppositions that capability and options are available, automatically gives the individual a *range* of possibilities, whereas the Yes/No question gives him only one. Of course, there are times when a Yes/No question is required, for example, when a final decision must be made. The habit of questioning one's questions would allow an individual to choose which kind of question might be most helpful in a given circumstance.

Solution-Seeking Questions   The individual who has not developed the self-observing habit of questioning his questions and beliefs is condemned to live in the reality to which he gives linguistic expression. In a sense, he has taken up residence in a "house that language built," and must remain in this domicile until he questions the old blueprints, designs new ones, and chooses to inhabit them. Question-centered therapy presumes that a key to personal freedom lies in constructing or reconstructing one's "home" by asking internal questions encoded with presuppositions of possibility, responsibility, the ability to choose, and the perception of multiple choices. However, invoking such keys to change depends first on questioning the limiting beliefs of which the "old home" was constructed, which includes questioning one's own questions. As Kelly wrote, "Each little prior conversation that is not open to review is a hostage (one) gives to fortune; it determines whether the events of tomorrow will bring happiness or misery" (Kelly 1963, p. 22).

Thinking, Question Asking, and Therapy   These discussions about thinking and question asking in relation to problem formulation, problem solving, critical thinking, learning, making distinctions, and issues of personal control position questions as central and fundamental in people's experience of having problems, as well as the possibility of resolving and growing beyond them. At the same time, this possibility also places a spotlight on questions as a source of therapeutic leverage with people experiencing many different sorts of difficulties, and further holds implications for those people who seek therapy with worthwhile goals and dreams, but no concept about how to make them come true.

How we humans feel, behave, and relate are all profoundly affected by the thinking constructs we bring to each. Whether we are able to bring ourselves to these domains in a sound and secure cognitive lifeboat profoundly influences the life journey ahead. For example, a leaky cognitive lifeboat is immediately evident in a client's affective life, and this, in turn, reciprocally affects how he feels, behaves, and relates. Therefore, it is the subject of feelings to which we turn next.

SECTION TWO: QUESTIONS AND FEELINGS

Our feelings and moods are inextricably linked with internal dialogue, as has been well established by cognitive theorists (Beck 1979; Burns 1980, 1989; Beck and Emery 1985; Ellis 1962). So far in this chapter we have reviewed examples of internal questions which affect people's feelings and moods. Basically, these questions fell into two distinct categories. In the first category were problem-focused questions such as: *"Why am I such a failure?" "When will the breaks start to come my way?"* and *"Why do I have all the bad luck?"* In the second category were solution-seeking questions such as: *"What can I learn from this?" "In what way could this be useful?"* and *"How can I take advantage of this opportunity?"*

The moods evoked by these two categories of questions result, in part, from the structure of the questions themselves. At the most basic structural level, an obvious difference is that two questions in the first category begin with *"Why,"* while those in the second category begin either with *"How"* or *"What."* However, the primary difference is not to be found in the structure, the words, or even the delivery. The felt difference is created by the presuppositions encoded in each kind of question. Next we examine those presuppositions, including how they relate to time, and to Seligman's descriptions of optimism and pessimism.

Feelings, Presuppositions, and Possibilities

Problem-focused questions, which can be characterized as negative, presuppose that something is seriously and pervasively wrong with the question-asker. The "fact" that he suffers from a permanent, negative personal fault strongly implies that his future possibilities are severely limited. In fact, there is a sense in which these kinds of problem-focused questions are not really questions. They can be seen as statements representing negative conclusions about self, others, life, and the future; the sentence just happens to end with a question mark. The questioner is not asking a genuine question, that is, one to which he doesn't yet have an answer. He asks a rhetorical question, seeking only an answer that could be generated from within the closed system from which the question was asked. The difficulty lies not only in the wording of the question; the limitations are also imposed by the attitude and judgments with which the individual asks the question. He has already reached a conclusion and concretized it by converting it into a belief.

Questions whose presuppositions confirm negative beliefs about oneself are particularly virulent and difficult to escape. Internally asking and answering questions such as these confines the questioner in a linguistic quandary that will likely continue as long as the language pattern is maintained. Escape becomes possible only by asking a metaquestion—that is, by assuming a position as observer of the languaging process. Only from a metaposition can one question the structure, content, and intent of the question itself. From here, one might ask himself, for example, *"Is this really true?" "Would anybody else agree?" "Does this belief support me or help me achieve my goals in life?"* or *"Can this question do me any good?"*

Furthermore, only from the vantage point of self-observation can the individual ask himself a *switching question,* that is, one that functions to switch him from "thinking track A" to "thinking track B." Examples of such questions are: *"What would I rather feel?"* or *"What other question can I ask to get me off this negative, dead-end track?"* or even *"What questions could empower me with resources and perspectives to make the changes I want?"*

While problem-focused questions are negative and limiting, solution-seeking questions presuppose that options, especially positive ones, are possible and available, that the asker is competent to take advantage of these, and further, that the question-asker is motivated and willing to do so. It is not surprising that the moods elicited by the second kind of presuppositions are optimistic and forward-looking. For these reasons, training an individual to observe his internal dialogue, and especially to question and revise his internal questions, is a powerful therapeutic intervention that is basic to the psycho-educational foundation of question-centered therapy.

Questions, Feelings, and Presuppositions about Time   Presuppositions about time and the passage of time are quite different in these two categories of questions. The problem-focused questions presuppose that things were bad, painful, and undesirable *in the past*; that they are *similar in the present*; and *will continue to be the same in the future*. With no fundamental distinction between past, present, or future, any experience becomes part of an infinite present, implying that negativity and limitation are a permanent, unchangeable state. Cognitively speaking, these presuppositions about time, which preempt the possibility of a positive future, contain a predictable recipe for the experience of hopelessness and helplessness. Such temporal presuppositions have also been associated with the experience of being out-of-control (Goldberg 1986), and were the basis of my interventions with Barbara, the librarian, whose presenting complaint I reframed as an ending to the unhappy second phase of her life, and an opening to a third phase—one alive with new positive possibilities.

The solution-seeking questions assume that whatever was the case in the past (or however events were interpreted in the past) can be *relegated to the past and left there*, hopefully to be learned from and/or appreciated, as appropriate. Further, the assumption is that the present, and certainly the future, can and probably will be *different* from the past. In other words, only the solution-seeking questions hold an assumption that change—especially intentional and positive change—is possible at all. The experience of hope *must* rest on the assumption that change is possible, and that there can be enough of a difference to make a positive difference. In other words, the very experience of hope and optimism rests on an individual's ability to make temporal distinctions that posit the possibility of a different and better future. Perhaps this is what Simone de Beauvoir meant when she said, "The whole meaning of life is in the question of the future that is waiting for us."

Learned Optimism and Pessimism   These observations are similar to those of Seligman on learned pessimism and optimism (Seligman 1974, 1991). Seligman found that the presuppositions underlying pessimism included the individual's conclusion that a negative experience or quality is pervasive and permanent in all areas of one's life. In addition, the individual cognitively seals his or her own dismal fate by assuming that any negative happening is actually his or her own fault. By contrast, an optimist considers difficulties or setbacks as temporary, specific to just that one category of activity, and not his or her own fault. These assumptions allow him to operate in life with the hopeful expectation that things can improve and change, and that he actually wields considerable power in making this happen.

SECTION THREE: QUESTIONS AND BEHAVIOR

In this section, we focus on the relationship between language, cognition, and behavior, or rather, on language use that facilitates action and behavioral possibilities. One of the ways to think about and categorize language, based on speech act theory, is to divide it into declarations, assertions, promises, and requests. The premise is that anything uttered by anybody must fall into one of these categories. However, it is possible to make the classification even simpler, since there is a commonality among the first three categories that is quite distinct from the fourth. Declarations, assertions, and promises are all statements, while requests are all questions. This distinction is fundamentally important, since a request is the only linguistic move that *predictably* stimulates or catalyzes action. Flores diagrams the stages of a conversation for action as beginning with a request and as being complete with a declaration of satisfaction (Denning and Metcalfe 1997, p. 182).

Since a request falls into the domain of questions, we can extrapolate that a *question* is the only linguistic move that predictably stimulates or catalyzes action. Statements can, and often do, function as a stimulus to action, but this is random, and certainly not predictable. This chapter has already offered illustrations of behavior as representing answers to internal questions. Conceiving of behavior as answering an individual's questions—whether these are conscious or unconscious, linguistic or nonlinguistic—grants access to a plethora of possible therapeutic interventions that place clients in line for action. This is part of the utility and economy of using questions to focus therapeutic interventions.

Behavior is also framed and driven by large-scale background, or contextual, questions, which may be cultural, social, and/or historical in origin. Earlier, we spoke of questions as part of the background that determines our actions. Despite their reality-creating power, these background contextual questions are nonlinguistic and nonarticulated, as invisible as the wind, though their effects are as omnipresent and distinguishable as the aftereffects of a hurricane. Naturally, such questions are the most veiled, illusive, and difficult to detect. Furthermore, the more deeply such contextual questions are embedded in the fabric of social and cultural assumptions, the more they hold us under their sway.

One way to capture context is to cast it as a question or a series of questions. This effort approximates what Kelly described as the job of the personal-construct psychologist: ". . . to describe accurately the highest levels of abstraction in his subject's system at the lowest possible levels of abstraction in his own" (Kelly 1963, p. 174). Since questions, by nature, call for answers, we can play this out by considering context as operationalized behavioral questions that call for behavioral answers.

The following example about nomadic societies illustrates that even histori-cally significant behavior can be thought of as answering questions expressed in nonlinguistic, nonarticulated form. While nomadic societies could be thought of as based on the question, "*How do we get to water?*", the feat of becoming stable, agrarian cultures became a possibility only with a new paradigm question, "*How do we get the water to come to us?*" (Gelb 1996). In a similar fashion, a family with an alcoholic or abusive parent may organize itself, behaviorally and emotionally, around questions such as: "*How can we hide this problem from anybody outside the family?*" or "*What do we need to do to protect ourselves, and keep any outsiders from interfering with us?*"

Such behavior-driving questions, if they can be discerned at all, could also be considered to mark out the parameters of the particular contexts, or paradigms, in which we live. Such questions may be thought of as a paradigm's operational motor, that which automatically keeps it mechanically functional unless the oper-ation is unconcealed, challenged, and transformed in some way. In fact, breaking out of a paradigm may be catalyzed by asking a question "inside" it that can be answered only from "outside" it, a formulation that would also describe the world-altering effect of Einstein's question about riding on the end of a light beam.

Automatic Questions and Behavior

These behavior-driving, contextual questions may also be thought of as auto-matic questions, *automatic* being the operative word. Something that is auto-matic occurs without conscious volition; it is rarely noticed, given much thought, or questioned in any way. Not only are contextual questions usually automatic, thus not thought about, they are also nonlinguistic. Therefore, automatic con-textual questions place even more than the usual obscuring veils over the various stimuli to behavior. Nonlinguistic questions such as these are best captured *after* the behavior, by means of a retrospective analysis which asks, "*To what questions might this (whatever behavior) be a logical answer?*"

To illustrate how this thinking could be used therapeutically, let's return to the example of the family with an alcoholic parent. Our hypothesis is that the behavior of the family members represents automatic answers to unsuspected, nonlinguistic questions, and that discovering those questions can help liberate the family for therapeutic success. Therefore, in the spirit of collaborative research, the therapist and family would begin by specifying a behavior to use in searching for negative, limiting questions. This example of the alcoholic family can be helpful in introducing this concept in therapy. Despite how complex this intervention may seem, clients usually accept these therapeutic directions easily. In this case, let's say the husband woke up sick with a hangover, and the wife called his boss with the excuse that her husband had the flu and couldn't make it to work that day. The behavior to be studied is that of the wife.

Having identified a behavior which might reveal a damaging background question, therapist and clients together brainstorm possible questions until they hit upon one, or even several, which seem promising. In this example, let's assume the therapist and clients agree that some such questions could be, *"How can I keep Bill's boss from discovering the truth?" "How can I prevent a blowup in my marriage?" "How can we hide our problems from outsiders?"* Once a behavior-generating implicit question is made explicit by giving it linguistic form, it can be examined for therapeutic utility.

Therefore, the therapist might then inquire of the family, "How does this question fit with your stated therapy goal of dealing with Bill's alcoholism?" Rich therapeutic conversation could follow this inquiry, especially if it is facilitated in a researchlike, nonjudgmental manner. Finally, the therapist might ask about new questions that could alter the paradigm keeping the family captive. In this case, a possibility would be, *"In the long run, will we be better off if this deception continues, or if we face our problems directly and resolve them?"*

SECTION FOUR: QUESTIONS AND RELATING

Naturally, it is in relationships that thinking, feeling, and behaving converge in the most complex and challenging ways. In this section, we focus briefly on how questions operate in relationships. We touch on just two kinds of relationships to illustrate the dance of this convergence: those between mother and child and between therapist and client. Other examples throughout the book focus on other kinds of relationships, most specifically in the four chapters on couples.

Mother-Child Communications

Communication and relationship training begin very early in life. The world of the youngest infants is bounded mostly by touch and sound. The earliest interactions of human beings, usually mother-child interactions, include a pattern of questioning and responding which commonly begins shortly after birth. Often, from the moment a mother holds her newborn, she begins to speak to her infant, although of course she knows that not a word is understood. The mother's speaking includes questions, to which she obviously doesn't expect any verbal response. However, the *sound* of a question being asked, with its rising inflection at the end of the sentence, is common in most of the earliest speech interactions of mother and infant.

Furthermore, mothers and other adults tend to ask more questions of infants than they do of other adults (Crystal 1987, p. 235). Their speech contains a high frequency of question forms and many utterances have that characteristic high-rising intonation, such as: "You're my precious little girl, *aren't you?*" "We're going to have a great time, Johnny, *isn't that right?*" or, "Are you *hungry?*" (p. 235). The mother asks many questions, followed by pauses, as if to show that a response is expected. The pause becomes both an expectation and an invitation for a response. This conversational pattern of "my turn–your turn–my turn" takes on the reciprocal nature of a dance where leading and following are fluid, subtle, and may be interchangeable.

This cyclical pattern of speech and silence also anticipates the fundamental structure of later, more mature conversations. It is difficult to tell whether these responses and patterns are instinctive and innately biological, or simply become automatic and "hardwired" due to early exposure to this kind of systematic training and learning. Regardless, by the time first words appear, infants have already learned a great deal from interactions, observations, and practice about the question-and-answer nature of conversation, and how to participate within its choreography.

Thus, from the very beginning of a person's experience of being human, questions and statements together form the very fabric of conversation. The vital elements of cloth are warp *and* woof; questions and statements interrelate and function in a similar way. Without either, only unrelated threads would remain. While sounds might be heard, little meaning or relating could occur. Most of our earliest experiences in being human, in communicating, and in relating are learned, and much of this resides in the conversational dance of questions and statements, or answers, that is fundamental for initiating us into the social world.

Therapist-Client Relationship

We use this specialized relationship to illustrate how external conversations, including questions asked of others, are generated from internal conversations, especially from internal questions, a relationship we have already discussed. In therapy, the clinician asks questions of her client in order to answer her own internal inquiries. For example, the questions a therapist might ask herself in an initial interview include: "*Is therapy appropriate for this person at this time?*" "*What kind of therapy and what kind of therapeutic relationship will best serve this person?*" "*What are the main motivators for this person?*" "*How cooperative might this person be?*" "*Is this emotional problem complicated by, or even caused by, a physiological cause?*" "*Might medication be called for?*" and "*Should psychological testing be pursued?*"

Of course, the therapist has initial concerns and questions about risk factors, especially with depressed clients. Let's also follow out that line of conversation, listening to the therapist's external questions as they are based on her internal ones. In order to assess the risk of suicide (i.e., to answer her own questions: "*Should I be concerned about this person being an immediate suicide risk?*" and "*If yes, what should I do about it?*"), the therapist might ask the client, "Have you ever considered killing yourself?" If she receives an affirmative answer, she might then ask, "Have you ever actually made a suicide attempt?" If this answer is "Yes," the therapist typically continues her investigation with something like, "Will you tell me specifically when that was, what you did, and what happened?" In other words, she asks her clients questions in order to answer her own questions about any current risk of suicide.

This therapist continues asking her client these kinds of questions until satisfied that he is not currently a suicide risk, or that he definitely is, or that more information and assessment are required before being certain. The first conclusion ends this series of questions. The second conclusion (that the client is at risk) leads the therapist to ask other internal questions regarding immediate therapeutic steps. In other words, the purpose of the evaluation interview is to collect information allowing the therapist to answer her own questions about the status, prognosis, and needs of her client. Only with all her questions sufficiently answered can the therapist be confident about her conclusions and the recommendations and actions she will accordingly pursue.

These examples of a therapist's internal questions in an initial interview offered a microscopic view of just a few moments in a single therapy session. This same process, with different content, occurs in every therapy session, and for that matter, in every conversation between two or more people. The fact that many people are unaware of this guiding subtext, and the extent to which it pervades our lives, does not negate its existence or its influence. Moreover, if internal questions are positioned at the source of how we think—as well as what we do, how we relate, and even what we conceive as possible for ourselves—then they are close to the origin of how we show up as human beings. Furthermore, by distinguishing our exploration of questions into the four areas of thinking, feeling, behaving, and relating, we may extend the possibilities of therapy itself, including creating new interventions and classes of interventions.

SUMMARY

This chapter considered the roles of questions in creating, maintaining, and resolving problems. These issues were pursued and illustrated through the four functional areas of thinking, feeling, behaving, and relating. In particular, we emphasized cognition, due to its pervasive influence in every other area of our lives. We focused on the role of internal questions as generating and/or influencing clients' feelings, thoughts, behaviors, and ways of relating. In the next chapter we turn to examine questions and question asking in therapy, as discussed and represented in the literature. This focus serves as a foundation for proceeding to explore question-centered therapy throughout the rest of the book.

3

What Are the Roles of Questions in Therapy?

*Ultimately, we are seeking a better understanding of what it means to
be human. In this quest, progress is not made by finding the "right"
answers, but by asking meaningful questions. . .*
— TERRY WINOGRAD AND FERNANDO FLORES

Because question asking is at the heart of all communication, it is also at the
core of therapeutic conversations. In these specialized conversations, it is
obvious that questions constitute our main linguistic tool for obtaining information about clients' difficulties, resources, and desired outcomes. However, the
role of questions as therapeutic interventions in and of themselves has not been
as thoroughly appreciated or explored. Making a distinction between these two
functions of therapeutic question asking strengthens the study of questions, as
well as the practical applications of using them for interventions.

This chapter examines the roles of questions in therapy in several different
ways. After discussing psychopathology from the perspective of internal dialogue
in section 1, we move on to examine questions used for gathering information.
Accordingly, in section 2 we review information-gathering questions in therapy
from three representative therapeutic perspectives: cognitive-behavioral therapy,
Neuro-Linguistic Programming, and systemic therapy as represented by the
Milan Group. In section 3, we open a general discussion about the use of questions as therapeutic interventions. Lastly, in section 4, we describe current uses of
questions as therapeutic interventions, returning to the lenses of the three therapeutic perspectives explored in section 2. Each of the four sections includes discussion and examples of questions from the literature.

SECTION ONE: PSYCHOPATHOLOGY
AND INTERNAL DIALOGUE

Psychology has taken for its own domain of study and practice the world of inner language, sometimes labeled *self-talk* or *internal dialogue*. In particular, behavioral-cognitive theorists and therapists have demonstrated the importance and influence of internal language as it relates to cognition, affect, behavior, and relationships. They have succeeded in making the case that the actual words, sentences, and concepts with which people think often function as blueprints for the external worlds they perceive, create, and inhabit.

Therefore, the therapist's goal—especially in cognitive-behavioral therapy— often includes helping clients develop competence in purposefully altering their internal dialogue. The initial challenge in presenting this concept to clients is that they may be unaware of the existence or the pervasiveness of their internal dialogues. Nevertheless, the ability to change one's thinking is generally predicated on the ability to consciously notice, without judgment, what thinking is already present. Unless one is able to self-observe in this manner, the possibilities of experiencing personal choice and realistic, thoughtful self-control could remain forever elusive.

The difficulty of bringing internal speaking into awareness is compounded when the goal is additionally to bring internal *questions* to the foreground. Even though the term "internal dialogue" is routinely invoked to describe the thinking process, it is rarely noted that a dialogue involves statements *and* questions. Discerning the often implicit or silent background questions helps undergird the robust awareness upon which much intentional change depends. Noticing statements (answers) alone tells only half the story, and allows only an incomplete understanding of the thinking process. Discovering these background questions usually requires noticing one's internal statements and reconstructing what questions might have preceded them, a process we refer to as *retrospective analysis*.

Automatic Thinking

The practice of paying close attention to one's thoughts follows psychoanalytic tradition, which directs patients to report their stream-of-consciousness, free-association thinking to the analyst. It was while listening to the free associations of his patients that Beck noticed the occasional appearance of thoughts that seemed unlike those he usually heard from patients. These "new" thoughts were most often statements, such as, *"You'll never make it"* or *"You don't deserve anything good."* Sometimes questions were noticed as well; for example, *"Will they decide I'm a fool?"* or *"Will they mock me?"* (Beck 1976, p. 41). Beck named this newly observed phenomenon *automatic thinking*, since it seemed as if there were two streams of thinking occurring simultaneously—the free-association thoughts and the newly discovered thoughts which seemed to appear automatically and randomly, like fish leaping out of a pond.

After much careful observation, Beck was able to report a myriad of features of automatic thinking. They were characteristically discrete and concrete, rather than vague or impressionistic. These automatic statements and questions were likely to be negative and undermining, and that they didn't seem to be preceded by reflection or deliberate thinking. They also seemed to precede or stimulate emotion, not to be the result of emotion. These negative automatic thoughts occur despite objective evidence to the contrary. The themes of these thoughts are relatively stable and internally consistent for various clusters of psychological difficulties. For example, many automatic thoughts of people who are anxious are distinct from automatic thoughts of people who are depressed. Finally, these thoughts display more distortion of reality than do other types of thinking. For all this, Beck found that his patients would report these thoughts only if requested to track them; otherwise, these influential messages about individual psychopathology remained in the background, their secrets and keys for therapeutic change remaining untapped and unused (Beck 1979).

The thoughts themselves turned out to be only the tip of the iceberg. Automatic thoughts are secured through a foundation of assumptions and conceptions about self, others, and reality. A psychological problem, symptom, or "bad mood" is likely to be the undesired result of distortions or mistakes in these assumptions and conceptions. Gaining access to these misconceptions gives therapists an invaluable tool for helping their clients; changing automatic thoughts provides little therapeutic benefit if change doesn't also occur at the deeper level of the assumptions and distortions which yielded the damaging thoughts in the first place.

Automatic Thoughts and Personal Rules   This foundation network of thoughts is shaped by a personal set of general rules that governs their content. An individual needs these rules to help him make sense of the complexity of life around him. These rules function as seemingly permanent lenses through which an individual views life. Accordingly, these rules operate in any direction an individual gazes, just as rose-colored glasses embellish everything with a rosy hue and gray-tinted glasses place a gray overlay upon one's whole world. Personal rules are like beliefs, and predict an individual's probable reactions to different emotions, people, and situations.

These rules operate with such power because the meaning of a person's experiences is strongly influenced by his expectations of the consequences to him (Kelly 1963, pp. 46–50). For example, an individual might receive a letter from the IRS and feel either excitement or anxiety depending on his expectations about the contents. The variable of the letter remains constant; it is the individual's *anticipation* of its messages and personal consequences that shape his mood. Perhaps, in this example, the individual's personal rule might be summarized as "expect the worst." Consequently, he would look at the IRS envelope through expect-the-worst lenses, and anxiety would be a predictable result.

Personal Rules and Personal Judgment An important kind of personal rule relates to the expectations and standards that an individual uses to judge himself and others. People typically, and almost compulsively, judge themselves and others in terms of "good" or "bad," and "right" or "wrong." Beck wrote that, "These rules not only guide the individual's overt actions, but also form the basis for his specific interpretations, his expectancies, and his self-instructions. Furthermore, rules provide the standards by which he judges the efficacy and appropriateness of his actions and evaluates his worth and attractiveness. He uses rules in order to achieve his goals, to protect himself from physical or psychological injury, and to maintain stable relations with others" (Beck 1976, p. 42). Discovering a client's maladaptive governing rules, including his rules for judging himself, is fundamental in cognitive-behavioral therapy.

Internal Dialogue and Psychopathology

The cognitive-behavioral literature offers many examples of how internal dialogue, both statements and questions, reflect, generate, and maintain psychopathology. In fact, cognitive therapy is based on the premise that thoughts, not external events, are what make people upset (Burns 1989). Cognitive therapists believe that this claim holds true to some degree for all classifications of psychopathology. This includes anxiety, along with panic attacks, depression, obsessions and compulsions, paranoia, hypomania, hysteria, and even psychoses (Beck 1976).

Anxiety provides a clear example of how other internal rules can contribute to problematic behavior. The thinking of an anxious person is dominated by themes of danger as well as fears of the consequences of these dangers. The maladaptive assumptions and thoughts of people experiencing anxiety center on three major issues: acceptance, competence, and control (Beck and Emery 1985, p. 288). Often, the harm anticipated is of a psychological nature, so the anxious client may be concerned that others, strangers as well as family or friends, might reject, humiliate, or depreciate him (Beck 1979). This makes him constantly vulnerable to the whims of others, although it would be more accurate to say that he is vulnerable to his *own* thoughts and expectations about the whims and intentions of others.

For example, an individual's concerns and beliefs about acceptance predict what kinds of automatic questions and statements he is likely to say to himself. An assumption about acceptance might be, *"I am nothing if I am not loved."* An automatic statement could be, *"Nobody loves me."* In question form he might ask, *"Will anybody ever love me?"* or even, *"Why am I so unlovable?"* An assumption underlying concerns about competence could be, *"I am what I accomplish."* The internal statement might then become, *"You have to make it"* and the internal question could be, *"What if I fail?"* or perhaps, *"What am I going to do wrong this time?"*

Regarding control, the assumption might be, *"I have to be perfect to be in control."* A statement reflecting this could be, *"You won't get it right!"* and a typical question could be, *"When am I going to go out of control?"* In each case, the ruling theme of concern remains constant whether it is reflected in the individual's assumptions or automatic statements and questions. A major goal of cognitive-behavioral therapy is to help clients identify and alter such undermining questions and statements into those which can support their therapeutic success.

SECTION TWO:
QUESTIONS FOR INFORMATION GATHERING

In its own fashion, every school of therapy and counseling places emphasis on the role of questions for information gathering, especially during the intake interview. The mandate to make a diagnosis and develop treatment plans, along with evaluating risk factors and therapist-client "fit," demands strategic question asking for gathering information. For this reason, initial interviews represent the situation in which therapists are usually most aware of the questions they ask, the kinds of responses that different kinds of questions may elicit, and the timing and sequencing of their questions.

Many of the details sought in an initial interview are standard, such as, education, sibling placement, and etiology of the current problems. However, therapists also ask questions designed to help them understand the client and his problems within a familiar theoretical framework. Therefore, the therapist's theoretical orientation, training, and experience constitute the background that suggests what kinds of information she will pursue. In addition, many of the therapist's questions in the initial interview, and throughout treatment, depend on her beliefs about causality, the goals of therapy, and the nature of being human, of change, and of health and healing.

In this section, we review representative question asking in the initial interviews from three distinct therapeutic perspectives. The first two of these, cognitive-behavioral therapy and Neuro-Linguistic Programming, focus primarily on individual clients. The third, the Milan School, represents family therapy and so provides an example of systems thinking in the intake-questioning process. Each of these three therapy orientations is also discussed in the fourth section of the chapter, which focuses on typical ways questions are used as interventions.

Cognitive-Behavioral Therapy

Multimodal therapy was selected to represent cognitive-behavioral therapy because its explicit questioning protocols deal comprehensively with different symptoms, levels of functioning, and social context. Lazarus, in one of the basic texts of cognitive-behavioral therapy, *The Practice of Multimodal Therapy: Systematic, Comprehensive, and Effective Psychotherapy* (Lazarus 1989), presents many specific questions for the initial interview. Lazarus also includes many queries for therapists to ask themselves about their clients; he recognized that therapists' external questions are asked in order to satisfy their own internal ones. Indeed, the assessment process is largely complete when therapists are satisfied that their internal questions about the client have been answered satisfactorily.

Multimodal Therapy   Lazarus presented a model to systematically organize thinking about assessment and treatment. The acronym that describes this model is *BASIC ID*. This acronym represents the myriad ways that human beings are products of the constant interactions between their *Behavior, Affect, Sensations, Images, Cognitions, Interpersonal* Relationships and *Biological* (BASIC IB) functions. By expanding the last descriptor, biology, to include drugs, nutrition, exercise, and medical diagnoses, Lazarus gained the advantage of changing the acronym from BASIC IB to BASIC ID. Lazarus wrote that: "The fundamental assumption is that BASIC ID comprises the entire range of personality; that there is no problem, no feeling, no accomplishment, no dream or fantasy that cannot be subsumed by BASIC ID" (p. 14).

Lazarus also emphasized that each of these modalities is present, to a greater or lesser degree, in every other (Lazarus 1981, p. 16). In the formal, initial information-gathering phase of therapy, the therapist systematically asks questions to satisfy her own concerns and questions within each modality. Upon completion, the therapist can be reasonably confident of having a comprehensive picture of the presenting problem, and this will become the foundation she translates into a road map for therapy.

While similar questions are asked by clinicians of all schools of therapy, it is the attempt to ask and answer them in a systematic and comprehensive manner using the BASIC ID that makes the multimodal conceptualization of assessment useful for our purposes here. The entire multimodal interview is keyed to answer this summary question: "Who or what is best for this particular individual?" (Lazarus 1981, p. 4). In order to answer this question, the therapist must learn about the specific and interrelated problems, as well as how they are maintained.

Lazarus also detailed the questions clinicians should be able to answer by the end of the initial interview (Lazarus 1989, pp. 45–46):

- Were there any signs of psychosis (e.g., thought disorders, delusions, incongruity of affect, grossly bizarre or inappropriate behaviors)?
- What were the presenting complaints and their main precipitating events?
- Was there evidence of self-recrimination, depression, or homicidal or suicidal tendencies?
- What was the client's appearance with respect to physical characteristics, grooming, manner of speaking, and attitude (e.g., friendly, hostile, sullen, acquiescent)? Was there any disturbed motor activity (e.g., tics, mannerisms, rigid posture, fidgeting)?
- What seemed to be some significant antecedent factors in this person's life?

- Who or what appeared to be maintaining the client's maladaptive behaviors?
- Was it fairly evident what the client wished to derive from therapy?
- Were there any clear indications or contraindications for the adoption of a particular therapeutic style? (For example, did a basically directive or nondirective initial stance seem preferable? At what pace should therapy best proceed?)
- Can a mutually satisfying relationship be put into effect, or should the client be referred elsewhere?
- What are some of the client's strengths and positive attributes?
- Why is the client seeking therapy at this time—why not last week, last month, or last year?
- Did the client emerge with legitimate grounds for hope?

Lazarus further identified questions therapists often ask themselves before the first meeting. His making such inquiries explicit and conscious allows a therapist to be certain that everything important has been covered. These questions include: *"What will this person be like?" "What problems will be presented?" "What will be withheld?" "What sorts of experiences will the client have about therapy in general?" "Will there be many hidden agendas?" "How much rigidity, defensiveness, resistance, or hostility will be evident?" "Will this be someone with whom a constructive therapeutic relationship can be established?"* (p. 45).

Information-Gathering Questions and Neuro-Linguistic Programming (NLP)

Neuro-Linguistic Programming, usually abbreviated as NLP, is a field of study which has generated many methods of working with people.* These methods are based on models rather than on theories. A model need not be right, true, or correct—it need only be *useful*. NLP originated in the early 1970s, when Richard Bandler, a mathematician, and John Grinder, a linguist, became curious about expert behavior, the structure of subjective experience, and the relationship between internal and external behavior. In search of these understandings, they modeled some of the world's most expert therapists, Fritz Perls, M.D., Virginia Satir, M.S.W., and Milton H. Erickson, M.D. They reported their findings in the *Structure of Magic, vols. I and II* (Bandler and Grinder, vol. I, 1975 and Grinder and Bandler, vol. II, 1976) and in *Patterns of the Hypnotic Techniques of Milton H. Erickson, M.D., vols. I and II* (Bandler and Grinder, vol. I, 1975 and Grinder, DeLozier, and Bandler, vol. II, 1977). A similar learning goal is what motivated

---

*I thank David Gordon for helpful conversations in preparing the NLP portions of the chapter.

Dilts to model geniuses such as Einstein, Freud, and da Vinci, which we discussed in chapter 2.

In modeling and in NLP, behavior is taken to encompass *internal*, as well as external behavior. Internal behavior includes our sensory and neurological processes, and how these are represented and sequenced into models and strategies expressed through language, physiology, and external behavior. Language, of course, refers to internal language, or thinking, and external language, or speaking. The metagoal of NLP is to use these understandings to help people overcome problems, accomplish and have what they want in their lives, and be happy. Accordingly, the field continues to develop through permutations of questions such as: *"What can we learn about optimum human functioning?" "How can we use what we learn to help others have similar accomplishments?" "How can people resolve what holds them back?"* and *"What makes for positive, ecological, generative change?"*

Many NLP methods of working with people are actually structured questioning practices. Therefore, clinicians trained in NLP methodologies recognize that questions intended for information gathering often simultaneously initiate a change process, and therefore also function as interventions. For this reason, organizing NLP questioning procedures into information gathering and interventions is somewhat arbitrary. In this section of the chapter, we focus on three questioning practices in NLP: the outcome frame, the meta model, and the virtual question. Each of these questioning practices functions for gathering information and making therapeutic interventions.

Outcome Frame   NLP is solution-focused rather than problem-focused. Clients usually come to therapy with a symptom, experience, or situation they *don't* want, but with much less certainty or clarity about what they *do* want. A premise of NLP is that if people don't know what they're going *for*, they may get lost along the way, not recognize their destination once they reach it, or perhaps never get there. For example, in an initial interview a client may say, "I don't want to be depressed." It would be unusual for him to add, "What I *do* want is to be happy and satisfied," and then to go on to offer details of how happiness and satisfaction would be demonstrated in his life.

The clinician's aim is to help clients think carefully and comprehensively about their goals so therapy can consist of putting energy into the right place for the right reasons. Therefore, the therapist helps clients develop explicit descriptions of the outcome to be approached—as distinct from the problem or experience to be avoided. In the process of making these descriptions, clients begin to build portrayals of a specific positive future, one that begins to feel real and compelling. In other words, these information-gathering questions *themselves* generate a change, thereby functioning as interventions.

For therapists trained in NLP, the questioning process of developing well-formed outcomes is considered vital for helping therapy get off on the right foot. Two related and standard question formats help clients specify outcomes that can be considered well formed. These questions are asked in the initial interview and returned to throughout therapy, as appropriate. The first set of questions helps clients select goals that are worth going after and with which they can be successful. These questions (Cameron-Bandler, Gordon, Lebeau 1985, pp. 78–79; paraphrased) include:

- What do you want?
- Is what you want *possible* for you?
- Is it *worth having?*
- Will it get you what you *really* want?
- Is it *worth doing* what it would take to attain this outcome?

The second set of questions helps clients specify their goals along with necessary conditions for success. The most helpful answers meet the following criteria: stated positively rather than negatively; stated in sensory-based terms; can be initiated and maintained by the individual; are ecological in all systems; and can be appropriately specified and contextualized. In addition, outcomes sought must preserve any positive by-products of the present system. Here are typical outcome-frame questions (de Torres and Sauber unpublished workshop materials, 1985; paraphrased):

- What do you want?
- How will you know you have it? (What will be a demonstration of it?)
- *When* specifically do you want, and *not* want it?
- In what contexts do you want, and not want it?
- What will happen if you get it?
- What stops you from doing and having this now?
- What resources do you have available to help you with this?
- How can you best utilize the resources you have?
- What are you going to *do* to get started?

De Shazer offered an interesting version of the outcome-frame process. He wrote that ". . . we take nothing for granted, and thus have questions for everything, including miracles" (de Shazer 1994, p. 95). The miracle question he suggested asking clients was: "Suppose that tonight after you go to sleep a miracle happens and the problems that brought you to therapy are solved immediately. But since you were sleeping at the time you cannot know that this miracle has happened. Once you wake up tomorrow morning, how will you discover that a miracle has happened? Without your telling them, how will other people know that a miracle has happened?" (p. 95).

Meta Model   When therapists talk about information gathering, they usually refer to three domains of information: the data and history of what happened;

what individuals think and feel about this; and the influences of the social system in developing and maintaining problems. While NLP-trained clinicians are, of course, interested in this information, they impose additional filters on the information-gathering process: how clients *use language* to express themselves and how this language use—if unchanged—could constrain or even prevent therapeutic success. Since NLP focuses on the nature of subjective experience, clinicians seek to understand specifically how clients presently represent their history, current situation, and chances for success to themselves. The reason for this focus is simple: Therapeutic success usually hinges on clients altering enough of their subjective experiences and perceptions to free them to make effective, satisfying choices and changes.

The meta model—or, model of models—was developed as a set of precise questioning tools for eliciting information about the nature of an individual's subjective experience. Clinicians also use these questions to help clients get more specific and detailed about the outcomes they want. The meta model focuses on reconnecting language and experience by amplifying, specifying, and/or recovering aspects of the client's direct experience. In other words, the meta model is a comprehensive, detailed, information-gathering questioning system for recovering, describing, and ultimately transforming an individual's experiences and possibilities.

An underlying premise of the meta model is that all language use, even the most everyday expressions, represent abstractions from direct sensory-based experience. Language in this sense is always metaphorical to one degree or another; it can approximate but never exactly represent the experiences it attempts to convey. For example, even a simple conversational phrase such as, "I sat on the chair," leaves significant aspects of the speaker's actual experience unspecified, distorted, or poorly represented. We do not know, for instance, the individual's posture when sitting on the chair, what the individual was seeing, feeling, or hearing as he sat there, or what he was telling himself about the experience. Any such details could be therapeutically significant (de Torres and Sauber workshop materials, 1985).

The therapist therefore listens to her client through meta-model ears in order to understand his linguistic and experiential model of the world. Keeping in mind the meta-model distinctions, the therapist stays alert to how her client may be deleting, distorting, or generalizing in such a way as to obscure important information, or unintentionally keep himself stuck or frustrated. The therapist also listens to language patterns to assess the degree of flexibility in the ways her client perceives "reality."

The client may say, for example, "I should always do it right." A therapist with NLP training will challenge the linguistic limitations in this sentence. She might typically ask questions such as: "*Who* says you should?" "Is it *really* necessary to do it right *every* single time?" and "What could happen if you didn't do it right?" She might also ask, "What does 'right' mean in this context?" "Who set those standards?" "Do you *really* agree with those standards?" and "How *else* might you think about this?"

The meta model is also used to identify the linguistic structure of illogical or magical thinking. Consequently, the therapist seeks to understand her client's understanding of cause and effect, including his general sense of internal and external locus of control. For example, if the client says, "It's *his* fault I smoke," the therapist might respond with, "How, specifically, does he do that?" or "In what ways might your smoking ever be your *own* responsibility?" If a client believes he *always* knows what his wife is thinking, the therapist might challenge such mind reading with questions such as: "How do you know you're right?" "Has there ever been a time when you weren't perfectly accurate?" and "Would your wife agree that this is true?"

The Meta Model as a Psycho-Educational Tool The meta model is a potent psycho-educational tool, as well as a vital therapeutic one. Therapy clients, like most people, are rarely aware of all that they say, much less *how* they say it. Clients certainly don't recognize how they contribute to the development and maintenance of their problems simply by the actual ways they speak. This is liberating and enlightening information. Teaching them how to use this information empowers them with a unique skill to employ in every context of their lives. As Gordon said, "Using the meta model to teach clients about the power of language gives them an experience of being capable and responsible for their changes during therapy. It also helps assure their confidence as successful problem-solvers for the rest of their lives. This is imperative in doing effective, long-term, generative change work" (personal communication, 1997).

Virtual Question Cameron-Bandler (1986), a codeveloper of NLP, discovered that people characteristically ask themselves unconscious questions containing repetitive personal themes leading either to suffering or fulfillment. She called these profoundly influential internal queries Virtual Questions™. While a virtual question is like a theme song, it is far more powerful because it simultaneously expresses an individual's multiple core beliefs and needs, along with idiosyncratic perceptual, emotional, and behavioral patterns. Cameron-Bandler discovered the virtual question within the framework of the Imperative Self Analysis™, which she also developed.

The Imperative Self is a model which provides ways to elicit and map out an individual's core perceptual, emotional, cognitive, linguistic, and behavioral patterns. Singleton described this model as providing ". . . a way to represent who the individual is, with the analysis of who she or he can become, which includes fulfillment, and the sequence of steps to get there" (Singleton 1986, p. 3). Virtual questions are the operational motor of an Imperative Self because our perceptions, beliefs, feelings, and actions represent answers to our internal questions, whether we are or are not aware of them.

The potency of the virtual-question process seems to center on providing clients with a new set of perceptual distinctions that allows them to observe and reflect on themselves in helpful new ways. Once they are no longer as identified with their limiting questions, they gain some emotional and cognitive distance from them, a move that simultaneously brings new choices and opportunities into view. The virtual-question process is used with couples as well as individuals. When this process is done with couples, it is with the premise that they are unconsciously asking virtual questions which clash with each other's, and that discovering and changing these can fundamentally transform the relationship.

A male client in individual therapy, a 35-year-old dentist, described the first part of the virtual-question process like this: "When I think about my old virtual question, I picture myself like Gulliver when he was captured by the Lilliputians, and he was lying on the beach, tied down with hundreds of little ropes. When we figured out my virtual question, and you wrote it down so *I could look at it*, that was the first moment I felt myself *separate* from it. I suddenly had the experience that all those ropes popped free at the same time, and I was able to get up and go about my business."

The following excerpt from materials from an Imperative Self Analysis workshop was suggested as an introduction to the Imperative Self process. It also can be used more generally to introduce clients to the concept and power of internal questions (Cameron-Bandler, L. and M. Singleton, *Imperative Self Analysis Training*. Unpublished workshop materials, 1988; italics added).

> To give you a simple experience of how a virtual question determines the ways in which a person responds, notice the immediate change in experience when you consider one of your upcoming tasks and ask, "*How will I make the most of this?*" You can notice this question compels you to recognize inherent opportunities in the situation, and to imagine how to maximize those opportunities. If instead you ask, "*Do I know the right way to do it?*", you will (unless the answer is yes) start questioning your ability to perform, being concerned about the consequences of not doing things right, and feel inhibited and anxious. These are the natural responses to a question that embodies the beliefs that there is a right way to do things and that a given task either cannot or should not be done unless you know the right way to do it.

Information-Gathering Questions in Systemic Therapy (The Milan School)

Family therapists think in terms of systems, and their information gathering as well as their interventions naturally reflect this assumption. Of the various schools of family therapy, the Milan Group has the most thorough and well-articulated theory and practice based on question asking. However, their representation in the information-gathering section of this chapter is brief, since the Milan Group believes that practically *any* contact with a family constitutes an intervention. Consequently, most of the descriptions of this work are included in section 4. The following comments are based on Karl Tomm's interpretation of the Milan Group's work (Tomm 1984a and 1984b).

Members of the Milan Group take great care in framing their questions since they consider practically any contact with a family as inherently therapeutic, and that every interaction can be understood as an intervention. Tomm gave an example of a mother calling to request therapy for her daughter whom she said was seriously disturbed. In response to such a request, a therapist of the Milan School might ask, "When did you start having problems with your daughter?" rather than the more conventional possible query, "When did your daughter start having problems?" (Tomm 1984a, p. 122).

The proponents of the Milan School always work together as a team, and much of what they focus on are questions. The team begins its systematic questioning and hypothesizing even before the initial interview, in the formal presession, when they focus on information gained in the intake call. The major goal of this meeting is to formulate hypotheses about the family that will be tested in the actual therapy session through questions the team develops to either validate or refute their first hypotheses. In order to develop their information-gathering strategy for the all-important first meeting with the family, the team considers some of the following questions about the initial intake phone call: "Who in the family called?" "What is the presenting problem?" "How did they construe the situation?" and "What overt and covert expectations did they convey?" (Tomm 1984b, p. 254).

SECTION THREE:
QUESTIONS AS INTERVENTIONS

The purpose of this section is to initiate the conversation about questions as therapeutic interventions. Following an orienting discussion of question-based interventions, we focus on the unique role of questions in conveying therapeutic presuppositions. This includes the opening questions therapists ask in initial interviews. Next, we make a brief tour of typical ways questions are used as interventions in conducting therapy sessions. Lastly, two clinical examples are presented. The first illustrates the successful, elegant use of questions as interventions. The second demonstrates the potency of therapists' questions through an example of one that was *counter*therapeutic.

There is a sense in which *every* question asked in a session, whether intended for information gathering, also operates as an intervention. In each instance, the therapist's query focuses the client in one particular direction, and by omission, not in any other. Moreover, the metacommunication of many therapeutic questions is that the question itself illustrates what the therapist considers important. A Jungian therapist thus trains her client to consider material on the collective unconscious as important; a Freudian "informs" her client that early childhood memories and oedipal material are significant; and a cognitively oriented therapist trains her client to be aware of the statements and questions that comprise his internal dialogue.

Furthermore, many clinicians believe that the most potent therapeutic interventions are delivered through questions. For example, in a study group in which I participated, Milton Erickson provided a masterful illustration of a question-based intervention that literally *forced* his patient to take a positive therapeutic step. This man was a psychotic patient at a state hospital who believed he was Jesus Christ. His skill in woodworking had earned him an assignment in the hospital wood shop, but no staff member had succeeded in getting him to go to work. With a twinkle in his eye, Erickson commented to us, "All I did was ask that patient a very 'innocent' question." With obvious enjoyment, Erickson described the laserlike precision of his single-question intervention. He simply asked the man, "I understand you're a carpenter?" Since the hapless patient had to answer "Yes," or admit he wasn't Jesus Christ, he was soon on the job as a carpenter and woodworker.

Questions and Presuppositions

The presuppositions in Erickson's question accounted for much of the impact of this intervention. Erickson accepted the patient's reality, and *used it* by presupposing that this man therefore *had* to have the carpentry skills needed to work with wood. This elegant use of presuppositions was one of the major distinguishing skills of the master therapists modeled by Bandler and Grinder, which we discussed earlier in the chapter. The speaking of each of these therapists was layered with presuppositions, including those that presumed clients' resources, capabilities, and choice. Bandler and Grinder identified 29 simple and complex types of presuppositions that these seeming magicians so skillfully employed (1975, pp. 211–214). Andreas later elaborated on the therapeutic use of presuppositions in a detailed study of the work of Satir (Andreas 1991, pp. 139–152).

Questions and Presuppositions in the Work of Satir, Whitaker, and Minuchin
While presuppositions are encoded in statements, they usually carry the most therapeutic impact when delivered in the form of a question. In fact, at one point when Andreas discussed presuppositions in Satir's work, he gave six examples, each of which was a question. Two of these were: "Are you aware that the bad feelings come, and then comes the anger?" (*You have bad feelings that come before anger*) and "What can you do about that?" (*You can do something*) (pp. 30–31; his italics). Andreas also recounted some inspiring interventions by Whitaker and Minuchin.

Whitaker saw a divorced couple with their "model" son, who lived with the mother. After observing the mother's sexy, animated conversation with and about the son, Whitaker gestured to her and her son as he said, "So your second marriage worked out much better than your first one?" and then gestured toward the father. Andreas, who observed the session, commented: "The mother looked as if her brain had stopped working for several seconds. Obviously she had never thought of her relationship with her son as a 'marriage' before; from then on it would be impossible for her to keep from thinking of it that way" (p. 140, and personal communication).

Andreas commented that even if the mother consciously rejected Whitaker's remark, it would still have an impact. Since most parents don't want to be married to their children, the mother could not avoid considering her involvement with her son in this new light. Before Whitaker's intervention, her questions had probably been similar to, *"Do I have a close relationship with my son or not?"* Now, she would additionally think, *"Is it too close?"* *"Am I treating him like a spouse?"* The consciousness aroused by these questions hopefully led to the mother's avoiding behaviors that were too intimate or enmeshed with her son. Most likely, the boy also developed more appropriate boundary-setting behaviors with his mother (p. 140; italics added).

Andreas described an equally elegant intervention by Minuchin, where the transforming presuppositions were delivered inside an innocuous, humorous question. The problem that brought the family for treatment was that the ten-year-old son was sniffing gasoline. Immediately after introductions, Minuchin turned to the boy and said, "I understand you like to sniff gasoline. What do you think you are, an automobile?" The immediate impact of this joking comment was that everyone relaxed a little, and the problem was one step closer to resolution.

The first presupposition in Minuchin's question was that serious matters can be discussed with humor. The more veiled second presupposition delivered the one-two punch. Minuchin planted a presupposition about volition and choice by using the words "you *like* to." If instead, he had used a phrase like "you have to" or "you feel driven to," he would have implied that the behavior was out of the boy's control. Minuchin's phrase, "you like to" presupposed that the behavior resulted from the child's own desires, was carried out by his own choice, and that he had the capability to make *different* choices. In a single masterful linguistic stroke, Minuchin transformed the problem behavior; it was no longer some kind of untreatable, crazy, or incomprehensible compulsion (pp. 142–143).

Opening Questions in the Initial Interview   The presuppositions in a sentence include everything that is assumed to be true, in contrast to what is stated directly. It is not possible to speak without using presuppositions, especially because every utterance is made in some context which inevitably influences the interpretation of what is said. Therefore, presuppositions are inherent in all our verbal communications with clients. For example, part way through the initial interview, a colleague of mine asked his client, a struggling 45-year-old consultant, "How come you're not running a multinational company?" With this one comment, my colleague let his client know that he considered him capable of major responsibility and that he wondered what might be interfering with such high potential. The therapist's comment also focused the rest of the interview in that direction.

Our opening remarks in initial interviews are especially important because they help set the frame for the session and ultimately for the course of treatment itself. The goal here is not to propose "right" or "wrong" openings in initial interviews, but to offer some questions for therapists to ask themselves in formulating these important communications. Such questions include: *"What do I want to convey to my client about himself, his difficulties, and the therapist-client relationship?" "Do I want to focus him toward the past, present, or future?" "How can I speak about his difficulties in such a way that he feels respected by me?"* and *"How can I let him know that I consider him capable of growing, resolving his difficulties, and making the changes he wants?"*

Following are some common questions that therapists use in the beginning of initial interviews. Of course, in practice any question is asked in concert with others, including specific follow-up questions. Each of these sample opening questions is followed by a list of some of the presuppositions encoded in the inquiry.

"How can I help you?" The presuppositions include: The client needs help; he can be helped; he already knows what he needs help for; and the therapist can help him.

"What do you want?" The presuppositions include: The therapist considers it okay to want things; she thinks this is a worthwhile reason to seek therapy; it's possible to get what one wants; and she can help the client do that.

"What do you want to accomplish in therapy?" The presuppositions include: Changes—plural—are possible; the client—not the therapist—is the active agent; and the client will continue to be proactive throughout treatment.

"How do you want things to be different in your life?" The presuppositions include: The client has thought about his future, compared it to his present, and concluded that these present conditions are unsatisfactory; the client can specify how and what he wants to be different; it's okay to want things to be different; and this difference can be accomplished.

"What kind of relationship do you want to have with your husband?" The presuppositions include: The therapist is more interested in the future than the past; it is possible to choose and create the form and content of one's intimate relationship; issues can be resolved and problems left in the past.

"What is the problem?" The presuppositions include: There is a problem; something is wrong; the client had not succeeded in solving his problems on his own; and perhaps he failed and would be admitting defeat by having to ask for help with the problem.

"Why are you here?" The presuppositions include: There is a reason for being here; and there's something the client wants and can have.

Ways Questions Function as Interventions in Guiding Sessions

The ways a therapist uses questions as interventions throughout therapy is a vital component of her therapeutic toolkit. In addition to question interventions in specific cases such as those illustrated by Erickson, Whitaker, and Minuchin, all therapists also conduct the flow of sessions through their questions. Following are some examples of ways a therapist guides and directs sessions with her queries:

The therapist directs attention by asking questions ("What else could you have done when he said that?" or "How about that issue with your husband we were talking about a few weeks ago?" or "How did you do with the driving assignment we discussed last week?"). She also makes inquiries to get more detail about an issue ("What were you thinking about when you made your first driving excursion by yourself?" or "Will you help me understand more about your reasons for making that decision?").

An especially potent use of questions is to plant ideas and suggestions ("Have you considered trying to drive on the freeway yet?" or "What accounted for your skillfulness in handling that situation?" or "When did you start getting better?"). A clinician implicitly marks out what she considers important about specific issues through the number of questions and follow-up questions she asks—or doesn't. Therapists also use questions as a device to change the subject by asking about something they consider more pertinent to address.

There are many other ways therapists intervene by using questioning techniques. For example, in order to reinforce cognitive flexibility and enhance relationship skills, therapists ask clients to consider issues from perspectives different from their own ("If you were in her shoes, what do you think she would have thought of what you did?" or "What would your best friend, Joe, advise you to say to your boss under these circumstances?"). A therapist also reinforces the client's internalizing her own problem-solving and relationship skills through questions ("What might I have advised you to do after he made that awful remark?").

Opportunities to make interventions through skillful questioning occur whether a client is reporting a success or a problem. In either case, it is important to underscore the cognitive skills useful and/or necessary for success. After a success, the therapist might inquire, "Do you remember what questions you asked yourself just before you did that?" or "What was the question that altered your behavior?" or "What was the question that showed you there were more options than you realized?" If, on the other hand, the situation is one where the client continues to experience difficulty, the therapist might ask, "In thinking back to when you had to confront your son, what questions could you have asked yourself that would have made the situation turn out better for both of you?" Finally, it is also important for the therapist to know when *not* to ask a question, as sometimes silence (the doing of not doing) is the most potent intervention.

Wait Time   Silence—the doing of not doing—is often a therapist's most potent intervention. This is especially true in relation to asking questions. *Wait time*, which has been studied extensively in educational settings, is the standard term for the interval between when a question is asked and when it is responded to.

Wilen wrote: "Essential to student thinking, especially at the higher cognitive levels, is the amount of time a teacher allots for student reflection after asking a question and before a student responds" (Wilen 1982, p. 20). Wilen reported that when Rowe trained teachers to increase their wait time from one second to three to five seconds, the quantity and quality of students' responses improved dramatically. Rowe found that "the length of students' responses increased, responses reflected higher-level thought, failures to respond decreased, student-student interaction increased, and the frequency of student questions increased" (p. 20).

A Successful Question-Centered Intervention   Often a therapeutic anecdote poetically captures what pages of abstract explanation can not. The following account is from *Undercurrents: A Life Beneath the Surface* (Manning 1994, pp. 182–183, and personal communication). This incident occurred in an initial session with a six-year-old named Ben, who was preoccupied with his infant brother, Stephen, who died six months earlier. Ben's parents contacted Dr. Manning because initially Ben seemed to be the one who responded the "best" to the death. Virtually every intervention in this anecdote is expressed in the form of a question. Many of these convey presuppositions that helped the session glide to a healing new image for this young client. The therapist's ability to wait patiently for her client's responses was also essential to the success of this session.

> Ben is a freckle-faced redhead dressed in a baseball shirt and jeans. He looks like the kind of kid who is probably harboring a member of the reptile family in one of his pockets. When I ask him what's on his mind, he tells me that he is "sad" because he can't stop thinking about his brother. I ask him how he pictures Stephen now.
>
> He answers, "Mom and Dad think he's in heaven with all the other kids that got dead." He gets very quiet and stares at the floor. I let the silence surround us for a while and he adds, "But I don't know about God and heaven. I can't see it in my head."
>
> "So Mom and Dad's picture doesn't help you like it helps them," I suggest.
>
> He looks ashamed and answers, "No." We are both quiet for several moments and I feel an aching sadness fill up the space between us. With wide eyes and a confidential whisper he tells me, "Some people think that when you die you come back as other things."
>
> "Really?" I ask. "Like what?"
>
> "Like animals and trees and flowers and stuff like that." He smiles as he says it, but then instantly pulls back and insists, "But, of course, I don't believe that!"
>
> I smile mischievously and prod him, "Yeah, but if you did, what would you come back as?"
>
> "I'd come back as a blue jay . . . because I like the bird . . . and I like the team."
>
> "And Mom?" I ask. "What would she come back as?"
>
> "A cardinal . . . and Dad would be an eagle . . . a bald one." We laugh. Things get quiet again.

"And Stephen?" I ask softly. "What would Stephen be?" He thinks for a moment and replies, "Stephen would be the water that we all drink from."

"The water? Like in a birdbath?" I ask.

"Yeah, but not just a birdbath. That would run out. Like the water in all the creeks and all the rivers and all the oceans. And the birds could drink from it and never run out . . . not never. . . . Stephen could be the water."

The sorrow on Ben's face turns to pleasure at the image he has created.

A Countertherapeutic Question-Centered Intervention   In examining the power of questions as therapeutic interventions, we are also forced to recognize that: *If skillful questioning leads to effective therapeutic results, it must also be the case that poor questions (or even a good question, delivered at the wrong time, or to the wrong person, or in the wrong way) can lead to negative, undesired, and even countertherapeutic results.* Tomm courageously illustrated this phenomenon with an instructive personal example that occurred during a session of marital therapy (1987, pp. 3–4):

At the same time, however, some of the therapist's questions can be countertherapeutic. . . . The latter became painfully obvious to me a few years ago while reviewing a videotape of a marital session. One of my "innocent" questions appeared to have stimulated the re-emergence of serious marital conflict. It occurred during a follow-up session in which the couple were talking about the fact that they had not had any arguments for several weeks. In other words, there had been a major improvement in the marriage. After a lively and enjoyable discussion about these changes, I asked, "What problems would you like to talk about today?" Following this seemingly innocuous question, the couple gradually drifted into a bitter argument about which of the two of them most needed further therapy. I (privately) reconstrued the improvement as "transient and unstable" and resumed my treatment of their chronic marital difficulties. I remained completely blind to the fact that I had inadvertently triggered the deterioration until a colleague pointed it out to me on the videotape. In retrospect, the assumption behind the questions, that problems needed to be identified and/or clarified before I could act therapeutically, turned out to be limiting and pathogenic. It limited the discussion to areas of dissatisfaction and served to bring forth pathological interactions. Instead, I could have capitalized on the new developments and asked questions that were designed to strengthen the recent changes. Unfortunately, I did not see that option clearly at the time.

SECTION FOUR: QUESTION-BASED INTERVENTIONS IN THE LITERATURE

In this final section we revisit each of the three therapeutic approaches discussed in terms of questions for information gathering in section 2: cognitive-behavioral therapy, Neuro-Linguistic Programming, and the Milan Group representing systems-oriented therapy.

Question Interventions in
Cognitive-Behavioral Therapy

Question interventions are so much a part of cognitive-behavioral therapy that Beck and Emery labeled one of the ten principles of cognitive therapy as the "Socratic method." They preferred a question-based approach for helping people correct damaging thoughts because "Questions induce clients (1) to become aware of what their thoughts are, (2) to observe and examine them for cognitive distortions, (3) to choose more empowering thoughts as substitutes, and (4) to make plans to develop new thought patterns" (Beck and Emery 1985, p. 177).

According to Beck and Emery: "Good questions can establish structure, develop collaboration, clarify the patient's statements, awaken the patient's interest, build the therapeutic relationship, provide the therapist with essential information, open up the patient's previously closed system of logic, develop his motivation to try out new behavior, help him to think in a new way about his problems and enhance the patient's observing self" (p. 177). Further, the therapist, in asking questions, models a way of being and interacting that is itself an important learning intervention with clients.

A major goal of cognitive-behavioral therapy is to correct the faulty logic assumed to be primarily responsible for generating clients' difficulties. Asking clients questions is the major way these damaging assumptions are brought to their attention. At first glance, it may appear that the following questions are meant simply to gather information. However, it is most relevant that the therapist's intention is to stimulate clients' self-observation, thinking, and further conversations between therapist and client. Beck and Emery provided this list of questions for challenging limiting thinking (1985, pp. 196–197).

- What is the evidence for or against this idea?
- Where is the logic?
- Are you oversimplifying a causal relationship?
- Are you confusing a habit with a fact?
- Are your interpretations of the situation too far from reality to be accurate?
- Are you confusing your version of the facts with the facts as they are?
- Are you thinking in all-or-none terms?
- Are you using words or phrases that are extreme or exaggerated?
- Are you taking selected examples out of context?
- Are you using cognitive defense mechanisms?
- Is your source of information reliable?
- Are you thinking in terms of certainties rather than probabilities?
- Are you confusing a low probability with a high probability?
- Are your judgments based on feelings instead of facts?
- Are you overfocusing on irrelevant factors?

Inquiry, or Question Asking, as a Listening Skill   Burns used questions as interventions in sessions and also trained patients to ask themselves questions. The latter questions focused on helping patients become self-observers with the skill of self-questioning, so they can learn to problem-solve on their own. Like other cognitive-behavioral therapists, Burns assumed an explicit educational model as part of psychotherapy. In *The Feeling Good Handbook* (1989), he reported training patients to use inquiry, or question asking, as a method of communicating, connecting, and listening. He wrote, "Inquiry is the use of gentle, probing questions to learn more about what the other person is thinking and feeling" (p. 390). Another virtue Burns cited for the inquiry technique was that, "Inquiry is not only used to learn more about how the other person is thinking and feeling, it can help transform vague negative reactions into concrete problems that you can deal with in a more productive manner" (p. 392).

"What If?" and "Why Is This So Awful?" Techniques   Burns especially recommended these question-based techniques for anxiety-prone individuals who were likely to catastrophize negative consequences for themselves. In order to prevent this anxiety-provoking habit, he trained patients to ask themselves specific internal questions that could forestall rising anxiety, and keep clients from buying into their own exaggerated and anxious thoughts. The core skill needed to do this is self-observation. For example, if a patient were certain that some social foible would be catastrophic, Burns suggested the patient ask himself: *"What are the worst possible consequences of this?" "What if they really did happen?"* (p. 287; italics added). Burns also trained his patients to challenge their own anxiety-based conclusions by asking themselves questions like: *"Why is this so awful?" "What if such and such happened, why would that be so bad?"* and *"Is that the very worst possible thing that could happen?"* (p. 287; italics added). When his patient had pushed his fears to the worst imaginable extreme, Burns suggested he ask himself two questions: *"How likely is this?" "Could I live with this if it did happen?"* (p. 287, italics added).

Troubleshooting Guide   Burns had his patients keep a Daily Mood Log to help them problem-solve difficult situations. If they were still upset after going through the exercise of challenging their own emotional thinking, Burns offered the following guide of self-questions (p. 86; italics added):

- *Have I correctly identified the upsetting event?*
- *Do I want to change my negative feelings about this situation?*
- *Have I identified my Automatic Thoughts properly?*
- *Are my Rational Responses convincing, valid statements that put the lie to my Automatic thoughts?*

Question Interventions in
Neuro-Linguistic Programming

In the earlier section on information-gathering questions in NLP, we noted that such questions often function simultaneously as interventions in the sense that they have a therapeutic impact. Therefore, dividing therapeutic questions in this way, though useful for studying questions, is also somewhat arbitrary in practice. Consequently, when we discussed the outcome frame, the meta model, and virtual questions, it could be seen that each of these questioning practices could help clients access or create resources for building new perceptions, beliefs, choices, and solutions. In this section of the chapter, we explore modeling, including its utility in making therapeutic interventions.

NLP was generated by modeling outstanding individuals to discover explicitly how they did what they did. Modeling also has many therapeutic applications, including helping a client acquire skills and achieve outcomes admired in someone else and desired for himself. NLP assumes, within certain constraints, that what is possible for one person is also possible for others. Constructing a bridge between these requires an explicit enough understanding of how the goal behavior, skill, or outcome was accomplished in the first place. Thus, modeling is a foundation for therapeutic change.

Gordon's description of modeling makes the relationship between modeling for learning and for therapeutic impact clear (Gordon 1989, p. 1). He wrote that modeling is for:

1. Discovering patterns in experience and behavior
2. Describing those patterns (which sometimes requires making new distinctions) in such a way that we can understand how they related to the outcomes they are connected to
3. Discovering ways of using those patterns
4. Creating formats for making those patterns available to another individual

Modeling, or learning about successful patterns in experience and behavior, need not be confined to modeling *others*. Clients are usually successful in many areas of their own lives, and have a problem in only one specific context. It would be helpful, as well as validating for them, to discover explicitly what works in their *own* experience and behavior. Therapy would then include helping them transfer their own capabilities into resolving the issues that motivated them to seek therapy.

Dilts (1995) provided a detailed questioning format for modeling another individual. It is presented here for two reasons. First, therapists can use these questions to help clients study their own successful behavioral, emotional, and cognitive processes. What clients learn would become a practical resource in other areas of their lives; they could come to understand how they learned something successfully in one area in order to become a better learner in another context. Second, if a client has a goal of learning something more successfully, he could be helped to model someone whom he considered to be a superb learner.

The modeling questions are generally consistent with different levels of experience as identified by Bateson and described by Dilts (Dilts 1994a, p. 293). Dilts wrote: "In our brain structure, language, and perceptual systems there are natural hierarchies or levels of experience. The effect of each level is to organize and control the information on the level below it. Changing something on an upper level would necessarily change things on the lower levels; changing something on a lower level could but would not necessarily affect the upper levels" (p. 293). These levels are: environment, behavior, capabilities, beliefs, identity, and spiritual or larger systems. Therapists who model someone, or instruct clients in studying themselves or someone else, could begin with the following: "As you think about (your behavior) or the behavior of this person, consider the following questions. . . ."

- Questions about "Environment": "*When* and *where* did/does the individual enact the behavior to be analyzed?" "What was the external context surrounding the individual and his or her actions?"
- Questions about "Behavior": "*What*, specifically, did/does the individual do behaviorally in those times and places?" "What are the details of the behavior?" "How did/does that behavior 'fit' or relate to the environment in which it occurred?" "Which behaviors, if any, do not seem to 'fit' with the typical assumptions related to the context?"
- Questions about "Capabilities": "*How* did/does the individual use cognitive or mental processes in order to carry out those behaviors?" "What capabilities were needed or presupposed in order to trigger or guide those actions in that place and time?"
- Questions about "Beliefs and Values": "*Why* did/does the individual use those particular cognitive processes or capabilities to accomplish those activities?" "What beliefs motivated or shaped the individual's thoughts and cognitive activity?" "What values were/are important to the individual when he or she was/is involved in those cognitive and behavioral activities?"
- Questions about "Identity": "*Who* was/is the individual such that he or she engaged those particular beliefs, values, capabilities and behaviors in that particular time and place?" "What was/is the individual's perception of his or her own identity and mission?"
- Questions about "the Larger System": "*Who else* may have shaped or influenced the individual's beliefs, cognitive strategies or behavior with respect to this activity?" "What was/is the broader vision that the individual was pursuing or representing?"

Question Interventions in
Systemic Therapy (the Milan School)

Family sessions conducted by the Milan Group depend almost entirely on the therapist's asking questions of family members. This therapeutic orientation is sometimes described as employing the Socratic method. For example, in the main part of the intake interview, the therapist does almost nothing except ask questions, many of which were generated by the team in the presession. These initial questions tend to be general and open-ended, to give family members the maximum possibility of expressing themselves. The therapist's questions become more specific and focused as the session continues and as important issues begin to be revealed.

In an attempt to remain neutral and nonjudgmental about the family or any of the family members, the therapist asks questions of everybody, and avoids any that would appear to create an alliance. When the therapist intervenes, she does so primarily by asking questions which cause family members to address issues they may not have noticed, or that they had been avoiding. For example, she might ask, "Who in the family is usually most supportive when someone shows sadness by crying?" (Tomm 1984b, p. 254). At the same time, the therapist asks questions that implicitly challenge the assumptions of the family; her aim is to facilitate more autonomy and freedom in the system. This serves the main goal of the Milan School which is to create metachange, or change in the family's ability to change itself.

In the Milan School, questions as interventions take other forms as well. The therapist's goal is to introduce "news of difference"—or new "information"—into the system, and these new perspectives are likely to be introduced nondirectly, usually through questions. This information about difference is intended to get the family to look at and think about their problems differently. These interventions are based on the pattern of thinking known as *circular epistemology*. It is assumed that the family's own explanations for its problems are based on a linear, cause-effect view which cannot give them the freedom necessary for change.

Three basic and interrelated principles have emerged as the foundation of the Milan team's thinking and interventions. These are: (1) hypothesizing, (2) circularity, and (3) neutrality. Questions and questioning, however, are central to each. Hypothesizing occurs first, since the goal of the team is to develop alternate theories or hypotheses about the family's difficulties. These hypotheses, which must be different from the family's own hypotheses about the situation, are intended to guide the therapist in asking the kinds of questions which can either confirm or refute the team's hypotheses about the family. The activity of generating hypotheses is an evolving one; new behavior or questions among the family will cause the need for updating this thinking.

About circularity, Tomm wrote: "Circular questioning reflects the executive aspect of the process of systemic hypothesizing. The activity of the therapist triggers the release of 'information' by asking questions. The types of questions asked are based on two fundamental assumptions: that information lies in differences and that the meaning of a behavior is derived from its context. Examples of these types of questions include difference questions, hypothetical questions, behavioral-effect questions and triadic questions" (Tomm, 1987, part II, p. 259). *Difference* is the important concept here, because "a difference always reflects a relationship (between whatever is being distinguished) that is reciprocal and hence, is circular" (p. 259).

There are two important kinds of difference questions: spatial and temporal. Here, we invoke Tomm once again: "Differences in space include differences between persons ('Who gets more upset, mother or father?'), differences between relationships ('Is father closer to Mary or to John?' or 'Does father show more anger when John misbehaves or when Mary misbehaves?'), and differences among ideas, perceptions, values, and beliefs ('When people get angry in this family does it mean that they care too much or not enough?')" (p. 259).

Temporal differences refer to changes between different intervals of time. Here are a few illustrations of questions demonstrating temporal difference, again described by Tomm: "Differences between one occasion in the past and another occasion in the past ('Was there more fighting before or after the heart attack last year?'), differences between the past and the present ('Was father closer to Mary when she was a little girl or is he closer now?'), differences between the past and the future ('If you had not had any children, do you think it would be more or less likely that you will still be together five years from now?) (p. 259). The Milan Group also uses triadic questions. A triadic question may be defined as a question addressed to a third person about the relationship between another two. These questions deliberately invite 'gossiping in the presence' of the person being described" (p. 260).

SUMMARY

The chapter began with a discussion of the role of internal dialogue in developing and maintaining psychopathology and the problems which impel people to seek therapy. Then we reviewed the multiple uses of questions in therapy, focusing on ways they are used for gathering information, as well as making interventions. We explored the role of presuppositions in strengthening the therapeutic impact of questions and included examples from master therapists Erickson, Minuchin, Satir, and Whitaker. In the next chapter, we turn to an orientation to question-centered therapy, which builds on the models, theories, and practices reviewed in this chapter.

PART TWO

Question-Centered
Therapy with Individuals

4

Overview of Question-Centered Therapy

We knock upon silence for an answering music.
— CHINESE POET, ANONYMOUS

All therapists have a question-centered orientation to some degree, although most do not think of themselves this way. All use questions as the basic linguistic instrument to conduct an interview, and all guide a session through their own internal questions concerning the client, the progress of the interview, and whatever they deem needs to be accomplished. Moreover, since questions are fundamentally interactive, they are at the heart of what Friedman calls "the healing dialogue in psychotherapy" (Friedman 1985). Clinicians differ with regard to question asking based on their awareness of the power of language, training in a methodology of question asking, their own life experiences, and the skill and intuition which comprise the strategic use of this essential linguistic tool.

The purpose of this chapter is to provide an overview of question-centered therapy. We begin by positioning this orientation as one which makes explicit some linguistic presumptions and characteristics that are often implicit in other therapy methods. We then explore the psycho-educational foundation of question-centered therapy that is meant to build on, and perhaps extend, the therapeutic utility afforded by an awareness of these linguistic distinctions.

Therefore, we begin in section 1 with a discussion about therapy and language. Then we focus on the therapeutic conversation, including its improvisational nature, and explore general goals of therapy from the clinician's perspective rather than the client's. Within this context, in section 2 we discuss the orientation and goals of question-centered therapy, as well as the characteristics of a question-centered therapist. In section 3, we introduce the model of the Learner Self and the Judger Self, which is the general organizing metaphor and theoretical background for this work. Finally, in section 4, we discuss how to present the psychoeducational material of question-centered therapy to clients. Included in this section are three handouts: the Choice Model, Observe-and-Correct Questions, and Switching Questions, all of which are based on the model of the Learner Self and the Judger Self. This section also includes clinical anecdotes.

SECTION ONE: THERAPY AND LANGUAGE

Our lives are comprised of continuous conversations, a multilevel, ongoing dance of questions and statements. Consistent with the assertion that statements represent answers to prior, usually implicit questions, we can consider questions as *partnered* with answers, engaged in the universal "my turn-your turn-my turn" structure of conversations. The therapeutic conversation is a specialized form of this dance. A musical metaphor invokes its rhythm—the ongoing mutual reciprocity of the conversation of these speakers and listeners in a therapy session. Therefore, in this section we focus on the therapeutic conversation as this dance of speaking and listening, especially as these operations are shaped by the internal and external questions of client and therapist alike. We note the improvisational nature of this dialogue, the courage and creativity required to engage in it, and also consider goals of the therapeutic conversation.

The Therapeutic Conversation

One universal element in therapy is that people speak, and of course, most of what we therapists learn about our clients issues from their speaking. Regardless of problem or personality, what clients say conveys their thoughts, and simultaneously reflects the ways in which they think. Both the content and process of this thinking and speaking must bend to the way that language, any language, shapes perception and reality. For example, the English language shapes a different possible reality than does, say, Japanese. However, regardless of the particular tongue, we are inevitably shaped by the language in which we live, a phenomenon Heidegger pointed to when he wrote that "language speaks us" (Heidegger 1971). In therapy we are primarily interested in the idiosyncratic ways our clients' thinking and speaking confine them to their problems, and at the same time offer fundamental keys to the changes they seek.

Another universal element in therapy is that people listen. Listening is always filtered and focused by what an individual is listening *for*, whether consciously or unconsciously. However, people are generally not aware of the questions through which they listen, interpret life, and make their choices of being and doing. Furthermore, the same individual listens through different questions depending on his role, concerns, and priorities, as well as the setting and context within which he listens. By example, jurors listen to a defendant through the question, *"Is he telling the truth?"* The mother of a newborn listens through *"Is my baby OK?"* Her attention is acutely framed by this question, and new mothers are known for hearing their baby's cries under otherwise "impossible" circumstances. The generic role of client stimulates listening questions such as: *"Does this therapist understand me?"* and *"Can she really help me?"* The listening of any specific client will, of course, also be focused by automatic, unconscious questions related to his difficulties and presenting problems.

This book is based on the assertion that our questions—often the ones of which we are unaware—hold fundamental power for shaping our personal, as well as collective realities. Our job as therapists requires that we help clients create more satisfying lives and worlds for themselves. The more skilled they are at speaking and listening, the more successful they can be. Therefore, it is incumbent upon us to understand how clients' current use of language restricts them to a limiting world, when what they desire and need is an expanding and inventive one. We can teach them to dance a splendid polka or an elegant waltz, and stop playing music that causes them to fall over their two left feet.

Clients engage therapists to conduct and orchestrate many complex variables in order to bring the music of a single session, or an entire course of treatment, to a satisfying and successful denouement. Beginning musicians and therapists alike must learn how to play their respective instruments most effectively and efficiently. Senior therapists, like master musicians, routinely play their instruments with prowess, finesse, and artistry. Language is the therapist's instrument, and the more skilled she is in understanding and using language therapeutically, the more effective and efficient she can be in fulfilling the mandates of successful therapy.

Therapy as Improvisation

Improvisational jazz, rather than scored music, best captures the interplay between client and therapist. At any moment the therapist's music represents her answer to the question, *"What's the best note to play now?"* rather than, *"How shall I play the notes written on this page?"* In fact, the whole experience of really good therapy is a lot like really good improvisational jazz. We hear the sounds of two musicians conversing and resonating with each other, creating in the moment. The therapist's music blends her training, experiences, intuitions, and therapeutic intentions, as she responds to the needs and goals of her client from moment to moment. She structures her therapeutic moves through her skillfulness in understanding and using language. She listens on many levels, including to the questions behind her clients' questions. Through her speaking she may strike a caring note, an inquiring note—or issue a challenging one.

Basically, the therapist responds in order to lead, recognizing how fully therapy is a skillful improvisation. She knows that despite the most detailed treatment plan, she must improvise to some degree because therapy occurs in the present encounter, in what is *actually* happening, not in what was *supposed* to happen.

Every therapeutic moment is an invitation, a request, and a question, with the therapist asking, *"Will you listen to me?" "Will you risk?" "Will you step past fear?" "Will you say what you really want?"*

The client, on the other hand, generally responds in order to be led, his music a blend of his concerns, beliefs, hopes, and fears. In truth, every moment in therapy between these two is a dialectical creation, a continual dance of invitations, expectations, risks, disappointments, and successes. In each moment, therapist and client meet each other, check each other out, invite each other, respond to each other, and sometimes dare each other. The client's questions in therapy take courage to ask: *"Is it safe to reveal myself here?"* Will you *really* listen to me?" *"Will you confront me when I need to be?"* "Can you really show me how to make my life work?"* However, there is a constriction in the client's music that goes beyond any psychodynamic or historical influence. His use of language limits him, especially those implicit, negating questions such as: *"Why am I such a failure that I had to end up in a therapy office?"* or *"Whose fault is it that I'm here?"*

Courage, Creativity, and the Therapeutic Dialectic   Courage and creativity characterize this dialectic, this questioning and responding between client and therapist, as between the two improvising jazz musicians. The moment would lose that sense of immediacy and encounter if either the therapy protocol or the musical score were followed note by precise note. It would also lack the creative condition necessary for something new to emerge. Courage in each moment— whether in therapy, jazz, or life—lies in choosing the risk of encounter in the face of not knowing the outcome. Rollo May wrote, "Creativity occurs in an act of encounter and is to be understood with this encounter at its center" (May 1975, p. 77). While the therapeutic encounter is between two or more human beings, it is also between what-is-known and what-is-yet-to-be. May quoted a Chinese poet, "We poets struggle with Non-being to force it to yield Being. We knock upon silence for an answering music" (May, p. 79). Optimally, the questions we therapists ask of our clients will call forth new answering music that is both creative and helpful.

The Goals of the Therapeutic Conversation

While therapy and improvisational jazz share important experiential components, the purposes of each differ in significant ways. In jazz, the moment of meeting and relating *is* the point, and that moment is often beautiful and complete unto itself. By contrast, while the therapeutic moment may be valuable and even transforming, alone it is usually insufficient to fulfill the goals for therapy. That contract involves the mutual expectation that one participant in the conversation will make desired personal changes as a result of the music created together. Evidence of success will not happen primarily in the therapy office; ultimately, it must manifest in our clients' lives.

The therapeutic conversation, that therapeutic dialectic, gets played out within a context that has goals, theoretical underpinnings, and a temporal structure. A therapist can only guide that score (or answer her internal questions with therapeutic interventions) in relation to the goals she assumes about therapy. Despite many diverging therapeutic orientations, a DSM-wide range of diagnoses, and multiple reasons that people seek help, most therapists would agree that there are only two basic, yet connected, goals in therapy. These are: resolving any presenting problem(s), and helping clients develop the cognitive, emotional, behavioral, and interpersonal attitudes and skills that constitute a foundation for satisfying and successful living. Any other goals—for example, developing appropriate boundaries, becoming more assertive, or creating a stronger sense of self—could be subsumed under these two more basic and inclusive therapeutic outcomes.

In a best-case scenario, therapeutic success is even richer than an expanded repertoire; the client develops the ability to create new musical scores for himself. He accomplishes more than changing and resolving problems; he develops skills of metachange. He will be able to *intentionally change the way he changes* in order to meet future challenges in a more powerful way. His therapeutic success therefore becomes generative; he "learns to fish," rather than having only "been fed." In these ways, the time he invests in therapy is like a pebble thrown in a pond, its ripples expanding outward into the client's future. This is what's meant by *enduring* therapeutic success.

SECTION TWO: ORIENTATION TO QUESTION-CENTERED THERAPY

Therapists with a question-centered orientation share an appreciation of the role of language in promoting or inhibiting change work. They also presume that an important goal of therapy is skill training and empowerment. Therefore, they seek to help clients discover or develop their own best answers to the dilemmas and questions which caused them to seek help. After all, ultimately, they need their own wisdom more than they need ours. Question-centered therapists also hold certain cognitive and developmental goals for their clients. These therapists recognize that changes in internal dialogue, including internal questions, are reflected in positive changes in clients' experiences, behaviors, and relationships. Therefore, such cognitive shifts are considered core to the process of desired, intentional change. In other words, question-centered therapists recognize the necessity of helping clients develop the cognitive lifeboat, needed to successfully navigate the inevitably stormy seas of life.

The goals clinicians hold for therapy are naturally related to some theoretical model, implicit or explicit, about optimal, healthy human functioning. With question-centered therapy, the fulfillment of these therapy goals finds a home in the model of the *Learner Self* and the *Judger Self*. This is a model of being human that posits that each of us "has" a Learner Self and a Judger Self, and that each of these mindsets is characterized by specific ways of thinking, feeling, behaving, relating, and using language.

In particular, the Judger Self and the Learner Self ask different kinds of questions, especially internal ones, and these divergent types of questions automatically place the questioner in disparate worlds of perception, experience, and possibility. Question-centered therapists formalize the psycho-educational aspect of therapy by explicitly assisting clients in developing the abilities of a skillful Learner Self. These include the ability to self-observe, think clearly and nondefensively, take responsibility for one's choices, and engage in relationships in a win-win, heartfelt way.

Choice and the Experience of Being in Control

Certain other skills are fundamental to the empowerment intentions of question-centered therapy. Personal power becomes most possible when people recognize that they make choices every moment, and that they have the ability to exercise much more control over the choices they make. Clients in question-centered therapy come to understand that while we have little control over what happens *to* us, we have *much* control in how we respond to whatever happens to us. This responsiveness is quite distinct from merely *reacting* to whatever comes our way. Beyond clients' recognizing that they always have a choice, at least in attitude, they also learn that they significantly increase the number of choices available by asking more, and better, questions. The recognition of the nature of choice contributes to clients developing a stronger sense of self-efficacy and of being in control, which, in turn, helps them to accomplish their desired outcomes.

Choice and Responsibility

The recognition of control and choice contributes to an individual developing another fundamental awareness—that he is *responsible* for his choices. These realizations about choice, control, and responsibility, are coupled with training in how to transform these abstractions into reliable, everyday skills. This is the basis of question-centered therapy.

Having access to these characteristic research attitudes and skills also gives meaning and muscle to the concept of taking responsibility for oneself, one's behavior, and one's life. Once an individual learns to appreciate how pervasively his internal dialogue and internal questions influence his experiences and results, he also knows one specific and concrete thing he can be responsible *for* that will actually make a difference. He can ask more questions. He can also examine his existing questions, or "question his questions," and design improved ones in keeping with his values and goals. These skills of attitude and actions belong to the domain of the Learner Self.

Strengthening the Learner Self   Planting seeds for strengthening the client's Learner Self is the fundamental orientation of a question-centered therapist. This success depends upon the client cultivating a researcher's mindset in relation to himself and his own life. When the client is able to observe himself, others, and the world around him (that is, report objectively without undue personal bias), then he can be a competent self-researcher. Among the skills of a researcher is the ability to experiment with different approaches to problem solving without condemning himself for having taken routes that "failed." His internal dialogue is characterized by self-questions such as: *"What do I want?"* *"How shall I get there?"* *"What might work?"* *"What shall I try first?"* and *"What would be useful?"* He avoids indulging in distracting and derailing internal questions such as, *"Why were you so stupid?"* or *"Why do you blow it so often?"* The question-based method for cultivating a researcher's attitude in question-centered therapy is called *observe-and-correct,* and is described later in this chapter.

Ideally, the completion of therapy finds the client having learned, among other things, that the ways he thinks, feels, behaves, and relates correspond to his internal dialogue, and especially the kinds of questions he asks himself at any moment. These awarenesses motivate him to be alert to his internal questions, which fortunately, he needn't do most of the time. Only when things go poorly need he backtrack to discover what ineffective guiding questions led him astray. With this information he is empowered to develop better ones. In this way, the client learns to approach life as a researcher — or a jazz musician — whose every moment is an experiment. Rather than judging the results of any experiment as negative, or as a failure, he simply wonders what he's learned and what corrections might work better next time.

For the individual who regards his life as continuous, promising research experiments, this modus operandi leads to a fulfilling personal and interpersonal life of response and creativity. It also leads to the ability to maintain healthy personal control, rather than living reactively, often feeling upset and out of control. Naturally, there's no guarantee that things won't go wrong, because in fact, they will. It *is* a promise, however, that these self-observing, thinking, problem-solving, and questioning skills enhance the skill, ease, and confidence with which one recovers and sets other courses.

Learning to be a competent critical and creative thinker does not turn one into a robotic Mr. Spock, as some clients fear. Nor does the commitment to live from a researcher's mindset mean one must be a cold, unfeeling scientist. Many researchers and scientists care passionately about their work. For this reason, they learn to discipline their thinking, feelings, reactions, and behaviors in order to stay on course for accomplishing their goals and fulfilling what is meaningful for them. A life of meaning for clients, as for anyone else, includes effectiveness and love, and these question-centered methods can contribute to both.

Characteristics of a
Question-Centered Therapist

As we have said, a therapist who is "question-centered" does not belong to or adhere to any particular school of therapy. Rather, this is an orientation that constitutes a way of thinking that can be a useful addition to any approach to therapy. Thus, the therapist with a question-centered orientation shares the same range of training, concerns, skills, and goals as any other therapist. The main difference lies in an orientation and training to take advantage of the power of language, specifically the shaping and guiding power of both internal and external questions. As a consequence of this linguistic focus, question-centered therapists impose additional filters, goals, and tasks on the process of therapy.

Since such therapists recognize that the person asking questions usually controls a given situation, they intentionally use this linguistic tool to guide the direction and shape of an interview, including inquiries designed to induce clients to think along new lines. A question-centered therapist maintains awareness of the questions she asks the client, how to formulate them, what presuppositions to embed in them, of course, and the most effective ways to deliver them. To this end, her consistent background questions include: *"What shall I ask?" "What do I want my question to accomplish?" "What wording will best help me accomplish that?"* and *"Is this the right time to deliver this question?"* Naturally, she also takes care to give clients sufficient time to absorb her questions and to muse over their responses.

Therapists' Internal Questions   In addition to making question-centered interventions, a question-centered therapist is aware that her communications, interactions, interventions, and questions to the client are designed to help her answer her own internal questions about that individual. She engages in moment-to-moment question-centered problem solving as she observes her client, his reaction to the last intervention, the emotion on his face, the text his body reveals. She asks herself questions such as: *"What's the most helpful thing to do now?" "Should I ask another question?" "Should I be silent to let him absorb what just happened?"* She might ask, *"What role shall I assume at this moment—supporter, educator, or perhaps challenger?"* In truth, this continuous internal process—observe, self-question, intervene (behaviorally answer), observe again, self-question—is the subtext that guides the entire musical improvisation of this session, or any session, for any therapist of any orientation. A question-centered therapist, having a heightened awareness of the power of internal questions, gains additional advantages. She skillfully monitors her own internal queries as she conducts a session and trains her clients in question-centered methods for thinking, speaking, and listening more effectively.

SECTION THREE: THE MODEL OF
THE LEARNER SELF AND THE JUDGER SELF

The model of the Learner Self and the Judger Self serves as the organizing metaphor and represents the theoretical foundation of question-centered therapy. This model is an elaborate description of being human that organizes thinking about the self into five categories: thinking, feeling, behaving, relating, and languaging and communicating. A sixth category summarizes the other five, and functions as an orientation to the model. This model stands in the background of assessment and treatment in question-centered therapy. It is also the basis of all the psycho-educational training, including the handouts. The model of the Learner Self and the Judger Self is most thoroughly displayed on the Learner/Judger Chart. Further elaboration about this model is found in chapters 8 and 9. Here, we explore definitions of the Learner Self, Judger Self, and skillful Learner Self.

The Learner Self, the Judger Self,
and the Skillful Learner Self

The terms "Learner Self" and "Judger Self" do not refer to actual people, but to *parts* of each of us—*everyone* has *both,* simply by virtue of being human. These terms are simply a convenient way to cluster characteristically related attitudes, behaviors, ways of being, and ways of using language. These terms also allow us to consider a theory of change designed to be simple and practical for clients to understand and use. In general, presenting problems are construed as more Judger-based, while Learner Self attitudes and skills are utilized for resolving problems and growing beyond them. The major goals of therapy focus on strengthening the Learner Self of the client, including the ability to subdue the Judger Self. This model is employed to help clients resolve presenting problems, integrate the concepts of choice and responsibility, and grow and evolve as human beings.

The designations Learner Self and Judger Self point to different cognitive and perceptual paradigms for orienting toward the world. Each subsumes many presuppositions and characteristics that are, in some loose way, internally consistent. One essential distinction is that the Judger Self is more oriented to the past, while the Learner Self focuses itself toward the future. These two paradigms result in the Judger Self asking questions designed to protect itself and preserve its identity, while the Learner Self asks questions which lead to sorting incoming data by criteria of usefulness and learning. This allows the Learner Self to change in relation to what it learns, including formulating revised growth goals.

Much of the change work based on the model of the Learner Self and the Judger Self is linguistically oriented, especially with respect to questions each asks self and others. In chapter 3 we explored how changing people's use of language grants significant leverage in the process of change in general. The

Learner Self and the Judger Self each have characteristic ways of using language. These are reflected both in internal dialogue, or thinking, and in speaking and communicating with others. Presuming that language structures reality, or at least how we construe reality, altering the way individuals operate linguistically should simultaneously affect the reality they perceive, and in which they operate.

It is important for clients to keep in mind that characteristics of the Judger Self and Learner Self are not considered permanent, although people do tend to operate predominantly from their Learner Self or Judger Self, especially with reference to the problems they bring to therapy. The point is that we humans can always learn, grow, develop new skills, make new choices, strengthen the Learner Self, and subdue the Judger Self. Clients can experiment with Learner Self attitudes and characteristic ways of behaving and relating. They can ask Learner Self questions and discover the results in their lives. Certainly, no model can solve people's problems; this one is meant to help strengthen the *ability* to resolve problems.

Of the two, the Learner Self's research attitude supports the individual's experiencing itself as more basically safe and effective in the world. Constantly asking, "*What's this?*" its present-centered focus helps it stay current with what is important to attend to in life. In general, the Learner, being realistically optimistic, asks, "*What's right, and/or useful about this?*" By contrast, the Judger, in general being unrealistically pessimistic, asks, "*What's wrong and/or bad about that?*"

The Judger Self   The term Judger Self refers to that part of us which is inflexible, problem-focused, past-oriented, and reactive. It tends to be blame-seeking, which can be focused either internally or externally, and sometimes, both. Typically, presenting problems in therapy are most associated with the client's Judger Self. "Judger," as we use the term here, does *not* imply objectivity, balanced evaluation, or discernment. Rather, it is meant in the sense of judgmental, or negatively biased. Our Judger Selves are often afraid of change, or do not believe positive, purposeful change is possible (those attitudes and abilities belong with the Learner Self). Judger-based relationships are typically win-lose.

The Judger Self can be thought of as having a "knows-it-already mindset," meaning that any new experience or information is likely to be judged in terms of whether it reinforces, invalidates, or threatens what was already known, believed, or accomplished before. The Judger Self part of us typically asks questions such as: "*Who, or what, is wrong?*" "*Who, or what, is to blame?*" "*How could I get hurt?*" "*How can I protect myself?*" "*How can I win (regardless of the other person)?*" and "*Why does this always happen to me?*"

The Learner Self   The term Learner Self refers to that part of us which is open-minded, flexible, responsive, solution-seeking, future-facing, and accepting of self and others. The Learner Self makes *active choices*, being aware that it chooses how to respond in any moment. The Learner Self part of us knows it can change purposefully, that change is inevitable anyway, and that the future can be brighter than the present. The Learner Self can be thought of as having a "beginner's mindset," meaning that it regards each fresh moment as an opportunity to discover, learn, and choose, regardless of how much the individual already knows, believes, or has previously accomplished. Relationships are typically win-win.

The focus of the Learner Self, therefore, is not on judgment, but on acceptance and usefulness related to some goal. This is evident in the basic kinds of questions it asks self and others. These include: *"What's going on here?" "What can I learn from it?" "In what ways might this be useful?" "What's useful or valuable about this?" "What's right (or what works) about myself, the other person, or the situation?" "What's the best thing to do now?" "How can we resolve this to our mutual satisfaction?"* The Learner Self basically directs and manages its life with questions such as these.

The Skillful Learner Self   What distinguishes a *skillful* Learner Self, in part, is mastering the discipline of approaching life from a beginner's mindset, coupled with the skills to hold the Judger Self at bay, when necessary. This allows the skillful Learner to be consistently proactive and responsive, rather than reactive. The skillful Learner retains much of the driving curiosity it exhibited as a child, determined to discover and make sense of the world. The skillful Learner also maintains the child's sense of wonder and delight in discovery from those early years. The skillful Learner intentionally maintains a mental and emotional state that is open, receptive, flexible, and inquisitive. It cultivates a mood of speculation, even wonder. This mood, along with critical and creative thinking skills, provides the skillful Learner a far wider horizon of choice than that confined by the usual either/or binary judgments—good/bad, right/wrong, correct/incorrect, and acceptable/unacceptable.

The Skillful Learner Accepts the Judger   Essential to establishing oneself as a skillful Learner is recognizing and accepting the Judger part of the self and acknowledging that it will always be part of the human condition. Maturity includes accepting this "reality," developing the skills to manage it, and even coming to appreciate the Judger for its contribution to the "whole self." After all, embracing this part of oneself is required for personal wholeness; it is essential for acceptance and compassion for self and others. The skillful Learner also recognizes that it shares these Judger characteristics with all others. Some of these aspects are our shadows, and part of what makes us all human. Moreover, the skillful Learner respects its Judger counterpart as it would a sleeping dragon. The ever present possibility of the Judger swinging into action keeps the skillful Learner alert, and present focused.

SECTION FOUR:
PSYCHO-EDUCATIONAL TRAINING

This is the practical, how-to section of the chapter. Its purpose is to provide a structure for the psycho-educational training that is at the foundation of question-centered therapy. The model of the Learner and Judger serves as the foundation for assessment and treatment in question-centered therapy. As the organizing metaphor, it is also the basis for all the psycho-educational concepts and materials the therapist uses with her clients. One of the goals of question-centered therapy is to render the conceptual, theoretical, and abstract underpinnings of therapeutic change practical and simple, so that clients can take purposeful advantage of this understanding. The handouts, all of which are illustrated, are designed to fulfill these goals. The therapist uses four handouts with individual clients. With the exception of the Learner/Judger Chart, each of the handouts is presented in this chapter. The chart, which is rather lengthy, appears in its entirety in chapter 9. Five additional handouts are used with couples, and these are presented and described in chapters 12, 13, and 14.

The section is divided into three parts. In the first, we cover how to introduce and set up the psycho-educational training with clients. This includes premises about the material and a list of teaching points for therapists to keep in mind when they teach this material. There are also some comments about the overall structure of the training sessions. In the second part of the section we present examples of teaching stories and exercises for therapists to use which help clients easily and naturally understand the various teaching points. The third part of the section presents the handouts. Lastly, a case example is presented.

Introducing the Psycho-Educational Training

The client already anticipates this psycho-educational training since it is usually discussed briefly in the initial interview, or shortly thereafter. Chapter 5 covers the initial interview, and includes suggestions for introducing the concept of psycho-educational training. This chapter covers the material as it is presented to individual clients once they are actually engaged in the psycho-educational teaching sessions. The same presentation of this information is used with couples. At the beginning of the actual training sessions, the therapist elaborates on the rationale for this intervention. Her remarks could go something as follows:

> The purpose of these educational sessions is to give you skills and tools to help you take care of the problems you brought to therapy. These skills and tools are basic, but they're also very advanced. They're designed to help you think more clearly about those issues and also think about them in new ways that can help you resolve them more easily. You will probably find that you also become a more effective communicator in general. What is unique and powerful about this training is the discovery of the major importance of questions in thinking and communicating. It turns out that the questions we ask—and that includes

the questions we ask ourselves even if we're not aware of it—generally program how we think, how we handle what happens to us in life, and basically how successful and happy we can be.

I'm going to teach you some easy and very practical ways to use this information. The bonus is that these skills and tools will benefit you for the rest of your life, and also in areas of your life other than where you want some changes. Another bonus is that this will probably shorten the length of time you'll need to be in therapy. Do you have any questions or comments about this before we get started?

Structure and "Tone" of the Training

The material that follows may be taught in several, relatively formal and structured educational sessions, or sprinkled through parts of "regular" therapy sessions, depending on what seems most appropriate for particular clients. Therapists are encouraged to experiment with different forms of presenting this information, in order to discover what fits their style and works best for them and their clients. The tone of these sessions is educational and informal, as would be typical of a seminar. It's important for the therapist/educator to be positive, even enthusiastic, about the material, letting her client/student know she believes the content is valuable and can make an important difference in their lives. To set the frame for these teaching sessions, I ask clients to consider several premises which we discuss until I believe these are understood and, at least minimally, accepted. These premises are:

Premise #1: Being a "Beginner" Helps Learning   I ask clients to imagine they are beginners at learning about thinking and communication in terms of question asking. Then I position this attitude as the most powerful one for learning. I explain to them that taking a beginner's attitude powerfully assists learning because beginners don't have preconceived ideas that could interfere with getting any value out of the new material. To underscore and reinforce the power of a beginner's perspective, I usually tell the story about the world-famous black belt karate master who, on his deathbed, requested that he be buried in his beginner's white belt.

It is important for therapists to emphasize that they are teaching how to refine and expand on something that clients already do naturally, easily, and well. After all, they've been asking questions successfully all their lives. People usually find this a comforting perspective because it affirms their competence as we begin these educational conversations. I also tell clients that I plan to keep my own beginner's mindset alert for the rest of my life because there's always more to learn, and learning can be exciting and fun, as well as necessary.

Premise #2: Taking Responsibility for One's Own Communication Is Empowering   While we study this material about language, questions, communication, and personal power, I ask clients to make the assumption that they are responsible for all the results of their communication. Even though this may not be the case, this assumption grants an individual the maximum power in a situation because it means there's *something he can do to alter it*. Otherwise, people easily fall into blaming and judging (self and/or other), and both of these behaviors prevent problem resolution.

Presuming personal responsibility in communicating also enables clients to take a researcher's and reporter's perspective, motivating them to figure out what worked, what didn't work, and what could work better. This strategy neutralizes defensiveness and helps an individual learn from any situation, which is empowering in itself. In asking clients to assume this premise about responsibility for the results of their communications, it is important that they understand the distinction between responsibility and blame. Taking responsibility gives people personal power and is a Learner Self characteristic. On the other hand, if a client engages in the Judger behavior of heaping blame on himself or others, he may unwittingly prevent positive behaviors and outcomes, either intrapsychically or interpersonally.

Premise #3: What to Expect While Learning   It is important that clients understand that learning and integrating this material may result, initially, in feeling less, rather than more, competent as a communicator. As strange as this may seem, such awkwardness is a positive sign that the client is successfully learning the material. With this understanding as a frame for the teaching experience, clients are not likely to get discouraged, and more likely to operate proactively as their Learner Selves.

One of the main teaching goals is for clients to learn to slow down automatic, streamlined internal dialogue enough to become aware of it. This is necessary because clients need to be able to "catch" the ongoing contents of their internal dialogue in order to change what they're telling themselves—especially their internal questions. However, even though slowing down an automatic process enables one to make new and finer distinctions (and thus have expanded access to new choices and actions), the experience also may feel clumsy at first.

The Teaching Points

There are certain fundamental concepts for clients to grasp so they can use this material thoughtfully, creatively, and successfully. The following points are meant to guide therapists as they educate clients about these question-centered methods. The goals include understanding themselves and others better, exercising more control with their emotions and behaviors, and having more success, especially with regard to their presenting problems. Each point includes an indication of what stories and exercises most contribute to learning and integrating that concept. All of these stories, exercises, and handouts are presented in this section.

The points may be summarized as follows: The fundamental goal is to establish an awareness of the *existence* of internal dialogue, the *prevalence* of internal dialogue, and the *power* of internal dialogue so clients can take advantage of this information not only in therapy, but also for the rest of their lives. The goals of the question-centered psycho-educational training are to demonstrate:

- The phenomenon of internal questioning, underscoring its importance in problem solving, decision making, and making emotional and behavioral choices. *See stories #1, #2, and #3, exercise #1, and all handouts.*
- That self-questions are omnipresent, prolific, and important—that effective solutions are best facilitated by the right questions to open those doors, allowing the options and opportunities behind them to become available. *See story #1 and the Choice Model.*
- How the structure (or wording) of questions, including the presuppositions embedded in them, influences an individual's perceptions, emotions, behaviors, and ways of being and relating. *See exercise #1 and story #4.*
- That the results of a person's efforts are influenced by whether he is asking himself effective questions, ineffective questions, or neglecting altogether important questions he should be asking about a particular issue. *See stories #2 and #3 and all handouts.*
- A model of how an individual makes moment-to-moment choices about how and what he thinks. The emphasis is on being a self-observer, and on the power of internal questions in choosing to operate either in the domain of the Learner Self or the Judger Self. *See the Choice Model.*
- The thinking strategy of observe-and-correct, which helps people move successfully toward their goals. *See the Observe-and-Correct Questions handout.*
- The cognitive operation of anticipating consequences, and avoiding danger by switching successfully to a safe thinking track. Switching questions are an elaboration of observe-and-correct. *See the Switching Questions handout, the Observe-and-Correct Questions handout, and story #3.*
- That the *statements* we make to ourselves and others represent answers to prior, usually implicit questions. This places the spotlight on those hidden questions as holding significant keys to change. *See story #4.*
- That our *behaviors* also represent answers to prior, usually implicit questions. Again, this places the spotlight on those background, usually silent questions as holding significant keys to change. *See stories #1, #3, #4 and the Observe-and-Correct Questions handout.*
- The unconscious, automatic nature of these prior, implicit questions which people "answer" with their statements and behaviors. This understanding helps motivate clients to search for and identify these questions. This, in turn, helps them make different, more effective choices about how they think, what they do, and how they relate. *See story #4.*
- That the *delivery* of a question makes the all-important difference in whether the individual can be effective in his communication. *See exercise #2.*

- That choosing to take a Learner Self or Judger Self mindset most fundamentally represents that person's choice of being at any moment. How a person behaves and relates issues first from this choice of being, which is often described as "where a person is coming from." *See exercise #1 and the Choice Model.*

Illustrating the Teaching Points, Anecdotes, Exercises, and Handouts

Story #1: Getting Dressed.   The process of training a client to recognize the phenomenon of internal questioning is essential in question-centered therapy. Such a training process works best if it is presented in everyday terms and made personally relevant to the client. The point is that all of us already ask questions all the time, and that our choices are based on the questions we ask ourselves. However, people generally don't realize they're even asking these questions, or how frequently they are doing so. It's important for clients to understand that their behavior can be considered as answers to their internal questions, even if, like most people, they're totally unaware of these influential questions.

I have adopted a simple, standard way of making this point with which everyone can identify. First, I tell my client I'm going to teach him about problem solving, decision making, and internal questioning. Then I usually engage him in a short conversation about why this is important, and how it could be relevant to him. Next I get into the subject by telling my client that I'm positive he's already asked himself many questions that very day. In fact, I'm willing to bet on it, and I can prove it. In response to this last comment, clients usually look at me quizzically, as if to say, *"What are you talking about, lady?"*

I proceed by saying that my certainty is based on the fact that he is dressed. That typically produces an even more puzzled expression, and I know that I've captured the attention I need to get my point across. I proceed by saying that I imagine that when he got dressed that morning, he went to his closet, or wherever he keeps his clothes, and asked himself a series of questions that included some of the following: *"Where am I going and what am I doing today?" "What's appropriate?" "What's the weather supposed to be?" "Can I get away with jeans?" "Do I have to wear a tie (or stockings)?" "What will I feel most comfortable in?" "What fits?" "What's ironed?"* and *"What's clean?"*

At this recitation, the client virtually always nods his head in agreement, as he recognizes some of the questions he asked without awareness only hours before. Then I ask explicitly, "Do you recognize any of these questions?" The answer is virtually always, "Yes." I speculate that this recognition occurs as clients become aware of a naturally occurring phenomenon, a cognitive process that has always been present, just below the surface of awareness.

Next, I point out to my client that he answered his own questions by taking an action, or rather, making a choice. He took something off the hanger or out of a drawer. That piece of clothing represents his choice, or his answer to those internal questions. In fact, one could even say he is *wearing* his choice. This point usually makes clients laugh and also nod in agreement. Then we talk about the implications of this way of looking at things, since one can extrapolate that essentially all of an individual's choices represent answers to internal questions, some of which were effective, some which were not, and others which were consequences of not asking necessary questions.

Story #2: Results of NOT Asking Necessary Questions   The point is that many of our decisions are made by default. They are "default decisions" because the appropriate question wasn't asked. Therefore, that particular issue was literally not raised, and the individual wasn't cued to think about it. To make this point, I use an example about a friend who used to go shopping, asking only the question, *"What do I like, and what do I feel like buying today?"* Then I ask clients what kind of shopping trip that was. They always laugh, and say something like, "Very expensive!" or "That sounds like my wife (or husband)." Then I reveal that eventually my friend learned to go shopping with another, much more useful question, *"What do I like, what do I need, and what can I afford today?"* Clients respond with comments such as: "Sign up my spouse for this training" or "That would be a good one for me, too."

This example gives us a platform to discuss the implications of not asking oneself necessary questions. I've been surprised by the number of divorced clients who've commented that if they had *seriously* asked themselves: *"Should I marry this person?"* or *"Is this a good decision for me at this time in my life?"* or *"How will I feel about this marriage in ten years?"* they would never have married the person they eventually divorced.

Story #3: Pilot Story   I begin by asking clients if they can describe the thinking process that helps an airline pilot navigate and arrive safely at his or her destination. Few clients figure out how to describe this unless they're pilots themselves. Then I ask them to imagine that I am an airplane pilot, flying my plane from New York to San Francisco, and that I'm going to mimic the pilot's internal dialogue. It goes somewhat like this:

"I'm keeping an eye on the instruments that mark my destination. There's San Francisco. Oops. I notice I'm 15 degrees off to the left. How do I get back on track? Now, I'm right on course. Oh, now I observe that I'm 20 degrees off to the right. What's the best way to make the correction? OK, back on course. Now I should check to see where I am in relation to my goal. Oh, I observe that I'm 25 degrees off to the left. How should I make that correction?"

In other words, I tell clients that a pilot's thinking strategy is to observe and correct all the way from liftoff to landing. It's a continuous monitoring process: simply observe, correct, observe, correct. The prevailing emotional state is neutral and calm. One is just doing the job, "just observe, and correct, observe, and correct." Then I say:

"Now let's imagine I'm a different pilot, flying the same plane, and on the same route from New York to San Francisco. This time I'm going to mimic the internal dialogue of the second pilot. As pilot #2, I look at my instruments, and say *"Where am I? Oh, I'm 15 degrees off to the left. OH NO!!! My mother was right, I'm just not smart enough to be a pilot! I should never have been stupid enough to think I could do this."* And the pilot continues in this kind of emotional, judgmental vein, commenting on her capabilities and the value of her performance, instead of simply doing the job, which *requires* observing and correcting from liftoff to landing.

Then I ask clients what they think will happen to this second pilot. Do they think she'll make it to San Francisco? Almost invariably they laugh, and say they expect a crash. Then I alter the conversation to talk about *their* personal thinking strategies. I ask clients to think of situations where they've been able to effectively observe and correct, in contrast with times when they judged themselves and got derailed and upset. Almost invariably they discover to their surprise that the observe-and-correct strategy was behind their effectiveness.

Story #4: Personal Guiding Questions   While general, content-free questions exert a strong influence on us, it's also the case that personal, often unconscious and automatic questions affect us in very specific ways. Of course, the most unconscious and automatic internal questions are rooted in difficult early experiences and ensuing protective decisions and beliefs. This effect can be powerful, unsuspected, and yet have many consequences and implications. The following story about Lorraine illustrates how self-questions, especially the ones we don't realize we're asking, influence our perceptions and the results we accrue.

Lorraine was a participant in a workshop I give entitled the Power of Questions. She told us she had a frustrating problem, and despaired of finding a solution. She said that she loved her job, yet disliked her boss so much she was considering quitting. She wanted help because she wanted to stay at her job. Together we figured out what questions she was *already asking herself that she didn't know she was asking*, and we discovered two real "troublemaker" questions. Every time her boss, Mr. Smith, walked into the room, Lorraine asked herself, *"What's he going to do wrong this time?"* or *"How's he going to make me look bad?"*

The workshop participants decided that Mr. Smith didn't stand a chance with Lorraine as long as she kept asking those same two questions about him. Lorraine concurred, and agreed to an experiment I proposed: purposefully asking herself a different question in relation to her boss. The query I suggested she try was: *"What can I do to make my boss look good?"* Although she was startled by this question, she agreed the experiment was worthwhile.

Several months later I ran into Lorraine and her husband, Todd, who was also in the workshop. Lorraine reported a "miracle story"—she had gotten a promotion *and* a raise at her job. Furthermore, she and her boss had chosen to work together on a committee, even though they previously avoided even being in the same room together. After Lorraine's recitation, Todd gave his view of the situation. While he applauded Lorraine's results at work, he was happiest that "she no longer complains about her boss for an hour every night." The interaction with Lorraine in the workshop lasted about 20 minutes.

Exercise #1: Questions and Moods   In the psycho-educational sessions I use a simple, five-minute exercise to demonstrate the power that questions have over an individual's feelings and moods. This exercise works equally well with individuals, couples, families, and groups. I also use it in the Power of Questions communications workshops.

I tell clients that I'm going to have them listen to two distinctly different sets of questions, and that I will deliver each in a neutral and similar manner. The clients' task is simply to note their own reactions and feelings, or the mood(s) in which they find themselves as a consequence of listening to each set of questions. It quickly becomes apparent that even content-free questions delivered in a neutral manner provoke an immediate felt difference in affect. The first set of questions includes the following: *"What's wrong with me?" "How come I have all the bad luck?" "Why do I have to be such a failure?" "Why did I have to be born into such a dysfunctional family?" "Why bother?" "Why me?"* This first set of questions routinely evokes mood(s) of helplessness, hopelessness, despair, negativity, and depression, as well as feeling trapped, passive, victimized, and out of control.

Conversely, the second set of questions elicits quite different responses. It includes questions such as: *"What's useful, or helpful about this?" "What can I learn from this?" "What are my resources?" "What are my choices?" "How can I get started on this project?" "How can this be accomplished in a win-win manner?"* Again, I ask what moods or feelings were provoked. Clients consistently report that this set of questions elicits feelings of being uplifted, positive, resourceful, active, energetic, willing, optimistic, and in control.

Of course, we discuss what makes the two sets of questions so very different, especially since they are content-free and were delivered in a neutral manner. The two sets of questions are distinguished by the presuppositions encoded in them. The presuppositions of the first set are of limitations and negativity, external control, and the temporal focus is mostly in the past. The presuppositions of the second set of questions are positive, control is localized *internally*, and the availability of new possibilities is implied. The temporal focus is present to future. This exercise is especially powerful with couples and groups, because the unanimity of responses makes the point even stronger.

Exercise #2: The Impact of Delivery   It's essential that clients understand that *the right question delivered in the wrong way becomes the wrong question.* A simple exercise illustrates this convincingly. I tell clients that I'm going to deliver the same question two different ways, and then I'm going to ask how each delivery affected them. First, I adopt an exaggerated condemning tone, and ask *"Why did you do that?"* Then I ask the same question again, this time in a neutral, calm, interested manner. Clients invariably report that these two questions are *defi-*

nitely not the same. In fact, the first query makes them feel attacked, defensive, and unwilling to answer the question. By contrast, the second question feels like an invitation from someone who's interested in them and what they have to say.

Clients quickly understand that the Judger Self asks questions that can be interrogating and condemning. The Learner Self asks questions that are inquisitive and curious, and presume that the receiver is a worthy human being, and any answer will be worth listening to. Naturally, these distinctions make the most difference in discussing clients' relationships, whether in individual or couples therapy.

Two points are important in using this exercise. First, I've learned from experience *never* to deliver the Judger question directly facing clients. Otherwise, even though this is only an exercise, they usually react viscerally and negatively, and may even have a difficult time recovering. I actually make a point of moving slightly, and looking off to the side when I deliver the Judger question. Also, I always deliver the Judger version of the question first, and then make sure my client has resumed a neutral emotional state before I deliver the Learner version of the question. This time, of course, I face my clients directly so they can be left with this positive experience.

Handouts

Choice Model   The Choice Model is at the heart of question-centered therapy. It illustrates the question-driven structure of choice by depicting the consequences of asking different kinds of questions. It shows that at any moment an individual makes question-based choices about whether to move into Learner Self territory or tumble into Judger Self territory. According to the Choice Model, everyone theoretically has the ability to choose, and is thereby positioned to take responsibility for his or her choices. The Learner Self, which occupies the territory at the top of the Choice Model, *responds* to life, and consistently uses effective self-questions to support attitudes and behaviors that are solution-seeking, and that offer the best possibility of realistically based experiences of self-efficacy, personal accomplishment, and win-win relationships.

On the other hand, the Judger Self *reacts* to life. Its attention is problem-focused, and relationships are win-lose. The Judger Self operates in the territory at the bottom of the Choice Model where choice exists, but is neither claimed nor taken advantage of. Since the Judger Self is either unable or unwilling to acknowledge this ability to choose, it makes passive choices, not recognizing that it is at the helm, and that its life is largely the result of such moment-to-moment choices. The consequence of this presumption is a habit of judging or blaming oneself, another person, or circumstances for one's difficulties, as well as feeling justified in making these attributions. This results in becoming caught in reactive patterns of thinking, feeling, and relating that keep one relegated to the bottom half of the chart, where the individual experiences himself as powerless. In fact, some clients have designated the domain of the Judger Self as "that blame-and-shame place" or "the blame-and-fear part" of the Choice Model.

The Choice Model basically depicts an internal focus for the Judger. A version of the Choice Model that is used with couples, the Marriage Context Model, illustrates the results of the Judger's external focus. Once the Choice Model is introduced to clients, it is frequently used as the background of therapeutic conversations. Chapter 6 presents a case centered around the Choice Model. (See Figure 4.1.)

Observe-and-Correct Questions Handout   Observe-and-correct is a "mantra" that clients learn in question-centered therapy. It becomes a reliable, easy way for them to think about their thinking and their behavior. The observe-and-correct thinking strategy also trains and reinforces the observer self, and helps clients problem-solve and make choices more effectively. Both of the functions of observing and correcting operate via a series of specific self-questions. These questions figure prominently on the handout. The illustration of the pilot visually reinforces the teaching story about the pilot that was covered earlier in this section.

Anecdotally, clients with a background in science or technology, such as engineers and doctors, often comment that observe-and-correct is reminiscent of the scientific method. Jim, an engineer, and husband in the couple whose case is presented in chapter 15, commented: "To me, observe-and-correct is like practicing the scientific method, only I'm shining the light on *me* instead of on research data. Myself and my thinking processes, *that's* what I'm learning to observe and correct." (See Figure 4.2.)

Switching Questions   The Observe-and-Correct Questions handout and the Switching Questions handout (Figure 4.3) are related. Switching questions actually represent the mental operation of choosing that occurs between observing and correcting. I designed these as two separate handouts in order to reinforce each concept separately. I want to anchor the term *observe-and-correct* so that it becomes a natural part of clients' self-questioning. I also want them to recognize how they can *choose* to rescue themselves even in difficult situations where they formerly felt out of control and helpless. Both handouts use illustrations to subliminally suggest to clients that *they* are in the driver's seat. The illustrations also place the viewer in a time trajectory of present to future; that is, *away* from focusing on the past, where problems and negativity reside, and *approaching* a future open to possibilities and solutions.

Learner/Judger Chart   The Learner/Judger Chart is the multipage handout that clients usually receive in the mid-phase of therapy. It provides a model for self-observation that helps them to be more perceptive and objective about themselves and others, including characteristics some construe as "negative." The detailed nature of the chart is intended to give them new distinctions, or ways of thinking about themselves and others. The chart can be considered a roadmap for therapy, allowing one to assess and acknowledge what has been accomplished, as well as focus explicitly on what more needs to be done. It can also

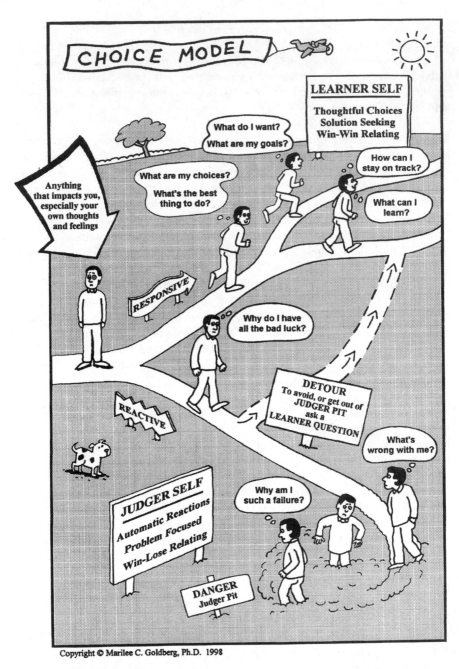

Copyright © Marilee C. Goldberg, Ph.D. 1998

Figure 4.1   The Choice Model

Figure 4.2   Observe-and-Correct Questions

Copyright © Marilee C. Goldberg, Ph.D. 1998

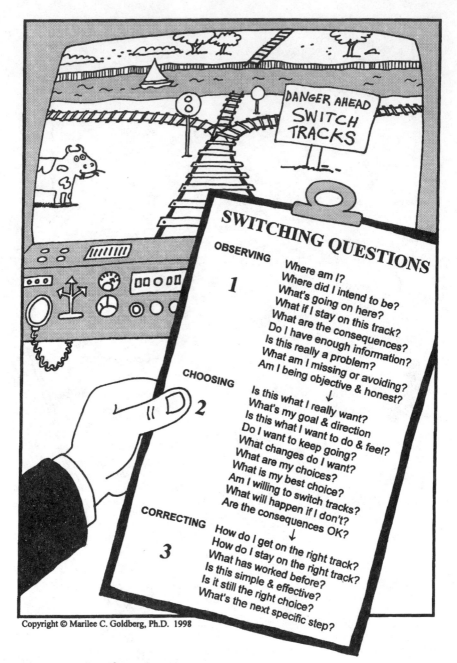

Copyright © Marilee C. Goldberg, Ph.D. 1998

Figure 4.3   Switching Questions

serve as the basis for designing new therapy and growth goals. The chart is presented in chapter 9.

A Case Example   Tom, an overweight executive, came to therapy with a goal of dropping 15 pounds in three months. He went through the standard psycho-educational protocol. Additionally, we worked with the outcome frame, as discussed in chapter 3. He developed a hypothesis that eliminating desserts would bring him the desired results. He was successful in eliminating desserts; that is, he tested the hypothesis adequately. However, the result was that he dropped only five pounds—this was his observation. He assessed his result and concluded that he needed to do more if he wanted to get rid of the remaining 10 pounds. He made a correction in his program by additionally eliminating fatty foods. This correction constituted his new hypothesis—that eliminating desserts *and* fatty foods would do the trick. Then he repeated the process, behaviorally testing this new hypothesis until he lost the desired weight. Observe-and-correct is the shorthand expression for this ongoing Learner Self cognitive and behavioral process, and Tom "observed and corrected" his way to success with his weight goal.

Let's look at how Tom used to deal with his overeating. Instead of exercising choice by observing and correcting, he reacted in a Judger-like way to any deviance from his commitment. Instead of simply noticing he had overeaten and saying, "*Oops, look what I just did. What correction would help?*" he was more likely to tell himself something like, "*What's the matter with me? I'm a fat idiot, and I just blew it again.*" He took any slip-up as evidence that he had failed, and then saddled himself with a stultifying permanent label—a "failure." This label made it even more difficult for Tom to observe and correct the next time his behavior was less than "perfect."

Several months into treatment, Tom made an unintentional detour away from his weight-loss goal when he reacted to an upsetting phone conversation with his girlfriend. Right after he hung up the phone, he binged on sweets. In his next therapy session, he proudly reported that soon thereafter he recovered his observe-and-correct composure. He asked himself, "*What actually happened here?*" The answer was: "*I got upset at something Beverly said, and after we hung up I dove into the cookies.*" Then he asked himself, "*Is that what I want to do? How could I have handled this better?*"

This answer was: "*First off, don't keep cookies around when you're not supposed to eat them anyway.*" His next question, "*Is this likely to happen again?*" brought an affirmative answer, which he followed up with the obvious correction question, "*What can I do about it?*" His first behavioral correction was to throw out the cookies. His second was to ask Beverly if she would be willing to attend a couples' therapy session with him.

From a question-centered perspective, Tom's new competence was based on becoming a more astute self-observer, and using the improved problem-solving and decision-making skills he learned through therapy. His comments about this incident were most telling: "It may not seem like a big deal to you, but the way I handled this situation was a triumph for me. Even though I wasn't so hot on that training about thinking and problem solving, I'm really glad you stuck to your guns. Being able to observe and correct is really what saved me. Otherwise, I wouldn't have realized I am at the center of my choices—and I'd probably still be fat and alone. But I'm not. I like my body now, and Beverly and I are engaged. I think I'm ready to be certified as an official 'Learner Self.' "

SUMMARY

This chapter opened with a discussion about therapy and language, and the therapeutic conversation in particular, including its improvisational nature. We placed question-centered therapy within a context of therapy in general, focusing on the leverage that using a methodology centered in language and question asking extends. We introduced the model of the Learner Self and the Judger Self, which is the theoretical foundation and organizing metaphor of question-centered therapy. It is also the basis of the psycho-educational training and of all the handouts. Finally, we reviewed practical aspects of presenting the psycho-educational material, through the teaching points, anecdotes, exercises, and handouts.

5

Unfolding the Map:
The Beginning of
the Journey

*Symptoms are not malignancies that attack from the outside but
"urgent questions, behaviorally expressed, which have somehow lost
the threads that lead either to answers or to better questions." (Kelly)*
—Jay Efran, Michael D. Lukens,
Robert J. Lukens

The beginning phase of treatment, like the middle and ending ones, is characterized by particular goals and interventions, and a distinct tone of relationship between therapist and client. In question-centered therapy, many of the seeds for achieving these goals are planted in the initial interview, and the chapter focuses on these goals. Section 1 discusses the goals of the first phase of therapy. Section 2 focuses on general considerations about the initial interview from a question-centered perspective. Section 3 covers the eight stages of the initial interview, and elaborates on how the issue of questions and question asking is introduced in this first therapy session.

SECTION ONE: GOALS OF THE BEGINNING PHASE OF THERAPY

Goals, other than those associated with the therapeutic relationship, fall into two categories in the beginning phase of treatment. The first category focuses on assessment. This covers diagnostic concerns beyond what can be explored in the initial interview, and includes an ongoing social assessment of how a client relates over time, as well as how fully he takes advantage of therapy, in general. Further, the therapist uses the opening phase to elicit a detailed representation of her client's desired changes, along with a thorough understanding of what has prevented those changes so far.

The second category of goals in question-centered therapy relates to the broad area of psycho-education. Clients are oriented to the psycho-educational foundation in the first interview. Much of this training takes place in the beginning phase of treatment, often within the first few sessions. The psycho-educational focus adds another layer to the therapeutic relationship, as the clinician takes on the roles of teacher and coach, in addition to therapist and healer.

SECTION TWO: CONSIDERATIONS ABOUT THE INITIAL INTERVIEW

Every clinician, regardless of training or background, faces certain tasks which must be accomplished by the conclusion of the first interview. These include establishing and maintaining rapport, gaining the client's cooperation and collaboration, learning about the client's history and current levels of functioning, getting a comprehensive understanding of the problem, and developing a treatment plan. To conclude these tasks satisfactorily allows the therapist to end the interview by giving feedback and recommendations intended to give direction, engender hope, and promote action by the client.

In this section, we explore the subtext of the therapist's and client's self-questioning through the initial interview. Then we introduce the concept of the Learner Self and the Judger Self as background for initial assessments. Finally, we consider advantages of converting statements of presenting problems into questions.

Question-Centered Thinking

This discussion of the therapist's and client's internal questioning represents a different cut at a phenomenon that always goes on in initial interviews. The difference is that here we aim a light on the complex background thinking that undergirds the external verbal and nonverbal expressions of each. It is useful to examine this thinking process through the context of the initial interview situation since this situation is standardized and familiar enough to assist in identifying many of these mental operations. In addition to exploring the external verbalizations of both individuals, we also examine samples of the specific internal conversations that form the substrata of what actually gets communicated externally. This complex internal mental operation occurs at lightning speed; an exegesis of the therapist's mental inventory in the initial interview simply slows it down enough for the components to be appraised.

The question-centered therapist organizes her thinking about the goals of the initial interview into a series of questions which guide her interventions from beginning to end. These are not the questions she verbalizes externally; rather, they are the internal questions that her interactions with her client are intended to answer. As noted in previous chapters, little of this takes place in conscious awareness. It would hardly be possible to hold these questions consciously in mind and still pay adequate attention to the client. (Such an experience might be akin to the centipede's stumbling response when asked to describe how it walked.) Yet the therapist's interview questions (for example, those explicated by Lazarus in Chapter 3) frame, guide, and give rise to her verbal and nonverbal behavior during this first interview, as well as in all others.

Any therapist performing an initial assessment interview goes through her own idiosyncratic version of this process. This assertion is based on the observation that any communication represents a series of internal decisions, such as: *"Should I stay with this topic (Yes/No)?" "Should I switch to another subject (Yes/No)?"* If yes, *"To what subject should I direct the conversation?"* Every decision strategy must have some exit point where the signal is binary. Here, the internal *"Yes"* leads to the therapist redirecting the focus of the session. A *"No"* leads to other internal questions, such as: *"What else do I need to know?" "Is it possible to get what I need in order to make recommendations today?"* or *"Do I need to follow up this interview with psychological testing or perhaps a consultation with a supervisor or colleague?"* These questions lead the therapist to her next decisions about subsequent interactions in the interview.

Toward the end of the initial interview the clinician performs a mental inventory, using her internal questions as a checklist to make sure she has adequately covered her basic goals in the session. For example, she might ask herself: *"Do I know enough about the antecedents to this young man's presenting problem of depression?" "Do I need to take a more specific sexual history?" "How much is his relationship with his family of origin influencing his present difficulties?" "Is there anything else I need to know about these relationships?"* Finally, she asks herself something like, *"Do I know enough at this point to make confident recommendations?"* Some personal signal that she recognizes unconsciously (something she sees, hears, and/or feels internally) gives her an affirmative answer equivalent to *"Yes, you can move on."*

During the interview the question-centered therapist also attempts to be conscious of questions her client might be asking himself. She strives to communicate her response to such probable questions through her verbal and nonverbal behavior. Though the questions themselves are silent, they are present in the atmosphere of the room and in the verbal and nonverbal behavior of the client. While the client's self-questions are rarely asked overtly, they shape the background of how he brings himself to the session, as well as how he conducts himself throughout the entire therapy process. Examples of self-questions the client might be asking in an initial interview include: *"What's wrong with me?" "Can I trust this therapist?" "How much should I tell her?" "Will this therapist accept and like me?" "Will she actually understand me and my problem?" "Can she really help?" "Can I be helped?" "Will she decide to accept me as a client?"* and *"Is this going to work out?"*

Assessment and the Model of
the Learner Self and the Judger Self

As noted in Chapter 4, the model of the Learner Self and the Judger Self gives the therapist an explicit frame for assessing her client in the initial interview, as well as to monitor progress throughout the different phases of therapy. We explore this in more detail in Chapters 8 and 9. Now, however, we simply consider three dimensions of the Learner Self which are particularly relevant to the therapist in the initial interview. The Learner Self knows it has the ability to choose and that it always has a choice, at least in attitude. The Learner Self knows it is responsible for attitudinal and behavioral choices. The Learner Self also recognizes that internal dialogue reflects, patterns, and generates an individual's moods, behaviors, and perceptions of available choices.

The model of the Learner Self and the Judger Self provides a basis for articulating such assessment dimensions. It gives a therapist the means to ask specific diagnostic questions such as: *"How much does my client take responsibility for his choices?"* or *"Does he tend to blame others for his misfortunes?"* or *"How well is he tracking his internal dialogue?"*

The therapist is also interested in discovering what questions the individual is *not* asking himself, since these represent blind spots that almost certainly contribute to his problems. Throughout, the therapist recognizes that her client is unlikely to be aware of these internal questions, despite the prolific number and pervasive influence of such internal questioning on how he thinks, feels, behaves, and relates.

In an initial interview, a question-centered therapist is naturally interested in the client's question asking in conversation with her. She includes this in her assessment of the client's social and communication skills. Along these lines, she may encourage her client to ask questions. Whether and how this invitation is accepted gives her additional information about him. For example, a reticent client who declines the invitation, or says he has no questions, may be frightened or untrusting, or in some denial about his difficulties. Since frequent question asking in relationships is a characteristic of the Learner Self, a client's reluctance to engage in this way may suggest that the question-centered psycho-educational training will be particularly helpful for him.

Symptoms, Problems, and the Question-Centered Initial Interview   The therapist keeps in mind that the situation that carries the label "problem" may be conceptualized or reframed in terms of questions to which the client has not yet found satisfactory answers, a concept that we explored in Chapter 2. The clinician also recognizes that the formulation of a problem in terms of internal questions is probably unfamiliar to her client. This leads her to help him consider questions he wants and needs to answer regarding the problem situation. Since the client probably will not have a ready response for this, the therapist helps him explicate a few questions of this nature. Two or three such questions may serve to show him the usefulness of this new thinking about his problems. Sometimes the perceptual shift that illuminates new ways to think about problems helps clients feel more hopeful about therapeutic success.

The possibility of this perceptual shift also represents an important potential reframe, in that clients can emerge from the initial interview with new ways to think of issues about which they have felt frustrated and defeated. Sometimes fresh perspectives are accompanied by relief and even physical relaxation. The therapist's questions also constitute an implicit metamessage and educational reorientation for clients. They recognize that the phenomenon of such questions exists, and that the therapist thinks questions are important and can be helpful. This suggests that clients might become more aware of their own internal dialogue, including their self-questions, and how these relate to presenting problems.

SECTION THREE:
STAGES OF THE INITIAL INTERVIEW

In the initial information-gathering interview the therapist must be efficient, all the while staying in rapport with the client. This interview is most easily thought of as having successive stages, each of which has rapport tasks and information-gathering tasks. However, any clinician knows that life is not so neat and well-behaved as to occur in discrete, sequential, and predictable stages. Therefore, the material presented in this section is simply a construct to organize the conversation about the tasks of the initial interview in question-centered therapy.

Sometimes a therapeutic task prior to the initial interview is to decide what unit of individual(s) to invite to the session. Occasionally, there is a difference of opinion between individual therapists and family therapists about which people constitute the basic unit to be seen in treatment. I generally see the individual, couple, or family who initiates the request for therapy. A pragmatic view of these differences of opinion holds that "It should not be a question of *whether* to treat the individual or the family but *when* to concentrate on one or both" (Lazarus 1989, p. 41; his italics). This chapter on initial interviews focuses on the individual adult client. The initial interview with couples is discussed in Chapter 13.

There are eight stages of a question-centered initial interview with an individual client. While the interview itself can be considered an intervention, there are some points in the session where a question-centered therapist also makes purposeful interventions. This material occurs predominantly in stages 3, 4, 5, and 7.

The eight stages are:

1. Getting acquainted and establishing rapport.
2. Problem stage 1, which garners a brief description of the problem.
3. Psycho-educational phase 1, wherein the therapist inquires about self-questions related to the presenting problem.

4. Problem stage 2, which covers standard history and mental status considerations. In other words, the therapist asks questions and makes observations that allow her to answer her own questions about diagnosis, prognosis, and treatment.
5. Feedback, which includes the therapist sharing hypotheses about possible questions the client may be asking himself, related to presenting problems.
6. Recommendations about therapy, which may include helping the client make a decision about committing to therapy.
7. Psycho-educational phase 2, when, and if, appropriate. I orient him to my theory of practice and make sure he anticipates some psycho-educational training near the beginning of treatment.
8. Closure.

The Eight Stages of the Initial Interview in Question-Centered Therapy

1. *Getting acquainted, establishing rapport.*   Every therapist knows that communication occurs most effectively in a climate of rapport and trust. The challenge in the initial interview is to establish that atmosphere within seconds or minutes of first meeting. Both client and therapist know that the client is expected to reveal intimate aspects of his personal life. This is a particularly daunting prospect in the face of his probable assumption that the interview itself constitutes evidence of his failure to solve his problems.

Therefore, the goal of the first stage is simply to assist the client in feeling comfortable and respected so he can participate fully in the interview. The therapist/host tends to the comfort of her client/guest. The metamessage is: *"You matter, your comfort matters, helping you is important to me."* At this early stage of the interview, the therapist often asks questions about impersonal topics such as the weather, traffic conditions, or whatever might serve as an icebreaker.

2. *Initial brief description of problem.*   This stage opens as the therapist shifts the session from a social mood to one that is purposeful; there is a sense of "getting down to business" (Haley 1976). The therapist invites her client to give a general description of his reasons for making the appointment. At this point, questions are open-ended and general; the goal is to obtain the client's own thinking about his concerns and problems. Possible opening queries include: "What brings you here today?" "What did you come here to resolve?" or "What's puzzling (troubling/frustrating) you enough that you decided to get help?"

Especially at the outset, the therapist's questions are few, simple, and brief. Her goal is to encourage clients to speak freely about whatever was important enough to make this appointment. Stage 2 itself should be brief, just long enough for the therapist to assess that she has a beginning handle on the situation, and that the client feels comfortable enough to begin to unburden himself.

3. *Psycho-educational phase 1: Inquiring about client's self-questions in relation to the presenting problem.*   After the therapist has an adequate beginning

sense of the problems, she shifts into the first psycho-educational stage of the interview by asking questions the client probably hasn't yet considered. Since the therapist is interested in internal dialogue, she asks her client what he has been telling himself about the problematic situation. She may need to help him identify self-statements, and may, if possible, use parts of what he has already said to help him retrieve or re-create some representational internal dialogue.

The therapist next asks a question such as: "And what *questions* have you been asking yourself about this?" She makes this query naturally, as if assuming her client knows the answers, as if it were the most ordinary thing in the world to be aware of internal questions. One of two things will happen. While it is possible, of course, that the client will report some internal self-questions, it is also possible that he will not understand what is being requested of him. In this case, the therapist might comment that his is a typical response to her request since most people are not aware of their internal questions.

Of course, the therapist adds that there are important advantages to learning about the power of questions. One is that questions lead more naturally to action and change than do statements. Another benefit is that new questions stimulate creative thinking. This is essential in therapy because often what keeps people from solving problems is thinking about them in the same old ways. After making certain the client understands and accepts this concept, the therapist adds that sometimes it is helpful to think about a problem as a series of questions — questions to which a person simply hasn't yet gotten satisfying answers. She invites him to join in a brief experiment of thinking about his problem in this new way of formulating questions that the presenting problem might represent.

It is important to accept any questions the client offers. If the therapist wants to include additional questions, she says something like: "Good. That's an interesting question. You might also consider X question and Y question." Her goal here, as in therapy itself, is to make new options available. For example, if a client's presenting problem were marital unhappiness, he might convert that statement into: "How can I get my wife to change?" The therapist could say, "Well, that's one way to think about it," and then comment, "How about including this question: 'What changes can I make that could change how I relate to my wife?' "

Despite how complex this aspect of the initial interview may appear, in practice it usually occurs easily and naturally. If not, the therapist simply comments, "We'll probably get back to this at some point" and moves on to further information gathering. The goal of introducing these question-based interventions so early in treatment is threefold. It elicits information specifically used by question-centered therapists. It subliminally alerts and educates clients about possibilities for change of which they were previously unaware. Finally, it sets up clients to be more comfortable with the notion of psycho-educational training that is introduced toward the end of the interview.

4. *Problem stage 2: History.*   Phase 4 takes up most of the time of the session. This is the investigative work that allows the therapist to address the diagnostic and prognostic questions she needs answered in order to formulate her

recommendations. It is assumed that standard history-taking and mental-status questions similar to those outlined by Lazarus are ordinarily covered, since they provide a comprehensive and necessary system of assessment. While the therapist asks questions about the history of the problem, she simultaneously asks herself questions about her observations to help her formulate her opinions and recommendations.

Question Asking in the Family   Our history-taking inquiries can shine light into hidden or unconsidered aspects of problems, and even induce new ways of thinking about them. For these reasons, a question-centered therapist often inquires whether question asking was encouraged or discouraged in a client's family of origin. The answers (if a client remembers) could hint at how individuation and free thinking were encouraged—or not. The same query is useful about a client's adult love relationships. These queries can uncover helpful information about clients' relationships as well as their communication skills.

In the family or relationship context, therapists could further inquire about the existence of unspoken rules about what questions were/are permitted to be asked, and of whom. Responses here could illuminate denial, secrets, or collusion in the family. Children learn early what is taboo. They learn, for example, not to ask questions about what happened to Aunt Helen or why Daddy sometimes comes home so late from the office. Couples also have arenas where restrictions and fears limit question asking. In other words, because questions and answers imply interaction and communication, a lack of question asking often points to restrictions in relationships.

5. *Feedback.*   After so much self-revelation, a client wants and deserves feedback. He wants the experience of having been understood, and he needs direction. The therapist's feedback includes an assessment of the level of severity and urgency implied in the client's problems. Her observations also cover evidence for hope garnered from what has transpired in the session and from what the client has shared about his life. If the therapist thinks that couples or family work should be included or pursued, this is usually discussed. Finally, if the client hasn't mentioned or indicated that the feedback seems correct, the therapist requests some verification that he experiences being understood. She might do this by asking a few simple questions such as: "Do you think I understood what you wanted to communicate?" or "Have I gotten the important points here?" or "Is there anything else you think is important for me to know, or that I should ask you about?" She might end by saying, "Is there anything you might regret not telling me after you leave here today?"

There is also an opportunity in this stage to plant seeds for harvest in future sessions. Regarding presenting problems, the therapist might include in her feedback some conjecture about the role of the client's internal questions in relation to these difficulties. For example, if the client is a depressed executive, downsized out of a job, and lacking much insight, the therapist could venture: "You might be asking yourself, '*How could this affect my relationship with my children?*' or

'*How am I going to get through this, <u>and</u> keep my relationship with my wife strong?*' " If the client is a woman seeking therapy for overweight and a bulimic eating disorder, the therapist might offer some of the following self-questions for the client to consider: "*How could I get more comfortable with my body?*" or "*How could I deal with my emotions without bingeing?*" or "*In what ways are these problems related to my family?*" By offering these questions, the therapist has already indicated three important areas to be addressed.

6. *Treatment options and recommendations.* The feedback phase flows naturally into the conversation about treatment. Even if a client is not ready to act yet, he wants our opinions and recommendations, and often the reasoning behind them. Sometimes clients need to be encouraged to ask questions in this phase. The more thoroughly they understand the journey upon which they are about to embark, the greater the likelihood of success.

7. *Psycho-educational setup for therapy.* Assuming the result of the initial interview is that this individual becomes my client, I take the opportunity to orient him to what he can expect in therapy. (If I am going to refer him to another therapist either for testing or for therapy, this stage is unnecessary.) In particular, I want a new client to anticipate that within the first three to five sessions we will pause from a direct focus on his issues in order to engage in psycho-educational training about thinking and problem solving. I mention that this is related to my earlier query about any internal questions about his problems.

I emphasize that knowing how to self-question effectively is a fundamental building block for success in general. I also explain that this training is standard in therapy with me because it helps make treatment quicker and often more effective. These lessons will either occur in a formal, structured sense over a few sessions or might take place as part of a few more sessions. Psycho-education seems natural if this expectation is set up before formal therapy begins. In fact, clients often look forward to the training sessions and sometimes ask if we can get to them right away.

8. *Closure.* At the end of an initial interview, I usually ask a client how he experienced the session, and if he has any new ways to think about his problems. This functions as a check and review for both of us. The question opens the way for the client to articulate what, if anything, he gained from the session. Any positive answer functions as an implicit acknowledgment that the interview has been helpful because some change (in the form of increased understanding) has already taken place. In this way the therapist plants the notion that since change has already occurred, therapy can indeed make a difference. Even a negative answer is useful; the therapist, through her question, planted the idea that change can begin very early in therapy, and that her client's changes are important to her.

This final stage of the initial interview takes on some of the same social sense characterized by the first stage. It includes being considerate of a client's reasonable need to talk about the session, especially if it has been a difficult one. The last part of the closure stage generally includes comments of a more social nature such as: "I'm looking forward to seeing you next Tuesday" or "You worked really hard today"—comments that are the verbal equivalent of helping a guest put on his coat.

SUMMARY

This chapter explored the beginning of the therapeutic journey by considering the goals of the beginning phase of therapy. We explored the subtext of the therapist's self-questioning through the initial interview, introduced the concept of the Learner Self and the Judger Self in relation to assessment, and discussed converting statements about presenting problems into questions. Lastly, we examined the eight stages of the first session in question-centered therapy, focusing on those stages most conducive to making purposeful therapeutic interventions.

6

Getting Started:
The Case of Andrea

Asking a question is the simplest way of focusing thinking . . .
asking the right question may be the most important part of thinking.
—EDWARD DE BONO

The aligned issues of choice and responsibility for one's cognitions, feelings, and behaviors are at the heart of therapy, whether it be focused on remediation, empowerment, or both. Certainly, these issues are central to dealing with severe anxiety, an experience where one often feels out of control. Yet, in reality, much anxiety is unintentionally invited by the individual's negative and limiting thinking. In addition, past circumstances—that is, how they were dealt with, and the life decisions that were made in reaction to them—often predispose an individual to feel victimized by his or her own emotions.

Andrea was such an individual. A married, 25-year-old woman, Andrea came to therapy after suffering with anxiety attacks for about six months. She described these anxiety attacks as occurring several times a week, including when she was driving, and occasionally took medication to help deal with them. She hated feeling anxious, and especially hated feeling out of control. Andrea and her husband, Ted, had been separated for about seven months, and she and the couple's two young children had moved in with her mother.

The most significant traumatic event in Andrea's history concerned her father. According to her, up until she was about 15 years old her father had seemed to be a normal, competent accountant. For no obvious reason that either Andrea, her mother, or brother can recall, he began acting in bizarre ways, and within a few months was briefly hospitalized for paranoid schizophrenia. He disappeared shortly after being released from the hospital, and no one in this large, extended family had seen or heard from him since. Andrea denied being upset or angry about these difficult circumstances, either in the past or in the present. She pointed out that after her father's disappearance, she maintained a straight A average in school and served as captain of the girls' basketball team. Andrea described her two biggest current fears were of being alone and of hurting her children, whom she loved very much. However, as she was preparing to leave her first interview, she stopped at the door, turned to me, and revealed what was obviously her deepest fear. In a hesitating voice she asked, "You don't think I'm crazy, do you?"

I told her directly: "No, I don't. But I can understand why you're afraid you might be." In the next four sessions we discussed her father's illness and her relationship with her husband, and worked on ameliorating the anxiety attacks. I believed her issues with both her husband and her father contributed to her anxiety, and both would have to be dealt with in treatment. She chose to work first with the anxiety and her marriage, which I encouraged. She was relieved that I agreed to put off conversations about her father until her anxiety had diminished.

Much of our time was spent discussing the specific sequence of thoughts, feelings, and behaviors associated with her anxiety attacks. Of course, we also reviewed how she could have averted or handled them better. I presented her with psycho-educational material about internal dialogue and the importance of self-questions, and gave her the Observe-and-Correct and Switching Questions handouts. After five or six weeks the anxiety attacks abated, and she decreased her medication to less than once a week. Since she used the psycho-educational information to handle the anxiety attacks, we were able to review carefully what she had done so she could learn from and reinforce what she had accomplished. Most attention was given to tracking her cognitions before, during, and after these episodes, and especially noting the questions she was asking herself—or that she should have been.

In Andrea's seventh session, we turned to her marriage. She and Ted had reunited and moved to a new home. Ted joined us for this session, at his own request. He especially wanted help understanding his wife's problems with anxiety. They said they loved each other, and wanted to stay married. In fact, neither could articulate why they had separated. It was clear to me, however, that in addition to myriad other factors, these spouses suffered from poor conflict resolution skills, and were also unaware of the impact of their communication on each other. Their decision at the conclusion of the session was that Andrea would continue to work individually, with Ted saying that he wanted to return to therapy later in order to work on improving the marriage. This fit his work schedule, which promised to be unusually pressured in the coming few months.

Reading the Transcript

This is the first of four chapters which are comprised almost entirely of transcript material. The format for each includes the therapist's and client's dialogue, as well as commentary about the process, which is separate. There are different ways for readers to interact with this material. Some people will find it most convenient to simply read all the material straight through, in the order presented. Another suggestion is to read the transcript twice, in a different way each time. The first reading should go quickly. Read it like it's a story, just to get the theme, flow, and sense of the process. Skip the intervening commentary, and pay attention only to the actual dialogue. Ask yourself questions while you're reading, as well as once you're done. Here are some sample questions:

- *What happened?*
- *What worked?*
- *Did anything not work?*
- *What are some of the specific ways the therapist used questions as interventions in this session?*
- *What was different from how I might have handled the same situation?*
- *What kinds of problems seem most amenable to this question-centered approach?*
- *What might I try now that I've read this transcript?*
- *What new question-centered interventions might I try, and with whom?*
- *What would I want those interventions to accomplish?*

The second reading of the annotated transcript reveals different dimensions of question-centered thinking. This time, read the commentary along with the dialogue. Remember that much of this textual analysis was available for me only *after* the interview. A session itself moves much too quickly to attend consciously and simultaneously to the background questions, one's client, *and* one's interventions. In fact, some of my supervisees who read early versions of the four transcript said that were overwhelmed by some of my commentary. They had assumed that I was aware of all my background questions during the sessions themselves. I assured them that actually, each time I reread a session, I recognized more background questions, those which would have had to be asked logically (albeit unconsciously) in order to give rise to the interventions I made.

Here are some additional questions to ask at the end of the second reading:

- *In what ways was my experience different the second time?*
- *What more did I notice about the therapist's interventions?*
- *Which of these interventions were familiar to me?*
- *Which ones were not familiar to me?*
- *What questions and/or observations do I have after reading the transcript?*
- *What new ideas and possibilities do I have after reading the transcript this time?*
- *What seemed more understandable, logical, and perhaps even easier to do?*
- *In thinking about a particular client, what internal questions might he or she have asked during our last session?*
- *What new idea or question might I experiment with sometime this week?*
- *With whom?*
- *What would I want to accomplish?*

ANNOTATED TRANSCRIPT:
THE CASE OF ANDREA

The session that follows, #8, occurred just after the couples' session.

[This is just a few minutes into the session. Andrea and I have started discussing patterns of painful interactions in which she and Ted often got stuck. In fact, he cited this as a primary reason for wanting a separation.]

THERAPIST: Andrea, you're saying that when Ted comes home and speaks to you in a certain tone of voice, you usually snap back at him?

CLIENT: That's right. He becomes sarcastic and says "Uh, *Andrea*" in a kind of belittling way. And that sets me off.

THERAPIST: And if you didn't react like that?

CLIENT: If I didn't snap back at him, and stayed calm, and said something nice? He might be like—

THERAPIST: "What happened to *her?*"

CLIENT: Yeah. (*laughing*)

THERAPIST: Well, that would be OK. I mean, you *are* coming to therapy because you want some changes, right? So, I think what you said was fine, that you want to stay calm. But what usually happens when he comes home after a hard day?

CLIENT: We start yelling at each other, blaming each other, really yelling. Nothing gets accomplished at all.

THERAPIST: Well, actually something *does* get accomplished, but it's negative. What's the negative thing that gets accomplished?

CLIENT: We feel further apart.

THERAPIST: I'm sure that's so—you end up feeling further apart. And I'll bet you *also* feel bad *about* feeling further apart. You're probably also upset that the kids heard you.

CLIENT: You're sure right about that.

THERAPIST: It *must* be disturbing to them, and they can't possibly know how to handle it. Besides that, later that night, it's probably harder for you and Ted to get back together. So, on the negative side, what you've accomplished is upsetting yourself, Ted, and the kids. And the evening, instead of being a nice family time, is terrible for everybody. (*She nods in agreement, and makes a disgusted-looking face.*) You see, Andrea, you *always* accomplish *something* by what you do, but you may not always like or want what you accomplish. There is *always* a result. There is *always* an outcome.

[It's important to reinforce to clients that there's always a consequence to their actions, and that they are responsible for their own behavior. This intervention sets the stage for the presentation of the Choice Model later in the interview.]

CLIENT: Um-hum.

THERAPIST: What are you smiling about?

CLIENT: Well, it's easy to admit you've accomplished something when it's good. But I hate to think that everything I do, even the bad stuff, accomplishes some result.

THERAPIST: To tell the truth, sometimes I hate admitting it myself.

CLIENT: Even when I didn't mean it?

THERAPIST: It's a bummer, isn't it?

CLIENT: You're not kidding!

THERAPIST: I can tell I'd better clarify something here. Andrea, do you know the difference between blame and responsibility?

CLIENT: *(She looks puzzled.)* Well, not really, I guess.

THERAPIST: Then I'm glad I asked the question. It's crucially important to make the distinction between them, and even some dictionaries aren't clear enough about it. What do you think *blame* is?

CLIENT: Blame means I did something wrong, like I was bad. Like I did something wrong and should be punished. Blame feels like guilt to me. It's almost like I committed a sin. Also, somebody else might think I did something wrong on purpose and get mad at me, or look down on me.

THERAPIST: That's a good definition. It's close to what people usually say when I ask them to define blame. What do you think *responsibility* is?

CLIENT: I'm responsible for anything I do, because I did it. Wait a minute. If I'm responsible for doing what *I* do, isn't Ted responsible for yelling at me?

THERAPIST: Sure. Only he doesn't realize it, just as you hadn't recognized your responsibility for how you've acted with him. However, *you're* the one I'm working with right now. Usually, when I work with couples, I teach *both* partners this way to think about responsibility, because this way of understanding it gives people so much more control. I'll probably do that with Ted later on. However, since *you're* the one who's here, you're the first of the two of you to get this. Anyway, gives us the opportunity to show you how to really be more in control. Learning about responsibility and choice will help with that a lot. Can I keep going now?

CLIENT: Yeah. But I hate to let him off the hook.

THERAPIST: I understand that. Most people would feel that way. But I also want you to realize that learning about responsibility will make you feel more in control. It's very powerful to realize that you, *by yourself*, can make things change, and that you don't have to wait and hope that something or somebody else will do it for you. Otherwise you could get into those powerless feelings again. I want you to know there's something *you* can do to make things better.

[Again, it's important to underscore personal, individual responsibility. At the same time, of course, therapists know that interactions in relationships happen systemically, and that where we punctuate these interactions defines the unit of cause-effect to be addressed. There is a delicate balance to be achieved here, and I like to cover my bases by taking both into consideration.]

THERAPIST: Can we get back to looking at the difference between responsibility and blame now? I promise we'll go over all this with Ted when he comes back for a session.

CLIENT: Do you really promise?

THERAPIST: Yes. I really do.

CLIENT: All right.

THERAPIST: Thank you. So what would you say is the difference between responsibility and blame now?

CLIENT: I guess I'm still not really sure.

THERAPIST: OK. Let me clarify these concepts for you. Once you know the difference, it will be easier for you to recognize what you're responsible for, and that will also tell you what you *can do* something about. Like you said, responsibility is simply acknowledging that you've done whatever you've done. It's also associated with feeling in control and in charge of yourself, and, of course, that goes along with good self-esteem. Blame has to do with a *judgment* about what you've done—and it's *always a negative judgment*. Blame is usually associated with feelings of unworthiness. It's no wonder it makes people feel bad, whether they're blaming themselves, or being blamed by somebody else.

CLIENT: I blame myself a lot. For my anxiety, for the problems in my marriage. And it does make me feel really bad.

THERAPIST: In addition to making you feel bad, blame doesn't get you anywhere. It's only related to something that happened in the past and it doesn't help resolve anything, or teach you anything that could be useful in the future. Only taking responsibility can do that. When you take responsibility for your actions, you're free to simply observe and correct. Remember, I taught you about observing and correcting?

CLIENT: Yes, in fact, I've even remembered to try to think that way a few times.

THERAPIST: Good. I'm glad to hear that. Now, the original reason you came here was those panic attacks. Can you imagine handling them without knowing how to be in charge of yourself, or without recognizing and taking responsibility for those negative things you were telling yourself?

CLIENT: Actually, no. But I never thought about it like that before we talked about it. When I first came here, I thought those attacks just happened *to* me. I felt completely out of control, and scared about it all the time. It made me feel like a victim. I blamed myself constantly. I didn't have any idea that *I* made the problem worse by my negative thinking. But in the last month or so, I've been able to control some of my scary thoughts, and I haven't had nearly as much anxiety as I used to.

THERAPIST: And it's been great to watch you learn to change that sabotaging thinking, and get back in control of yourself. You've been using this information well.

Let me tell you about some research that helps explain why learning about thinking is so important. There's a researcher named Martin Seligman who has studied what attitude and thinking have to do with the experiences of what he called "learned helplessness." Later, he wrote a book called *Learned Optimism* which was about how to change your thinking and *not* feel helpless or depressed. Seligman said that one of the most important things that psychology has learned in the last 20 years is that people can *choose the way they think*. And that the way we think is tied up with how we feel. Negative thinking helps cause anxiety, and that's how come teaching people how to change their thinking is a treatment of choice for anxiety. Of course, how you think is also tied in with blame and responsibility, and that leads us back to how important choice is. Let's get back to talking about the concept of choice now.

CLIENT: OK, fine by me. Anyway, I get what you're saying about being responsible, even though I still don't like it all that much. I do see where it helps me be in control.

THERAPIST: Good. Here's what we've established so far. First, *anything* you do accomplishes *something*—even if it wasn't what you wanted. Second, you have a *choice* about what you think and do. Third, you're *responsible* for what you do. The fourth thing is that your *results are your responsibility*, whether you intended them or not, because they resulted from what you did. That doesn't mean you should be blamed for them, or that you're bad. It just means that you did what you did, and the results were what they were. Are you with me?

CLIENT: Yeah. It makes sense so far.

THERAPIST: Now, we're getting to the fifth point. There is a specific technique for helping you make choices more easily and successfully. This has to do with asking yourself the right kinds of questions, and doing it on purpose, and at the right times. This is where choice comes in. You can *always* stop, and ask yourself a question. The questions might be like, *"What's going on?"* *"Do I want this?"* And if you don't want it, you could even ask a question to switch your thinking to another track, like, *"What can I do to change what's happening?"*

CLIENT: I can identify with that. I know I ask myself questions. Especially after that session we did on question asking. Actually, that handout on Switching Questions is what helped me short-circuit the anxiety attacks.

THERAPIST: Good. I'm pleased that you used it on purpose, and I'm so glad that it worked. Of course, you've always asked yourself questions. The difference is that you're learning to ask *helpful* questions, and to do it a *lot*. That's a foundation for learning to make choices more powerfully. Let me show you a diagram that helps make this more concrete. OK?

CLIENT: Sure. OK.

THERAPIST: *(I went over to a file cabinet and took out the Choice Model.) (See Figure 4.1)*

[For the next 5 to 10 minutes we discussed the various elements on the Choice Model. I find that clients readily understand these concepts when they are described verbally, visually, and concretely, which was my reason for converting these complex concepts into a user-friendly cartoon. The Choice Model is most useful for clients when it's used to discuss a specific situation, so they can relate to it personally.]

THERAPIST: I call this the Choice Model because it shows specifically when we have a choice and how to make consistently successful ones. The diagram shows *how* we make choices based on the questions we ask ourselves. And it shows how to make *active* responsive choices which are positive and focused on solutions instead of passive reactive ones, which are almost always negative, and focused on problems.

[Note that I used the pronoun "we." I purposefully underscore that the Choice Model illustrates how *human beings* make choices; it is not just about how clients make choices.]

CLIENT: Before you go any further, I sort of have a confession. I *hate* words like choice and responsibility. I feel like I've been hemmed in and beat up with those words all my life.

THERAPIST: Andrea, I admire you for telling me that. Many people feel that way, and frankly, lots of people *have* been beaten up with those words. It's really unfortunate, because the truth is completely the opposite. *Freedom* is what you get when you know you have choice, and you take responsibility for yourself. Choice is not what puts you in prison; *choice is what lets you out of prison.* Maybe that's where the phrase "freedom of choice" comes from.

CLIENT: Well, it sounds nice, but I still don't really get it.

THERAPIST: How about if I give you an example by using what you just did? *(Andrea looked quizzical, but nodded her assent.)* When you told me you had a confession, that was actually a big moment of choice for you, even though you might not have realized it. Do you remember a few weeks ago I showed you that what we do and say comes from questions we ask ourselves, even when we don't know we asked them?

CLIENT: You mean like that story about getting dressed, and picking what to wear after asking myself questions like, *"Where am I going today?"* or *"Will this sweater be warm enough?"* With two little kids, my usual question is, *"What do I have left that's clean?"* And that's what I end up wearing. *(She laughed, and looked pleased with herself.)*

THERAPIST: Exactly. So about this confession you made. Andrea, that was an important choice, even though, like I said, I doubt you thought about it that way. You *chose* to make that comment to me after asking yourself a question like, *"Will I get anything out of this session if I don't tell Marilee how I feel about those words?"* The answer was *"No."* Then you might have asked something like, *"Will Marilee get mad at me if I tell her how I feel?"* That answer would also have been *"No."* Then maybe you said, *"Well then, should I say it?"* Obviously, you answered *"Yes,"* because you did tell me your "confession."

CLIENT: This is so weird. Are you a mind reader? Everything you just said makes perfect sense, but I didn't know all that was going on. All I knew was that I got this funny feeling in my stomach, and knew I had to say something to you.

THERAPIST: *(I laughed.)* No, I'm not a mind reader. And soon you'll be able to do the same thing. That's why I'm teaching you all this stuff about questions. Of course, Andrea, those questions I told you were not actual sentences in your mind. This all happened in a millisecond. But the questions were back there anyway. All I had to do to find them was think about what you said about a confession, and ask myself, *"What questions must she have asked herself in order to decide to say that to me?"* I call that a retrospective analysis, but what I call it doesn't really matter. It's just a fancy name for what you're learning to do with yourself, and even with Ted. Being able to catch all those little moments of choice is like waking up and realizing what is actually possible. It's what makes you able to make powerful, *helpful* choices, and not just react to everything, like for example when Ted comes home from work and says, *"Uh, Andrea."* How might learning all this affect you, Andrea?

CLIENT *(Long silence.)* Well. Oh. *(Another long silence.)* Well, I guess that changes just about everything. This is going to take some getting used to.

[It's vital to grasp the concept of "wait time" in order to get optimal mileage from asking questions in therapy, or anywhere. Wait time has been researched extensively, mostly in educational settings. The accepted wisdom gleaned from this research encourages teachers to *wait three to five seconds after asking a question* in order to increase the frequency and duration of student responses, and to encourage higher-level thinking. We therapists could take note. Certainly wait time is as important for learning in the intimacy of the therapy room as it is in the classroom.

In fact, the issue of wait time brings up an even more important concept in therapy, that of the *presence* of the therapist. Often, the best we give clients is the still point of our attentive presence, simply *being* with them in their pain, troubles, and confusion. In truth, it's more challenging to train "being" than "doing," yet clinical competence calls for just that (Welwood 1977). I have noted that supervisees learning to wait patiently after asking questions also develop more ability to sit comfortably in silence with a client, trusting the organic unfolding of the self in the natural process of healing and growing.]

THERAPIST: You're right. It *does* change everything. Fortunately, you have the rest of your life to get used to it, and take advantage of it, too. But for now, I'd like to get back to the Choice Model. Andrea, can you live with the word "choice," now? Did we take care of this enough so we can move on? (*She nodded "Yes."*)

[I often ask clients if they are complete with an issue or concern before moving on. The point is to be certain they can be available, present, and undistracted for whatever is next. In other words, why would anyone even speak to another person without being sure there was an opening to speak *into?* Sometimes when discussing this with clients, I'll invoke the well-known story of the Zen master who filled his student's teacup to overflowing, and commented: "You, like that teacup are so filled that there isn't room for anything else."]

THERAPIST: Good. Let's start by looking at that person standing at the crossroads on the left side of the chart. He has to decide which way to go. That's you. It's also me. Actually, it represents any human being. This arrow to his left represents *everything* that could possibly happen to a person. Andrea, what do you think goes into that—everything and anything that happens to you?

CLIENT: The people around me, and how that makes me feel.

THERAPIST: Right. So, if the telephone rings, that affects you. If your mother calls, and you don't want to talk to her, that affects you. If your father called, that would *definitely* affect you. When your husband comes home from a difficult day, or yells at you, it affects you. If the kids wake up in the middle of the night, that affects you. If you have a dream the night before, that affects you. Also, *what you say to yourself affects you,* maybe more than anything else. So, if you tell yourself it's going to be a bad day, that affects you. See, the arrow on the Choice Model says: "Anything that impacts you, especially your own thoughts and feelings." If you tell yourself you're going to have a panic attack, that affects you, too, as you've learned recently. If you ask yourself questions such as *"Why am I such a weakling?"* that affects you by getting you to feel weaker.

CLIENT: Geez. It makes me feel like a target for everything and everybody— including myself. *(laughing)*

THERAPIST: In a way, you're right. And it's true for everybody. But *nobody* could handle everything that comes at us all the time. In life, every one of us has the job of sorting out all that stimuli, and making sense of it, of deciding what to pay attention to, and what not to pay attention to. Now, it's a little tricky, because when things first happen, let's say your husband yells at you, you will have some kind of *physical* reaction. You might tighten up or your stomach might turn over; sometimes people even get a headache.

CLIENT: That's true. Now that you mention it, I *can* feel myself tense up sometimes when I'm mad at him. *(pause)* Oh. I just realized I also get tense when Ted's mad at me.

THERAPIST: Sure. In other words, our emotions always affect us physically, even if we're not aware of it. In fact, we have physical reactions to everything, but it's pretty subtle, so most people don't realize it. And you really can't do much about it anyway. It's like when the doctor taps your knee and your leg jerks up. You know what that is—it's called a knee-jerk reaction. That's *supposed* to happen. You're "wired" physiologically like that. You'd be startled if there were a sudden loud noise outside, or your pupils would dilate in bright sunlight. These are normal physiological reactions. Andrea, it's very important to understand the difference between when you don't have a choice and when you do. You don't have much of a choice when your body is having one of those normal physiological reactions. You *do* have a choice at the instant *thinking* comes into the picture. As soon as you can ask yourself, "What's this?" that's when you become a conscious human being.

CLIENT: It *does* help to see there's a difference. (*She points to the figure on the Choice Model.*) I see that if I take the high road, I'm acting like a Learner. If I take the low road, I'd be choosing Judger, only I wouldn't realize I was choosing anything because I'd be having a knee-jerk reaction. I guess I've been a jerk sometimes. *(laughing)*

THERAPIST: No more than anybody else. We all end up acting our Judger Selves sometimes. That's not the issue. The issue is how long we stay as Judgers, and how quickly and well we recover ourselves. OK. Let me give you one more example. Let's say you planned a special picnic. That morning when you woke up, you looked out the window, found out it was raining, and got upset. In this instance, the arrow on the left represents the rain, because it says "*Anything* that impacts you." You have *no* choice about the rain. It's raining, period. That's it. Then, you have two possibilities. You could stay disappointed and upset. Where would that put you on the chart?

CLIENT: At the bottom, in Judger Self territory, because I would just be reacting and feeling sorry for myself, and not doing anything about feeling better.

THERAPIST: Right. You're a quick study, Andrea. What's the *other* thing you could do?

CLIENT: Oh, I get it. I could ask myself a question like: *"What are my choices?"* or *"Do I want to be feeling this?"* or *"What else could we do today that would feel special?"* Then I would be my Learner Self. *(Andrea looks pleased with herself.)*

THERAPIST: That's great. I think you have the concept. The rain just *is*. There's nothing you can do about it. But you have a *lot* of control about what you do with the fact that it's raining. You can let it ruin your day, or you can take matters into your own hands by asking active Learner questions, like the ones you just said. You can't do anything about the rain. But you *can* do something about what you think. You *are* responsible for how the rest of your day goes. You can't blame a bad day, or a bad mood, on the rain.

CLIENT: That's too bad. *(laughing)*

THERAPIST: Here's the most important point, Andrea. Imagine that it's *you* standing at the crossroads on the Choice Model. There's almost *always* this moment of choice. It's like a window of opportunity. *This* is the place of power. When something first happens to you and you react physically, that's when you don't have choice. But at the instant you *notice* you're experiencing something, and you say something about it to yourself, then all of a sudden, it's like choice pops up. You *do* have a choice.

So, when Ted comes home, and he's in a bad mood, and he first goes, "Uh, *Andrea*," your stomach tightens up. What you used to do was get upset, and just continue to react. You didn't know you had any choice not to. So, it wouldn't have occurred to you to think about how you could change your reaction into a positive response. Notice that the Choice Model has an arrow that says Reactive and it's pointing into Judger territory, OK? *(She nodded "Yes.")* What are some of the ways that you used to react when Ted came home in a grumpy mood?

[Notice that I spoke of the behavior to be changed in the past tense. If she answers the question it will imply that she accepted the presupposition about the behavior being in the past.]

CLIENT: It started when he said, "Uh, *Andrea*" in that tone that drove me nuts. Then we'd start arguing back and forth. And I'd get defensive automatically, even if I didn't think I did anything.

[Good. She accepted. Also, she used the past tense.]

THERAPIST: Okay, this is a great example to use with the Choice Model. Here's what I think has been happening typically between you two. Ted would say, "Uh, *Andrea.*" That's the big arrow coming at you from the left side of the diagram. This is what you don't have any choice about. It was his behavior, he just did it. And, this *(pointing to Judger Self territory)* is where you usually went as a result. No choice, automatic reaction. It ended up going around in circles, and sometimes feeling like getting into quicksand. *(She nodded vigorously.)* What do you feel when you look at the area I labeled the Judger pit?

CLIENT: Like getting upset. Going around and around in a circle. Using a lot of energy and going nowhere.

THERAPIST: A client once told me it looked like her whole life, going around in circles, in a rut that kept getting deeper and deeper. No way out.

CLIENT: Right. That's just what I meant.

THERAPIST: The good news is that where you *thought* you *didn't* have a choice, and you went into an automatic reaction, you actually *do* have a choice. You *always* have a choice. The trick is to catch the moment, because those opportunities go by so fast. And if you start going down the road toward the Judger pit, people tend to get stuck in those feelings. After that it gets harder to remember that you can always choose a positive direction by asking a Learner question. That's why the sign says *Detour. (Andrea was staring intently at the Choice Model.)* Andrea, here's how you know you have a choice. The first thing that has to happen is you say something like, "*Oops, I'm mad again. Am I reacting?*" The answer would be, "*Yes.*" So, then you say, "*Do I want to be reacting?*" What's the answer, Andrea? Do you want to be reacting? *(She shakes her head, "No!")* I didn't think so. *(laughing)*

Here are some other questions you could ask: "*Do I want to feel this way?*" "*Do I like the I feel and behave when I'm reacting?*" "*Do I want this situation to go the way it's about to go?*" You ask yourself those questions, and the answer is "*No.*" So, what gives you choice at that moment is *first noticing that you're having a reaction,* and then you ask a really quick inside question, "*What's going on?*" "*Do I want to feel like this?*" The answer would be "No," and then, "*Do I want the evening to turn out the way it always does when I feel this way?*" The answer would be "No." Andrea, the *question is the pivot point.* You can rescue yourself from reacting and just being on automatic by remembering to ask a Learner question. OK. After you've asked one of these questions, that's sort of the first in a series. And, the next part of the series might be a switching question such as, "*What could I do instead?*" Then you could say, "*How do I want the evening to go?*" or "*Is it going to be more fun if it goes the old way, or do I want to try something new?*" Oh. I just thought of a good question for you, Andrea: "*Do I want to be controlled by the situation, or do I want to be in charge of how things turn out?*"

CLIENT: That's interesting.

THERAPIST: *"Do I want to be controlled by the situation?"* Is it clear that when you are just reacting, like down here (*I'm pointing to Judger Self territory*), you *can't* be in control, and you *can't* be in charge. You'll feel like a victim to everything that happens to you.

CLIENT: Is that true?

THERAPIST: What would make it true or not true?

CLIENT: Because you can *choose* how to react to something. It might seem in that instant that that's just your reaction, but with me I can hear myself after a while even though I can't catch it in the beginning yet. But after a while, I can *hear* myself, and I can *hear* what's going on.

[This is an important point. Andrea is reexamining old behavior in terms of these new distinctions by identifying when she's been in observing mode in the past. However, she didn't have any training or skill then in how to take advantage of what she observed.]

THERAPIST: And then what do you do?

CLIENT: And then, I usually calm down, and I start speaking in a softer voice.

THERAPIST: OK. Let me describe what I think happens in those situations. This is in the past now. Ted would say, "Uh, *Andrea.*" You would react by getting defensive and upset, which meant you were going down this road (*pointing to the domain of Judger Self*). After a while, you realized what was happening.

At one of those points, whether you realized it or not, you asked yourself, *"Do I want to stay down here, or do I want to <u>change</u> things?"* That's like earlier in the session when you asked yourself, *"Should I tell Marilee that I hate the words choice and responsibility?"* and *"Do I want to get anything out of this session?"* When you asked yourself those Learner Self question they took you straight up into Learner territory. You got yourself out of the reactive, territory in the Judger pit, and back up here to the responsive territory of the Learner Self. That's what the Detour road in the dotted line indicates. It shows that a Learner question takes you straight up into Learner territory. The Detour road takes you from that instant of waking up, realizing you have a choice, and asking a Learner Self question. It takes you into the territory where you can *keep* being effective if you keep asking Learner questions. That road actually represent moments of freedom. Can you guess why that would be so?

CLIENT: Well, I have a sense of it, but I don't think I can put it in words yet.

THERAPIST: OK. It'll be more obvious once I explain a few things about Learner Self questions. A lot of what makes questions effective is that they're actually *real* questions. A genuine question is one you don't already know the answer to, and *you're willing to be open* to a *new* answer. It is this *openness* and *willingness* that gives new freedom. So when you ask yourself an effective question, *it is the question itself,* your *open mood* in which you ask it, and the *new options that show up* that are so freeing. That's what it means to be open-minded—your mind is actually *open* to something new. This is also the essence of successful problem solving and creativity. It gives you the possibility of something new and different, something you hadn't thought of before.

CLIENT: I get what you're saying about being open to something new. But sometimes I *do* realize I'm in the area below. I do see where it's going, and I really think I'm open to something different. But then I still don't change direction and go the other way. I choose to just keep being my Judger Self.

THERAPIST: What do you think makes you do that?

[There are two reasons why I didn't ask, "*Why* do you do that?" "What" and "How" questions often generate richer, more detailed answers than "Why" questions. Also, my wording suggests that anything she offers will be her *theory.* Therapeutically, it's often more fruitful to discuss clients' theories, rather than the "facts" as they saw them. People usually feel they have to defend "facts," but not so much their theories.]

CLIENT: If Ted is doing something that's driving me crazy, and I'm desperate to get my point across, but he's not listening to me. And it's just that he's said some things that really made me angry. Then I decide: "*I'm not going to let this go for now. I'm just going to keep on it.*" My mind is thinking in the direction: "*If I do this long enough, maybe I'll get through to him. I want to change things. Can I change things?*"

THERAPIST: OK. This is worth paying attention to. Let's figure out what happens when you chose to stay at the bottom of the chart, even when you realized where you were, and even when you might be open to something new. Here's my guess, Andrea. Let's say you're stuck in Judger Self land. You see what's happening, and you even asked yourself a question, "*Can I change things?*" However, since you haven't been able to do anything in the *past,* you didn't *believe* you could make changes so your answer was, "No." It was your *belief* about not being able to change things kept you from asking a Learner question.

CLIENT: That *is* right. And then I felt defeated, and out of control again. I could practically see my marriage going down the drain at that instant. God, it felt awful! I was really stuck in the Judger pit.

THERAPIST: Would you like to go over how you can get out of it?

CLIENT: I really would like that. I'm sick of it. And I'm sick of feeling like I don't have any control.

THERAPIST: I understand why you're sick of it, and I'm *glad* you're sick of it. *So let's change things.* What do you think would happen if you asked the question, "*Can I change things?*" a little bit differently? What about if you asked yourself, "_How_ can I change things?" (*Andrea looked startled, and stared at me.*)

CLIENT: Wow. That's wild. Why does that question make me feel so different from the first one? *This* question makes me think about what I *can* do, rather than *whether* I can do anything. The first question just made me feel awful.

THERAPIST: *(laughing)* Andrea, you just answered your own question, but you don't know it yet. Let's go back over this because it's really important. Think about these two questions. What's the difference between them?

[I am seizing another psycho-educational opportunity. What I'm about to teach her will make an important, empowering difference.]

CLIENT: Obviously, they're worded differently, although they're still a lot alike. Except one makes me feel depressed, and the other one makes me feel hopeful, like I can be in control.

THERAPIST: Of course. The first question is usually a Judger question. The second one is a Learner question. There is a subtle, but *fundamentally important* difference between these two questions. The first, which is the one you asked when you were with Ted, can be answered only with "*Yes*" or "*No.*" Since you didn't believe you *could* do anything, you *had* to answer "*No.*" Unfortunately, that answer also meant you were defeated. No wonder it made you depressed.

CLIENT: You're not kidding.

THERAPIST: But look at the Learner question. It *assumes* there *are* things you can do, and now your job is just to choose from among those options. This *forced* you to think about your options, and maybe make up new ones. Options and possibilities always make people feel better, like there's hope the future could be better.

CLIENT: This is gold, it really is. But I'm afraid I'm not going to remember.

THERAPIST: Don't worry. We'll go over this many times, and practice it, too. Soon it will become almost second nature. Also you have the Choice Model to take home and refer to. Remember you already have the Observe-and-Correct and Switching Questions handouts. I've even had clients teach this material to their friends and their kids, and it worked. How about if we go back over the Observe-and-Correct handout?

CLIENT: OK. I think it would help make this more real for me, especially now since we're using an example that's so close to home.

THERAPIST: Observe-and-correct is a way of thinking that you could be doing practically minute by minute. Remember the example of the pilot? She navigates by observing the instruments and correcting when they're slightly off-course. She observes with the simple question, *"What's here?"* and chooses with a question like, *"Is this correct and on-course?"* Then she corrects with a question like, *"What's the best way to fix this?"* It's a three-stage operation. First is observe, second is choose, third is correct. For shorthand I call it observe-and-correct. A pilot arrives safely to her destination by observing and correcting all the way there.

CLIENT: I remember. *(laughing)* Not like the pilot who sees she's off-course, and instead of just making the correction, starts asking herself stupid questions like, *"Why didn't I listen to my mother when she told me I was too dumb to be a pilot?"* If a pilot asked a lot of questions like that, it would be the end. Crash and burn!

THERAPIST: Do you see the similarity to yourself? When you've asked the kinds of questions you just called stupid?

CLIENT: Oh brother. Yeah, when I blame myself, or doubt myself, or when I put myself down. I've asked these kinds of questions millions of times, like, *"Why are you so dumb?"* or when I feel even a little anxiety and ask myself, *"Am I going to die?"*

THERAPIST: Good, you're understanding the concept. Let's get back to this situation with you and Ted. Here's another powerful question I'd like you to have. It's about thinking ahead. *"If I don't do anything different, how is the evening going to turn out?"*

CLIENT: That's easy to answer. Awful, as usual.

THERAPIST: Right. When you're standing at the crossroads, it's vital to look ahead down *each* road, so you can predict what will probably happen each way. That's what really makes it easy to choose. Then, you could ask yourself: *"What do I really want?"* or *"What's best for both of us?"* Andrea, I know we're getting very detailed here. We're actually breaking this tiny, ordinary incident down into split seconds, sort of like freeze-framing it. I'm doing it to show you how many places there are to make new choices that will work lots better than some of your old ones. By really slowing down the process, we're taking it off automatic. That makes so many opportunities become visible that were hidden before. Those new opportunities represent fresh new choices, and give you lots of options and strength.

OK. I really want to make sure you're getting this. Let's go over it again. Ted comes home; he's had a bad day. You know it's not any serious argument, it's just the usual sort of static. How would you *want* it to go?

CLIENT: I'd like it to go nice and smoothly.

THERAPIST: And what would that be like?

CLIENT: Well, if he started with, *"Uh, Andrea"* I'd like to be able to figure out how to respond so I'm calm, and I calm him down, and we accomplish something; we *settle* the problem.

THERAPIST: Great. So, you want to know how to accomplish having the evening turn out different and better? (*Andrea nodded "Yes," and smiled.*) OK. So, first you would ask yourself, "*What do I want?*" And then in an open-minded mood you would answer, "*I want it to be different, and I want to be calm.*" Oh, Andrea, here's another important point, sort of like a word to the wise. *Whatever* he's upset about, this really isn't the time to deal with it anyway. It really isn't.

CLIENT: I think that's the hardest part.

THERAPIST: It is? How come?

CLIENT: Because, let's say, I'm feeling like a Judger Self, where I tell myself: "*OK, I'm going to keep going; it's the only way.*" If I didn't do that, I'd feel like, "*OK, now he has won.*"

THERAPIST: Now *he's* won? What does that mean?

CLIENT: Well, let's say I don't agree with anything he's saying, and he's telling me I did all these things wrong, and I don't believe I did. The usual way to get him calm is to agree with him, even when I really don't.

THERAPIST: In which case, you feel like you've lost.

CLIENT: Right. I feel like: "*I lost, and now he's just going to do the same thing next time.*"

THERAPIST: Oh, I'm glad I asked you about that. This kind of thing goes by really, really fast, because our reactions become automatic. It's so important to catch this. See, a person who's in control *steps back* from a situation and asks: "*Is this the best time to deal with this?*" The answer in this case is obviously "*No.*" So, what if Ted says, "Uh, *Andrea?*" and it's about something you ostensibly did wrong, but you *know* you didn't. Then, you could ask yourself: "*Is this the time to deal with this?*" The answer is clearly "*No.*" So, then a smart person tells herself: "*OK, I'm going to remember to bring this up again because it's important, but if we get into it now while he's still upset, it's not going to work out. We won't connect right, and we'll upset the kids. Anything he wants to talk about is not going to get resolved, if we try to do it now. And, if it does get resolved, it will be in a way that he won, which is going to not change anything the next time. So it's an all-around bad idea to deal with this now.*"

CLIENT: That helps a lot.

THERAPIST: Good. Now Andrea, it's important for you to realize that Ted is not aware that he's starting a long chain of things that will probably make the evening a mess. He's not aware of it, all he's doing is being upset and saying, "Uh, *Andrea.*"

[I'm reinforcing her Learner attitude toward her husband, and her responsibility for problem solving in this situation.]

CLIENT: Yeah. I know. I realize that now. He's really a wonderful man and a terrific father. He's not upsetting me on purpose. In fact, when he comes home and does that, he doesn't even know he's starting on something that used to make me nuts.

THERAPIST: Good for you to realize that. You see, by toning down blaming thinking, you're freed up to have a positive feeling about your husband, and to get a whole different picture of the situation. Which gives you new ways to deal with him. Now you can imagine a whole new positive ending to an evening with your husband and children.

[Teaching clients about false attribution is an important component of the psycho-educational process, whether in individual or couples therapy.]

THERAPIST: The point of what I was saying is that you have a *lot* of control here, because what you can do is say to yourself: *"This isn't the time to deal with it."* You asked if it were, and you answered, *"No."* So you've made that decision. Then you tell yourself: *"We'll get back to that. I'm not even going to respond to it right now. Because anything I respond to is not going to work out right now."* Though it does depend on how upset he is. If he's really upset, and you say, "Look, we'll deal with that later this evening" he might say, "Oh *no*, we're not." *(She nodded.)* So, your best defense right there is probably not to respond at all. See, you always have this question, which is an important one, *"Should I respond to his words, or to his mood?"* Why do you think that's an important question, Andrea?

CLIENT: Because lots of times, if he's had a bad day, what he's upset about has nothing to do with me; it's just a bad day. Then some little thing I did annoyed him on top of that. If he's in a good mood, it wouldn't bother him. He would probably just laugh it off.

THERAPIST: And you wouldn't feel attacked.

CLIENT: Right. But if he was in a bad mood already, then he is likely to come at me with whatever it is.

THERAPIST: In other words, you would become responsible for the one little tiny thing, and everything else, too. Which doesn't belong to you. So, if you react to what he's saying, then what would happen in the old scenario?

CLIENT: What would happen is what always used to happen when he said, "Uh, *Andrea.*" It would be a circus. Actually, more like a horror show.

THERAPIST: What if you say to yourself: *"Should I let myself react like I used to, or should I respond to his mood, and remember that this moment could set the tone for the whole evening?"* You're nodding your head, *"Yes."* So now you can ask yourself: *"In that case, what's the best thing to do?"* OK Andrea, so what *would* you do?

CLIENT: I guess try to ignore the issue, and try to calm him down first. Wait a minute. I think before I even try to discuss it calmly, I should think about when would be a good time to deal with it. Anyway, I have to calm him down first.

THERAPIST: Which would be a real step in maturity for you. That would put you up here in Learner Self territory. Everything you asked yourself, and everything you did would be in this range up here. Now, let me tell you a secret about calming people down. There are *lots* of ways to do it. One is to do something entirely different from what they expect. He comes in, and he goes, "Uh, *Andrea?*" which used to be the trigger for the bad feelings we've been talking about. What would happen if you just gave him a big hug and a kiss?

CLIENT: *(She grinned.)* It would definitely throw him off. And knowing Ted, he would *love* it!

THERAPIST: Great. Another thing you can do is ask him a question, but *not* one about whatever he's upset about. Let's suppose you asked him if he wanted a back rub after the kids go to bed. Andrea, here's the big secret about questions. A <u>*question* asked in the right way, at the right time, to the right person, can change practically anything</u>. It's amazing how much control you have when you ask questions. Does that make sense? *(She nodded "Yes.")*

CLIENT: It makes sense because for a moment, he has to pay attention to the question. He'd be thinking about the back rub, and not about that other stuff.

THERAPIST: Bingo. That's right. And what would happen if you made a statement instead of asking a question?

CLIENT: It would probably go in one ear and out the other. *(laughing)*

[Without overtly pointing to it yet, I'm teaching her what I've been doing and modeling all along, making interventions in the form of questions. I want her to include this in her tool kit of communications skills.]

THERAPIST: Exactly. For some reason, people feel forced to answer a question, or at least to think about it for a second. Getting back to Ted—if you responded to his sour mood by asking, "Honey, how was your day?" what would happen next?

CLIENT: He would probably say "Terrible" or something.

[More psycho-educational training. Of course, I'm pointing to a strategy for changing emotions and situations in general.]

THERAPIST: But he would answer the question in either case? *(She nodded "Yes.")* And how do you think he would feel if you asked him, in a really concerned, caring way, "Honey, how was your day?"

CLIENT: I guess it would depend on how bad his mood was. Maybe he would stop and think: "*Wow. My wife's <u>concerned</u> about me. Andrea's interested in my day, and what happened to me.*"

THERAPIST: In that case, would you be on the same side in the conversation?

CLIENT: Sure. We would both be concerned about how his day went. I would be wanting to get involved in what happened to him during the day.

THERAPIST: And, although he may not realize it, he would be thinking: "*Oh, my wife loves me. She wants to know what happened today. She recognized the signals that I had a hard time.*" And then he'll probably be relieved and go "*Phew.*" (*Andrea's smiling broadly.*) Now, what happened to the whole discussion that began with, "Uh, *Andrea*, what did you do wrong?"

CLIENT: Forgot about it for a minute.

THERAPIST: Yes. And, you've *broken the pattern*. Once you've broken the old pattern, you have *lots* more time to think about how you want things to go, and to make them work out. It puts *you* in control. Remember, Andrea, you have control almost all the time, but if you don't know it, you can't use it. That's why it's so important to learn to recognize those tiny little moments when you can grab control. And that's what these techniques teach you to do, they teach you to grab control, especially with yourself.

CLIENT: That's what I did with those anxiety attacks. Now we're applying the same techniques to my marriage. This is cool. I like it. It puts me in the driver's seat, and I can make sure we both win.

THERAPIST: That's exactly what we're doing. Let's go back to the moment Ted comes home and says, "Uh, *Andrea*." We've written a new play now. What happens in the new play?

CLIENT: I know how to make it turn out OK for both of us. Ted and I can be together. We can be on the same side instead of opposite sides.

THERAPIST: You will feel connected. You're partners. How are the children going to be then?

CLIENT: Happy. Not affected by it.

THERAPIST: Right. And in the background, their feeling will be: "*My parents love each other.*" Which makes them feel more secure. That means they'll be less likely to get into a fight, or compete for attention. And then, Andrea, after the kids are in bed, and it's just you and Ted, what's more likely to happen if you've done all this, and you're being your Learner Self?

CLIENT: We'll have a good evening; we'll get along great.

THERAPIST: What kind of things will happen?

CLIENT: Well, the kinds of things that happen when we're having a good evening. Sometimes he puts his head on my lap and asks me, "Sweetie, will you massage my head?" I really like that.

THERAPIST: So, you're *together*, you both *feel good* about being together, the kids are calm. And Andrea, *you* were the one who determined how the evening would go when Ted came home and said "Uh, *Andrea*." Of course, you've *always* determined the course of the evening, it's just you didn't know it. Ted determines the course of an evening, too, but he doesn't recognize it yet. Since you do, it's more up to you.

CLIENT: All right. This is really making sense now.

THERAPIST: Andrea, we are spending a lot of time on something that is really only a tiny little moment, but, this kind of thing can make an *enormous* difference in which way things go in your life. The way I see it, the sooner people realize how much control they have, no matter what happens to them, the better their lives are going to turn out. It's amazing that something as simple as the right questions could make so much difference.

In fact, Ted might start looking forward to coming home more. It's even possible that after a while he wouldn't even come in with that old greeting, "Uh, *Andrea*." He'll feel good about coming home, sort of like, "*It's going to go great when I walk in the door. It's going to feel really good to see my wife and kids.*" Rather than the old way. I'll bet it used to be that as he got closer to the door, he wondered, "*What pain-in-the-neck things are going to happen when I get in there?*"

CLIENT: Right. In fact, he actually told me that. But it never occurred to me that I had any responsibility in what used to happen, or that I could do anything to make it turn out different.

THERAPIST: See, Andrea, you're changing a lot by changing this little thing. Now, let's look at the Choice Model again. See where the arrow's hitting the guy, and there's that fork in the road? The reactive road goes to the Judger pit. The sooner you catch yourself before you go down that road, the better it will be. If you've fallen into a knee-jerk Judger Self reaction, the sooner you catch it the better. Now, does that mean that you can't make a change if you end up in the swamp at the bottom of the chart?

CLIENT: No. Of course not.

THERAPIST: Good. It's important for you to remember that. How *could* you change the situation, if you've gone all the way down to the Judger pit?

CLIENT: Well, it *is* going to be a lot harder, because I'm sure we both have said some awful things.

THERAPIST: That's probably true. You would be reacting to things you've both said that didn't feel very good. There are lots of techniques for rescuing yourself from being stuck down there in Judger territory. But we'll save that for another session. There's not enough time left today. I promise you, there *are* techniques that can rescue you, even when you're really stuck in the Judger pit. Learning those techniques can make a huge difference, and they're pretty easy, too. We've already done a *lot* today.

CLIENT: You're right. (*Smiling.*) I feel really different. In fact I can't believe what I'm about to say. But I can't wait for Ted to come home in a bad mood so I can practice all this!

Epilogue

Andrea's anxiety attacks abated significantly, and she stopped taking medication. She did get her chance to practice these new skills with Ted, and was surprised at how successful she was. She learned to have far more control over her internal dialogue, especially the negative questions, and this was reflected in the positive turn her marriage took. She reported that she and Ted were much happier and optimistic about their marriage. She also said the children were calmer, more affectionate, and doing better in general.

SUMMARY

In the beginning phase of treatment, the question-centered therapist helps clients develop the skills, attitudes, and perspectives required to overcome presenting symptoms. She assesses the client's level of functioning with the goal of strengthening the Learner Self. She also begins teaching her client the relationship between their problems and internal dialogue, especially self-questions. The detailed emphasis on the concepts of choice and responsibility are the cornerstone of question-centered therapy. Question-centered therapy emphasizes the question-driven nature of choice and the importance of learning the results of asking Learner questions in contrast to Judger questions. The case of Andrea illustrated how the Choice Model and the Observe-and-Correct and Switching Questions handouts were utilized as psycho-educational tools for facilitating this process.

7

Midway on the Road:
The Case of Beth

The big question is whether you are going to
be able to say a hearty "yes" to your adventure.
—Joseph Campbell

C linicians often refer to the middle phase of therapy as the "guts" of the process: the time when much of the actual work takes place. It begins only when enough foundation has been laid in the beginning phase, and ends only when enough has been accomplished that the home stretch is practically in sight. This chapter focuses on the goals, therapeutic relationship, and interventions of therapy's mid-phase, and these are initially addressed in section 1. Section 2 introduces the case of Beth, a woman suffering with severe depression who was a client in question-centered therapy. Some background information about her is followed by a summary of sessions 1 to 10, representing the beginning phase of her therapy. Next is a summary of mid-phase sessions 11 to 19. Section 3 presents an annotated transcript of Beth's session number 20.

SECTION ONE: GOALS AND
INTERVENTIONS OF THE MID-PHASE

The primary goal of the mid-phase of therapy is to ameliorate the presenting problem. A secondary goal, from a question-centered perspective, is to continue strengthening cognitive, emotional, behavioral, and relationship skills. The model of the Learner Self and Judger Self stands in the background, especially as it enhances self-observation, self-responsibility, and internal locus of control. The therapeutic relationship provides the medium in which this all takes place. Interventions of the mid-phase use information elicited in the beginning stage to design strategies for achieving therapeutic goals. This section opens with a discussion of the goals, therapeutic relationship, and interventions of the mid-phase.

Goals of the Mid-Phase of Therapy

The first goal of the mid-phase of therapy is to continue to ameliorate the symptoms and causes of the presenting problem. Depending on the complexity of the case, this target requires the prior achievement of supporting subgoals. For example, successfully addressing Beth's depression depended on a confluence of factors, including biological, physiological, cognitive, emotional, social, and even vocational ones.

The secondary goal, contributing to the developing life skills of the client, is interwoven with symptom-specific interventions. In addition, a therapist with a question-centered perspective helps her client develop the ability to discover his or her own best answers and solutions, a habit which will help with resolution of the presenting problem, and endure as a generative life skill.

Interventions of the Mid-Phase of Therapy

Each of these goals calls for strategic interventions—some sequential, others simultaneous. Central to mid-phase interventions are challenging old thinking and beliefs, and developing appropriate behavioral rehearsals for assignments outside of session. Psycho-educational training is an important part of the mid-phase in question-centered therapy. At an appropriate time, the therapist introduces a number of handouts, including the Learner/Judger Chart. Because of its importance, the Learner/Judger material is explored extensively in the next two chapters.

Therapeutic Relationship in the Mid-Phase of Therapy

We assume in the mid-phase that a strong therapeutic relationship has already been forged, allowing the client enough trust to permit the therapist to introduce escalating challenges and more demanding behavioral assignments. The therapist's role as supporter, educator, and coach becomes even more important as she introduces new psycho-educational material and continuing growth-inducing emotional and social challenges.

SECTION TWO: THE CASE OF BETH

Beth was an extremely bright, perceptive, and attractive 28-year-old woman who felt hopeless about getting relief from a serious depression she had experienced for almost a year. Despite her strong desire to get better, and six months hard work in therapy with a highly regarded psychologist, Beth was discouraged, feeling she had made little progress. When her therapist took a job in another state, her family doctor referred her to me.

Beth said that our first interview represented grasping at her "last straws of hope." Her life "was in a shambles." The depression had forced her to take a disability leave from her career as an engineer. Her symptoms included poor memory, as well as an inability to concentrate, read, or even take care of routine maintenance. She regularly slept 14 hours daily, woke up tired and dreading the day, and often cried for hours at a time. She showered irregularly, and rarely left her apartment, now in chronic disarray, except to see her previous psychologist or the psychiatrist who was unsuccessfully supervising her medication. Beth also developed an obsessive fear that her apartment would burn down if she left anything plugged in, resulting in the compulsive need to check and recheck everything dozens of times before leaving home. This made her habitually late, adding to her feelings of being a failure and an embarrassing disappointment to her parents and herself.

Beth was the oldest of two siblings from an intact home in Iowa. She described her parents as caring, prudish, and "very negative." She had never seen them hug or kiss and they acted embarrassed if she or her brother asked them anything personal, even about their courtship. When Beth broke up with her high school sweetheart upon leaving for college, her mother made a comment indicating that she would have been shocked if Beth had even held hands during this two-year romance. Beth's brother was a physician practicing in Los Angeles, suffering from a mild depression and an obsessive focus on a failed love affair.

Beth was valedictorian of her high school in Des Moines, and went on to graduate with honors from a prestigious Ivy League college. There she majored in engineering, a subject she abhorred, because her parents refused to pay her college tuition if she majored in anything else. After her freshman year, Beth revolted, refusing to return to college unless she were allowed to major in psychology or religion. Her college boyfriend persuaded her to return, and she began her sophomore year as an engineering student several weeks late in the semester.

After graduating, Beth felt ill-suited for any job other than engineering, and took a position in a small construction company. As usual, she was a perfectionistic, hard worker who soon distinguished herself. Eventually, she was courted and won over by a large engineering firm in New Jersey. She relocated, and was doing a superior job, giving her managers the confidence to heap increasing responsibilities on her.

However, turning out top-drawer work in a field she disliked, and for which she was poorly suited despite her brilliant academic performance, required Beth to work literally 80 to 90 hours a week. Naturally, this left her little time, energy, or interest in a personal life, friends, or dating. Around the time that job pressures were mounting even further, Beth, a virgin, was violently raped. The combination of these factors triggered this severe depression, resulting in the disability leave. It was at that point that the human resources department of her old company referred her to the therapist she had been seeing until his recent move.

The Beginning Phase of Beth's Therapy
(Sessions 1 to 10)

The first order of business with Beth was to develop a therapeutic relationship she could trust, and to accomplish some small, but measurable, success that would serve as evidence for hope and a foundation for future work. Toward this end, our beginning work was structured, concrete, and directive, as well as supportive and encouraging. For example, we worked on strategies for cleaning up her apartment, beginning with moving several untouched piles of books away from her bedside. By the fifth session she reported having had four "good" days in a row. We had conversations about authenticity and individuation, and the development of a meaningful interior life, including the need to shift from seeking others' approval to caring about her own.

We broached the subject of the rape only briefly at this point. It had not been addressed in her previous therapy. I came to believe her depression had been either catalyzed or complicated by a posttraumatic stress reaction to the rape. Of course, it would be necessary to deal with this directly—eventually. However, first we had to attend to the more practical requirements of getting her back on her feet. Beth seemed relieved to discuss the rape, and also that more in-depth conversation would be put on the back burner until the time was right to deal with it.

Interventions in the Beginning of Beth's Therapy

In the initial interview I asked Beth what she was telling and asking herself about this depression. I also asked about her theories regarding her symptoms and present life circumstances. While these questions may appear to be information-seeking, I was also beginning to teach her about questions and inviting her to think from new perspectives about her problems. She was initially unaware of any specific internal dialogue, either statements or questions. In her first interview we talked about this for only a few minutes, and I ventured some guesses about her actual self-statements. She was able to identify some of them, and sense that they were thematically, if not specifically, accurate. I continued my queries about specific examples of internal dialogue in subsequent sessions, asking her what she was asking or telling herself about most topics that we discussed. She began to identify and even volunteer examples of such internal dialogue. When she wasn't sure, we worked it out together, until she, as the final authority, could say in agreement, "Yup, I recognize that now."

Developing the ability to identify one's self-talk, either in retrospect, or as it is occurring, can be considered cognitive training in formal operations. After all, the ability to think about one's thinking must rest on being able to notice or observe it in the first place. In this way Beth began to absorb both the realization that her internal dialogue existed, and that it correlated with, and sometimes even generated, her behaviors and feelings, including her sense of hopelessness and helplessness.

As Beth developed these cognitive skills, we also focused on shifting perceptual positions. She considered what advice I might give her about situations or questions she brought up in therapy. When she didn't know, we would discuss it. I wanted her to understand the reasoning and principles that gave rise to the suggestions I offered. Sometimes, we role-played situations that were troubling to her. First, I played myself to give her a direct, explicit means of internalizing me, including my problem-solving skills. Also, it was important for her to hear the psycho-educational concepts turned into specific dialogue, since she initially had difficulty making the leap from psychological abstractions to actual words and phrases. She also role-played therapist while I coached her. This kind of behavioral rehearsal is an important element of the session which comprises most of this chapter.

Discovering Her Own Answers   Training Beth to think from my perspective started in the very beginning of therapy. An example occurred with the early issue of cleaning up her apartment and moving those piles of books next to her bed. She thought it was a trivial issue compared to the suffocating problem of her depression. I dealt with her objection by asking how she felt when she woke up in the morning and those piles were the first thing she saw. She admitted she felt overwhelmed and defeated, not only because the piles were messy, but also because these were books she wanted to read, but couldn't, since she was too depressed to concentrate.

When I asked her to turn those feelings into statements she might have told herself, she readily recited: "*Beth, you're never going to get better. You can't even read the books that could help you. Anyway, you've turned into a slob. You're going downhill and getting worse.*" She added, "*What makes you think you'll ever get over this?*" Then I asked why she thought I wanted her to clean up those piles and move them away from her bed. This time she said, "Because you don't want me to see evidence of my problem first thing in the morning. You think I'll feel better if my apartment doesn't keep telling me I'm sick."

Another of my goals was to impel Beth to explore and develop some insight about her relationship with her parents, and her brother. As is often the case, I did this in an indirect way by asking many questions about them, and how they related to her. Many of these questions were intended to plant ideas about issues she could and should be thinking about. I wasn't looking for any change at this point; I was preparing the soil for new perceptions and behaviors to grow. My questions appeared to be merely information-seeking, and indeed I was interested in any information I could unearth. However, through these questions I also planted ideas about her relationship with her parents and benignly provoked her into questioning many of her assumptions about them and how they related to her.

The process of awakening Beth's awareness of self-questions and their potential for healing as well as growth was helped through using questions of another type that I sprinkled into these conversations. I would ask her, "What questions might you have been asking yourself about your parents in that situation?" Not surprisingly, her initial questions were along the lines of: *"How can I keep them from being disappointed in me?"* or *"What would they think if they knew I have sexual feelings?"* After we discussed the implications of these kinds of self-questions, it was easy and logical for her to transition into asking herself new queries, such as: *"What's appropriate for my parents to know, and what's not appropriate for them to know?"* or *"What's the best way to tell them I plan to leave engineering, even though they won't approve of my decision?"*

When Beth began reporting similar new self-questions she was asking outside of therapy, I was convinced that some of these new perceptions were taking root; that is, she was increasingly objective about her parents and less enmeshed with them. Relationship patterns that had been automatic were being questioned and altered. At the same time she was becoming more emotionally separate from her family, she was also developing some understanding and compassion for their personal dilemmas. This did not stop her, however, from beginning to experience anger over some ways they treated her.

By the tenth session, we agreed that significant progress had been made. Her apartment and paperwork were organized, and she was paying her bills. She was exercising regularly at a gym, and felt better for it. She was reading, absorbing, and enjoying books she had previously been unable to read at all. She was also beginning to be aware of feelings other than the numbness which seemed to have characterized most of her life. She sadly recalled having had no pleasure or emotional reaction upon hearing that she had made high school valedictorian. Instead, she had only thought: *"That's good. Now, what's next?"*

The Middle Phase of Therapy (Sessions 10 to 19)

There was much more evidence of progress by session 19. Beth took a rejuvenating two-week vacation with a friend (around session 12). She matriculated in a certificate program to prepare for nursing school, having decided this career would allow her to express the "soft, people-loving" side she had denied for so long (around session 14). She was stabilized on medication, and accepted that she still needed it. She was learning to distinguish between the self she had developed to gain her parents' approval, and her own authentic feelings, thoughts, and desires. She was learning to be patient and even compassionate toward herself, as contrasted with the cruel taskmaster she was previously in order to shine in a field she described as being ". . . totally opposite everything I am, and that I care about." In session 17 Beth began to talk about using therapy for growing and taking advantage of life, rather than simply as an emergency measure to fix her because she was "sick."

In the name of learning to "trust my own gut," Beth began noticing incidents in which she felt invisible, controlled, and angry, especially with her parents, with whom she had some successful, confronting interactions. She was increasingly comfortable saying and doing things she considered right for her, even though her parents would have been dismayed. However, Beth was also discovering a developmental lag in some of her social skills, having difficulty with interactions she recognized should be simple and easy for someone her age.

The question-centered approach supported many of these shifts. This was especially apparent in four areas where we focused much of our work together—learning to accept and validate herself and her feelings, learning to see her parents realistically and accept them for themselves, learning to act assertively and set boundaries with others, and learning to trust her own instincts, both self-preservative and creative.

Beth began to ask herself pertinent self-questions routinely and consciously. She was clearly incorporating some of my perspectives, thinking, and standards into her own. She developed the habit of commenting, "We're making progress here" or "We're doing a good job of getting me well." Her handling of a challenging incident demonstrated how well she was doing this. She enrolled in a workshop she thought would strengthen her ability to be a caring, compassionate nurse. To her dismay, however, she found the instructor consistently inconsiderate and disrespectful during the Friday night session. She asked herself: *"Does he represent the way I want to interact with patients?" "Could I handle it if he treated me the way he has most everybody here?" "Would Marilee think this was good for me?"* and *"Would she want me to stay in this workshop?"* Beth decided not to return on Saturday morning after answering *"No"* to each of these questions.

Notes on Reading the Transcript of Beth's 20th Session

I would like to share some of my experiences and thinking in this session with Beth. Obviously, by this interview, she was feeling and doing significantly better, and had good reason to trust my directions for therapy. I enjoyed her eagerness for learning, and the initiative she exhibited, frequently exceeding my homework assignments and tackling new challenges. By session 19, Beth had come to appreciate the usefulness of the radical break that this depression imposed on her life—even though she hated being depressed. She admitted that unless she had been pushed to the breaking point, where it was really physically and emotionally impossible for her to continue as she was, she would never have voluntarily made the life changes she was now accomplishing and enjoying.

At this point in her course of treatment, many of the needed internal changes were well under way. Now it was time to deepen our work on relationships. Naturally, this would be where her growing sense of authenticity, identity, and internal locus of control would be most tested—and needed to be. The only interpersonal situations we had dealt with up to this time concerned those with her parents and brother. Therefore, when Beth told me in session 20 she felt like withdrawing from her previous colleagues, I recognized the opportunity I had been waiting for. Up until now she had good reason to hide and avoid these kinds of interpersonal challenges. In fact, she would not have handled them with aplomb, and that might have left her feeling humiliated given her previous reputation as a high-ranking manager at the ABC Corporation.

In the beginning of the session, Beth was adamant that she wasn't avoiding her former colleagues. However, my opinion was that "she doth protest too much," and that she was actually very frightened, and not at all willing to deal with them. I had a number of therapeutic choices. I could have taken the route of dealing directly with her fear, since this was where she was already focused. However, I was certain she was ready to be coached into action, even though she certainly didn't know it. I asked myself: *"Would it be more productive for her to experience and deal with her fear, or move into a corrective interpersonal experience?"* I chose the action route; that is, a cognitive and behavioral rehearsal for the real thing. My goal was clear: to prepare her to handle at least one of these social situations successfully in real life. However, I first had to get her to agree that this was important, and that she was willing to take up the challenge. As you will see, it took almost half the session to move her to this point.

There is no obvious confrontation in the session, although I challenged her almost every step of the way. This is simply testimony to the power of questions to sidestep a conflict which could distract from achieving a goal. If I had thought that a direct confrontation would have been more efficient, I would have taken that route. For approximately the first half of the session, my experience was of politely parrying with her—or, more accurately, of subtly wrestling her to the mat. At each juncture, as she tried to slip away, I indirectly confronted her by merely (!) asking her to consider some further questions. Each time I did this was equivalent to cutting her off at the pass; I blocked her attempted exit from having to face doing what she wanted to avoid.

When she finally did acquiesce and agree to the session goal of getting ready to deal with her former colleagues, her shift from *"No"* to *"Yes"* was so subtle as to be practically imperceptible. This occurred right after I offered her two new self-questions, giving her the choice to align with one of them. She picked the one I hoped she would: to confront this situation and use the therapy session as a safe place to ready herself. Not only did she now agree to this route, she also took ownership of it as if it were her own idea.

SECTION THREE: ANNOTATED TRANSCRIPT OF BETH'S SESSION #20

[We enter the conversation early in the session when Beth and I are discussing her fear of expressing herself.]

CLIENT: OK. I have to admit that I've been more withdrawn recently. I've noticed there are certain people in my life whose phone calls I just don't want to return, even though I thought of them as friends before. They are good people, but they fit in with a model of a person I used to be, and that I want to get away from. I just don't want to get on the phone and feel like I have to justify what I'm doing professionally because it's so different from when they knew me.

THERAPIST: *(After gathering some relevant information about this situation)* I'm glad you're telling me this. It might be useful if I generate a list of some questions to consider in dealing with these kinds of situations, and maybe we'll put some to play.

CLIENT: Should I write them down?

[Beth's possible self-questions here: *"What does Marilee want me to do with what she says?"* *"Will I remember what she says?"* *"Would it be safer to write these down because I might forget them otherwise?"*]

THERAPIST: I don't know what I'm going to say yet, but, yes.

[This remark represents my *"yes"* response to the following self-question: *"Would it be helpful for her if I risk modeling that "not knowing" is OK?"*]

THERAPIST: Beth, these questions would go something like: *"Is this person, or was this person, a friend to the old model me?"* *"How willing would this person be to accept and embrace who I am becoming?"* What other questions might you ask, Beth?

[My self-question: *"How can I involve her as a partner in the session?"*]

CLIENT: *"Were they really friends to begin with?"*

THERAPIST: Okay. That's good.

CLIENT: I'm just sensing that everything leads to this, like when you asked, *"How willing would they be to embrace the person I'm becoming?"* My instinctive reaction was, *"Well, maybe a few of them."* It would be easy to say I'm not willing to chance it, but that's not it.

[Beth demonstrates that when I suggested this question in the grammatical form of a self-question, she had thought it was important, had asked it of herself, and come up with an answer. Note that she made my suggested self-question her own by using my exact words.]

THERAPIST: Well, if that isn't it, what questions could you ask yourself to find out what's going on?

[This intervention is in answer to my internal self-question: *"Would it be more fruitful to challenge her unwillingness to risk, or simply offer some questions to help her become more aware of her thinking?"*]

CLIENT: Okay. *"What could be stopping me from telling these people what I'm really doing professionally?"*

THERAPIST: Good question.

CLIENT: It just comes to mind that anything I've ever done goes back to that perfectionism. It goes back to that feeling that I *have* to have it all together. For example, if somebody gave me a project and said they wanted status reports at various times, I wouldn't want to give that status until the end point, until I could say: "This is it, it's beautiful. The best I could do." It's like when I would play in these little concerts in high school, and I didn't want my parents there. Now, were they really going to disown me if I played an F sharp rather than F flat in measures 3 or 4? Of course not. That was *my* worry.

Now, obviously something in their needing perfection was striking a chord with me—this made me scared. And I think that applies to what's going on now, because I don't have the answers, and I don't think I'll get it right. I'm out on another planet right now, as far as these people are concerned. And they're going to ask me a lot of questions, and I don't have those answers. There is a vulnerability there, that I feel could pull me back; there's a risk there.

THERAPIST: That is exactly the point. There *is* vulnerability there, and risk here, and that's some of what it takes to be in relationship. Beth, we're really talking about the old model you versus the new model you're becoming. It's like the Judger versus the Learner. The old model fixed herself up to look perfect, so that people could respond to her as being perfect. The trouble is, it was mostly a mask. The new model is somebody who's courageous enough to risk the vulnerability of whatever happens. And sometimes the process of being human is very messy.

[I reframe her fear into something desirable that we've talked about in past sessions—discovering herself under all the layers she developed for her parents' and others' approval. Also, I posit authenticity as being a positive goal. I want her to recognize that working on this would be evidence that she was getting better, and that she would win more of my approval by taking up the risk of this challenge, regardless of the outcome.]

CLIENT: I think the trouble that I'm having is that intellectually I know every interaction carries a risk. But there's something here that feels like it's beyond risking a friendship, or risking somebody's opinion or image of me.

It's more a risk of not feeling like I'm on solid ground. I'm afraid that if I'm around people I know intrinsically won't agree with what I'm doing professionally, I'll be risking something healthwise, that I'm going to be pulled back to the old model of me.

[I don't challenge the accuracy of what she's saying. However, it represents a restricted way of thinking, one that could keep her stuck, because it is black and white, and offers only limited possibilities for actions she could take. Also, I want to get past her emphasis on feelings of fear, and instead suggest alternative ways of thinking that could let her safely test her ability to handle these kinds of situations. I'm betting she would discover unknown capacities within herself, and expand her positive opinions and beliefs about herself.]

THERAPIST: You're also thinking in black and white, which, as you know, is Judger Self thinking. It supports your fear and keeps you in the old model you. But if you were thinking from the new model as a Learner Self—which you are learning to do very nicely—you would be asking different kinds of questions such as: *"Who would be the best person to research this with?" "In terms of risk taking, does this make sense?" (Beth nodded in agreement to this last question.)*

[My comment about black/white thinking again underscores a psycho-educational approach. I want to reinforce her thinking about her own thinking, to build her "observer muscle," now and for the future. The self-question which generated my earlier two offerings was: *"How can I get her focused on the logistics of this possible experiment in a way that also gives her confidence?"*

I chose not to focus on her feelings which might have kept her stuck in them. I had asked myself, *"Would she benefit more from 'getting in touch' with her feeling of fear, or in achieving something important that would contribute to her sense of self-efficacy?"* I was also making these points:

1. The importance of focusing on an action or behavior.
2. That it was *possible* to research this, probably with any of these people of whom she was afraid.
3. That she didn't have to do it perfectly because it would *only* be research.
4. That this choice offered a path of growth I would approve of, regardless of the outcome. I would applaud her merely for taking on this research.]

THERAPIST: And then, you would ask yourself questions such as: *"What would be the best way to go about this?" "What resources do I have?" "How can I get sup-*

port in doing this?" "How can Marilee help me practice this, or research this?"
"Could she use this situation to coach me in doing better in relationships?"

[I'm educating her about a way of thinking. Under the guise of offering new questions, I'm actually planting specific new ideas. I want her to open up to include new possibilities for successful accomplishments. Her fear was, in part, a natural response to not having any real ideas about how to go about doing this.]

CLIENT: I just don't want to continue these relationships. I *am* thinking about what you're saying, but I had a chance to make this idea gradual to my parents.

THERAPIST: What idea?

[I want to distract her from the notion of discontinuing these relationships simply because she was afraid of them. My question to her, "What idea?" also suggests that I respect her objection, and want to learn more about it. I do respect her objection. This is not "merely" resistance. It was clear she had more in mind than I knew, and I needed more information so I could continue moving her to action. At this point, I have definitely chosen my goal today: for her to be ready and willing to deal with one of these people by the end of the session. Many of my interventions from now on will answer this contextual question: *"What will it take for her to be ready and willing to engage with one of these people?"*]

CLIENT: About going to nursing school. Two months ago when I told my parents I was going to leave engineering and go to nursing school, I had the chance to build up to that idea and soften it for them. I was trying to keep them from getting too angry or disappointed. I had a chance to tell them gradually. I've widened the circle of people who know, and now there's just a few people left from my old corporate life who don't. I think they're going to really look down on me for this. They're not bad people—I don't find them repulsive. It's just there's a repulsion there.

THERAPIST: Repulsion of what?

[This question forces her to specify. I am not interested in her feeling of repulsion. I am interested in the *idea* she's carrying that's creating this feeling. Also, if she doesn't specify it, she'll have no ability to challenge it herself and she'll just stay stuck with this vague, unpleasant (yet distinctly limiting) feeling.]

CLIENT: I'm talking totally out of my gut now. Maybe that's a good thing that I'm talking from my gut—because my head says there's nothing wrong with getting in touch with these people. *"You talk to them, you don't talk to them;*

whatever happens, happens." But there is something in my gut that says, *"Why bother? Leave it in the past. It doesn't matter."*

THERAPIST: There are a couple of ways we can go here, Beth. Let me tell you what I'm asking myself. Part of me is asking: *"Should I support you in just going from your gut for now?"* because in truth, it's great for you to be even talking like that. I'm also asking myself: *"Would it be helpful for you to pick just one of these people for us to check this out?"*

[These questions represent two disparate choices, and it was this technique that moved her beyond the fear that had kept her immobilized previously. The wording basically forces her to handle the situation in one of two ways. Among the questions I had asked myself to arrive at this intervention was, *"Although I have a preference about which course she chooses, how can I word the questions so she gains something positive from either choice?"* I'm also being careful not to invalidate her feelings or her instincts. She was so intellectualized before, and so remote from her feelings, that she didn't have the concept of "gut" in her repertoire. Also, notice the word "us." I am letting her know clearly that I'll be there to help her, and even subtly, that if this doesn't work, I'll share the responsibility. She won't need to be perfect, I won't judge her negatively for that, and she will not run the risk of disapproval.

This technique of sharing with a client several different positions (in this case, in the form of self-questions) is an internal, cognitive version of a family therapy technique I learned from Peggy Papp. In this situation the therapist is observed by a team behind a one-way mirror. They give her suggestions by phone or in a quick conference when the therapist steps out of the room. Then the therapist tells the family: "Some members of the team think 'X.' Other members of the team think 'Y.'" This allows the therapist to present several choices without being identified with any of them. If the client(s) pick the idea the therapist didn't identify with, they're not resisting her, or risking her disapproval. Also, this prevents their picking a position other than hers just to be oppositional. This technique helps free client(s) to make their own choices.]

CLIENT: I thought of that already. I think that's what I was leaning towards, too, to try to clarify for me and you why I'm feeling the way I am. And maybe if you look at the relationships I am talking about, we can get some tangible reasons as to why my gut is saying what it is.

[Success, finally. She changes direction here, as I hoped she would. The shift is subtle, but definite. She doesn't appear to notice that a few moments before she was trying to avoid this confrontation. Now we can

really go to work together. My goal for the first part of the session was to
get her to this point. Beth now indicates that I am verbalizing and validating a question she had already thought of, but hadn't been able to
share yet. Somehow, the way I presented this possible route allowed her
to make this choice *and* to take ownership of it. She also lets me know
that she considers us a therapeutic partnership, working together for her
benefit.]

THERAPIST: That would be helpful. We'll consider this a research period,
which means that at the end you might come to the conclusion, *"I was right,
this isn't somebody I want in my life right now."* And that would be perfectly
legitimate. That's how your Learner Self would think.

[Validating her again, making this whole challenge easier, and reinforcing my sincerity in labeling this as research. Again, this underscores that
we're doing this together, we share the responsibility, and that she
doesn't have to be perfect to keep my approval. The goal is not to be
right or perfect, but to learn something from whatever happens. I had
answered *"Yes"* to my self-question: *"Would it be worthwhile to further
underscore this as research?"*]

THERAPIST: Beth, I hear you telling me: *"I'm going to take a courageous step
and get my hands a little bit dirty, and approach this like it's a piece of living
research. And, it's safe enough to try."* By the way, this is a good question to
remember: *"Is this safe enough?"*

[Direct, strong validation. Also, I'm introducing the distinction "safe
enough," instead of just "safe." Safe/not safe is black/white thinking. "Safe
enough" provides shades of gray. The question, *"Am I safe?"* demands a
"Yes" or *"No,"* black-or-white answer. So if Beth doesn't think she's *completely* safe, the linguistic structure of the question would force her to
declare herself unsafe, a declaration which would actually contribute to
her *feeling* unsafe, which could then keep her from acting at all.
    I crafted the term "safe enough" from Winnicott's distinction of
"enough." He talked about a woman being "a good enough mother"
(Winnicott 1958). I've long considered this to be an empowering and
kind phrase, extending some cognitive and emotional relief from impossible, perfectionist, punishing ideals. My intervention of underscoring
the utility of this phrase is another example of my psycho-educational
predilection in therapy. I directly suggest she add this new question to
the lifetime tool kit of skills she is building in therapy.]

CLIENT: Okay. That's good. I do feel safe enough to risk this. Do I have to deal
with all my old colleagues right away?

[Her question suggests her old paradigm. One of her old operating questions was something like: *"How can I do everything that needs to be done, in the fastest and most perfect way possible?"* Since a person's perception of available choices and all her consequent behaviors are in response to such questions, the one she has just asked would have gotten her into the same overwhelming, impossible predicaments as before.

I choose *not* to raise this point, having asked myself, *"Should we take a teaching side road here, or move into action?"*]

THERAPIST: No. Let's just pick *one* person. But to start with I need to know how many of these people there are.

[Here, I'm making the task easier and more manageable by suggesting a smaller chunk to work with, which is also something I want her to learn. Dealing with a manageable unit size is something she'd do automatically in managing engineering projects. However, this didn't occur to her in thinking about personal "projects." Also, I do need to know how many of these people she's going to have to deal with eventually. My self-questions: *"Are there any difficult situations brewing that could create problems if we don't address them now?"* and *"Will she have trouble staying focused on the one person she chooses to deal with if there are other troubling situations which I don't know about?"*]

CLIENT: Twelve?

THERAPIST: A dozen people. How many are people you might want to keep in your life?

[I'm asking myself: *"What question can I ask her to make this list smaller, thus less overwhelming and more manageable?"*]

CLIENT: Four.

THERAPIST: Good. That's a much more manageable number for now. Which one would you like to start with?

[Getting her to select one person, where some behavioral intervention is possible. I'm asking myself: *"How can I move this to a real situation?"*]

CLIENT: Steven is somebody I met at XYZ Corporation six years ago. Probably for the first five years of our interaction, I had in the back of my mind that this guy was my soul mate. I really felt that way. It was like one of these comic relationships that you see on TV—when they put on the little sitcoms with two people who always eye each other a certain way, and tease a certain way. And the audience always says, "Would you just go for it?" But for this reason, or for that reason, or the next reason, it never happens.

THERAPIST: Are you saying soul mate in the sense of somebody you would date or marry? Or soul mate in terms of personality?

CLIENT: In terms of date or marry. That's how I felt since I met him. We've had lots of conversations about this for five years. But now, in my mind he's the model of who I *don't* want to be. You know, brought up in a very conservative, religious, ethnic family, valedictorian of his class, Stanford, and another engineer just like me. Always has to succeed, wants to dabble in absolutely everything, and be the best at absolutely everything. I would also say immature comes to mind when I think of him, emotionally immature.

THERAPIST: Do you *still* feel he's a soul mate?

[This question is for double-checking. I suspect her relationship with this man represents her biggest concern about interacting with former colleagues from her corporate life. I'm also curious why she hasn't told me about him before, but mentioning that now would distract us from the task at hand.]

CLIENT: Not at all. Actually, he's very much of a Judger with himself, like I used to be. He can also be very judgmental of me.

THERAPIST: Okay, now I understand.

CLIENT: That's what the issue is. The person I was, or the model of person I was then, which was high-test Judger Self, made us just perfect. We could have been brought up in the same family. We could have had the same genes. I mean it was perfect. So, I'm sure you can understand why he makes me so anxious. He's the old me in masculine form, and I'm afraid to be around him. We've had so many things happen, and when I say emotionally immature, I really mean it. He's got a million and one hang-ups with relationships. I found it cute and endearing during our years of bickering back and forth at 2:00, 3:00, or 4:00 in the morning. I just thought he was so cute, and very innocent sexually. I really found it endearing.

And right now I feel like: *"I can't be bothered with this bullshit."* (spoken emphatically) That's just honestly how I feel. I have cried, I don't know how many nights, over one interaction we had. We had this one evening. God knows what got into us, but we were physically intimate even though we didn't go all the way. I called him two days later, because we had known each other such a long time, and I wanted to know how he was feeling about me and what had happened between us. He was a total spaz on the phone. He said something like, "Yeah, we will have to get together sometime, and I don't know—the month of February is looking busy for me, the month of March is looking busy for me." I thought about this a few days, and I called him back. I pretty much shocked myself with my behavior. I said, "Forget it, Steven. I can't put up with this. We have had this interaction back and forth forever, and now you either know if you want to go forward or you don't."

THERAPIST: Wow. Good for you.

CLIENT: Well, it was good, but it was also around the same time as the beginning of my complete depression and downfall at the beginning of last year. Actually, I can't believe I never told you about it. Even when you asked me what was going on in my life when I got depressed, I completely blanked out on this. I guess it's because no matter what was going on in my life, in the back of my mind I always had the assurance that this was the guy I was eventually going to end up with. That's how we always talked to each other.

THERAPIST: And then when life confronted you with the reality of what it might be like to be married to him, the whole thing fell apart. Is that accurate?

[I don't want to make presumptions. I let her know I've made an interpretation that I recognize as an interpretation, and that she is the *real* authority, and should have the last word. Also, I am modeling asking questions for information and clarification. Again, I imply that it is acceptable not to know something, and am willing to show that by asking a question.]

CLIENT: To tell the truth, even then I felt at some time in the future we would be together. He just wasn't at that emotional level yet. And here we go again—I get hurt.

THERAPIST: Okay. I'm going to put us on a fast forward because there is a limited amount of time left in our session.

[I asked myself: *"Is there enough time left to finish this situation, and also address her belief about always getting hurt?"* My answer was "No." I had also asked myself: *"If we move faster, can we accomplish our goal for the session?"* Answer: *"Yes."*]

THERAPIST: Beth, let's look at how this situation can be useful for you. You don't really know whether there's something in the future with this guy. But I don't think that's your issue at this point. (*She nodded affirmatively.*) So here's a question for you: "How could you have an interaction with him, either on the phone or in person, that would validate your friendship from the past, let him know you need to be separate right now, and do it in such a way that was compassionate toward him?"

[The question would probably have been better if I had phrased it in the first person singular, and possibly had made it two questions. However, I was really thinking out loud—there were so many criteria I was trying to crowd into this one question.

I'm hoping she will hear this as a self-question, and will find it easier to answer and also feel more compelled to do so. I assumed that she previously felt so anxious and confronted about the situation that she hadn't considered how to *do* it in practical terms. So I plant the idea that she could do it on the phone, and that instead of feeling awkward and possibly even hurting him, she could communicate in a way that worked for both. Her idea was that she would just tell him the harsh truth. She had no concept that she could communicate honestly, protect her boundaries, and still be genial.]

CLIENT: What you said is probably more important. In my gut I've been feeling like he deserves the respect of my returning his phone call, and I also want to tell him what's been going on with me. But I also have to let him know that he just can't be part of my life right now.

THERAPIST: Right. That's a clear boundary, but it's also a caring action.

[She's just learning to put in effective boundaries, though still afraid of doing so because it seems mean and selfish to her. So I tell her explicitly that it's possible to take care of herself without hurting someone else at the same time.]

CLIENT: But then my mind says: *"Why does it have to be black and white?"* You know, I did see him maybe two months ago, and it wasn't awful.

THERAPIST: This is one of those times you should tell your mind to be quiet. Right now what your gut says is: *"It's not good for you to be around this guy, period." (spoken emphatically)*

[I side directly with her gut, with her need to have clear boundaries, and a period of healing unimpaired by having to deal with Steve, or anyone in that category, from her former life. I'm in the role of protector and teacher here. I'm helping her say what she wants to say, but is timid about saying. I'm also aware of how little time is left in the session.]

CLIENT: Loud and clear. *(She says this emphatically and seems relieved.)*

THERAPIST: Loud and clear. But then the question is: How can you behave toward him in a way you will respect?

[This time I repeat her exact words, "Loud and clear," reinforcing the boundary. In a subtle way, I also acknowledge her for taking the lead. There have been several points in the session where she echoed me verbatim. Now I'm returning the favor. I also want to build in the criteria and experience that establishing a boundary doesn't have to be uncaring toward the other person.]

CLIENT: In a way I can respect? Help me.

THERAPIST: Well, tell me what you respect and what you don't. I'll make this more specific. Would you respect yourself if you just never returned any of his phone calls? *(She shakes her head "No.")* The answer is "No"?

[When I tell her I'll make this more specific I am answering "No" to this self-question: *"Do we have enough time left in the session to elicit her criteria for respect?"* With this question, I'm checking to make sure my idea of respect matches hers. Also, I'm highlighting her criteria for respect *in this situation*, so they can be conscious and clear.]

CLIENT: I know I have to get in touch with him. My Learner Self knows I have to handle this.

THERAPIST: Okay, so part of respecting yourself here includes knowing you have to get in touch with Steven? *(She nodded.)* Okay. When you get in touch with him, how would you treat him, that in retrospect you would respect?

[Checking her criteria. Also, helping her build an interaction that is congruent with what she wants. I assess that I can ask her questions directly now, rather than couch them in the easier-to-respond-to form of the self-question.]

CLIENT: I feel like I have to explain what my gut is saying, but I want to do it so I really get my point across.

THERAPIST: Oh, so you're planning your criteria. You want this to be it, the conversation that completes things with him? *(She nodded.)*

[I'm also planting the idea that it's a good idea to specify one's criteria for success in a situation, that she can make this boundary, do it well, and complete this in one clear conversation, and really close this issue about Steven.]

THERAPIST: Knowing you as I do, I think you'd be most comfortable sharing your personal decisions with Steven in a way that doesn't put him down. That would include taking responsibility for it in a sense, as in saying to him: "This is where I am now. This is what I need. This is what I am going to do." This is very different from saying, "Steven, you're too immature for me to be around right now."

[I am planting ideas again, explicating what I know would be her own criteria if she weren't so anxious. Also, I'm modeling how to take responsibility for one's own feelings and decisions rather than blaming or putting down the other person. Ordinarily, coming out of my psychoeducational frame, I also would have asked her something like, "Beth, can you tell me what's the difference between the two comments to

Steven that I just gave you?" I didn't do this here because I had asked myself if there were time for this and answered "*No.*"]

CLIENT: What you're suggesting is what I feel I should do. But I know this guy is a very thinking-oriented person. If I talk from my gut, and say, "This is what I need right now" he's going to say, "Why? Explain it to me, give me the details."

[This is a place where therapists might inquire, "How does that make you feel?" I intentionally do not. I want to complete this behavioral rehearsal before the end of the session.]

THERAPIST: And, what will you say?

[I'm wanting her to come up with ideas; I'll help only if she needs it. The more she thinks this through on her own in session, the more easily and naturally she'll be able to interact with him in vivo.]

CLIENT: That "You need to respect my bottom line."

THERAPIST: You could say that. You could also say: "Steven, I'm not clear about all of the 'whys.' I wish I could tell them to you, but I don't know them. Nevertheless, I *am* clear about what I need to do for myself."

[I am avoiding invalidating her suggestion, even though I knew that her statement wouldn't work well. Instead of commenting on the content of her suggestion at all, I simply accept it, and suggest something to add on to it.]

CLIENT: That will work. That works for me. As simple as that line is, I would not have come up with it. *(laughing loudly)* I would not have come up with it.

[She's saying: *"I really needed this explicit, step-by-step rehearsal. I didn't know it was OK to just tell somebody 'No' without being sure of all the reasons why."*]

THERAPIST: Therapy is partly educational. And by the way, this line about what works and what doesn't is a wonderful catchall line. It works in a lot of different situations because it allows you to draw a respectful boundary.

CLIENT: I don't need to spend four months thinking about "Why?" I can just say, "I really don't know why, and you need to respect that." *(She sounds amazed.)*

[Her question is not a question so much as a restating of what she's hearing. The concept of not having to obsess about a communication or interaction for months appears to be a novel, and welcome, idea.]

THERAPIST: No. He *doesn't* need to respect that, but you can *ask* him to respect that. Beth, you can't tell other people what to do or how to feel. You *can* say what you *hope* for. For example, "Steven, I hope you'll respect that, I hope you'll understand. It's probable that sometime in the future, I'll be comfortable talking with you again, but this isn't that time."

[More psycho-educational focus. I dropped the ball slightly here. It would have been better if I'd commented on her former statement about not needing to obsess, to actually allow the possibility of spontaneous, safer interactions. However, I hadn't asked myself a question about this, so naturally it did not "occur" to me to say anything. It would also have been better if I had not started out by saying "No" here. She might have experienced it as invalidating, and retreated. Luckily, she didn't. So she was able to absorb my teaching point.]

CLIENT: I know his next question: "When will that be, seven days, ten days, two months, or three months, and can I put that date on my calendar?"

THERAPIST: And you're going to laugh and say: "There you go Steven, thinking just like an engineer. I can't give you a hard answer, I can only give you a soft answer, which is 'When it's right.' And, if you want to check in with me in six months or a year, that's fine. I wouldn't do it before then, because I don't think I'll be ready to give you an answer."

[I have asked myself: *"Does she really need to hear some actual wording of how to respond?"* As my answer was *"Yes,"* I did so. Also, I'm continuing to monitor the time left in the session; I want to be certain we can achieve closure with this issue.]

CLIENT: Yeah. That works.

THERAPIST: And what about it works?

[I'm interested in what she's specifically absorbing and learning. Also, by having her describe what she's learning, she makes the various points more conscious and reinforces them for herself. Further, I'm checking my own work to see if she has really gotten what I intended. Finally, I will need this information anyway in our continuing work.]

CLIENT: What about it works? Getting and confirming that I need to be true to me, and I also need to get in touch with him. And I need to speak to him as the friend that he has been for five or six years. I need to share what my gut is saying, and I don't have to give any more explanation.

[Notice she repeats my exact question as a prompt to herself, probably as a way to generate starting the answer. This is a common thing for people to do, in and out of therapy.]

THERAPIST: Right. And, that you will feel more solid as a person for not having run away from this. *(She nodded.)*

[This is a reinforcement and a setup. I am future-pacing, and making a subliminal suggestion about her increasing self-esteem by using the word "solid." She has not run away, which is what she had been doing by withdrawing from contact with people from her old corporate life. The previous statement was an answer to this internal question: *"How can I demonstrate how well she did in this session, and let her know that it would have positive ripple effects in the future?"* Also, *"What evidence of self-efficacy would she accept that is behavioral and unequivocal?"* She cannot deny that she faced up to this in today's session, rather than withdrawing or running away.]

THERAPIST: So, let's test something out here. When we began talking about this potential interaction with Steven—on a scale from 1 to 10—what would have been your level of anxiety about it?

[I often test my work, and often share with my client that that's what I am doing. This habit is long ingrained from NLP training. I want Beth to have an explicit representation of what she's accomplished, and underscore for her that she can move from severe to mild anxiety on purpose, and do it skillfully, calmly, and in a relatively short amount of time. Naturally, I wouldn't have done this particular check if I didn't think it would give helpful and reinforcing feedback. Also, this kind of scale will mark the experience in her memory more than if she had just said something like, "I feel much less anxious about this situation now." Further, this technique gives me explicit, useful information.]

CLIENT: Nine point five.

THERAPIST: Nine point five was your starting level of anxiety. Wow! *(laughing)* Okay, and now what is your level of anxiety?

CLIENT: Point five.

THERAPIST: Really? Point five, not plain five? *(She nodded emphatically.)* Good work, Beth. You really did great. *(She grinned.)*

[I'm a little surprised that she rates her initial anxiety that high and her ending anxiety level so low. However, I asked myself if there were any point mentioning it and the answer was negative, so I didn't. I simply give her the credit she deserves for her accomplishment.]

Epilogue

Beth reported that the feared conversation with Steven went smoothly and easily. She was surprised to find that his favorite aunt was a nurse, and he had respected and appreciated her his whole life. She was also impressed to hear him say that while a parent might be proud if her child were an engineer or a lawyer, Steven thought it was more important to answer the question "Is she happy with what she does?" Beth said they talked and laughed like the old friends they are, and she even felt comfortable with the possibility of getting together for coffee after a few months. We later discussed the remaining colleagues she had been avoiding, and she also handled these situations quite competently.

SUMMARY

In the mid-phase of therapy, the question-centered clinician works on resolving the presenting problem(s) and building the client's abilities as a skillful Learner. Using psycho-education as a foundation, the therapist teaches the client how to self-question effectively in order to interrupt maladaptive thinking and behavior patterns, and to gain choice over his or her conduct along with a positive sense of control with regard to the future. The case of Beth focused on demonstrating how question-centered methods empower clients to access their own wisdom in making positive choices.

8

The Learner Self and
the Judger Self

Q: *What one word should I carry with me for the rest of my life?*
— PETER B. BLOOM

A: *Observation!*

— MILTON H. ERICKSON

Chapter 7 referred to the mid-phase of therapy as the guts of the therapeutic process, and so it is. This chapter, and the next, further explore the mid-phase with particular emphasis on the model of the Learner Self and the Judger Self. This chapter focuses on how this model is used as the backdrop for both assessment and treatment in question-centered therapy. The model is most fully expressed by the Learner/Judger Chart, which is presented in chapter 9 along with clinical anecdotes that illustrate its clinical utility.

Section 1 of this chapter elaborates on descriptions of the Learner Self and the Judger Self in previous chapters. Section 2 deals with how the therapist uses these concepts as the undergirding of her question-centered therapeutic work. Section 3 explores how the construct of the Learner Self and the Judger Self is used for assessment and treatment. Section 4 covers how the Learner/Judger Chart is introduced to clients as a psycho-educational tool to strengthen their success in therapy.

SECTION ONE:
THE LEARNER SELF AND JUDGER SELF

In this section we explore the origins of the model of the Learner Self and the Judger Self, including my own questions about therapy and change which led to developing it. Following this, we elaborate on this construct of these two "selves" that are part of each of us. We include a discussion of the relationships typical of the Learner Self and the Judger Self.

Origins of the Model

My ideas about the Learner Self and the Judger Self grew during many years of doing therapy with a population of clients who were obsessed about eating, body weight, and appearance. My questions about this population evolved into my dissertation, a phenomenological study entitled: *Out of Control: The Subjective Experience Associated with Binge Eating Among Obese Females* (Goldberg, dissertation, 1986).

What I learned from this research provided the foundation for a psycho-educational therapy model that could be used with individuals, couples, families, and groups. It also turned out that this approach had broader applications and was not limited to the population that had originally sparked my questions about the experience of being out of control. That research revealed common cognitive and emotional patterns that were grounded in my subjects' unconscious and limiting beliefs about time, life, reality, choice, change, and self-efficacy, as well as the experience of living in and relating to their bodies. Their unconscious conclusions about these complex topics were encoded and summarized under the painfully experienced self-attribution, *out of control*.

Regardless of the historical origins of my subjects' problems, they shared an experience of being overwhelmed and victimized by their own emotions, which they felt *forced* them into behavior they hated and also feared. In other words, my subjects' experience of not having any control was equivalent to their perception of not having any choices, other than to feel and behave as they did. Interestingly, their belief in their own inadequacy, failure, and out-of-control nature had calcified to the point that it was as rigid as their standards for being *in* control. In addition to the commonalities in their beliefs about being out of control and lacking personal choice, they also exhibited similarities in their all-or-nothing thinking and their experience of time. These observations led to my asking the following questions:

- *What beliefs about reality, change, time, and choice kept my subjects and clients imprisoned in their experience of being out of control?*
- *What cognitive and emotional characteristics and patterns kept them from making the changes they wanted?*
- *Of what would a functional model of self-control, self-management, and personal choice be comprised? What beliefs, attitudes, and skills would it embody?*

The answers and speculations stimulated by these questions led to my early thinking about the model of the Learner Self and the Judger Self. Then I wondered whether each of these positions might show up differently in language, given the powerful role that language plays in shaping experiences of reality and possibility. Therefore, I further asked myself:

- *Are there distinguishing <u>linguistic</u> keys to the Learner Self and the Judger Self?*
- *(If yes) Would the habitual use of "Learner language" extend to an individual the perceptions, attitudes, skills, and possibilities of a Learner Self?*

The answer turned out to be "Yes." The language properties and patterns of the two stances had many distinguishing characteristics, and this was especially evident in the kinds of questions each asked themselves and others. Furthermore, we discovered that certain kinds of internal questions, asked from the being of the Learner Self, could function as a reliable bridge to help clients move out of the Judger's constraining perceptual world and its paradigm of inherent limitation. Using questions encoded with Learner presuppositions, clients could cross over to the brighter world of the Learner Self with its invitation and promise of more spacious possibilities. In other words, the right question, asked in the right way, at the right time, and to the right person (especially to themselves), seemed to offer clients the potential of a transformation in experiences, behavior, and possibilities.

The Model of the Learner Self and the Judger Self

The model represents my attempt to synthesize and represent a broad spectrum of psychological wisdom in a way that could be instructive and helpful to clients. The concepts of the Learner Self and the Judger Self constitute a construct, or a way to cluster related attitudes, thoughts, and behaviors, in order to help clients understand themselves and others better and be more effective and successful in general. My goal was to develop everyday descriptions of the various points that would make intuitive sense to clients and that they wouldn't find off-putting, or label as psychological jargon. This was apparently successful, as clients describe the material as "user-friendly" and find it helpful, practical, and easy to use.

The terms *Learner Self* and *Judger Self* are capitalized in order to help clients think about themselves and others objectively, without becoming overly identified with these aspects of themselves. The word *Self* after Judger and Learner is important because it reminds clients that everybody has these two parts, or *Selves*. It is vital that clients recognize that these terms subsume all of the possibilities exhibited by human beings. In practice, these terms are often abbreviated to Learner and Judger. In therapy, even when a client says: "I was being a Judger in that situation," or when therapists inquire, "What attitude would you need in order to act like a Learner with your boss?" we recognize these as abbreviations of the longer terms.

In general, Judger Self attitudes, characteristics, cognitions, and behaviors may be associated with earlier developmental stages through which we all must pass. For example, we learn to think concretely before advancing to abstract reasoning. A client may be able to think about his problems only in concrete terms because they are so emotionally laden. He may, therefore, need to activate or advance his abstracting abilities to get past feeling "stuck" with his problems and discover new options in resolving them.

Of course, all of us are intrinsically Learners. Otherwise, none of us would have even learned to walk or talk. Practically everything we've acquired or developed has been the result of learning of some sort or another. Thus, being a Learner is natural; it is the foundation for growth, a resource every client brings to therapy, to some degree or another. It is with the Learner part of our clients that we make the therapeutic alliances that ultimately lead to therapeutic success.

Question-centered therapy presumes that presenting problems are most associated with clients' Judger Selves, and that solutions will develop from their Learner Selves. In therapy this means developing the skills to strengthen one's Learner Self and subdue one's Judger Self, an accomplishment that becomes the metagoal of question-centered therapy. The Learner Self part of our clients can be potentiated by helping them develop the skills to learn intentionally, which is sometimes called "learning how to learn." This is one of the distinctions I make when referring to a *skillful* Learner Self. The skillful Learner Self also possess some of the skills of metachange, that is, the ability to *generate* personal changes in order to meet future challenges.

The Judger Self

According to the Judger Self, there is an objective reality and it knows what it is. As a consequence, uncertainty, ambiguity, or even the beginning of a learning curve may cause anxiety of its own unintentional construction. Another person's disagreement or disapproval may bring the same unfortunate result, since the Judger-dominated individual assumes that he should be able to successfully control his emotions and behaviors. Any evidence to the contrary may provoke him to make harsh global pronouncements of himself, another person, or even a situation as either bad, wrong, unacceptable, or out-of-control.

The Judger Self orients itself to the world according to the belief that an individual should be able to achieve his version of what is right, good, correct, and acceptable in any particular arena of life, and at all times. With these rigid and impossible standards, the Judger Self places itself in a position of constantly seeking to confirm that it is right about its judgments. Any doubt about these standards or opinions might be experienced as dangerous by threatening to undermine or challenge the entire cognitive system upon which they are based. It is these characteristics which earn the Judger Self the nickname, knows-it-already mindset.

Whichever way the Judger Self's judgmental spotlight is aimed, anything it illuminates will be tainted by the same paradigmatic assumptions prescribed by these black/white, good/bad, right/wrong, acceptable/unacceptable conclusions. Moreover, since the Judger Self also presupposes that the future can represent only variations of the past, such conclusions are assumed to be permanent. The emotion of fear—acknowledged or not—is part and parcel of the Judger Self's experience of life. This emotion prevails whether it results from developmental difficulties, trauma, a lack in the sense of basic security, or simply from the erosion of self-acceptance that comes with constant self-judgment. Within such a closed, self-referring system, neither compassion nor paradigmatic change may prevail.

By example, my research subjects were convinced of the validity of their negative self-assessments. According to their rigid standards, they had totally failed, a fact over which they felt no control—that is, no choice. A mistake, such as absolutely failing to control their eating or even the size and appearance of their bodies, earned them a permanent self-imposed characterization, a label of being "a failure." Since they unconsciously assumed the future would only repeat the past, the labels "failure" and "out-of-control" became unintentionally permanent, saturating their sense of self and functioning as both condemnation and prediction.

These individuals operated predominantly out of self-questions with negative presuppositions, such as, "*What's wrong with me?*" and "*Why am I such a failure?*" Their despair and pessimism were understandable responses to the negative and limiting questions which focused their attention in these dismal directions. In part, through such linguistic habits, they unwittingly sealed themselves in a prison that could admit no possibility outside of the paradigm it recognized. If we assume that ". . . the self includes everything that passes in consciousness, (and) it follows that what we pay attention to over time will shape that self" (Csikszentmihalyi 1993, p. 217), then Judger Self questions automatically contaminate future attempts at change by functioning as self-fulfilling prophecies.

Focus of the Judger Self   The Judger Self plays out its role as judge and jury in different ways, depending on where it focuses. It may turn judgment inward, as my research subjects did, and judge *themselves* as unacceptable and unworthy failures. This may include an assumption that everyone else is "right" and only they are "wrong." We have all had clients who *insisted* that their negative self-opinions were accurate and deserved; they were defending being "right about being wrong," not recognizing the logical inconsistency of tenaciously defending what they came to therapy to change. Certainly, many of us have experienced the futility of attempting to "convince" them of anything else.

Alternatively, or simultaneously, the Judger Self may direct its judgment *externally*, as a harsh and unaccepting critic of others. Behaviors that result from this include blaming others for one's own woes, not taking responsibility for oneself, reacting defensively to feedback (however well it might be delivered or deserved), and sanctimonious justification for whatever one does. By so doing, the Judger

Self unwittingly fulfills this admonition from the New Testament: "Judge not, that you be not judged. For with the judgment you pronounce you will be judged, and the measure you give will be the measure you get" (Luke 6:37).

Transforming the Judger   Yet, making one single change could free the Judger-dominated individual, along with the others with whom he interacts, from the tyranny of his inherently limiting conclusions. He could question his own beliefs and assumptions by asking, for example: *"What's my belief here?" "How do I know it's 100 percent true?" "Are there any exceptions?" "Is there anyone who might see things another way?" "What might that be, and how come?"* and *"Is there something about myself, this situation, or that person that I don't know enough about yet?"*

However, with the Judger's mind and heart clamped shut to the perceptions and responses such inquiries might bring, the worlds accessible only on the other side of such questions remain invisible and unavailable. The openness and possibility inherent in that single self-questioning propensity would let the Judger glimpse and even step into the world of the Learner Self. Lacking the habit of that cognitive strategy, the Judger Self continually condemns itself to remaining in a frozen, limited reality, at least in relation to the problems which motivated the individual to seek therapy.

The Learner Self

A question-centered therapist considers the model of the Learner Self as a "portrait" of an actualized human being. The Learner Self is secure and fully self-accepting. Since it need not focus internally to find out if it's OK, it can afford to direct its attention externally to learn, connect, produce, and create. The Learner Self recognizes that it makes choices constantly, and this gives it a great deal of personal power. In taking responsibility for itself and its choices, the Learner Self garners the strength and possibilities that only this mindset can extend. It responds, rather than merely reacts, to whatever life throws its way. The Learner Self has a personal rebound strategy, which is aided by its beginner's questing mindset. The habitual use of effective self-questions such as: *"What's useful or valuable here?" "What can I learn?"* and *"What is the next best specific step?"* is what makes it so buoyant. The Learner Self resembles those toy punching bags that are weighted down to the floor. Regardless of how hard or often they are hit, they keep bouncing back.

The Learner Self and Self-Observation   The Learner Self's cognitive mode of self-observation is the pivot that liberates it from the Judger's paradigmatic prison. Without judgment or defensiveness, the Learner can observe and comment upon its own thinking, feelings, behaving, relating, and circumstances. Free to simply observe and correct, it habitually switches its thinking to the track most likely to lead to effectiveness and acceptance of self, others, and circumstances of life. The cognitive sorting strategy of the Learner is for what's right or valid, what it could learn, what could be useful, and what might be the most effective next actions.

As we've already pointed out, the Learner Self takes a researcher's stance toward life, generally keeping it in a mental and emotional state of openness and flexibility. The skillful Learner knows it is responsible for its own emotional state, is able to choose or create this experience to some degree, and proactively takes advantage of these insights. It takes a stance towards its life somewhat akin to that which a meditator takes towards his mantra. When something enters its field of consciousness that could distract or pull it off course, the Learner simply observes and corrects its focus back to the goal and the course of action consistent with this purpose.

In this way, the Learner Self *lives* its commitment to observing, learning, correcting, and creating. Recognizing that total control is an illusion, its concept of self-control is realistic, flexible, and self-accepting. Because it appreciates that life is in constant flux, it also knows that risk and loss are inevitable. While the Learner may easily be as attached as its Judger Self counterpart to the people, situations, totems, and material objects in his life, it doesn't make the error of believing it *is* any of these. Nor does the Learner make the mistake of believing there are guarantees of permanence or total predictability in life. Moreover, since constant change is the natural state, the Learner Self assumes that intentional change is possible.

The Relationships of the Learner Self and the Judger Self

Both Judger Self and Learner Self tend to relate to others consistent with the paradigms in which they typically operate. The Judger Self, assuming its assessments about others to be accurate as well as permanent, concludes that all others are also Judger Self–dominant. This places a severe limit on the possibility of making positive changes in relationships, especially intimate relationships, since this all-or-nothing thinking excludes the possibility of acceptance, negotiation, or mutually satisfying, win-win solutions. Thus, win-lose relationships are typical of the Judger Self, a natural consequence of being mired in a paradigm in which the only perceived interpersonal choices, under duress, are either to attack or to defend.

When individuals focus their Judger attention *internally* in the context of intimate relationship, they may feel inferior, unworthy, or even unlovable. As a consequence, they may behave subserviently and without appropriate assertiveness. They may also conclude that a mate's negative behavior toward them was justified or deserved. One such client told me that she felt "like a walking apology" no matter what her husband was upset or angry about. On the other hand, when individuals direct their Judger focus *externally* in the same relationship context, they may feel superior and self-righteous. As a consequence, their behavior may be demeaning, arrogant, or verbally or physically abusive. In the marital context, *either* an internal or external judgmental focus functions to keep spouses' feeling separate from, rather than connected to, their mates.

The Learner Self, on the other hand, assumes that others are flexible and open to change, responsibility for themselves, and have a goal of win-win relating. Thus, the possibilities of change, growth, and satisfying win-win relationships are kept fresh and alive. In chapters 12 through 15 we explore in further detail the implications of the model of the Learner Self and the Judger Self in working with couples in therapy.

SECTION TWO: USING THE
LEARNER/JUDGER CHART IN THERAPY

The model of the Learner Self and the Judger Self is usually taught during the mid-phase of therapy, usually within a few sessions of the Choice Model. It is presented to clients in the form of the Learner/Judger Chart, the extensive psycho-educational handout that functions as a kind of worksheet in sessions, and as a take-home for reference and study. The therapist uses the six categories and their contents as a backdrop for her observations, assessments, interventions, and recommendations. Once introduced as a formal part of treatment, the Learner/Judger Chart becomes a point of departure for further therapeutic interventions, as well as for conversations about possibilities of further learning, development, and growth. Thus, the Learner/Judger Chart serves as the foundation for an empowerment model of therapy, as well as an explicit means for therapist and client to assess progress in creating satisfying solutions to presenting problems.

In this section we first explore goals of using the chart in therapy, with emphasis on developing the observing self of the client. Then we explore the relationship of the Choice Model and the Learner/Judger Chart, how these reinforce each other, and how they are used in therapy. Finally, we explore the first part of the handout, the Introduction to the Chart, which helps clients make optimum use of the material.

Goals of Using the
Learner/Judger Chart in Therapy

The Learner/Judger Chart is designed to help people think about themselves and others in ways that enhance their ability to make the changes they want. The two mindsets of the Judger Self and the Learner Self represent the extremes of a continuum of the characteristics, attitudes, and behaviors that generally either limit or promote success in therapy as well as in life. The Learner/Judger Chart helps clients think about themselves and others as researchers and investigative reporters; that is, in ways that are nonjudgmental and seek to learn.

The educational nature of the chart supports and reinforces clients' ability to develop their observing selves. The goal is to strengthen the Learner Self and calm

the Judger Self. Few people have opportunities in life to review and assess themselves in such a comprehensive and objective manner. Furthermore, some items
on the chart probably refer to characteristics, attitudes, behaviors, and skills which
the individual hadn't previously distinguished or considered important. The very
act of establishing items as worthy of consideration and self-reflection creates new
distinctions and opens further possibilities for self-observation and change, thereby
creating openings where the skill of observe-and-correct can be usefully employed.

The Observing Self and Therapy   The prime purpose of the Learner/Judger
Chart is to activate and/or reinforce the observer self, with the expectation that
this is the pivot upon which maximum therapeutic success depends. This is tantamount to the cognitive accomplishment of being able to think about one's self
and one's thinking in an objective, accepting, and open-minded way. In fact, the
chart itself could be thought of as a way of formalizing, or elaborately operationalizing, how the observing self plays out in everyday life.

Deikman noted that: "Observing the processes of the mind is the basic technique of almost all psychotherapies . . . and that cognitive techniques of therapy,
in particular, can be understood as strengthening the observing self, extracting it
from the processes in which it tends to be submerged" (1982, pp. 97 and 98).
This same ability of self-observation is also called self-awareness by Goleman who
told us: "Self-awareness is not an attention that gets carried away by emotions,
overreacting and amplifying what is perceived. Rather, it is a neutral mode that
maintains self-reflectiveness even amidst turbulent emotions. . . . This awareness
of emotions is the fundamental emotional competence on which others, such as
emotional self control, build" (1995, p. 47). This nonreactive, nonjudgmental
attention to inner states is also primary in question-centered therapy; it is *the*
foundation upon which the Learner Self stands, and from which it operates with
itself, others, and life in general.

From the perspective of the Learner Self, the chart's presentation of the criteria and characteristics of the two paradigmatic orientations operates somewhat
like a checklist. When operating "from" their Learner Selves, clients naturally
ask themselves questions such as: *"Does this describe me?" "How is this like me?"*
and *"How is this not like me?"* It is particularly potent for clients to ask these questions about themselves with reference to Judger Self characteristics on the chart.
This automatically implies a shift into being less defensive, more honest with
themselves, and more open to change. In other words, by taking a Learner Self
stance toward their own Judger Self propensities, clients gain the opportunity to
consider whether any particular characteristic seems familiar, has been harmful
or useful in the past, and whether it is still desired. In this way, the chart functions
as a detailed, ongoing, nonjudgmental report card and action plan, substituting
subjects like math and science with personal attitudes, thinking patterns, and
ways of behaving and relating.

Furthermore, although clients "enter" the chart in the section most related
to their presenting problems, they soon observe that these issues are reflected to
some degree in virtually every section. Thus, they receive an implicit education

about themselves across all the contexts of their lives. Finally, with these educational purposes established, the chart is also meant to function as a prescription for the goals and tasks of therapy, as a means of assessing whether therapeutic success has been fulfilled, and as a blueprint for growth.

The Learner/Judger Chart and the Choice Model

The Learner/Judger Chart and the Choice Model operate in tandem. The lengthy chart is actually an elaboration of the Choice Model, while the Choice Model is a visual summary of the Learner/Judger Chart. The advantage of presenting the Choice Model to clients first is that this gives them an introduction to the essential and pivotal concept of choice.

According to the Choice Model, everyone theoretically has the ability to choose, and is thereby positioned to take responsibility for his or her choices. The Learner Self, which operates at the top of the Choice Model (and the right side of the Learner/Judger Chart), responds to life and consistently uses effective self-questions to support attitudes that are solution-seeking, and that offer the best possibility of realistically based experiences of self-efficacy, personal accomplishment, and win-win relationships. However, the Judger Self reacts to life where attention is problem-focused and relationships are win-lose. It operates in the territory at the bottom of the illustration (and the left side of the Learner/Judger Chart) where choice exists but is not claimed or seized. Since the Judger Self is either unable or unwilling to acknowledge this ability to choose, it makes passive choices, not recognizing that it is at the helm and that its life is largely a result of such moment-to-moment choices. The consequence of this presumption is a habit of judging and/or blaming oneself, another person, or circumstances for his difficulties, as well as feeling justified in making these attributions. This results in the individual's becoming caught in reactive patterns of thinking, feeling, and relating that keep him relegated to the bottom half of the chart, where he often experiences himself as powerless. In fact, some clients have designated the domain of the Judger Self as "that blame-and-shame place" or "the blame-and-fear part" of the Choice Model.

Case Example   The Choice Model also serves as a visual metaphor of the more elaborate Learner/Judger Chart. For example, Alan, who owned a construction company, was discussing his problems with his parents. We were talking about his relationship with them while referring to the Relating section of the Learner/Judger Chart. The Choice Model was also on my desk; Alan pointed to the Judger Self domain at the bottom of the handout and commented: "That's where I used to be with my father all the time. Now our relationship is about 70 percent in Learner Self and only 30 percent in Judger Self. I wish I could say the same about my mom. She and I are still in Judger Self about 90 percent of the time." In other words, the Choice Model optimized his ability to understand, accept, and use the concepts from the Learner/Judger Chart.

The Introduction to the Learner/Judger Chart

The handout of the Learner/Judger Chart is divided into two main parts: an introduction to the chart and the six categories into which the chart is organized. The Introduction has two purposes. The first, of course, is to make the therapist's job easier, since he or she can assume that any relevant introductory comments about the material can be found on the handout itself. Clients also say they find it helpful to read over the Introduction to the chart from time to time.

The second purpose of the Introduction is somewhat subliminal. It is meant to help clients develop the meta position of an *observing self in relation to the chart itself*, in contrast to the contents of the chart. The Introduction tends to diminish defensiveness to the content that follows, a result also sought when a hypnotherapist comments, "There are a few things I'd like to go over with you before we get started today." Without the setup of the introductory comments, clients tend to approach the chart with understandable Judger Self fears, expressed through internal questions such as: *"What will I find out that's bad or unacceptable about me?" "Does my therapist think I'm a Judger?"* or even, *"Will I find out I'm really crazy?"* The material is much more helpful when clients read and study the chart through neutral, self-observing, Learner questions such as: *"What's here for me to learn?"* and *"How could I use this information?"* The Introduction to the chart facilitates this inquisitive, learning attitude.

These two sets of questions illustrate once again the importance of context, that where a person is "coming from" inevitably influences how he "brings himself" to any particular situation and "what" he will find there. Since the metagoal of question-centered therapy is to help clients develop and strengthen their Learner Selves, the Introduction to the Learner/Judger Chart is meant to "stack the deck," giving both therapists and clients more tools to contribute to the client's growing Learner Self attitudes and capabilities.

Case Example   Carla was a client in a group where the Learner/Judger Chart and the Choice Model were presented. Shortly thereafter, she tearfully described how she had "blown" a difficult interaction with her boyfriend. Launching into a litany of what was wrong with her, as well as what she had just done wrong, the tears flowed faster. Suddenly, she looked startled, stopped crying, and started to laugh. Intrigued by her sudden shift in affect, I asked what happened. She grinned, saying she had a sudden insight that made the whole drama make sense and seem silly at the same time. In explanation, she told us: "I realized what happened that made me start crying. I pictured myself like I was that person on the Choice Model. I was running down the Judger road, asking myself all those dumb Judger questions we talked about last week when you gave us that long chart. No wonder I got upset. I had a Judger Self attack, that's all."

We laughed with her, and then I asked: "In order for you to recognize a Judger Self attack, where did you have to be looking *from?*" She looked startled, and then answered shyly, "I was acting like a Learner Self. I had to be *watching* myself and my own feelings, instead of just reacting to them, and believing them like I used to do all the time." Carla had made her first successful foray into the perceptual and experiential world of the Learner. An awake, observing self was born.

SECTION THREE: THE LEARNER/JUDGER MODEL IN ASSESSMENT AND TREATMENT

In this section, we explore the Learner Self and the Judger Self in terms of assessment and diagnosis. Then, we examine some practical applications of including this thinking in treatment.

Assessment

The therapist's background thinking in the initial interview includes the model of the Learner Self and the Judger Self as part of her assessment process. Of course, she continues to consider customary diagnostic questions such as: *"What is his DSM diagnosis?"* and *"Are the antecedents of his depression more biological, cognitive, or interpersonal?"* Simultaneously, keeping the six categories of the Learner/Judger Chart in mind, the therapist asks herself questions such as: *"How rigid or flexible is his thinking, especially with regard to the presenting problem?"* *"Does he blame either himself or others for his troubles?"* *"Does he recognize and take responsibility for his own role in this situation?"* and *"What questions might he be asking himself about his problem?"*

As therapy progresses through its beginning stage, the therapist has many further opportunities to assess her client in light of the Learner/Judger material. As she focuses attention on the unfolding therapeutic relationship, she also deepens her understanding about how her client operates as a Judger Self in relation to his presenting problem. For example, the therapist may ask her client, "Have you thought about your boss's behavior from *his* point of view?" or "What other motives might he have had other than what we've discussed so far?" Here are three ways her client might reply: "He's just a stupid jerk, that's all there is to it" or "What are you doing, taking *his* side now?" or "That's interesting. I never thought about it that way before." The first two responses are typical of an individual whose perceptions are tainted by the Judger Self. The third response lets the therapist know her client already operates from some of the requisite open-minded, inquisitive attitudes of a Learner Self.

Treatment

Furthermore, each of these three hypothetical responses suggest distinctly different therapeutic paths, representing divergent answers to the therapist's self-questions about directions to pursue in therapy. In the first instance, she might ask herself, *"Can he tolerate any challenge to his thinking or his beliefs?"* followed by asking her client in a neutral tone, "Has there ever been a time when your boss didn't act like a jerk?" In the second example she might ask herself, *"What can I do to recover whatever trust we had?"* and then express her behavioral answer by saying gently to her client, "I'm sorry if that's the way it felt. It wasn't my intention. Sometimes people feel that way when someone suggests a different way of looking at things."

In the third instance, she could ask herself, *"What's the best way to take advantage of the opening my Learner-dominant client just gave me?"* and say to him, "It's great you're able to look at the situation from a new point of view. What do you know about your boss that could help us think about his concerns and motives?" Each of these three possible interventions takes place against the backdrop of the Learner/Judger Chart. Each intervention also represents an answer to the therapist's internal questions about assessment and treatment with that particular client.

Potential therapeutic interventions are expanded after the therapist introduces the Learner/Judger Chart in treatment. Once the client is familiar with its contents, the therapist can ask questions such as: "In that supervisory interview with your boss, were you acting more from your Learner Self or a Judger Self?" or "What could you have done to respond to him as a Learner instead of reacting to him like a Judger?" or "How do you think he would have responded if you had put on your Learner mindset when you talked to him?"

In other words, by using the chart as an intermediary, the therapist reinforces her client's ability to self-observe, make personal corrections, and think about others without undue references to himself. This also allows him to consider different points of view and new possibilities in a particular situation. Furthermore, the more the therapist explicitly uses the chart as a reference in therapy, the more consistently the client comes to use it as a reference and guide outside of therapy, thus helping him further integrate its distinctions and possibilities into everyday life.

SECTION FOUR: INTRODUCING THE LEARNER/JUDGER CHART

In this last section, we discuss the presentation of the Learner/Judger Chart to clients. We also explore how the chart may contribute to the therapeutic relationship. The section ends with sample comments that a therapist could make in introducing the chart.

Presenting the Learner/Judger Chart

The fact that the Learner/Judger Chart obviously existed prior to the client's beginning in therapy helps him recognize that it represents a model, rather than a description of him personally. This helps clients, both in individual and couples therapy, to approach the material impersonally enough to minimize defensive reactions. The attitude the therapist models toward the chart is somewhat like: "*OK, let's study this together, and see where you fit with this. It's useful to locate some attributes which you experience as part of your presenting problem. This is fascinating information, and can make a big difference for you, as it has for many others.*"

The therapist's nonjudgmental, inquisitive attitude is an essential element promoting the likelihood of clients taking the same stance towards the material on the chart, and by implication, toward themselves. Her attitude toward the Judger Self is particularly important, since the Judger encompasses the characteristics that are sometimes considered the dark, or shadow side of the human psyche. The therapist's neutral, objective, and accepting attitude also belies the negative, rejecting judgments that clients may fear from her.

The Therapeutic Relationship

Additionally, the therapists' accepting attitude toward the various items covered by the chart may serve as a beginning point of conversation about the therapeutic relationship, as well as about transference issues. The question-centered therapist may also selectively share personal examples of both Judger and Learner characteristics and behaviors. For example, sometimes I share with clients a personal experience that was both humbling and eye-opening. It occurred the time I realized I was being judgmental about someone *else* being judgmental!

This kind of sharing helps define the therapist as a human being who continues her own journey of intentional growth. This allows her to function as an *attainable* model for clients, rather than an impossible and therefore defeating one. The therapist may also share examples of successful personal transformations, of having left a Judger mindset in favor of a Learner one in relation to a particular issue. This helps normalize the material, placing the items on the chart in a human context rather than a pathological one. Ironically, an experience that occurred while I was writing this chapter provided a personal story that illustrates the usefulness of asking Learner Self questions. Here's what happened:

Anecdote   Bob was a very good, longtime friend who died suddenly and unexpectedly. After a lengthy time of grieving, I began to suspect that in addition to feeling sad, something else was going on with me. When I asked myself what assumptions I was making, a belief emerged that I would be damaged by my friend's death. After examining this, I realized there was no foundation for this thought, and anyway, such a belief could not lead to anything positive for myself, or anyone else. In fact, I could feel my mood plummet every time I allowed my thoughts to wander down the path prescribed by the question, "*How will I be hurt by Bob's death?*"

In true Judger Self fashion, my self-questions reflected, "*What's wrong?*" and "*How could I lose?*" rather than, "*What's right?*" and "*How could I win?*" Recognizing the importance of actively contradicting this Judger Self thinking, I decided to develop a question encoded with the opposite Learner presuppositions, even though I didn't believe them. To my surprise, the contrived question, "*What positive things might happen as a result of Bob's death?*" brought unexpected insights and ideas, as well as a welcome elevation of mood. Only after going through this intentional exercise, did I realize that I would *continue* receiving gifts from my relationship with Bob, even after his death. In this instance, he gave me a poignant and somewhat provocative anecdote to share with certain clients, as well as to use in this book. He would have loved it.

Introducing the
Learner/Judger Chart

Here are some sample comments a therapist may use, or paraphrase, in introducing the Learner/Judger Chart to clients:

> You've graduated. You're ready for the next step, and we're going to use another handout for it. It's called the Learner/Judger Chart. You're already familiar with the Learner Self and Judger Self from the Choice Model. (*Therapists may initiate a brief conversation here, perhaps recapping the Choice Model.*)
>
> This chart is like a curriculum of the school of life. You can think of it as a summary of the things that could help resolve the problems you came to therapy to handle. It can also help with growing beyond your present difficulties. It will help you identify and understand the progress you've made so far, and also show you where you might still be stuck and have things you want to learn and accomplish. The chart will help you understand other people in new ways, as well as how to have better relationships with them. This chart will also give you a basis for thinking about what's next and setting new goals later, if that's something you want to do.
>
> I know this handout has a lot of pages and it might feel intimidating at first. Other clients have felt that way, but they soon find it easy to use. Not to worry. This isn't something you're expected to learn or memorize overnight. In fact, I hope you'll use it for the rest of your life. This is your copy to keep. You can take it home and read it over as many times as you want. Some of the information will make sense right away, some of it may not. You may also find things you disagree with. That's fine. We'll work together with this material in session. Today I'll show you how the whole thing is set up and then we'll go over a few items that most obviously relate to the problems you came to therapy to solve. It's also OK if you want to show it to somebody else, but I suggest you wait until you have a chance to get familiar with it.
>
> Please remember that the Learner Self and Judger Self are not actual people and nobody is all one way or the other. These labels simply represent different ends of a continuum of human nature and human behavior. More or less, everybody in the world fits here. That's you. It's also me and everybody we know. Not only that, we all move across the continuum, from side to side, depending on circumstances, or fears and desires, as well as our attitudes and

skills. OK. Let's get started with the Introduction to the Chart. It goes over some of what I just said. By the way, lots of clients have told me they found it helpful to read over the Introduction a few times and even go back to it later for a review.

SUMMARY

This chapter focused on the model of the Learner Self and Judger Self, which is the psycho-educational foundation and organizing metaphor of question-centered therapy. We began by discussing the origins of the model and elaborated on descriptions of the Learner Self and the Judger Self. The model is most fully expressed by the Learner/Judger Chart and we explored how it may be used for both assessment and treatment. The chapter concluded by presenting ways to introduce the Learner/Judger Chart to clients. In the next chapter the Learner/Judger Chart is presented, along with clinical examples in each of its six categories.

9

The Learner/Judger
Selves in Action

How shall I live the life that I am?
—ABRAHAM HESCHEL

A s we have seen, the model of the Learner Self and Judger Self is in the
background of every intervention made in question-centered therapy.
The purpose of this chapter is to present the chart itself and bring it to life
through case material. Therefore, the Learner/Judger Chart in its entirety comprises the first part of the chapter. The second part focuses on clinical material
illustrating each of the six categories of the chart: Orientation, Thinking, Feeling, Behaving, Relating, and Language/Communicating. Additionally, two of
these categories, Feeling and Language/Communicating, include theoretical
elaboration about the category itself.

In reading the case material, it becomes obvious that the six categories of the
chart are somewhat arbitrary, since each exists, more or less, with reference to
each of the others. Ultimately, of course, everything is connected to everything
else, and nothing can be grasped fully unless considered in light of its context.
Thus, it is important to remember that the whole person stands in the background whenever we discuss one of his or her characteristics, behaviors, and/or
ways of being and relating. This is apparent in the clinical examples that follow;
virtually any one could have been chosen to represent any of the dimensions of
the chart.

The Learner/Judger Chart begins with the introduction to the chart that was
discussed at the end of the last chapter and is followed by the six categories in the
order indicated. Each page of the chart is illustrated. Clients report that this helps
them feel more comfortable with the material, making it friendlier and easier to

understand and use. At the top of the first page of each category is a hat rack with Judger and Learner caps hanging on it. This is meant to reinforce the fact that a person chooses whether to "put on" a Judger mindset or a Learner mindset at any particular moment. Each of the six categories contains examples of both Judger and Learner questions, which are located under the picture of the bridge with the Judger and Learner caps hanging off their respective sides. This illustration suggests that an individual operating on the Judger Self side can cross the bridge to get to Learner Self territory by asking a question that represents that mindset.

Reading the Chapter   The customary way to read a chapter is from beginning to end. In this case, it might also be instructive to read by moving back and forth between the clinical examples and the chart itself. For example, one could read the category on the chart and then the illustrative case material or vice versa. The chart is presented separately from the text. Therapists are encouraged to copy the Learner/Judger Chart and give it to their clients. When working with couples, it is useful to give each partner his or her own copy.

SECTION ONE: ORIENTATION

Stuart, a client with obsessive-compulsive disorder (OCD), illustrates the usefulness of the Orientation section of the chart. A 39-year-old business consultant, Stuart often traveled, leaving his fiancée, Susan, an architect, at home. While he was away on one of his trips, his mother invited Susan to her home for dinner. Knowing this would pose a problem for Stuart, Susan called and asked for his instructions, which she followed explicitly. These included two important details: hanging up and retrieving her own coat so Stuart's mother wouldn't touch it; and not touching her future mother-in-law at all.

With the assistance of the Learner/Judger Chart, Stuart and I reviewed this incident with Susan and his mother. We focused on the issue of control as it appears in the Orientation section; this stimulated a conversation about his concept of self-control. Stuart recognized that his rigid, authoritarian concept of control resided on the Judger side of the chart, even though he wanted credit for being flexible enough to let Susan go to dinner with his mother in the first place! I agreed that he had made progress, and pointed out other examples of his developing observing self and his new ability to think strategically about managing his OCD symptoms.

However, since he had improved, more was being asked of him. I then shared a metaphor about self-control derived from my years of working with biofeedback, especially the electromyograph (EMG), which is used to monitor muscular tension. I drew a picture of the scale of the EMG which resembles that of a nondigital bathroom scale and showed him how I trained people to be in *real* control by learning to relax to a *specific medium range on the scale*. Many of those

THE LEARNER/JUDGER CHART

Introduction to the Chart

Welcome to the Learner/Judger Chart. Please read these introductory notes before going on to the chart itself. This makes the chart easier and more comfortable to use. Also, it may be helpful to reread this Introduction from time to time.

About the Chart

The Learner/Judger Chart is an elaborate description of being human. It is also a practical tool to help people make more effective choices — and to help them understand themselves and others better. This includes learning what's required for resolving problems and finding satisfying solutions.

The terms *Learner Self* and *Judger Self* represent different mindsets. They do not refer to actual people, but to *parts* of each of us — every human being has *both*. These terms are a helpful way to cluster characteristically related thoughts, behaviors, and ways of being and relating. The items on the Judger Self side of the chart are characteristic of a person with reference to a problem or concern. They do not describe the person as a whole, and it is unlikely that anyone would experience or express every aspect of either the Judger Self or the Learner Self. At any moment, we are each a blend of our Learner and Judger Selves, sometimes with the Learner Self predominating, and sometimes with the Judger Self predominating.

The chart consists of six categories. The first, Orientation, summarizes the other five. These are: Thinking, Feeling, Behaving, Relating, and Language and Communicating. Each category describes the Judger Self on the left side of the page, and the Learner Self on the right. At the end of each category is a list of questions typical of the Judger Self or the Learner Self in that particular category.

For maximum benefit, put on your Learner Self mindset as you read the chart.

Copyright © Marilee C. Goldberg, Ph.D. 1998

Figure 9.1

The Learner Self

Learner Self refers to that part of each of us that is open-minded, flexible, responsive, proactive, solution-seeking, and accepts ourselves and others. The Learner Self makes thoughtful choices, being aware that it can choose how to respond in almost any moment. This gives the Learner Self a sense of internal strength, personal control, and many choices. The Learner Self takes responsibility for itself and its actions. It also knows it can change intentionally, and that the future can be brighter than the present. Learner relationships are typically win-win.

The Learner Self has a "beginner's mindset," meaning it regards each fresh moment as an opportunity to find out what's new to discover, learn, and/or do — regardless of how much one already knows, believes, or has accomplished. The Learner Self typically asks questions such as: *"What's useful about this?" "What's right about myself, the other person, or the situation?" "What are my choices?" "What are my goals?" "What can I learn?"* and *"How can we both win?"*

The Judger Self

Judger Self refers to that part of each of us that is inflexible, problem-focused, reactive, and tends to be blame-seeking. The term Judger is used in the sense of judgmental or negatively biased. The Judger Self does not evaluate objectively. The Judger Self focuses judgment internally and/or externally.

When the Judger Self focuses judgment *internally,* it may be self-doubting and afraid of change, or not believe positive, purposeful change is possible (those attitudes and abilities belong with our Learner Selves). If the Judger Self focuses judgment *externally,* it often labels others negatively, is unaccepting of differences, and believes that control is necessary in dealing with other people. Judger relationships are typically win-lose.

The Judger Self has a "knows-it-already mindset," meaning that any new experience or information might be judged in terms of whether it reinforces, invalidates, or threatens what was already known, believed, or accomplished. The Judger Self typically asks questions such as: *"Who, or what, is to blame?" "How can I defend or protect myself?" "How can I avoid losing?"* and *"How can I win (even if someone else loses)?"*

Your most important choice in any moment is whether to "put on" your Learner Self mindset or your Judger Self mindset. When necessary, you can always ask the right questions to take you over the bridge to the Learner Self side of the chart.

Copyright © Marilee C. Goldberg, Ph.D. 1998

Figure 9.1   *(Continued)*

When and Why to Consult the Chart

- To find the right questions to help in a particular situation
- To find ways to satisfying solutions
- To reinforce and strengthen your Learner Self
- To become a more skillful self-observer
- To have more opportunities and choices
- To reinforce learning the information on the chart
- To stimulate creativity and accomplish goals
- To have more win-win relationships

Miscellaneous Information about the Chart

- The terms Learner Self and Judger Self are sometimes abbreviated to Learner and Judger.
- Items on the Judger side usually refer to the characteristics or effects of an internal judgmental focus. They sometimes also refer to the characteristics or effects of an external focus.
- Sometimes similar questions appear in different categories or on both sides of the chart. This is because the mindset *behind* a question determines its meaning, as well as the words.
- An item on one side of the chart may not have a counterpart on the other side. Also, items opposite each other are not always opposite in meaning.
- Most items are worded in an extreme black-and-white way. However, it is important and respectful to remember that people are really "shades of gray."
- Questions listed are only samples of that category. There are always more questions.
- Usually more questions are on the Learner's side since the Learner asks more questions.

Be careful not to judge the Judger Self — that would be acting as a Judger Self. Instead, the Learner accepts its Judger characteristics as normal expressions of its humanness. After all, every one of us has a Judger Self.

The more we accept and manage our Judger Selves, the stronger and more successful our Learner Selves can become.

Copyright © Marilee C. Goldberg, Ph.D. 1998

Figure 9.1   *(Continued)*

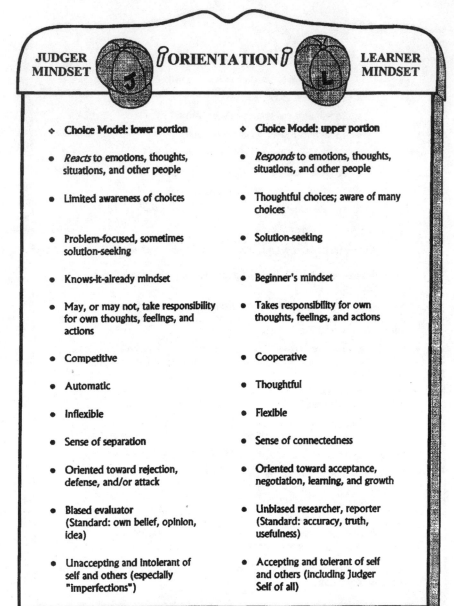

JUDGER MINDSET	LEARNER MINDSET
ORIENTATION	
◆ **Choice Model: lower portion**	◆ **Choice Model: upper portion**
● *Reacts* to emotions, thoughts, situations, and other people	● *Responds* to emotions, thoughts, situations, and other people
● Limited awareness of choices	● Thoughtful choices; aware of many choices
● Problem-focused, sometimes solution-seeking	● Solution-seeking
● Knows-it-already mindset	● Beginner's mindset
● May, or may not, take responsibility for own thoughts, feelings, and actions	● Takes responsibility for own thoughts, feelings, and actions
● Competitive	● Cooperative
● Automatic	● Thoughtful
● Inflexible	● Flexible
● Sense of separation	● Sense of connectedness
● Oriented toward rejection, defense, and/or attack	● Oriented toward acceptance, negotiation, learning, and growth
● Biased evaluator (Standard: own belief, opinion, idea)	● Unbiased researcher, reporter (Standard: accuracy, truth, usefulness)
● Unaccepting and intolerant of self and others (especially "imperfections")	● Accepting and tolerant of self and others (including Judger Self of all)

Copyright © Marilee C. Goldberg, Ph.D. 1998

Figure 9.1   *(Continued)*

- Sense of scarcity
- Rigid concept of control, worries about going out of control

- May consider change dangerous, and resist it (even when wanting it)

- May get upset or defensive if doesn't know something

- Often unable to conceive of future as potentially different from past or present. Possible difficulty conceiving of intentional change

- Major focus on past. May consider:
  (a) past negative experiences as exerting total or undue influence on present and future, or
  (b) past as better than present. May result in belief that present or future inevitably dissatisfying

- Objectifies self, body, time. A person is static, like a noun or a still photo

- Attributions about others and their behavior made in relation to self, and often negative

- Sense of sufficiency
- Adaptable concept of control, trusts self to recover if ever out of control

- Accepts change as constant, everything in flux, including self

- Accepts "not knowing," admits it, can embrace it

- Conceives of future as potentially distinct from present or past. Considers intentional change possible

- Major focus divided between present and future. Past to be remembered, resolved, learned from, appreciated, and left in past. Present to be experienced, appreciated, utilized. Future to be created

- Conceives of self, body, time as process. A person is like a noun *and* verb, a movie

- Able to assess and hypothesize about others and their behavior without undue reference to self

JUDGER ORIENTATION QUESTIONS LEARNER

- *What's wrong with this?*
- *Whose fault is it?*

- *What's right about this?*
- *What are my choices?*
- *What can I learn?*

Copyright © Marilee C. Goldberg, Ph.D. 1998

Figure 9.1   *(Continued)*

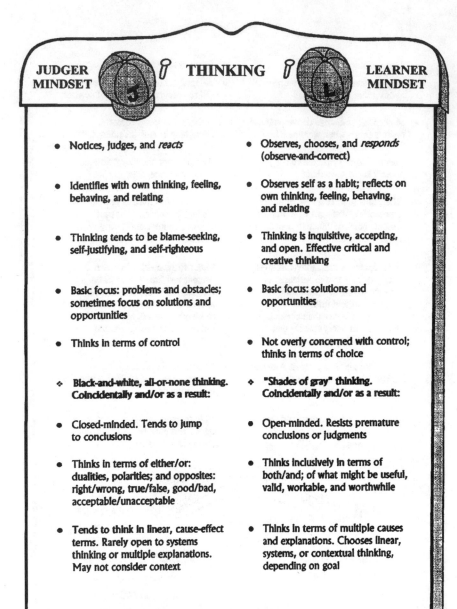

JUDGER MINDSET	THINKING	LEARNER MINDSET
• Notices, judges, and *reacts*		• Observes, chooses, and *responds* (observe-and-correct)
• Identifies with own thinking, feeling, behaving, and relating		• Observes self as a habit; reflects on own thinking, feeling, behaving, and relating
• Thinking tends to be blame-seeking, self-justifying, and self-righteous		• Thinking is inquisitive, accepting, and open. Effective critical and creative thinking
• Basic focus: problems and obstacles; sometimes focus on solutions and opportunities		• Basic focus: solutions and opportunities
• Thinks in terms of control		• Not overly concerned with control; thinks in terms of choice
❖ Black-and-white, all-or-none thinking. Coincidentally and/or as a result:		❖ "Shades of gray" thinking. Coincidentally and/or as a result:
• Closed-minded. Tends to jump to conclusions		• Open-minded. Resists premature conclusions or judgments
• Thinks in terms of either/or: dualities, polarities; and opposites: right/wrong, true/false, good/bad, acceptable/unacceptable		• Thinks inclusively in terms of both/and; of what might be useful, valid, workable, and worthwhile
• Tends to think in linear, cause-effect terms. Rarely open to systems thinking or multiple explanations. May not consider context		• Thinks in terms of multiple causes and explanations. Chooses linear, systems, or contextual thinking, depending on goal

Copyright © Marilee C. Goldberg, Ph.D. 1998

Figure 9.1 *(Continued)*

- Personal reality, opinion, interpretation—only one correct, so is always "right" (even about being wrong)

- Paradox, contradiction, ambiguity, and/or confusion not tolerable or acceptable

- Overlooks or collapses distinctions, leads to overgeneralizing, possible stereotyping

- Accepts own assumptions, often without noticing or questioning them

- Thinking may be concrete and literal in relation to symptom or problem

- Thinks negatively of any person or position with divergent positions

- Looks for other points of view; recognizes simultaneous possible realities, opinions, and interpretations

- Paradox, contradiction, ambiguity, and/or confusion tolerable and acceptable

- Habitual search for distinctions and new categories to think in. Actively seeks to understand, appreciate, and utilize differences and exceptions

- Habitually questions own assumptions

- Able to reflect on and think abstractly about own problems or symptoms

- OK to disagree; may be curious and inquire about other viewpoints

Copyright © Marilee C. Goldberg, Ph.D. 1998

Figure 9.1 *(Continued)*

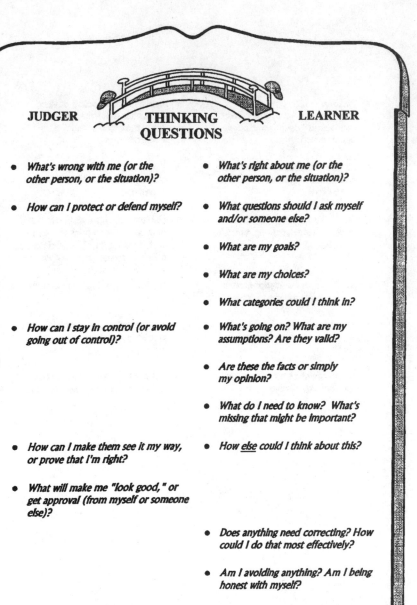

JUDGER

THINKING QUESTIONS

LEARNER

- What's wrong with me (or the other person, or the situation)?

- How can I protect or defend myself?

- How can I stay in control (or avoid going out of control)?

- How can I make them see it my way, or prove that I'm right?

- What will make me "look good," or get approval (from myself or someone else)?

- What's right about me (or the other person, or the situation)?

- What questions should I ask myself and/or someone else?

- What are my goals?

- What are my choices?

- What categories could I think in?

- What's going on? What are my assumptions? Are they valid?

- Are these the facts or simply my opinion?

- What do I need to know? What's missing that might be important?

- How else could I think about this?

- Does anything need correcting? How could I do that most effectively?

- Am I avoiding anything? Am I being honest with myself?

Copyright © Marilee C. Goldberg, Ph.D. 1998

Figure 9.1   (Continued)

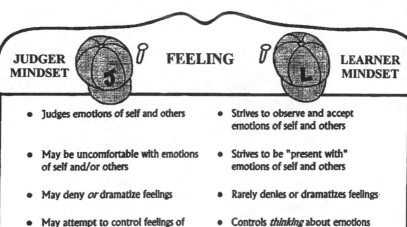

JUDGER MINDSET	FEELING	LEARNER MINDSET
• Judges emotions of self and others		• Strives to observe and accept emotions of self and others
• May be uncomfortable with emotions of self and/or others		• Strives to be "present with" emotions of self and others
• May deny *or* dramatize feelings		• Rarely denies or dramatizes feelings
• May attempt to control feelings of self and/or others		• Controls *thinking* about emotions (not the same as controlling emotions)
• Afraid of submitting to, or being overwhelmed by, emotions (as if they were tidal waves)		• Can choose to surrender, submit to emotion; thus, is self-possessed in face of emotions. (Considers emotions as ocean waves; they come and go—and any feelings that come will also go)
• May consider emotions unnatural, unhealthy, even as enemies. Or, may select some feelings as OK, reject others		• Considers emotions as natural, healthy, possibly helpful, as friends. Values and accepts feelings, even if uncomfortable with some of them
• May be dissociated from physical or kinesthetic experience. May not use body signals for information, feedback, or guidance regarding emotional life, decisions, and health		• Consistent awareness of physical and kinesthetic experience. Respects and listens to body for information, feedback, and guidance regarding emotional life, decisions, and health
• Time: Emotion may be experienced as "expanded present." Possible fears that "bad" feeling will never end		• Time: "Present" with emotion, so doesn't push away or try to hold on; knows emotions like waves—they come and go
• *Sexuality:* for enjoyment, own pleasure most important. May or may not consider sexuality natural and healthy		• *Sexuality:* for enjoyment, pleasure of both important. Considers sexuality natural and healthy

Copyright © Marilee C. Goldberg, Ph.D. 1998

Figure 9.1   *(Continued)*

JUDGER **FEELING QUESTIONS** **LEARNER**

- *How can I avoid, stop, or control this (negative) feeling? How could I get hurt by this feeling?*

- *What am I feeling? How can I accept what I'm feeling?*

- *Will I go out of control? How can I stay in control?*

- *How can I calm myself? What's one small thing I can do to help me feel better?*

- *Is this something I can handle myself? Could I use support or help?*

- *What will people think if they see me feeling this?*

- *Is this the time/place/person to be safe feeling like this? If not, what can I do to take care of myself?*

- *How can I make people change so I don't have to feel this?*

- *Is this feeling related to the current situation, or is it a throwback to some old situation, person, or feeling?*

- *What could I learn from this feeling about myself, someone else, or this situation?*

Copyright © Marilee C. Goldberg, Ph.D. 1998

Figure 9.1 *(Continued)*

JUDGER MINDSET **BEHAVING** **LEARNER MINDSET**

• Behavior attempts to prove self as right, good, acceptable, worthy	• Behavior attempts to meet a goal or provide a solution
• *Blames* self or others for own thoughts, feelings, behaviors, and circumstances. Rarely takes responsibility for any of these	• Takes *responsibility* for own thoughts, feelings, behaviors, and circumstances
• Purpose of behavior often to "look good" in opinion of self and others	• Purpose of behavior usually for accomplishing, enjoying, contributing, partnering
• Information examined and judged as right/wrong, good/bad, true/false, acceptable/unacceptable. May examine information for usefulness	• Information examined for usefulness, learning, curiosity; not only from moral perspective
• Behavior may attempt to control self in rigid, inflexible way; may react or compensate by going out of control	• Self-control expectations realistic; knows "total" control illusory
• Behavior may attempt to control others, especially partners and children	• Behavior attempts to make situations work in cooperative, win-win way

Copyright © Marilee C. Goldberg, Ph.D. 1998

Figure 9.1   *(Continued)*

JUDGER **BEHAVING QUESTIONS** **LEARNER**

- *How can I prove I'm right?*
- *What's the most appropriate and prudent way to do this?*

- *What do I need to do to "look good" in this situation?*
- *What's my responsibility here, and what's the best way to fulfill it?*

- *How can I make them do what I want?*
- *How can I contribute to getting this done?*

- *How can I get my way?*
- *What would be a win-win way to get this done or to resolve this?*

- *How can I get what I want NOW?*
- *What are the consequences?*

- *What do I need to be feeling in order to handle this situation or person effectively?*

- *How can I avoid dealing with this (feeling, person, situation) when I know I should?*
- *How can I handle this most expeditiously, even if I don't feel like it or want to?*

Copyright © Marilee C. Goldberg, Ph.D. 1998

Figure 9.1 *(Continued)*

JUDGER MINDSET   **RELATING**   **LEARNER MINDSET**

JUDGER MINDSET	LEARNER MINDSET
• Relationships: win-lose	• Relationships: win-win
• Competition	• Cooperation, partnership
• *Reacts* to other people	• *Responds* to other people
• *Reacts* to own thoughts, emotions, and situations	• *Responds* to own thoughts, emotions, and situations
• Unable or unwilling to shift perceptual positions	• Habitually shifts perceptual positions (walks a mile in other person's moccasins)
• Sense of separation	• Sense of connectedness
• Reacts to others based on distortions from past (near or remote)	• Responds to others based on current situation and relationship
• Attributions about others mostly in relation to self, and often negative	• Able to assess and hypothesize about others without undue reference to self
• Unwilling to admit being wrong, or to apologize	• Willing to be wrong and to apologize
• May be unaware of, or not take responsibility for, personal effect on others	• Mostly aware of own effect on others; takes responsibility for this
• Tends to be intolerant, critical, judgmental, nonforgiving; holds grudges	• Basically accepting, tolerant, compassionate, forgiving; able to let go, move on

Copyright © Marilee C. Goldberg, Ph.D. 1998

Figure 9.1   *(Continued)*

- May consider self either superior or inferior
- Overly dependent or overly independent
- Boundaries tend to be extreme, either rigid or "mushy"
- Feedback considered as attack or criticism, often assumed to represent anger and/or rejection; may be defensive
- May have difficulty thanking, acknowledging, or supporting others
- Difficulty *accepting* acknowledgment, gratitude, or thanks (may block or deny). Yet may be approval-seeking
- May feel diminished by, or competitive with, success of others
- Prefers similarity to self in other people; differences may be threatening
- May see people as stereotypes, and mostly in relation to self
- Thinks others are basically like self, making them Judgers (that is, judgmental, unchanging, inflexible, and so forth)
- *Delivery:* tone may be neutral, or accusing, demeaning, condemning

- Considers self and others equally valuable and worthwhile
- Interdependent
- Boundaries semipermeable and appropriate
- Feedback considered useful; solicits, welcomes, and considers it (even when not liking or not agreeing with it)
- Habit of thanking, acknowledging, supporting others when appropriate
- Accepts acknowledgment, thanks, gratitude, and support from others
- Enjoys and applauds success of others
- Differences interesting and appreciated
- Sees people for who they are
- Thinks of others as Learners, or potentially so (that is, people are flexible, can learn, grow, and change)
- *Delivery:* tone generally intended as neutral, inquiring, interested, accepting

Copyright © Marilee C. Goldberg, Ph.D. 1998

Figure 9.1   *(Continued)*

JUDGER   **RELATING QUESTIONS**   **LEARNER**

JUDGER	LEARNER
• *How can I win?*	• *How can we both win?*
• *What's wrong with him/her?*	• *What's right about him/her?*
• *In what ways is he/she less (or more) important, worthy, or significant than I am?*	• *In what ways are we alike? How could our differences be a contribution to each other?*
• *What's the best way to protect or defend myself?*	• *How can I help, serve, support, and empower him/her?*
• *How is his/her reaction connected with me?*	• *Should I take this personally?*
• *How can I get what I want (regardless of how it affects others)?*	• *How can I get what I want? What is he/she feeling, needing, or wanting right now?*
• *How is he/she like X who hurt me?*	• *How is he/she different from X?*
• *Who (or how) do I have to be to get people to like and accept me?*	• *How can I enjoy sharing myself appropriately and authentically?*
	• *Am I giving him/her the benefit of the doubt?*
	• *What's the kindest possible interpretation of him/her or this situation?*
	• *Are we in an attack-or-defend mode?*
	• *Is either of us on automatic right now?*
	• *Is there anything I should apologize for?*
	• *What am I grateful for in this relationship?*

Copyright © Marilee C. Goldberg, Ph.D. 1998

Figure 9.1   *(Continued)*

LANGUAGE/
COMMUNICATING

Communicating

• Discussion/debate	• Dialogue
• Communication may be manipulative and/or self-aggrandizing	• Communication intended for achieving goals, delivering information, or sharing something, including about self
• May be unaware of, or unconcerned about, effect of own communication on others, unless for benefit of self	• Recognizes and takes responsibility for what and how it communicates, including own effect on others
• Communication may be irresponsible; may assert something without certainty of facts. May gossip	• Communication intended to be responsible; if uncertain, indicates so. Doesn't gossip
• May not notice or pay attention to own internal dialogue about others	• Attempts to be aware of, listen to, and "observe" own internal dialogue about others
• May not realize own power to alter internal dialogue about others, or the difference that that would make	• Recognizes own power to alter internal dialogue about others, and does so in realistic, positive, solution-seeking manner
• Requests to self and others may be unreasonable and win-lose	• Requests to others intended as reasonable and win-win
• Promises to self and others may be unreasonable and unreliable	• Promises to self and others intended as reasonable and reliable
• Rarely checks or confirms that other person understood communication	• Habitually checks to make sure communication was understood
• May not check to confirm that it understood a communication	• Habitually checks to make sure it understood a communication

Copyright © Marilee C. Goldberg, Ph.D. 1998

Figure 9.1 *(Continued)*

Language Use

- Presuppositions tend to be negative, limiting, and/or self-preoccupied

- Use of inclusive adverbs such as *always* and *never,* which provide no basic difference between past, present, and future; may assume future will be repetition of past

- May use extreme descriptions that interfere with needed distinctions

- Predominance of nouns, many nominalizations (the noun form of a word, rather than the verb form)

- Much labeling of self and others

- More "you" statements than "I" statements

- May speak of self and circumstances in passive voice ("It happened to me.")

- Presuppositions tend to be positive, expansive, self-*and*-other-centered

- Uses qualifying adverbs, thus allowing distinctions between past, present, and future—assumes future can be different, possibly better

- Habitually uses descriptions that provide distinctions and gradations, often with qualifying adverbs

- Predominance of verbs, action-oriented

- Avoids labeling

- More "I" statements than "you" statements

- Speaks of self and circumstances in active voice ("I made it happen.")

Listening

- Listens first for how a communication might affect self, rather than to the communication itself

- May not consider how well other person is listening

- ❖ Listens through questions such as:

- *What's wrong with this, me, the other person, or the situation?*

- Listens for context and content of communication, as well as how it might affect self

- Considers how well other(s) listen, and designs communications to be understood

- ❖ Listens through questions such as:

- *What's right about this, me, the other person, or the situation?*

Copyright © Marilee C. Goldberg, Ph.D. 1998

Figure 9.1 *(Continued)*

- Might this make me "look good" or make me "look bad"?
- What might be useful or valuable about this?

- How might this challenge me?
- What's my responsibility here?

- How can I protect/defend myself?
- What are my choices?

- How can I win?
- How can we both win?

- What could I learn from this?

Questioning

- Asks few questions of self and others
- Asks many questions of self and others

- Rarely questions own questions, internal and interpersonal
- Habitually questions own questions, internal and interpersonal

- Questions usually for verifying or confirming own opinion or belief, protecting or seeking advantage to self
- Questions for obtaining information, learning, and creating; may be seeking advantage for self (not at expense of another)

- Asks few genuine questions of self and others
- Asks many genuine questions of self and others

- Rarely asks questions to check assumptions of self or others
- Often asks questions to check assumptions of self or others

- May be afraid to ask questions, even when needing information (fearful of seeming dumb, ignorant, "not in the know")
- Usually asks questions, even when fearful or uncertain, or when question reveals not knowing

- May get upset or defensive if doesn't know answer(s) to question(s)
- Accepts "not knowing," admits it, can embrace this state

- Intent of questions to others may be to prove them wrong or prove self right
- Intent of questions to others to get information, learn about person's intentions, feelings, and desires, and/or move toward effective action

Copyright © Marilee C. Goldberg, Ph.D. 1998

Figure 9.1 (Continued)

highly stressed clients were so out of control with tension that the needle flopped off-scale.

Getting the message, Stuart said, "You mean, like me?" Then he added: "I guess you're telling me that to be in more control, I have to be flexible enough to *choose* my *level* of control?" This realization served as the basis of a series of behavioral rehearsals, homework assignments, and relaxation trainings, each designed to give him a healthier, more flexible, and varied experience of self-control, as well as less anxiety in situations that had been troublesome. We also developed some new internal questions for him: "*Realistically speaking, how controlled do I need to be at this moment?*" and a backup question: "*Would Dr. Goldberg agree with me about how much control I really need right now?*" His success was emphatically demonstrated a few months later when he and Susan had dinner with his mother, and they both hugged her goodnight.

SECTION TWO: THINKING

Frank, a 45-year-old computer programmer, began therapy when he feared his hard-won relationship with his father was threatened by his new stepmother. The time factor in this case was urgent since the father had recently had a debilitating stroke, and his condition was worsening. Frank commented, "I feel paralyzed. Everything I try ends up in a mess. It would break my heart if my father and I were estranged when he dies." Frank agreed that the ways he was thinking about the situation seemed to be making it worse, and even humorously admitted that one of his questions about his stepmother was, "*How can I put a muzzle on the wicked witch of the west?*"

I introduced the Learner/Judger Chart almost immediately, and we turned out attention to the Thinking Section. Frank chuckled when he recognized himself as firmly ensconced on the Judger side in this situation. He remarked, "No wonder I've been paralyzed. I've been asking every one of those Judger Self questions. It's actually a relief to understand why I've screwed up so far." Then he implored, "I've got to figure this out quickly. Please just tell me some Learner questions that will help."

I responded, "Frank, I understand your eagerness, but slow down a minute. I don't want to shortchange you by giving an answer that may be simplistic. This situation is too complicated, and you're going to need to be able to do some quick thinking on your own to get through it. Do you know that expression about giving you a fish versus teaching you *how* to fish?" He nodded "*Yes.*" "Good," I continued. "I can show you how to fish pretty quickly. Do you still want me to just throw you a little fish?" He answered simply, "You're on. Let's do it."

I redirected Frank's attention to the Learner Self questions, and pointed to one in particular: "*What categories should I think in with this situation?*" I explained that generating a list of categories in a particular circumstance gives a person a comprehensive view instead of a narrow one, and makes him less likely to miss something important. I told him: "Think of the situation as if you were creating a directory in your computer. Then every category you come up with in that context is like a new file you can fill up with all kinds of things to consider, as well as suggestions for solutions."

Among the categories Frank thought of were: his relationship with his stepmother, his relationship with his mother, a family reunion that was coming up soon, how tense and anxious he got before seeing his stepmother, what kind of relationship he wanted his sons to have with his father, and what was the optimal possible relationship with his dad at this point in their lives (especially factoring in his father's health and his stepmother's intrusiveness). Frank seemed amazed that there were so many different issues to consider, and said: "Before I was just a big emotional jumble, and I couldn't see anything clearly enough to figure out what to do. Now, I have tons of ideas just from thinking of these categories."

I told him, "I'm glad about that; however, you'll be happy to know you'll get at least as much mileage from the next step. Now let's come up with questions in each category that will set you in motion to resolve these issues. Please pick one category that's a priority and we'll use it to go through this exercise." Frank immediately selected the one about developing an optimal relationship with his father. I made sure he understood the differences between Judger Self questions and Learner Self questions, and he joked, "I can tell I'd better keep my Learner cap on while we do this." Among his most important new questions were:

- *How can my father and I communicate with each other since he can't talk very well anymore?*
- *How can I arrange the most advantageous circumstances for being with him?*
- *What kinds of things can we do together that would feel good for both of us?*
- *How can I make sure my Dad knows I love him?*

Frank realized he was letting his negative reactions to his stepmother distract him from focusing on his relationship with his father. He started visiting more regularly, even if only for a few moments, and arranged those visits so he and his father could be alone together. He brought photo albums of happy times for them to reminisce over, and he also brought music his father particularly enjoyed. At our last contact, Frank commented, "I still don't like my stepmother, but I just don't bother myself with her—she's not that important. With my father, most things have gotten pretty simple. I can sit with him peacefully and not feel like I need anything from him anymore. I know he knows I love him and that I'm grateful for everything he's done for me. It's like there's a circle around us and when we're together we're really together. It's better than I ever hoped it could be."

We met Andrea in chapter 6, when she and I worked with the Choice Model in reference to her responsibility in her relationship with her husband, Ted. A few sessions after that I introduced the Learner/Judger Chart, using the Relating section and the Thinking section as her entry points into the material. She easily identified how the chart operates as an elaboration of the Choice Model. In fact, she pointed to the items about how *Judgers react* and *Learners respond* and commented, "That's what I learned in that session when we changed how I used to deal with Ted after he has a bad day." The following story shows how she successfully used the chart in thinking through another situation with her husband.

Andrea told me she loved to read in bed until she got drowsy and fell asleep. Marriage interfered with her cherished ritual and she missed it. One night, Ted had some work to finish, and she grabbed the opportunity to go to bed early and snuggle up with a favorite book. She was annoyed with herself when she inadvertently slammed the bedroom door, and wondered for an instant if Ted might think she were angry. But she shrugged off the thought as she got comfortable under the covers. To her irritation, however, she couldn't lose herself in her book because that tiny incident kept nagging at her.

Andrea recalled that she finally sat up in bed and said to herself, "*All right Andrea, let's think this through, and get it over with.*" She got out the chart and noticed the item in the Relating section which says, "Aware to some degree of effect of self on others and takes responsibility for it." Then, still using the chart, she altered one of the Learner Self questions to make it fit the current situation. She asked herself, "*What might Ted think and feel, not just what do I think and feel?*" She also wondered what other questions a Learner Self might ask in this situation. That list included the following:

- *Does Ted think the slammed door means I'm mad at him?*
- *Is it really important to get up and check this out?*
- *If I don't, could this cause a problem?*
- *If it does cause a problem, would it have been worth a few minutes extra reading time?*
- *If this happened the other way around, would I want Ted to get up and make sure I wasn't worried about him being angry?*

Somewhat ruefully, Andrea admitted she knew all along she should get out of bed and check this out with her husband. However, she also said she probably wouldn't have done it without forcing herself through this thinking exercise using the chart. The clincher questions for Andrea were: "*What could be the worse consequences if I don't do anything?*" and "*What do I need to do so we both can win?*"

Andrea concluded her story by saying: "It's a good thing I made the effort, because Ted *did* think I was mad at him, but couldn't figure out what for. I can predict what would have happened, too. Ted would have been hurt, but not said anything, of course. Then, when he came to bed, he wouldn't have cuddled up with me like he usually does. Then I would have gotten hurt, which would have turned into me being mad. Then I would have moved over to the far side of the bed. Then he would have moved all the way over to *his* side of the bed. Then we would have slept separate, and that's how we would have woken up, too. Separate. Neither one of us would have known why we didn't feel right together in the morning, so there wouldn't have been any way to fix it."

When I asked Andrea specifically about the usefulness of the chart in this situation, she commented: "To be honest, if all that bad stuff had happened, it would have been *my* responsibility if I hadn't bothered to check whether the slammed door made him think I was mad. I hate to think how many times stupid little things like that happened in the past before we separated. The chart helped me see Ted *and* me starkly right there on the page. It was obvious that I was acting like a Judger Self because I was thinking only about what I wanted, and not how it would affect "us." It was so glaring, even *I* had to admit it, and that forced me to *do* something about it."

SECTION THREE: FEELING

The Feeling section of the chart differs from the polarized definitions and examples given in the other five categories, both conceptually and in visual presentation. For this reason, we discuss the category itself before moving on to the clinical examples. The feeling category is different, of course, because no feeling belongs exclusively either to the Learner Self or the Judger Self. Both experience fear, anger, and sadness, just as each also experiences calmness, enthusiasm, and happiness. The difference lies not is where particular emotions might fall on the chart, but more in the individual's *orientation* toward emotions altogether. Therefore, in this section, we first explore how to present this material so it neutralizes clients' fears about feelings in general, and some of their feelings, specifically. Next, we discuss the goal to orient clients to the presumption that we humans have responsibility, and at least some choice, about the feelings we experience. Then, we examine the affective life of the Judger Self, including case material. After this, we focus on the affective life of the Learner Self. Finally, we explore the home-base residence of the Learner and Judger with regard to their feelings.

"Depathologizing" Emotions

Most of us are capable of almost any emotion, given the right circumstances or provocation. No particular emotion is evidence that we are "good" or "bad" people; no specific emotions *prove* that one is crazy or not. In fact, emotions themselves do not cause problems. Rather, how we relate to our emotions, and what we do as a consequence of experiencing them, are at the core of most human difficulties. This is not to say that many emotions are not uncomfortable—because many are. Nor is it meant to imply that emotions are always easy to deal with—because, of course, this is often not true. Emotions simply are what they are; it is the judgments and interpretations we make about them that create difficulty. Negative judgments about emotions cause people to resist and deny some feelings, even while attempting to hold on to others. To judge ourselves or others for the feelings that do show up simply complicates any difficulties of dealing with those feelings in the first place.

Furthermore, many people believe any discomfort is negative and must be avoided or buffered. Nevertheless, discomfort lives at our growing edges, and some growth cannot happen without it, as any serious athlete would tell us. For example, learning how to discipline oneself and delay gratification sometimes requires tolerating anxiety and discomfort. In fact, Goleman (1995, pp. 81–82) reported that the ability to delay gratification—as early as age *four*—turned out to be a significant predictor of SAT scores as well as personal effectiveness. The Learner/Judger Chart can help here; a therapist can take advantage of the Feeling section to initiate conversations to help understand feelings.

Feelings and Choice

When discussing the Feeling section of the chart, I often invoke the metaphor of a piano keyboard. Just as a keyboard is comprised of all its white and black keys, human beings are capable of most any particular emotion—and perhaps even most behaviors, as some of the studies on authority and obedience (e.g., Milgram 1974) have shown. A piano has no choice about how it is played. Human beings, on the other hand, *can* choose many of the keys we play, once physiological reactions to incoming stimuli have passed. Because emotions register in our bodies and minds virtually simultaneously, we have little choice about most initial reactions. A sudden noise startles almost anyone; a bright light normally causes one's pupils to dilate. These reactions are physiological; they are hardwired, and we have little, if any, control over them. However, we *do* have choice about what we do *next*, by virtue of how we orient to emotions through our perceptions, interpretations, beliefs, and the questions we ask ourselves. This is the lesson of the Choice Model.

The Affective Life of the Judger Self

The Judger Self's orientation toward its emotional life is expressed in two ways that appear to be opposite. On the one hand, it is fearful of feelings, and so resists them. On the other hand, it may overidentify with its feelings, being certain their importance is paramount, and the Judger may therefore end up getting "lost" in feelings. It is obvious that in neither case has the Judger-dominated individual securely attained the level of formal operations with respect to his affective sensibilities.

In the first case, the Judger Self—operating from the belief that it must resist, avoid, or control its feelings—is poised as an antagonist to a natural emotional life. At best, it is able to manage its emotions, but most often attempts to repress or deny them. However, doing so requires both conscious and unconscious attention to affective experience, and so operates to keep the Judger Self somehow attached to the very experiences it wishes to avoid. Paradoxically, the Judger Self, feeling the imperative to control, deny, and/or resist its feelings, often ends up being stuck with them, and stuck *in* them. The Judger Self in the second instance may *appear* to be in touch with its feelings because it seems so expressive. The problem is that it never questions the beliefs or conclusions that led to the feelings in the first place.

If only it could learn and remember that human beings are capable of playing all the keys on the emotional keyboard, and that feelings, like every other aspect of life, come and go, like waves on the shore. This is not bad or even good; it is simply a description of the way it is. This understanding might allow the client who is dominated by his Judger Self to recognize that he *has* feelings, rather than having the experience of being victimized *by* his feelings. Such a realization could help catalyze his movement from the Judger Self to the Learner Self side of the chart, especially if he asked himself questions that empowered *him* rather than whatever he was reacting to at the moment. Unfortunately, when a person operates as Judger, he often blocks access to the full range of human feelings that give life its richness, including acceptance and integration of his shadow side. Accordingly, he also loses potential experiences of wholeness or full authenticity, either with himself or others.

Case Examples   For Sarah, questioning the beliefs that sparked her feelings would be quite helpful. Sarah, a bulimic college sophomore, felt insecure in her relationship with Mark, a senior on the football team. When Mark called to break a date because the coach called an emergency meeting, Sarah hung up the phone and cried hysterically. In session, she was initially inconsolable. Her conclusion was that Mark didn't really like her, that this was an attempt to reject her, and that he planned to end the relationship soon. I insisted, quite contrary to Sarah's desire, that we consult the chart to find out what we could learn from this situation, and also to get some guidance about how to best handle her next contact with Mark.

In the Feeling section of the chart, Sarah reluctantly pointed to the items that mentioned dramatizing feelings and being afraid of being overwhelmed by feelings. Then we turned to the Relating section and I asked her to pick one Learner Self question that might make a difference. She modified one and came up with, "What did *Mark* feel when the coach told him he had to stay late?" This led Sarah to realize that Mark might have been disappointed, annoyed with the coach, and maybe even unhappy about not seeing her. When I asked Sarah what she had learned from this experience she said: "I always think about myself first, and then get stuck there. My first impulse is to think that the other person wants to hurt me, but I guess that isn't always true. It would help a lot if I asked myself about the *other* person's feelings and didn't stop with my first reactions. It's no wonder I feel like one of the 'walking wounded' so often. I overreact when I feel like I've been rejected—even if I haven't been."

Another client, Bill, assumed that his boss, Patrick, was disappointed and angry when he walked out on an important seminar that Bill had been preparing for months. My client was distraught when he came to his therapy session that evening, and angry at me for insisting that it was important for him to speak to Patrick, and simply ask the obvious questions, "Why did you leave my presentation?" and "What did you think of what I did?"

Bill was suitably sheepish the next week when he reported that Patrick had received a note during the seminar saying his wife had gone into premature labor and had been rushed to the hospital. Patrick told Bill he was impressed with as much of the seminar as he had seen. Bill commented, "If I had just asked myself two questions, '*Do I need more information?*' and '*Should I take this personally?*' I would have checked to find out what actually happened. I could have avoided being so upset; I even ruined the evening with my wife. That whole situation was based on nothing." After a moment of silence, he added: "Well, it wasn't really based on nothing—it was based on stuff I made up. It was also the result of my not asking just one or two questions that would have made all the difference. Man, do I feel dumb."

It is important to note that while Sarah and Bill both experienced strong feelings, the feelings were inappropriate and unjustified, based as they were on unquestioned assumptions. No amount of emotional expression a therapist might encourage would make any growth difference for Sarah or Bill, either in a session or any future situation. In fact, such a therapeutic intervention would hinder their progress because the cognitive mistakes at the source of these difficulties would remain unexamined and unchallenged. Sarah and Bill had similar self-centered conclusions—that the other person's behavior was referenced toward them, that it was negative, and they would somehow lose or be hurt. These incorrect conclusions left them both mired in negative feelings, with no available strategy to take any effective personal or interpersonal action. The Learner Self questions *forced* them to shift perceptual positions, and stand in the other person's shoes. As both the Choice Model and the Switching Questions handouts illustrate, people can effectively rescue themselves from what has been called "the kinesthetic swamp" by going meta, assuming an observing self-position vis-à-vis themselves, and asking Learner Self questions.

The Affective Life of the Learner Self

The Learner Self stands in a different and healthier relationship with its affective life, and it is the ability to habitually self-observe that grants it this difference. Grounded in the twin recognitions that life is constantly in flux, and that difficult experiences and emotions are unavoidable, our Learner Selves accept the inevitability that wholeness in living requires accepting the whole range of possible emotions and experiences that are part of being human. The Learner Self knows that feelings register in our bodies and minds like waves on the shore. In constant repetitious motion, they rush in, peak, and recede. Similarly, the

Learner Self recognizes that *any* feeling, good, bad, or neutral, will come *and* go. While the Learner Self takes its feelings seriously, it doesn't worry that it has them in the first place or get overly attached to them. This allows it to "go meta," to stand as a self-observer in relation to the vast terrain of human emotion. The Learner Self is also able to see the present in relation to the future. Like a diabetic experiencing low blood sugar, the Learner Self is able to say: "*I feel awful now, but this, too, shall pass.*" In a sense, the Learner Self *has* emotions while *emotions* have the Judger Self.

When I was an adolescent I used a similar strategy to cope with a fear of going to the dentist. I kept reminding myself, "*This will probably hurt, but it will be over by 4:00 o'clock. It really will. There's life after this dentist appointment.*" Of course, I didn't know at the time that those reassurances were based on recognizing the future as distinct from the present, or that I was asking what I would later identify as a Learner Self question, "*What can I do just to make it through this experience?*" This is the same cognitive strategy that works so well in training individuals suffering with anxiety attacks to tell themselves: "*This is just an anxiety attack. I'm not going to faint. I'm not going to die. If I just hold my own, it will pass, and everything will be OK.*"

"Home Residences" of the Judger Self and Learner Self

While both Learner Self and Judger Self have potential access to the full range of emotions, it is also the case that they tend to have different base states or some emotions which are more typical for them to experience on an everyday basis. Clients seem to easily identify with this metaphor about the emotional home state of the Learner and Judger—it's as if they have different "permanent residences" illustrated by the human continuum that the chart represents. While they spend most of their time at home base, they also inevitably take excursions to the other domain. In fact, the empowerment goal of question-centered therapy focuses on the client's "shifting residences" to the Learner Self home base with reference to his presenting problems. Of course, this includes accepting that his humanness will automatically send him to Judger Self territory from time to time. While it is certainly predictable that we all will continually make "Judger Self excursions," advancing personal growth finds us making fewer such trips, and recovering from them faster and more naturally and easily.

SECTION FOUR: BEHAVING

Peter, the client of a therapist whom I supervised, was raised by an abusive, alcoholic father, and a "wimpy, depressed" mother. He seemed condemned to repeating a personal history he hated. Separated from his wife, Peter himself was abusive with his small son, and faced the possibility of a court order depriving him even of visiting rights. Peter worked hard to build his small electrical engineering firm, he loved his wife and son, and was desperate to make any changes that might bring his life back into order. His therapist reviewed the material on the Learner/Judger Chart with him, and trained him in the self-questioning methods. They began in the Behaving section with the item that reads "Behavior attempts to control others, especially partners and children."

The next week Peter reported that his first "test" with the chart came sooner than he expected, and that he was pleased, as well as surprised, at his success. During the weekend he had become typically impatient and angry while bathing his rambunctious three-year-old son. These feelings ordinarily led him to handle the boy roughly and often to slap him—and much worse. This time, however, Peter reported that he stopped what he was about to do, and some Learner questions "just popped in my head." The first was, *If I hit him, how will that affect him when he grows up?*" and the other was, "*What else can I do right now?*" Then Peter asked himself: "*What is he feeling?*" "*What does he need?*" and "*How can I work this out so we both win?*" He proudly told his therapist that he answered this last question by getting a cold soda, taking some deep breaths, and telling his son, "Daddy's upset, but he still loves you."

SECTION FIVE: RELATING

In addition to her weight management and self-esteem issues, Ellie had a volatile temper. She was always contrite and regretful afterwards, but felt she had no control whatsoever while in the heat of the fray. Her hotheaded flare-ups upset many weekends with her boyfriend, Chris, whom she desperately wanted to marry. So Ellie was understandably concerned that Chris might decide that putting up with her outbursts wasn't worth it anymore and so end the relationship.

Ellie seemed to have an affinity for the self-questioning material and began using it successfully in most areas of her life. To her disappointment, however, she initially made no headway in using it in her relationship with Chris. Then an incident between them demonstrated how much of a Learner Self and a natural self-questioner she had become. Ellie and Chris had planned to spend the weekend together, beginning with a romantic dinner on Friday night. Chris was to pick her up around 7:00 P.M., so it's easy to imagine how angry Ellie was by 10:00 when he finally called and apologized, explaining that he was so exhausted from his job as a construction worker that he fell asleep fully clothed on the sofa.

Ellie giggled as she told me what happened next. She said that after hearing the reason Chris was so late, she asked herself a question that never occurred to her prior to reading it on the Learner/Judger Chart, "*Should I take this personally?*" She answered "No," and decided that Chris's fatigue had *nothing* to do with her, nor did this incident mean he was ignoring her, abusing her, or abandoning her. So Ellie just said sweetly, "Well, that's OK, Honey. What time can you get here?" Then she looked at me, slapped her knee, laughed, and said: "You should have heard the shock in his voice. I thought he was going to faint! To tell the truth, I was pretty amazed myself. The next day Chris told me I was a 'new woman.' We had a great weekend, and I don't think he's gotten over it yet!"

Another client, Beth, whom we met in chapter 7, benefited from using the Relating and Feeling sections of the chart. This incident occurred near the end of her therapy when she was having difficulty with her parents. Beth wanted to move in with her boyfriend, a nice young man whom she met subsequent to the earlier session. Her parents opposed this move. In discussing how upset she was by her parents' attitude, I asked Beth how she was feeling, and all she could say was "mad and upset," although her tightly crossed arms and set jaw led to my opinion that she was also feeling stubborn and resistant.

When I asked what her body would say about how she was feeling she simply repeated "mad and upset." My next ploy was to suggest she exaggerate the way she was holding her body, and then tell me what questions she was asking herself. The questions came out in a torrent: *Do they think I'm still a child?* "Why do *they treat me like an imbecile?*" "Why don't they trust me?" "Don't they think I can *make my own decisions?*" "Don't they see that I've grown up?" A long pause followed that last question, then she relaxed visibly, looked at me wryly, and commented: "I'm not *acting* very grown up, am I?"

I laughed in agreement, noted that her question was definitely a Learner one, and asked whether she was acting like a Judger Self or a Learner Self with her parents. When Beth said, "I'm judging them like crazy and reacting like crazy," I knew we were almost home free. Then she added: "Here's another question I just realized I was asking: 'What's stupid and old-fashioned about how they *reacted to me last night?*' " When I suggested she cast the same incident in light of the chart questions, "What's the kindest possible interpretation of their behavior?" and "What would I say if I were giving them the benefit of the doubt?" Beth realized that her first-generation Irish parents were simply ignorant about typical women-men relationships at the end of the twentieth century in the United States. In fact, their negative, prudish-sounding reaction was largely based on their fear that their daughter would be hurt by this "modern" living arrangement.

In response to this realization, Beth commented that she could understand why they were worried, admitted that she was also, and that she owed them an apology. Then she asked me to help her plan a more constructive conversation with them, one that would allow them to talk honestly about their feelings and concerns, as well as the pros and cons of the situation. Beth realized that ultimately the choice was hers alone, and that she would have to make up her own mind, regardless of their opinions. However, she recognized she would be free to do so only if she were no longer reacting defiantly to her parents. She commented: "It's very obvious that if I want an adult relationship with my parents, I have to *stop reacting* to them as my Judger Self, and *start responding* to them as my Learner Self."

SECTION SIX:
LANGUAGE AND COMMUNICATING

This section on language and communicating is necessarily the most complex since each of the other five categories is expressed through it. The material itself is also complicated because the study and alteration of language, *any* language, is multidimensional, its intricacies touching, perhaps creating, virtually every nuance of experience and behavior. A clinical anecdote points to the relationship between language and "reality." A Japanese couple sought help for escalating marital stress and communication difficulties. Quite fluent in English, they had been in the United States for a few years completing their respective doctoral studies. After several therapy sessions, the husband confessed that a few months after they arrived in the States he decided he would argue with his wife only in Japanese, a decision based on his observations that he never won a fight if it took place in English!

This section of the chapter is divided into three parts. First we focus on language and change, including how to strengthen the ability to listen to clients' use of language. We also consider the importance of presuppositions in the therapist's thinking and speaking. Second, we focus on the importance of verbs and adverbs in giving clues for successful therapeutic interventions. Lastly, a long clinical example illustrates the power of language in inducing successful change.

Language and Change

For the sake of expediency as well as practicality, in this section we presuppose that language that occurs externally in communicating with others is basically isomorphic with our internal dialogue. This is akin to saying that a client's external speaking is relatively equivalent to putting his thinking processes on loudspeaker—which, of course, is not literally true. However, there is enough congruence between internal and external speaking that therapists gain a therapeutic advantage by making this assumption. The implication is that every intervention the clinician makes in helping her client increase his awareness of his external speaking has some simultaneous corrective impact on his ability to think more clearly, effectively, and creatively.

We also presuppose that most pathology (or its limiting characteristics and patterns), if it exists, can be found in linguistic expression. In fact, a careful examination of the cases presented in the preceding five sections of the chart reveals that each of my clients exhibited language usage (especially questions and verbs) that unintentionally sabotaged their possibilities for change. For example, Peter, who frequently lost control and hit his three-year-old son, illustrated this phenomenon. His damaging behavior was driven by unsuspected and silent self-questions such as: "*What's wrong with him (referring to his son)?*" "*What's wrong with me that I can't control my son?*" and "*What's the quickest way to get rid of my frustration?*" These internal Judger questions preempted Peter's ability to cope with his own emotions effectively and to shift perceptual positions to discover what his son might be feeling. The Judger questions also diminished his ability to anticipate consequences of his own behavior and kept him from dealing with his child in a win-win manner.

Listening to Language for the Sake of Change   As we discussed in chapter 4, one of a therapist's most basic skills is the ability to listen carefully to her client. Listening skill is associated with what one is listening *for*, and a question-centered therapist listens for linguistic processes as well as for psychological and historical content. Her basic listening question is some version of the following, "*Does this sentence, or any of its components, increase or decrease my client's personal power, or his ability to change and get what he wants?*" When the therapist asks herself this question, she refers to the actual words, as well as to the presuppositions of any particular sentence under consideration. The therapist could also ask other variations of that question, such as: "*In what way(s) is my client's language use (especially verbs and questions) sabotaging his possibilities for positive, healthy, desired growth and change?*" and "*Is my client speaking or thinking as a Learner Self or a Judger Self right now?*"

Three further questions narrow the scope of this rather general initial inquiry about the client's speaking. These are: "*Is my client _deleting_ anything that should be considered or included?*" "*Is my client _distorting_ anything that could prevent him from observing or understanding himself, another person, or some situation accurately?*" "*Is my client _generalizing_ anything such that distinctions that could lead to changes in perception might be overlooked or obscured?*" With reference to the last question, it is worth noting that the tendency to generalize without questioning one's assumptions correlates with the limiting, impoverishing effects of black/white, all-or-nothing thinking. The answers to any of these questions could easily lead to therapeutic interventions that would be rich in their ability to induce change.

If pathology is often found in linguistic expression, then the opposite presupposition must also be true—that principles leading to healthy, desired change would advantageously become integrated and embedded in a client's speaking and thinking. To support this, the following questions are offered for therapists to include in their repertoire: "*What linguistic changes (especially in verbs or questions) could liberate and extend my client's possibilities for positive growth and change?*" and "*What linguistic interventions would help my client speak and think like a Learner Self instead of a Judger Self?*"

Using Presuppositions for Change   The use of presuppositions, both generally and specifically, is one of a therapist's most powerful strategies. For example, a therapist takes advantage of presuppositional thinking when she asks her client, "When did you begin to get better?" In answering this question, the client automatically assumes that he *is* already getting better. In question-centered therapy, the therapist generally assumes that her client can operate from his Learner Self, and therefore presupposes resourcefulness, willingness, capability, and openness to learning and growing. She thereby builds these presuppositions into her speaking. She also asks herself questions such as, "*What presuppositions will facilitate a shift in my client at this moment?* Then she may ask her client questions such as: "What will it take for you to activate your Learner Self when you're upset with your wife?" or "How will you calm down your Judger Self if you begin to experience an anxiety attack?"

Verbs

The purpose of therapy is positive change. Change implies action and difference, as well as some passage of time. Linguistically speaking, change, action, difference, and time are most catalyzed by, apparent in, and identified with verbs in contrast with nouns. Furthermore, questions, as contrasted with statements, are also intrinsic to change, action, difference, and time. However, despite the fact that clients seek therapy because they want change, they usually inhibit that very possibility through their use of language, especially with regard to how they use questions and verbs in both internal and external speaking.

We have already spent considerable time focusing on the impact of various kinds of questions with which the Learner Self and the Judger Self create their disparate worlds. Therefore, here we concentrate more on verbs, as their usage either facilitates or impedes therapeutic change. While it may be convincingly argued that much of the interference to which we refer may be dynamically or unconsciously motivated, it is the linguistic impediments to change, which can be transformed into therapeutic possibilities, on which we focus here.

We consider just a few of the myriad ways that clients' misuse of verbs and adverbs can interfere with their success in therapy and in life. The first concerns the issue of personal responsibility as it is associated with active versus passive verbs. We also consider how verbs affect time perception and how verbs lose their power for action when they become disguised and/or reduced to nouns.

Active and Passive Verbs   Most therapists would agree that successful therapy includes at least a small positive change in a client's experience of self-efficacy and self-esteem. Both self-efficacy and self-esteem depend, in part, on a person's owning or taking active responsibility for his own thoughts, feelings, and actions. One could even argue that the more habitually and consciously a person actively assumes responsibility for himself, the more personal power he accrues. Yet simply by speaking in the passive versus the active voice, an individual *removes* power from himself, while attributing it elsewhere. The Judger Self comment, "My report got there late," versus the Learner Self statement, "I was late getting my report to him" illustrates how speaking in the passive voice simultaneously removes responsibility for one's actions and inhibits the chance that one can, or will, take a proactive stance to do anything differently next time. In the therapy context, based as it is on the goal of positive change, that humorously delivered expression, "The devil made me do it," turns into a very poor joke.

Verb Tenses   Unthinking and unskillful use of verb tenses also impedes the possibility of change. For example, if a person continues to speak about difficult emotions and situations in the present tense, he may unconsciously and unintentionally "program" himself to expect the problem situation or feeling to *continue as is*, into an indefinite future. For example, when a husband declares, "This is the way I *am* with my wife" or, "This is what she *does*," he unintentionally assigns permanence to his presenting problem. In other words, when a client makes these kinds of assertions, he actually speaks about the future as part of an *expanded present*, unconsciously inhibiting his expectation and belief that the future could be distinctly different, much less better, than the present. These statements are typical of clients at the beginning of therapy and indicate a lack of progress in treatment if they continue.

This underlying presupposition about the elasticity of present time undermines hope in depressed patients. It was apparent in the cognitions of the women in my research study, all of whom "lived" unhappily on the Judger Self side of the chart with regard to their worries about weight and feeling out of control. In their experience of time, my subjects somewhat resembled the much more extreme experience of Ellen West, of the well-known "Case of Ellen West" by Binswanger (May 1958). Ellen West, a bulimic, weight-obsessed woman, described her inability to see the future, or only a dark one. She eventually killed herself. While this was a complicated case, further understanding of how people code experience, linguistically and otherwise, might have suggested different ways of conceptualizing her difficulties as well as with working with her. (See James and Woodsmall 1988.)

It is important for therapists to be alert to ways that people come to therapy wanting different and better futures, and then speak in ways that interfere with this possibility. Knowing this, the therapist may take advantage of psychoeducational interventions to interrupt and/or correct unintentional verb-related linguistic sabotage and directly address issues about time. Therapists may also experiment with some subtle interventions such as referring to a problem in the past tense. If a client "doesn't notice" or "buys it," this may signal that he unconsciously accepted that presupposition.

Adverbs   Because adverbs express a person's sense of time, adverb usage can also be problematic therapeutically. For example, those "sabotaging" adverbs *always* and *never* contribute to a client's sense that whatever condition he wants to change, can *not* happen if the future is presumed to be an extension of the present. The following sentences: "I *always* get depressed when my mother visits" or "My wife *always* yells at me in front of the children" or "He is *never* nice to me when he comes home from work" or "I'll *never* be happy," represent versions of black/white thinking that significantly undermine possibilities for change. With each statement the client posits a total homogeneity in some ongoing series of situations and experiences. Not acknowledging or even noticing variations in his own or someone else's affect or behavior prevents him from asking helpful self-questions to challenge his own thinking. These could include: *"Is it true that he has never been nice to me?" "Have there ever been any exceptions?" "What is different in the times when this doesn't happen?" "What could I learn that would help things change?"* or *"What could I do to help myself feel even a little bit better right now?"*

Verbs Disguised as Nouns   While verbs inherently relate to action, time, and possibly change, this is not the case with nouns. In fact, objectifying a verb process into a static noun conceals many possibilities for action and change, a process that linguists call *nominalizing*. It is easy to discern nominalizations, as these are nouns that don't specify anything concrete; that is, the noun doesn't refer to anything that can be seen, heard, touched, or even smelled. Nouns such as education, discipline, and love fall into this category. To activate each of these nouns and release their potential for therapeutic interventions, one can convert them into the verbs to educate, to discipline, and to love. For example, if a client laments not having enough *love* in his life, or wonders where he can get more of "it," a therapist can help him retrieve his power for action by asking questions such as: *"How could you act more loving (to yourself, or to someone else)?"* or *"What behaviors feel loving to you?"* or suggest her client ask himself each evening, *"Have I loved well today?"* If the answer to the last question is "No," then the therapist might suggest follow-up questions such as, *"What got in the way?"* or, *"What will I do differently about that tomorrow?"*

Self-esteem is also a nominalization with which linguistic interventions can be very helpful. Self-esteem is a noun. To esteem is a verb. A client who complains that he "has" low self-esteem can be helped to assume responsibility for himself, and take specific action steps to address and change how he feels. New questions can initiate this process. Examples include: *"What have I done today to express positive esteem for myself?" "What more can I still do" "Do I have any reluctance about that?" "What's that about?" "What is one thing I can do in the next hour that would demonstrate caring for myself?"*

Nouns and Labeling   Labeling is a particularly lethal verb-into-noun habit, since it can damage self-esteem and limit possibilities for action and successful change. This problem is rampant, for example, among people who suffer with eating disorders, and attempt to harshly control their eating behaviors and their weight. If such an individual should fail, or not keep a behavioral promise, he will typically *label* himself "a failure," rather than saying, "I failed at keeping this promise this time." In other words, by converting his behavior into a noun with which he labels himself, he attributes to himself the *identity* of a failure. He thereby saddles himself with the assumption that he will naturally *continue* to fail at any such behavioral goals in the future. Adding insult to injury, the label of being "a failure" all too often becomes a self-fulfilling prophecy.

Case Example

The last clinical example in this chapter provides illustrative material about self-questioning. While all the anecdotes so far have emphasized the importance of self-questions, the example that follows additionally shows a client using this psycho-educational material to empower others in her life. This example also illustrates that clients generally find the Learner/Judger Chart accessible and user-friendly.

Allison came to therapy with issues centering on self-esteem, weight management, and resolving problems with one of her three married children. Although she made significant progress on all fronts, the following anecdote demonstrates what Allison did with the Learner/Judger Chart in her professional capacity as a resident house mother in a shelter for abused women. She told me she decided to experiment with the Learner/Judger material after getting affirmative answers to the following self-questions: *"Would any of this be helpful to the women I work with?" "If I told them I used it myself, would that make it easier for them to accept?" "Would this material be consistent with what they're already getting in individual, group, and family therapy?"* Finally she asked herself, *"Well then, why not?"* and went to work the very next morning.

Allison made a copy of the chart, posted it, and announced that she would teach it to any woman who was interested. About ten women showed up at the designated time and Allison began her informal experiment. She used the chart to show the residents how both they and their husbands were behaving like Judger Selves, though of course in very different ways. Allison and her group worked through the six categories of the chart and figured out that the men in their lives were often rigid, reactive, righteous, superior, and out of control. They blamed others, took no responsibility for their problems or behavior, and thought about relationships in a win-lose way. Their behavior seemed to answer internal questions, such as: *"How can I keep from looking (or feeling) weak?" "How can I come out on top in this relationship?"* and *"How can I show her who is boss?"*

As a group, the women saw that they had been acting as Judger Selves at the other extreme. Rigid in the belief that they were unworthy, inferior, and powerless, they acted passive and overdependent. Rather than take responsibility for their predicament, they usually blamed themselves, and denied that choice was possible, thought of themselves as victims, and of relationships as inevitably win-lose. Their internal questions echoed and perpetuated these themes. Behaviorally answering questions such as: *"What's wrong with me?" "Why bother, what's the use?" "What do I have to do to get him to approve of and accept me?"* only served to further entrench them in their sorry and unfortunate circumstances. Allison was particularly pleased that a few of the women commented that if they were going to start taking responsibility for themselves, they would have to think about the fact that they were attracting and *keeping* these particular kinds of men in their lives.

Once Allison and the residents went through the chart and identified these characteristics, she opened the possibility that they could *practice* becoming Learner Selves. Modeling what I taught her, Allison told the women that none of us become Learner Selves overnight, and that it's a challenge for anyone, including herself, to shift residence from the Judger Self to the Learner Self side of the chart. She suggested they begin by making some short excursions in order to check out the territory. She told them that certain kinds of self-questions would help them bridge the gap, and together they composed new questions to add to those already on the chart. These included: *"What's my limit?" "At what point is my dignity compromised?" "Did I do anything to aggravate this behavior?" (If yes) "What did I do, even if it wasn't intentional?" "Do I want to keep acting like my mother did with my father?"* and *"Am I being fair to my children if I let this go on?"*

After Allison worked with her informal group for about a six weeks, she proudly surprised me with the information about what she had done and her results so far. She said the women reported that this information was helpful because they discovered options they never considered before and therefore didn't feel hopeless. They especially liked the self-questions because they are so practical and could be experimented with right away. Some had tentatively tried new ways to relate to their husbands, and in a few instances, some had discovered how to assert themselves gracefully enough to cool down some potentially volatile situations. While these women obviously required far more intensive and comprehensive therapy, they were proud of these small behavioral changes, and said that learning about the Learner and Judger gave them some of their first concrete reasons for hope.

Clients' Comments about the Learner/Judger Chart   I was impressed that a client was able to use the chart so successfully, especially without any coaching or instructions. I asked Allison to interview the women informally about using the chart, focusing on what worked for them as well as anything that hadn't. Summarizing their responses, Allison told me that they liked the organizational structure of the chart because the contrasts between the Judger Self and Learner Self positions were stark, which makes it easy to identify and understand the differences. The women said it made sense to read straight down each column, thinking about how each characteristic related to them personally and also to others. They also liked the brevity, specificity, and everyday language of the descriptions. Further, they found the distinctions made by the six categories helpful because this led to specific questions they could ask themselves. Their only complaint was that they wanted to remember to think about the material more, especially in times of stress. They would also have liked the opportunity to discuss some of their personal situations as they related to the chart with a therapist.

Since Allison's experiment, I have encouraged other clients to share this material in whatever natural personal or professional contexts seemed appropriate, especially because teaching the material is reinforcing to the *teacher*. When we discuss this possibility, I remind clients of the old medical school adage: "See one, do one, teach one—and it's yours." Of course, I emphasize the importance of taking an accepting, compassionate Learner Self's attitude about the material on the chart, as well as to anything their "students" might tell them. Clients quickly learn that if they present the Learner/Judger material in a way that seems judgmental, their students reject both them and the helpful information they want to convey.

It is interesting to note that Allison originally came to therapy with a weight management issue. While the model of the Learner Self and Judger Self was helpful in her own therapy, we never discussed her professional life. Yet she saw a possible application of this material and ran with the ball independently, creatively, and successfully.

SUMMARY

This chapter introduced the handout of the Learner/Judger Chart. The chart is taught to clients as a means of activating and/or reinforcing the observer self and the Learner Self. This includes helping clients understand, accept, and work with the Judger Self, in themselves and others. The chart is used to facilitate cognitive, emotional, and behavioral change, and functions as the backdrop for interventions in sessions and for homework assignments. The chapter also presented many case examples for each of six categories of the Learner/Judger Chart. In the next chapter, we meet Sophia, a former client, who now "qualifies" as a skillful Learner Self.

10

Therapy as Journey
and Destination:
The Case of Sophia

*We grow up never questioning that which is
unquestioned by those around us.*
— MARGARET MEAD

ntering the end phase of therapy is like coming 'round the bend on the
last leg of the journey. Most journeys have a destination, and the therapeutic one is no different. Whether one has taken the short route or the scenic
tour, the whole process was begun with an end in mind. Other than the amelio-
ration of any presenting problems, the explicit metagoal delineated by question-
centered therapy is the empowering possibility of learning and integrating the
attitudes and life skills of a mature Learner Self.

The end phase of therapy operates simultaneously as a completion and a
launching. Section 1 of this chapter examines the goals, therapeutic relationship,
and interventions of this last phase as they contribute to the formal closing of
therapy. Section 2 explores the life that was launched for Sophia, a client whose
successful, nine-month-long therapy with me ended about five years ago. Since
most of Sophia's individual and group therapy was explicitly based on the psycho-
educational material presented in this book, I asked if she would agree to be
interviewed with the goal of discussing the Learner/Judger material and the
impact it had made on her life. She accepted enthusiastically, saying this would
be a "good review" for her, and that she would enjoy the opportunity to be helpful to others. The goal of this chapter, which focuses on Sophia, is to breathe life
into an understanding of question-centered therapy, and to satisfy some questions
about outcomes, at least in this one instance.

SECTION ONE: THE END PHASE OF THERAPY

Goals of the End Phase of Therapy

The goals of the end phase of therapy focus on assessing an individual's readiness for termination, preparing him for this event, and reinforcing the possibility of his continuing success in the future. Usually a therapist's evaluation of her client in the end phase of treatment is based on the resolution or dissolution of the presenting problem(s). With question-centered therapy, the therapist's assessment will also be based on specific evidence of the client's established and increasing perceptual, cognitive, and behavioral orientation as a Learner Self. Some of this evidence appears in the level of responsibility he takes for himself, on his receptivity and use of feedback, and in his use of language. It is also evident in how the client conducts himself in the therapeutic relationship. Examples of successful behaviors and results reported by the client about situations outside the therapy room supplement and reinforce the therapist's evaluation.

The therapist is especially alert to the client's increasing and natural use of Learner Self self-questions to direct and navigate his life. Ample evidence of naturally occurring Learner self-questioning will also be emblematic of the client willingly and competently assuming responsibility for his mindset, moods, behaviors, and choices—and thereby his interpersonal, intrapersonal, and situational outcomes. Because conscious, goal-oriented, self-correcting self-questioning is operational evidence of an individual's commitment and ability to live as a Learner Self, this crucial aspect of internal dialogue is highlighted in the case of Sophia in section 2 of this chapter.

Therapeutic Relationship

The therapist, of course, continues to be a "Learner model" for her clients in the final phase of therapy, just as she did throughout the beginning phase and midphase. This reinforces clients' ability and habit of taking that stance towards themselves, thereby further loosening remaining Judger Self attitudes toward themselves and others. The therapist may also continue offering examples of personal shifts from Judger Self to Learner Self behavior or attitudes, thus underscoring that the chart is a model about human nature which functions as a blueprint for growth, and is not merely an elaborate prescription to fix what's wrong. Neutral queries the therapist might pose to her clients are intended to support their thoughtful, honest, nondefensive researcher's stance toward themselves and others. Examples of such questions would be: "How might an advanced Learner Self have handled that situation with your wife?" or "What Learner Self question could get your thinking on a better track?" or "What advice do you think I would give you in this situation?"

While her attitude of respect, positive regard, and encouragement remain constant, the role of the therapist shifts in the end phase of therapy. It's as if the training wheels are removed in order to assess whether, and how well, the client can travel on his own. The therapist becomes less of a teacher, as well as less of a transferential object. She operates increasingly as a respected colleague, offering challenges and applauding successes. In effect, she passes the baton of self-therapist and self-supporter back to her client. Of course, the therapist also recognizes that the more her client has introjected, integrated, and now practices her own attitudes, expectations, skills, and ways of relating, the more confident she can be of her client's success in the future. In other words, the therapist's metamessage in the final phase of therapy is somewhat like the following:

> *You have demonstrated your ability to resolve a difficult problem. You have significantly strengthened your problem-solving skills. You have learned how important it is to continuously ask yourself helpful questions, like those for observing and correcting. Your answers will generally be trustworthy, and in the highest interest of yourself and the people with whom you relate. However, you are not perfect, and you are not Superman. You are human, and for this reason you will have disappointments, failures, and losses. Thankfully, and through your own hard work, you also know how to recover yourself and get back on track, and how to recognize when you need help or support. You also know that it takes strength to ask for support, and you know how to do that when you need to.*
>
> *Because, to some extent, you have developed the skills, attitudes, and operating questions of a skillful and trained Learner Self, you know that your experiences and outcomes are essentially your choice and your responsibility. You have the basic tools you need to take advantage of this realization, including the ability and inclination to be more accepting and forgiving of yourself and others. At the same time, you may ask and expect more in your desire to live life to the fullest. You know that life is constantly changing, that new challenges inevitably appear, and that opportunities for learning, growing, and fulfillment never end. I have confidence in you, and you can, too.*

Interventions

The therapist consistently uses the Learner/Judger model to reinforce the client's awareness that whether he operates in the Learner's paradigm or the Judger's paradigm at any moment is a choice—even if he doesn't initially recognize this or doesn't like it. The therapist emphasizes this attitude, knowing that personal power results from acknowledging choice and using it responsibly to build and live one's life. This recognition reflects a quote from Albert Schweitzer: "The greatest discovery of any generation is that human beings can alter their lives by altering their attitudes of mind."

Because people generally turn to therapy only when they have run out of perceived resources and options, one of the therapist's main tasks is to train clients to think in more discriminating ways about themselves, others, and the issues before them. Therefore, the question-centered therapist takes advantage of the handout material, including the Choice Model, observe-and-correct thinking strategies, and the Learner/Judger model to educate her clients to multiple distinctions of perception, attitude, and behavior. She does this in order to strengthen their ability to consistently discern and create options and opportunities for effective action.

The therapist knows that dependable, high-level cognitive functioning depends on making finer and finer distinctions, and that these appear only to those who habitually look for them. The primary way of operationalizing this search, of course, is through self-questioning. For example, the Eskimo's multiple, narrowly defined descriptions of snow help him survive. He *needs* those distinctions, and creates them by asking himself questions such as: "*Has the color of the ice on the river reached the level which I recognize as safe to walk on?*" By the same token, if a client asserts, "That was the *only* thing I could do under the circumstances" his therapist might insist on deeper thinking by inquiring of him: "What other options might you have noticed if you had asked yourself a question like: '*What other possibilities might my therapist (or boss, or wife, or colleague, etc.) have come up with in that same situation?*' "

Such interventions challenge a client to broaden his perception of options by minimizing judgment and expanding his thinking to include multiple points of view. This self-questioning, including questioning one's own assumptions, depends on observing and correcting both internal statements and internal questions—a cornerstone ability of the trained Learner Self. In the mid-phase of therapy, the clinician reviewed these practices repeatedly and in detail. However, in the end phase she expects her client to have advanced to the point where he usually does this for himself, while her job as therapist has shifted to merely reminding him from time to time. Of course, the therapist recognizes that refining this high level of cognitive self-monitoring and self-managing is an ongoing human challenge, one that she herself will also be practicing for the rest of her life.

Naturally, the number as well as the character of the therapist's interventions also change in the final phase of therapy. This includes the fact that choosing to be less active is itself a powerful intervention. The end phase of therapy is rarely a time for introducing new data, concepts, or skill training. Rather, it is a period of reinforcing and refining, for anticipating future challenges and rehearsing different attitudinal and life-management skills.

The therapist's choices about pacing and timing of sessions are also important interventions. There is often lengthening time between sessions, as clients are encouraged to meet life on their own. They may be enjoined to make up their own homework assignments, and give themselves challenges that require advanced skills. The therapist is likely to respond to clients' requests for advice by suggesting they practice functioning as their own therapist and anticipate what suggestions or advice may have been given.

SECTION TWO: SOPHIA

Sophia was my client about five years ago for a nine-month stint of individual and group therapy. She had heard about my work with people suffering with eating disorders, and thought only such a therapist could possibly help her. Matronly appearing at age 36 when she began treatment, Sophia had been married to Ray for 16 years, and they had two children, a boy and a girl, ages 15 and 14, respectively. Although she presented in therapy with concerns about her weight, it quickly became apparent that the real issues were a serious depression and a very troubled marriage. Sophia confided that what she had *really* wanted was to "find out who I was, be able to make my own decisions, and develop personal strength."

Sophia grew up as a nomadic army brat, the eldest of three sisters. The intense cocktail party scene of military officers provided a setting that contributed to the probable alcoholism of both her parents. Family life was "awful — they fought and yelled and screamed all the time." Although she "never did anything right, and was never acceptable," when her father went off to war (she was five) he admonished her "to be responsible and take care of your mother and sister." Since her mother even then was an unstable, overdependent, emotionally labile woman, this caretaker role was a real one. It was also one which Sophia maintained long after her father returned home; it was still a strong element of her personality when she began therapy.

In fact, when Sophia married at age 20, having realized two weeks prior to the wedding that she was making a mistake, she went through with the ceremony ". . . for my mother's sake. It was her wedding; she was a great hostess and had planned every detail," Sophia explained. Besides, she also thought that her fiancé, Ray, had stomach cancer, and so the marriage would be a short one. In this convoluted way, Sophia decided to marry and achieve her goal of leaving her parents' home, though still acting out the caretaker role. At the time, she and Ray agreed not to have children, and if they did, Sophia could continue her work as an administrator with the government, a job which she loved.

But Ray did not have cancer. Sophia got pregnant one month following the wedding, even though they were using birth control. A second child was born 10 months after the first. Within two years of her wedding, Sophia found herself depressed and a full-time mother, having had to quit her job to care for the children, and living in an isolated rural community. She recalled, "The big event of the day was getting dressed," and described one particularly gloomy period when she sat at the dining room table for hours, crying, day after day, with her dog on her lap.

Clearly, Sophia's marriage, undertaken in hopes of liberation, had become a prison and a cruel disappointment. While her husband, a struggling lawyer, was a caring father, he was also an angry man who drank too much, and abused her emotionally and sexually for the first half of their marriage prior to therapy. He was the kind of man who "always looked for what was wrong, never for what was right," Sophia told me. She didn't remember his exhibiting this negativity or anger before the marriage, but when he "snapped out and began throwing and smashing the ornaments off the tree our first Christmas," Sophia recalled that she "just withdrew, and basically lived in fear from then on."

Sophia had a hysterectomy about seven years into the marriage. At the time, she said she prayed for a miracle, and it came in the unexpected guise of her husband becoming impotent and less abusive following the operation. She also recounted that at certain points during her marriage she had been nearly suicidal, adding that her emotional reaction to several life-threatening antibiotic reactions early on was to hope she would die.

Sophia decided she had to do something to rescue herself when she recognized that God wasn't going to get her off the hook by letting her die. She made her timid beginnings by attending a woman's church group one night a month. Desperate for approval and contact, she began accepting the small jobs they offered her, rapidly demonstrated her capabilities, and told me, "I was like a flower who hadn't seen any sunlight in a long, long time." The church organization proved to be a lifeline, and Sophia began reconstructing herself within its embrace about a year before she came to therapy. The church experience ignited a glimmer of hope against the background of despair that characterized most of her life. Finally, an insight from a small incident related to her husband prompted Sophia to pick up the phone and call for help.

Sophia was highly motivated for therapy, and she immersed herself in the Learner/Judger material. Her therapy would have continued and evolved into work with her and her husband together, but I moved away from Washington after she had been in treatment for about nine months. The total number of contact hours was a little over 100, with the overwhelming majority being in group therapy. Although this termination came sooner than Sophia wanted, and preempted couples therapy, she had already made significant progress. She was grateful for the psycho-educational training and the materials she could keep for reference and study. She told me, "I wasn't about to stop growing just because you left, and I was afraid of going backwards. So I used all those handouts to keep learning, and reinforcing what we accomplished, though I think I relied on the lists of questions the most."

In our three-hour interview, Sophia and I discussed what she had accomplished in therapy, what changes she had made, who she had become subsequently, and how her training as a Learner Self had contributed to the satisfying life she had at the time of this meeting. Her marriage had improved substantially, and she was no longer depressed. In fact, I noted to myself during the interviews and in reviewing the transcripts that she used the word "happy" a number of times, and even referred to "joy" twice. In the years since her therapy, Sophia filled her time with more intense church involvement, a growing number of good friends, fulfilling her lifelong desire to become an artist, and participating in several intense educational programs. Because her husband had a drinking problem and refused to go to therapy, Sophia also decided to join Al-Anon when I left Washington, and the support had been helpful to her.

[The interview that follows is condensed from about three hours of time that Sophia and I spent together. I wanted to get an accurate picture of what had happened over time, as well as her reflections about the psycho-educational aspects of treatment. I found myself asking her many of the questions I had asked myself about her, some of which are listed below. Of course, I was mindful that Sophia had been my client, and my approval and acceptance were still important to her. Following are some of my internal questions as I conducted the interview:

- *Is she __really__ doing as well as she appears to be?*
- *Is she reporting accurately, or could she be skewing her report for my approval?*
- *What specific data and evidence can I get about her changes?*
- *What specific behavioral evidence can I collect about the cornerstones of living as a Learner Self (objective, nondefensive, compassionate self-observation, choice, personal responsibility, a win-win attitude, and positive self-esteem coupled with internal locus of control)?*]

THERAPIST: Sophia, when you came to therapy you told me that your weight and eating felt out of control to you, that you had been depressed for a long time, and that your marriage was in trouble. Was there any one incident that got you to pick up the phone and make that call to me?

CLIENT: Well, one day I came home and wrote down a list of everything my husband told me I couldn't do. Like breathe, walk, talk, dance, you know, we're getting real basic here. And I realized that that's pretty much what my mother had told me. So, anytime I would try anything, even really basic things, I would judge myself. "Am I doing it right?" "Who will see me?" "What have I done wrong this time?" And that's very draining. I just felt defeated, like I couldn't go on anymore.

[Sophia unwittingly demonstrates her current "status" as a Learner Self as she relays this pivotal moment in her life. The ability to self-observe, or assume a metaposition to her own process, has become a natural part of her thinking. Accordingly, note that she has integrated representative Judger self-questions into her memories. She certainly was not aware of them at the time, as she will tell us later.]

CLIENT: I had been living a life where every year I hoped my husband would leave me. At the point when I began therapy my kids were old enough that I knew they would be all right. It was hard to trust the good experiences I had at the church group, and I couldn't see any real alternatives for myself, so I thought, *"If this is life, it's not worth living because there's really nothing here."* Intuitively I knew at some level that life wasn't to be a struggle and painful. But if this was it, well I was out of here.

THERAPIST: Would it be fair to say then, that making that phone call was an attempt to discover that life *could* be something *more* than struggle and pain? (*Sophia nodded "Yes."*) Well then, it was certainly a courageous move.

CLIENT: Now I can see that you're right, but I would never have said it at the time. I was just desperate. I would say I lived out of fear, only I didn't know it, because I was so numb about everything. A lot of fear, anxiety, feeling helpless, feeling hopeless. Numb to the point where I didn't feel anger. Forget feeling my body. Body? What body? There was a lot of repression.

I felt like my problems were all my own fault. Of course, I never questioned it. I never questioned anything. It was like I was to blame, and I was always guilty about it. It seemed like no matter what I said to my parents or my husband, I was wrong, everything was my fault. The idea of being angry was just horrible to me. You know, I was really like the ultimate doormat, and I was sure I deserved to be.

THERAPIST: In other words, you thought that any problems you had with your husband and your parents were because you had done something wrong, or weren't good enough, and you could be blamed for everything? (She nodded "Yes.") You're also saying that you had a lot of feelings, including anger, but you had numbed yourself to your feelings, and in a way, to yourself?

CLIENT: I didn't have any idea who I was—I was just a swirl of bad feelings that I kept trying to push away. It was like not connecting to any emotion because I would be afraid I couldn't control it. I wouldn't allow myself to be angry. It would be too much.

THERAPIST: You wouldn't allow yourself to be angry out of fear that . . .

CLIENT: It wouldn't stop. And I wouldn't allow myself to cry, because I was afraid I couldn't stop, and to tell the truth, there were times when I couldn't stop. Anyway, sometimes crying actually gave me an asthma attack, which would give me an infection, and then I would be sick for weeks.

*   *   *

THERAPIST: You said you didn't question anything or anybody else. Were you aware that you asked *yourself* questions all the time?

CLIENT: No. Not at all. But after we went over that material, especially in the group, I realized I actually *did* ask myself questions, but they were not self-serving—they were self-defeating.

THERAPIST: Was it hard for you to become aware of your internal dialogue, in particular those self-defeating questions?

CLIENT: Actually, it was easier than I would have expected. It made me realize a big reason why things were such a mess in my life was because I was constantly asking the wrong questions.

THERAPIST: What kinds of questions did you ask? Can you give me some examples?

CLIENT: They were the victim, blame-and-shame, and guilt-type of questions, like: "What have I done wrong now?" or "What's wrong with me?" or "Why *bother?"* So, I was either asking those kinds of stupid questions, or, like I said, I didn't question anything. It was very depressing. *(She laughed, shook her head, and rolled her eyes.)* I would feel very nonfunctional and stuck.

THERAPIST: Oh. They were the kinds of questions that put you down in some way and didn't lead anywhere?

CLIENT: Yeah, but really, I don't remember questioning a lot because I didn't think I had the right to question, which to me is having the right of choice. In fact, that's one of the reasons I got married. See, I didn't realize I had a choice. It's like I didn't question the way my parents put me down all the time. I just figured they must be right. I didn't know I could think differently from them. It's hard to believe now, but back then it never occurred to me that I could say "No." It's like I was constantly giving away my power because I didn't know I had any.

[Here Sophia connects her previous lack of awareness of self-questions, her ignorance about having any power to make choices, and the negative impact this had on her experience of self-worth, her behavior, and her life.]

*   *   *

THERAPIST: It sounds like you're equating knowing you have the right and ability to make choices with having personal power. Is that true? *(She nodded "Yes.")* OK then, could you give me an example that occurred during therapy when you recognized you had a choice about how you handled a specific situation that worked out well?

CLIENT: *(Pause.)* OK, I've got one. To someone who hasn't had the experience of being timid or scared all the time, this may not sound earth-shattering. But it was a victory for me because I *did* something totally different than I would have before I started therapy. I remember being startled when I realized how different I'd acted than I would have before. I also remember how shy I felt when we talked about it in the group.

THERAPIST: Are you talking about that parking lot incident with your car? *(She smiled broadly, and nodded "Yes.")* I remember it, too, because it became a symbolic breakthrough for the whole group. In fact, afterward several group members said they used that incident for inspiration when they needed some. I think that was about midway through therapy. Will you describe what happened?

CLIENT: Sure. I remember it like it was yesterday, I guess because we all talked about it so much. It was winter because there was snow on the ground, and it was really cold. I had to run into a store to pick something up, and the only parking spaces were miles away from the door, and I *hate* to be cold. So I parked illegally, put on the blinkers, and ran in the store. Naturally, I got delayed, and when I came out I saw that someone had backed up into my car, and the police were there.

At first I just stood there and stared at the car, and I thought I was going to throw up. I *knew* Ray was going to kill me. Anyway, the old me would have had an anxiety attack on the spot, and blubbered all over the place. But then there was this tiny little moment when I realized I didn't have to act like the old me, that I could *choose* what I was going to do. My stomach settled down and I asked myself, *"How do you want to handle this?"* I even asked, *"Do you want to act like a baby or a grown-up?"* I guess by that question I had already decided. I walked over to the policeman and told him it was my car, and I was responsible because I was illegally parked, even though the other guy hit me. He give me a ticket, of course. Fortunately, the damage wasn't too bad for either car, so we just got each other's numbers and insurance information, and were able to drive away. At that point I should have been really proud of myself, but I knew I still had to face Ray.

On the ride home I worked myself up into a tizzy imagining all kinds of awful things. But I *was* able to stand outside of myself enough to realize that my fear was way out of proportion. I actually pulled over to the side of the road to think. Suddenly I heard your voice in my head. You were saying something like you always used to say. Probably like, *"Is the way you're thinking hurting or helping you?"* So I tuned in to how I was talking to myself and I heard those old self-defeating questions like, *"How could you be so stupid?"* and *"How will he punish me for this?"* I realized I was making myself sick and upset and more afraid by what I was imagining and how I was talking to myself.

So I asked myself what advice you would give. Right away I knew you would say, *"What kind of question could you ask yourself that would let things work out OK?"* So I asked, *"What would make him less angry?"* That might sound like my old question, *"How can I placate him?"* but this was different. I was figuring out a plan.

(Long pause.) Oh. *(She grinned.)* I just now realized there must have been another question. It was probably, *"How can I talk to Ray and work this out so I can respect myself in the end?"* Come to think of it, I probably also asked, *"How can we both be OK at the end of this?"* This is neat. I just learned something about that situation I didn't realize before. That question about self-respect is important for me to keep around.

THERAPIST: Sophia, that was elegant; I take my hat off to you. You just demonstrated *being* a Learner Self while you were describing how you *learned* to be one. Let's finish the story now. What happened with Ray?

CLIENT: I realized he wouldn't be as bothered if he didn't have to pay for fixing the car. So I decided that when I told him what happened, I would also tell him that since it was my responsibility, I would pay for it from the few paintings I had sold. And that's what happened. He wasn't great, but he *was* a lot calmer than usual. He just muttered about how stupid I was for a few days. But he didn't turn red and scream at me as he usually did. What was more important was I didn't cower and cry and apologize the way I would have before. All things considered, I stayed in pretty good shape. And I learned *a lot*. To tell the truth, at the time I could hardly believe I had done so well.

That was the first *real* awakening, that there was another way to look at life, and I could make choices about what I did. I guess I needed to *experience* that that was true by *acting* that way before I could really believe it. Hearing it from you was important, but it wasn't enough. I had to actually *do* something new. Before that I lived in a very victim role. But once I realized I had choice, that's when I could choose to switch to questions that could help me. That whole experience was the turning point in therapy. I felt like I had met a new me.

[Many clients present in therapy with catastrophizing cognitions. Commonly, they are in the form of very negative, unrealistic statements and defeating, limiting Judger-type questions. Because self-talk and especially self-questions are at the root of so many kinds of problems, it is important for therapists to make sure their clients are aware of their internal dialogue and the impact it has on their lives. These learnings set the stage for teaching to observe and correct and for the Choice Model. It is clear from Sophia's comments that she has integrated both.]

✳   ✳   ✳

THERAPIST: Sophia, in addition to the depression that brought you into therapy, and your marriage issues, you also had a problem with overweight and bingeing. You said you felt out of control a lot of the time. Can you remember any changes in that area that occurred during therapy?

CLIENT: Yes. I think this was right near the end, just before you left Washington. I had finally accepted that this weight and eating stuff really *was* complicated and tough. You know me, I was always looking for some magical "quick fix" before that. But I had come to terms with the fact that I binged to stamp down emotion, and also to avoid emotion. Anyway, Ray and I were at my brother-in-law's house. That's James, Ray's brother.

I was annoyed at being there. I hadn't wanted to go, and I let Ray pressure me into going with him. I shouldn't have gone, but I did, and Ray was in a bad mood, and picking on me, so I had to figure out how to handle myself. I tried to get away from him, and I went out to the kitchen, and there was this *gorgeous* tray of fudge on the counter. It was practically magnetic. I couldn't take my eyes off of it.

[Note: She's speaking responsibly and proactively, not reactively. She said, "I let Ray pressure me." The Judger version of that statement would be: "Ray pressured me into going."]

CLIENT: I kept staring at it, and finally I said to myself: "*Sophia, Stop! Why are you staring at this tray of fudge?*" "*What good is this going to do you?*" I knew

I was just plain ticked off. Not totally angry, but definitely annoyed. Ray followed me out to the kitchen, and he really *was* in a foul mood. He didn't feel like helping his brother move the old furniture out of the attic, but he got himself into it. Fortunately, I realized it wasn't my problem. Anyway, he started being nasty and sarcastic because I was always the safe one to get mad at in the family. The more he talked to me like that, the more I could feel myself drawn to the fudge.

But instead of giving in to the cravings as usual, I decided I had to do something about this, that I had a choice about whether to be a victim to his bad mood—or not. I knew I had to stand up to him, not angrily, but matter of factly. And I did. I told him he was really mad at himself, or his brother, but it wasn't me, and I didn't want to hear about it. I told him I didn't like that kind of treatment, and I didn't deserve it. I even told him not to do that to me again. And you know what? He stopped. He got this weird look on his face, and turned around and walked out of the kitchen.

[Again, she has spoken responsibly about her own feelings. She was active in speaking about her old habit of giving in to her cravings, making the assumption that power resided with her, not with any cravings. If she were in a Judger mode she would have spoken this passively. For example, she might have said, "the cravings got me." In this incident, Sophia has given us a demonstration of internal locus of control mirrored in the way she uses language, including the presuppositions embedded therein.]

CLIENT: What I was happiest about was I didn't eat the fudge. I knew that eating it would have been avoiding dealing with him, which was what I wasn't ever willing to do before. It seemed like I used to always be afraid. That was a big part of my eating. If I'd been an alcoholic who had stopped drinking I would have just been able to tell myself "No," but I was upset, and that tray of fudge sort of glowed at me. It even had some pieces cut out so nobody would have noticed if I'd taken a few. I think the way I was able to avoid the fudge and deal with the real issue was that I'd started to develop what you called "*intelligent* self-control" instead of the old kind when I just forced myself to go on those rigid, fad diets that always ended up with me out of control and bingeing.

THERAPIST: I do remember your telling us about that now. You really *did* do great. Sophia, you said this happened near the end of our work together. What do you think would have happened if the fudge incident had happened at the beginning or around the middle of therapy?

CLIENT: Impossible in the beginning. That kind of thing was what I came to therapy for in the first place. After a few months I already had a lot of what you taught us under my belt, so I was beginning to handle myself better. But you're missing something here. There was nothing special about the fudge. Those kinds of incidents happened *all* the time. Which means that I'd had zillions of opportunities just as good as that one. It's just that all the elements hadn't come together before. In fact, that's why I was at James' in the first place; I hadn't been able to say "No" to Ray. Maybe that was the straw that broke the camel's back. By the time the fudge thing got added on top of that, I was over the edge and *had* to do something. I was ready and what I did really worked.

THERAPIST: It sure did. You noticed the temptation. You observed yourself and your reaction. Instead of just getting mad, and putting the blame on him, you realized your reaction was *your* responsibility. Instead of giving in to old automatic *reactions*, you *responded* by asking yourself questions that helped you make a choice about your behavior and how to deal with your husband effectively.

[Note that the language I used here refers specifically to the Choice Model. (See Chapter 4.)]

THERAPIST: Sophia, this is a terrific example of acting from your Learner Self and asking yourself the kinds of questions that help people make good choices. I'd like to go back and explicate the process you took yourself through. OK? *(She nodded "Yes.")*

CLIENT: You want to know what questions I asked myself, I'll bet. *(I nodded "Yes.")* Well, I can't pretend to remember them exactly, but it doesn't really matter. This will be a good test. You taught us to backtrack logically and figure out what questions *had* to have been there to get us to wherever we were.

THERAPIST: Good. That's right, I'm glad you remember that. This is another aspect of thinking in an observe and-correct manner, which was the basis of so much we did. It's important to remember that good correcting *depends first* on good observing. And an important aspect of observing is figuring out how you got wherever you are in the first place. I don't mean *why* we might have gotten there—that's an explanation and an interpretation. I'm talking about *how* we get to any particular mental/emotional place. That's *operational*, and happens in some sequence, like left foot, then right foot, then left foot, or first I thought this, then I asked myself that, then I answered this other way.

Obviously, the "how" refers mostly to language and self-talk. The "why" part might have something to do with our upbringing, or how we found out about sex, or anything like that. Now that kind of thing is critically important, but it's not what I'm talking about here. What I asked you and the other group members to do was separate the psychological path you traveled to this moment from the linguistic, sequential one. This is tricky, in fact almost impossible to do completely, because we express ourselves psychologically *and* emotionally through language.

CLIENT: Well, I see that you still get on a soap box when you're talking about this stuff. *(She said this teasingly.)* What is it you want me to talk about?

THERAPIST: *(I laughed with her.)* I do have that tendency, don't I? Thanks. So we're talking about being a good observer and figuring out the sequence that got you to whatever you're observing in the moment. A retrospective analysis helps you figure that out. Do you remember what it is? *(She nodded "Yes.")* Good, will you describe it then?

CLIENT: It's how a person goes about finding the background questions, or the questions you're answering with whatever you're doing right now. It would work the same way if you're wondering about what questions led up to something you did last week or last year that you want to understand better. What you do first is observe whatever result you've got. Then you ask, *"What questions must I have been asking myself in order to end up here?"* Then it's just a matter of logic and thinking backwards, which becomes almost automatic pretty quickly. We learned how to do this in the group. It helped us find the actual questions that set us off on the right or wrong track, depending on whether or not we were happy with where we ended up.

THERAPIST: You did that very well, Sophia. You said this thinking backwards becomes almost automatic. By thinking backwards, I assume you mean simply wondering what questions must logically have been in the background to lead naturally to where you are? *(She nodded "Yes.")* Was it difficult to learn to do that?

CLIENT: Actually, it's amazing how natural that's become. I can't imagine not being able to do it now. All right. Here are some of the questions I must have been asking myself in that situation with the fudge: *"Why are you in the kitchen, looking at that fudge when you just ate an hour ago?"* *"Do you want to go backwards?"* *"Is this going to help you deal with him?"* Also *"How will you feel in an hour if you dive into the fudge now?"* *"Will you respect yourself?"* *"Are you going to take the coward's way out?"* *"Come on, Sophia. What's going on here?"* Finally, I said, *"What do I really want?"* How's that? Not bad, huh? *(She looks obviously pleased with herself.)*

THERAPIST: Great. Let's keep going. How did you answer yourself, especially the last question?

CLIENT: I realized I wanted this situation over with. And I wanted Ray to feel OK about himself, even though it was very important that he got my point. I wanted him to realize I've changed, and figure out how I expect to be treated now. I also wanted him to see that I could be fair and in control even when I'm upset. I think what I actually asked myself was: *"What can I say to end this situation without making it worse, and feel OK about it?* and *"How can I tell him how I feel without putting him down?"*

THERAPIST: This is very helpful because it demonstrates how simple it is to think out these questions and understand how they lead us to behave as we do; and in this case, succeed as you did. Thanks.

*   *   *

THERAPIST: Sophia, when we spoke on the phone to set up this interview, you mentioned that you still consult the Learner/Judger Chart every once in a while, and that you continue to find it helpful. Would you comment on what works for you about it, and *how* you use it?

CLIENT: Well, it's hard to know where to start. Maybe with when you first gave it to us? (*I nodded.*) To be honest, when you handed it out, I looked at the thing and it seemed so *long*. I remember wishing you'd just give me some answers about what I should do with my life, rather than making me work this hard. You must have read my mind, because right off you said that the chart might look overwhelming, but it was actually much simpler than it looked. You also said it was important to teach people *how* to fish, rather than just giving them fish to eat. You said you wanted to give us something *substantial* that would help with whatever reasons we came to therapy, and that we could use for the rest of our lives. You said you would teach us this stuff, and it would become obvious and easy after a while. I remember saying "*Sure*," under my breath, but I'm glad to say you were right.

THERAPIST: I'm glad to hear it, too, because that means you *have* continued to find it simple to use, *and* helpful. (*Sophia emphatically nodded "Yes."*) Can you think of a specific situation that happened with Ray or your children during therapy where the chart made an obvious difference?

CLIENT: Yeah, as a matter of fact something happened with our older son, Tim, just before we ended therapy. I remember being upset because I couldn't get an appointment with you the day it happened, so I really felt like I was on my own. I was *forced* to use the chart, and it turned out to be a good thing because we handled the problem pretty well. In fact, I think I did a great job. (*She grinned at this last statement.*)

When you asked to do this interview I went back over some of the notes I made during therapy so I could remember things better. There was even more material than I remembered. Guess you really do like handouts! I came across some stuff I had written down when we had that problem with Timmy.

THERAPIST: It's good to hear you give yourself a pat on the back. I do recall that incident. Would you refresh my memory please and go over what happened?

CLIENT: We got a call from school that Tim was caught in the bathroom smoking marijuana with some of his friends. The call came during the day, so I was home by myself. I remember I was trembling when I got off the phone. I thought my kids had survived our difficult marriage, and now it seemed like it wasn't true. I know I shouldn't have done it, but I ran upstairs to Tim's room, and tore it apart, and found a small bag of that stuff in his dresser drawer. Then I sat on his bed and cried.

THERAPIST: That could throw any parent for a loop. What did you do next?

CLIENT: At first I just sat there, I was in such shock. Then I realized I had to tell Ray, and I should do it before Tim got home from school. So I called my husband at his office. I knew he was going to be upset, but I didn't expect him to go *that* ballistic on me. Especially not on the telephone. But he just went out of control. It's a good thing his secretary had gone to lunch, because if she'd heard him, she might have quit. But it wasn't how loud he got that really upset me, it was that he *blamed everything* on *me*. He said I babied Tim and made him into a "Mama's boy," and that if it weren't for me, Tim would be getting better grades, and on and on and on. Then he said he was coming right home, and slammed down the phone.

I could hardly breathe. To tell the truth, that was the worst moment. It dawned on me that Ray was not going to help—in fact, it was more like I was going to have to deal with *two* children—my son *and* my husband. Not only was my husband not going to help with the problem, he was going to make it worse if I didn't stop him. I wanted to call you, but you were gone to some conference. It was really a rude awakening, I can tell you. But at least I woke up. I realized this was *my* job, nobody was going to help me, not you, not Ray, not anybody. It was all on *my* shoulders.

I was having a hard time getting my thinking straightened out about what to do, and I *had* to get myself back together before Ray got home— which gave me only about 45 minutes. I desperately wanted to talk to you. I think I actually asked you a question out loud: "Well, what would you do about *this* one?" Much to my surprise, I got an answer: "*Look at the Learner/Judger Chart.*"

Of course, I did go get the chart, and on the first page, *bam*, there was Ray. He was definitely reacting, he was stuck on what was wrong, on how bad things were—he was fixated on problems and on what was negative. He was *sure* that he was right about how bad I was, and that everything was *my* fault. On the phone at least, he had taken no responsibility for *his* effect on our son, he blamed me only for *mine*. Then I looked at some of the other sections. He was being critical, judgmental, and blaming. To tell the truth, I was starting to enjoy finding him plastered all over the Judger Self side of the chart. And then suddenly I realized *I* was acting like a Judger Self, that I was looking at the chart for what was wrong with *Ray*, rather than figuring out what I could do to help resolve this mess, which is how a Learner Self would obviously act. I decided to skim over the chart to get help about what I should do.

[Note that Sophia, acting as a skillful Learner, observed *herself* coming from the Judger position. She did *not* put herself down, or judge herself for being judgmental. She simply put herself into the consciousness of a problem-solving mode.]

CLIENT: I wrote down just the things on the Learner Self side that jumped off the page at me. That one about the difference between responsibility and blame was one of the first things I noticed on the chart. Another thing that made a big difference when I thought about Tim was that Learner question: *"Is this situation with Tim personal to me?"* I thought about that hard and decided it wasn't. I really didn't believe that Tim did this to get back at me for anything. So I didn't think it was personal that way. Also, no matter how much my husband tried to stick me with the blame for ruining our son, I knew it wasn't true. And I certainly didn't believe our son was "ruined" like my husband said. Yes, I was responsible as a parent, but I wasn't to *blame*. I didn't *cause* this problem, it was much more complicated than that. So anyway, while there were certainly issues to think about, I could separate myself from them enough that I *could think* objectively.

Believe it or not, I still keep the list I made that day. After everything worked out, I was so pleased with myself that I decided to keep it as a souvenir for future reference. I put it in my folder of handouts we used in the group. Do you want to hear the rest of my list?

THERAPIST: Are you kidding? That's the best offer I've had all day.

CLIENT: OK, here it is. *Respond* instead of *react* to situations. Be a problem solver. Be active and flexible. Take responsibility for self, instead of blaming self or others. Look from different points of view—that's like walking a mile in somebody else's moccasins. Most important, you said ask *genuine* questions—that means questions you don't already know the answer to. You said that to be a Learner Self, we had to ask questions with curiosity, and not ask them like we were condemning or accusing people, especially before we had all the information we needed. That last thing was a big key in this situation.

I asked myself if I knew everything I needed to know, and I realized there was a *lot* of information we didn't have about this problem with Tim. We didn't know who the other boys were, or whether Tim had been doing this a long time, or whether he was a follower or a leader. We needed to talk to the school, to Tim, to the other boys and their parents, and find out all kinds of things. I also realized that Ray *and I* were both overreacting. Then I realized that if we started jumping all over Tim, he would just decide we were against him, and clam up, and we might never know what really happened. It wouldn't have been fair to Tim. And it would have been *terrible* for our relationship.

I knew I had to get Ray to act like a Learner *with* me, and also with Tim. Otherwise, everything was going to blow up even worse. That thought made me depressed for a minute. I just didn't see how I could get Ray to be different. I obviously asked myself that question, because I got an idea. Since Ray is a lawyer, I could appeal to his logical, problem-solving mind—which works great in relation to everybody except us, his family. That thought helped me relax. Since I seemed to be the only functioning adult around, I needed to take charge right from the start. If I didn't stop Ray from going on a tirade, we might never get on a good track. I had to think and act like a problem solver. I had to stay calm, which also meant *not* to react emotionally if he accused me again of being responsible for everything. We needed to have *something* worked out before Tim got home, or it would be an awful mess.

By the time Ray got home, I was still a little shaky, but I was ready for him. Also, thankfully, he had cooled off a little, though I hate to think how the other drivers on the road had to pay for it. My strategy of appealing to Ray as a logical, problem-solving lawyer worked. We decided we would talk to Tim together the minute he got home, and tell him exactly what happened. And that before we jumped to any awful conclusions, we should find out the truth.

To make a long story short, in the end it turned out not to be such a big deal. Tim had tried marijuana for the first time only a month before, and he told us it made his throat burn, but he hadn't wanted the other guys to think he was a sissy. He was holding on to the bag of dope for his friend Jonathan, who was really the leader. We talked to the school, and the other parents, especially Jonathan's mother. We ended up grounding Tim for the month. And that was that.

At least, that was that with Tim. For Ray and me it was an important time. He actually complimented me on my cool thinking, and admitted he overreacted. I think that's when he started showing me more respect. But it would never have come from him if I hadn't acted like I did. I had to *prove* myself—and that could happen only if I had changed *first*. I also recognized that if I treated Ray less like a Judger and more like a Learner, it would help him *become* more like one. This was a sweet victory.

THERAPIST: And an impressive one at that. I was sure after that parking lot incident that you were also becoming capable of handling much more complicated situations. This thing with Tim is living proof.

*　*　*

THERAPIST: Now, I have some questions about the chart itself, not the content of it. Did it make a difference for you, having the chart to look at and take home and study? Did you like the way it was laid out? Or would it have been just as helpful if we had just talked about all that material?

CLIENT: Oh No! You've got to give people the chart! They have to have it. Don't change the chart! It really helped me to have everything so concrete, written out in black and white, and in those two separate columns. Those columns make me remember that I always have a choice about how to *be*, and they show me what my choices actually are. It's sort of like having a cheat-sheet about life. Just about everything's there, if you look hard enough. When I have it in front of me, I can just look at it, and ask myself: "*Am I there (pointing to the Judger Self side) or there (pointing to the Learner Self side) right now?*"

[Note that with this last question, Sophia used layperson's language to describe the formal operations stage of cognitive development. The cognitive position she took was meta to herself, simply nonattached, non-judgmental self-observation. She was able to wonder about whether she was operating as a Judger Self without blaming herself or putting herself down in any way.]

CLIENT: I would never have remembered most of what was there if it weren't written down. I like consulting with it; it's sort of like an old friend at this point. I used to go back to look at it a lot. I still do, but not so much anymore because when I do look at it I find that I already know what it's going to say. Another reason to give people their own copy of the chart is that all this information doesn't usually make sense all at once. At least it didn't for me, and that's what some of the other group members said, too. Some of the stuff on there didn't become obvious, or important, until later on.

THERAPIST: Well, you're certainly clear about that! *(We both laughed.)* Do you remember that I used to talk about people having permanent residence on one side of the chart and taking vacations to the other side? And with regard to our problems, we mostly start out with permanent residence on the Judger Self side, so the goal of therapy is to get free from there and activate the Learner Self side? Did that analogy work for you?

CLIENT: It did because it made it safe for me to risk.

THERAPIST: Please tell me more about that.

CLIENT: Even though I was coming from the Judger Self side, which was a familiar home at that time, it was like I could open the door and take this little trip, and try thinking a different way, try feeling a different way, asking questions a different way. And if it wasn't comfortable, or it became threatening, I could go back to my little Judger Self hole. But more times than not, I found I enjoyed it over here *(on the Learner Self side).* It was fun. There was some juice to it, and I just started visiting more often.

THERAPIST: Can you remember some of the Judger questions that used to keep you from taking risks?

CLIENT: Oh, that's easy. Questions like: *"How am I going to get hurt now?"* *"Where's the danger?" "How can I protect myself?" "How can I get safe?" "How can I stop the fear?"* Back then, I *didn't* ask myself questions like, *"What could I gain from this risk?"* or *"Is it worth it?"* But I do now.

THERAPIST: Could you actually feel the difference in yourself when you moved over to the Learner Self side? *(She nodded "Yes.")* What *is* the difference?

CLIENT: It's lighter. More joyous. For me, it's more grounding. It's like, I can come over here, and I can stick my toe in the surf. Maybe I don't know how to swim yet, but I can sure get my feet wet. And then, if I feel like it's getting too deep, then I don't have to go all the way back there. I can go back just part way, knowing I'm going to try again.

THERAPIST: So it was a way for you to practice taking on a new identity without feeling you had to leave everything you knew behind?

CLIENT: Yeah. But it was more than that, too. It was really important that I didn't feel like you were judging or rejecting me, or anybody in the group, for being on the Judger Self side. It was just something that was so, and we were going to study it. I think that made me freer to observe myself when I was over there. And then I began to realize that if I was less critical and more just noticing, I was actually waking up the Learner Self in me, which made me really happy. It was almost like when I observed myself being a Judger Self—this might sound strange—but it was like I was observing myself observing myself. I know that sounds weird, and it *felt* weird at first, but then it just became normal. I think that more and more, when I was acting like a Judger Self, I was taking my Learner Self eyes with me. That's what I try to do all the time now. And nowadays, if I fall into my Judger Self, I *do* take my Learner eyes with me. I am not who I was before.

* * *

THERAPIST: I'm interested in more detail about what's happened for you in the years since we worked together. I'm especially interested in areas where you feel like you've made significant changes. Will you go into that?

CLIENT: I was trying to think back on that, and what came up most vividly was what I did with the church pretty soon after therapy ended when you moved to New Jersey. In my church group, I had worked my way into being a delegate for our region. Right after therapy, I was asked to be president, and if they had asked me before, I would have said, "Oh, no, I can't do that." But therapy gave me the ability to *think through* the opportunity. So when I was given that opportunity, I asked myself about the people, the support system I would have around me, and how much I could grow. Finally I thought, "*I can do this.*" My thinking was that I could try it, and if it didn't work, "*Well fine.*" If it did, that would be fine, too. In fact, it would be great. And I would learn some important things no matter what happened. Before therapy, failure would not have been acceptable. In fact, I didn't do a lot of things because I was so afraid of being a failure.

THERAPIST: Sophia, this is very impressive.

CLIENT: Thanks. And I went on and accepted the position of president of my church organization. I was the first and *only* woman president of the region, up until today. I still have people coming to tell me I was the best. It was a wonderful opportunity because I had a chance to use my new skills. I had come to realize that my quietness was a gift, even though I had been told all my life it wasn't right. But I had finally accepted it as the gift it was. And I discovered that I could use it to be a peacemaker, which was exactly what was needed at that time. Being president gave me a viable way of using everything I had learned. It also gave me an arena outside of home where I could discover things about myself, which was very important. That was one of the ways I discovered how much I had grown, and how much I had changed. It was a process of discovery; it didn't happen all at once.

* * *

THERAPIST: You told me your marriage is much happier, and you expect to stay together with your husband, which is a real turnaround from where you were. You've already described some situations that help me understand the progress you've made in your marriage. Can you tell me more?

CLIENT: It's true. Our relationship *has* changed a lot, and I'm still a little surprised about that. That started when I was in therapy, which we've already talked about. That was the beginning, and it's picked up steam. What happened was that as I've changed, he's changed. It's funny—because I tried to change him for such a long time, and I finally realized I couldn't make anybody else do what *I* wanted them to do. Therapy also helped me focus on what was *his* and what was *mine*. So when some issue came up, I started asking myself, "Is this *his issue or is it mine?*" I had to learn to detach from him. I had to remember to do it a lot, rather than just now and then. Doing that consistently made a big difference. Then I could think about the relationship differently. Throughout therapy and especially afterwards, I kept asking myself questions about the relationship, and what I wanted, and what I could realistically do about that.

THERAPIST: That's quite a process. What did you ask yourself?

CLIENT: "*Why was he in my life?*" and "*What good can come from this relationship?*" instead of old questions like, "*How did I get myself into this mess?*" It finally dawned on me that I needed to change the way I looked at my husband if this marriage was going to have any chance at all. At some point during therapy I realized that I could think of him as a gift because he supported me financially, and this allowed me to take advantage of opportunities to grow, like being in therapy.

And slowly, I started *looking* at him as a gift, and he *became* a gift. When I decided I wasn't going to react to him out of fear anymore, it was almost like a door spinning. That incident with the fudge, and the one with Tim and the dope, and some of the other stories I've told you were the beginning of that. Suddenly there were more choices about how to be. I started feeling good about myself more and more. Even happy sometimes. It was like all of a sudden I was connected. I was in my body, and I was connected, mind, body, and spirit as one.

From that, when things would happen between Ray and me, I would go back to who *I* was. I would ask myself questions like, "*What's true to me?*" "*Is this who I am?*" "*What's good for me?*" "*How do I want to respond to this?*" And sometimes, I would be mad as hell, and I would just step back, observe the anger, and think, "*Will this serve me if I react, if I meet his anger with anger?*" And sometimes I let him know I was angry, but that was because I thought it would be helpful. Anyway, it was good to finally *feel* anger—and even better to know how to handle it.

I went through a phase of that—which I needed to do—because I had repressed my anger for so long. But I was turning this around in my head, and I also realized being angry and reacting wouldn't serve either of us. So, I just kept supporting him, and his anger started disappearing. Once he actually told me that I wasn't as much fun as I used to be! I think he really likes to argue, and I wouldn't play anymore. I met the energy but I didn't engage. This didn't happen as fast as it's sounding right now, but as long as I stayed aware of my goal to be true to myself and also support him, it was OK with me. Like I said, I started relating to him differently while I was still in therapy, as you know, and then it kept gathering steam afterwards.

THERAPIST: That's pretty remarkable.

CLIENT: And then he had a choice of whether he wanted to escalate and try to fight or not, and it got so that he chose: *"Oh, that's okay. It's not that important."* And so, his anger just started disappearing, and mine did too.

THERAPIST: That's a beautiful example of being responsible for yourself, working on your *own* changes, and then Ray had to accommodate to the new you in some way.

CLIENT: Um-hum. It helped to think about the chart and remember that a Learner Self thinks of everybody else like they could be strong in their Learner Self, too. I had Ray pegged as a really stuck Judger for so long, and I *know* I treated him that way. When I opened my mind to think about him another way, I think I started treating him differently. It also helped that he slowed down his drinking. He's still a maintenance drinker, but it's minimal, and his personality doesn't change as much now when he drinks. Plus, he has a lot less anger when he doesn't drink.

THERAPIST: It's amazing to see how much our expectations can script how we relate to people and how that affects them. When you made your switch from Judger Self to Learner Self you could see other people as having the potential of changing, too. I mean, you played it right out.

CLIENT: Yes, but don't get too carried away here. We *are* doing well, but we still have a ways to go.

✳   ✳   ✳

THERAPIST: Is there one thing you can isolate that made the biggest difference in how you're being in your marriage, and in your becoming the person who's sitting here with me today?

CLIENT: I know you think that's a hard question, but it's not really. Because if I didn't know I have choice all the time, then none of the other stuff would have fallen into place. Realizing that is what woke me up. If I didn't know about choice, how could I be responsible for what I say, and do, and think in my life? I don't think I could. I don't think it's possible to be in charge of your own life if you think someone else is doing it to you.

I think my previous life was all reaction, because I didn't have a dialogue with people. I would just react to what they said, and then I took it on. Now I know I have a choice about what I do, and I don't just automatically take on other people's stuff any more. If somebody dumps on me, I have a responsibility to myself to make a choice not to accept that, or to work it out with the other person. If my goal in life is to maintain my integrity and live from my heart, then I'm responsible for my actions with other people. I think the gift of life is being able to make a choice. So, when I go on automatic, I give away my right to a choice, which was like giving away my life, only I didn't know I was doing it. That used to be me all the time. That's not me anymore.

THERAPIST: That's an important statement about who you are now—a strong, confident, caring woman. This helps me see what has helped your marriage improve. At least, here is my understanding of it. Now when you give to your husband, it's because you *choose* to, not because you *have* to like in the old days when you felt like you had to take care of everybody because you felt guilty if you didn't. You're not just acting out that caretaker role, or giving to him in hopes that he'll then be able to, or want to, give to you. *(She nodded.)* I can see how this change on your part could be liberating for *both* of you.

CLIENT: I think that *is* what's happened, and it's made all the difference in the world. The funny thing is, if you had described this process to me before it all happened, I'm not sure it would have really made sense. Having traveled down that road, it now makes a lot of sense. In fact, it's the only thing that *does* make sense; that is, if I want to respect myself and *also* have my marriage work.

* * *

THERAPIST: Let's change the focus here. Is there anything you're disappointed about? Anything you haven't accomplished, or still wish were different?

CLIENT: Well, I'm not perfect yet, but I'm still trying! *(She laughed.)* Oops. Cancel that! Actually, I've mostly given up trying to be perfect. I know for sure now that's a way to punish myself, *not* help myself, and I try not to let myself go down that road. But, to tell the truth, I'd have thought I would have finished losing weight by now. That's what I'm disappointed about.

I hated it when you said that sometimes healing happens from the inside out, and that overweight and overeating were often signs that something was out of balance in your life, that other things needed to be handled first. But you were right.

THERAPIST: Has becoming slimmer become a different priority for you?

CLIENT: It really has. I've spent these last few years cleaning up my life and my marriage. I discovered that getting back to the weight I was when I got married was pretty low on the totem pole when I compared it with the goal of getting my life together. I also realized that my weight expectations weren't realistic for me. After all, I've had two kids, and I'm over twenty years older. Another good thing is that I'm much more comfortable with my body, and also my sexuality, and *that* really makes a difference. But I guess the truth is that with summer coming, I'd still love to look better in a bathing suit.

*   *   *

THERAPIST: What do you do these days when you find yourself in a bad mood, or you are upset or down, how do you deal with it? How do you get yourself out of it?

CLIENT: I have a lot of little things I do when I want to take care of myself, whether it's just sitting in the bathtub, listening to music, walking in woods, calling a friend, maybe reading. In the past, I would never take the time to do that for myself. I would think I had to sink in the mud, or tough my way through it. Where now, I know that if I don't attend to myself, I'll just make life miserable for me and everybody else, too.

THERAPIST: Well, that's true. Let's go back and see if we can identify the process, because what you are describing now is very good problem solving. First, I'm curious, how often do you get these kinds of feelings?

CLIENT: Not very often. Not even weekly; I don't know if it's even monthly anymore.

THERAPIST: Goodness. How much was it before?

CLIENT: All the time. Every day. Most of the day. Well, only when I was awake. *(She laughed heartily.)* It's like being a new person, but I have the memories from the past.

THERAPIST: That's a neat description. On those rare occasions now, when you find yourself upset, or in a bad mood, assuming you notice it, what's the next step after that?

CLIENT: I say something like, "Oh, *dear, what's going on?*" I can sense something is out of whack. I'll take extra time to check in with myself, which is sort of like observing. Then I'll ask questions like: "*What could possibly be affecting me like this?*" "*Am I missing something?*" "*Is there something I need to do today?*" to make sure it's not an external pressure, like it might be a meeting that I'm not real keen on going to, or something like that. So, I try to zero in on exactly why I might be stressed out.

THERAPIST: Then what do you ask yourself?

CLIENT: *"What do I need to do to shift this mood?"* Then I would move into a plan of action.

THERAPIST: Do you *really* think of it that way? That's one of the questions we talked about in the group. What would a plan consist of?

CLIENT: It would depend on the answer to: *"What do I need to do to shift this mood?"* Maybe I need to be outside in nature that day; maybe I need a quiet day alone. I guess I ask, *"What do I need to do to take care of myself?" "Why am I feeling out of sorts?" "Do I need to connect with a friend?" "What needs to be fed?"*

THERAPIST: *"What needs to be fed?"* That's nice. *"What part of me needs to be fed?"*

CLIENT: Right. Is it emotional, physical, mental, maybe even spiritual?

THERAPIST: And you would go through a process like that, very quickly mentally? What percentage of the time are you able to shift out of that mood?

CLIENT: Oh. Most of the time. Sometimes it's almost instantaneously. It usually shifts within a few hours. In a situation where I have to actually go out of the house because there's something I have to attend to, like meetings or something, I can just set it aside. I can leave the mood home and say, *"I'll take care of you when I come back home."*

THERAPIST: At this point, I sense that you trust yourself to do that.

CLIENT: Right. Right. And I can just go out and be in the world, and I'll be fine. Sometimes, when I get home I'll have changed enough so there's no longer a need. I think it depends a lot on my schedule. But there are also times when I sense there's more to it than that, and I just want to be with my mood. Then I'll ask, *"What is this mood trying to tell me?"*

THERAPIST: Is that like asking, *"Is there some value to staying in this place right now?"*

CLIENT: Right. That's when my Learner questions are really important. Because maybe there's something I'm avoiding, or something I have to deal with. I'll ask myself: *"What's really going on here?" "Is there something I need to resolve?" "Am I being honest with myself?" "Is there something I need to learn?" "What do I want to do about this?"* And then I have to be very quiet, and wait for my answers. The key is that I really *do* want to know, and that I really do want to get back to a good place. What's so important for me now is that I really do know what a good place is for me, and I know how to get there. You know what? Being the way I am now—how I handle myself and my marriage and my life—is something I couldn't have even imagined before I started therapy. It's like the whole world has opened up for me. It was there all along, but I didn't know how to get to it. Now I do.

THERAPIST: Sophia, this has been very helpful, and it's been a pleasure to see you again, and find out how well you're doing. Thank you so much.

SUMMARY

The end phase of therapy operates simultaneously as a completion and a launching. The goal of this last part of therapy is to further empower the Learner Self aspects of the client, so this becomes his or her dominant mode of operating in the world. In order to achieve this goal, the therapist must begin to move out of the role of expert, and focus on reinforcing her clients' ability to apply Learner Self thinking to their lives, especially in situations outside of therapy sessions. The case study of Sophia was presented to illustrate this process.

11

A Single-Visit Stop on the Trip: The Case of Brian

What does e.e. cummings say? "Always the most beautiful answer, who asks the more difficult question." You see I am not asking another question each time. I am making the same question bigger.
— GREGORY BATESON

There are several circumstances, other than "therapist-shopping," which lead to intentional and successful single-session contacts with clients. For example, a client may solicit advice for a narrowly defined problem, or seek verification of a path already chosen. A colleague may refer a client for a consultation, desiring the secondary therapist's viewpoints and suggestions. Or a colleague may refer a client for work she doesn't consider within the realm of her own expertise. The referral could also be a strategic move on the part of the initial therapist if, for example, he or she presumed that a different therapist, as a new authority, might stimulate a more effective result.

In any case, it is an interesting discipline to assume that a single session "cure," or intervention might be all that's needed in a particular instance. Whether it is warranted, this presupposition allows for some creative interventions that may not have occurred to a therapist had she been making different assumptions. This is illustrated in the case of Brian, whose single-session consultation comprises this chapter. The referral of Brian to my practice was a strategic move on the part of Dr. John Brown, his former therapist, who had worked successfully with Brian and his wife, and felt that his previous client would be better served by seeing a different therapist for the current issue.

Since large context shifts also result in smaller, second-level changes, I constantly ask myself questions, such as, *"What's the most encompassing intervention that could alter everything within it?"* as well as *"What's the smallest intervention that could make the biggest impact?"* In a single-session consultation, I would pick only a small behavioral detail to work with if I considered it emblematic of a large contextual shift that could be accomplished through it. There are other questions that I typically ask myself in a consultation situation, as well as in an initial interview, and during ongoing therapy. These include: *"What is this client not seeing that is keeping him stuck?" "How could he be led to view or consider this situation anew that would bring him relief and/or resolution?"* and *"What question(s) is he not asking himself, the asking of which could be helpful or even open the door to a breakthrough?"* This latter question turned out to be helpful with Brian.

The Case of Brian

Brian was a 37-year-old attorney in Washington, D.C., who had been married to his second wife, Elizabeth, also an attorney, for twelve years. This was Elizabeth's first marriage. They had two sons, ages 8 and 10. Brian also had one son, age 17, from his former marriage. Up until about a year before our session, Brian and Elizabeth had been in couples' therapy with a colleague of mine, Dr. John Brown. At that time, the presenting issue had been an extramarital affair on Brian's part. That therapy concluded with Brian choosing to reembrace his marriage and completely severing ties with the other woman.

Brian recently contacted Dr. Brown, and reported that he was depressed. Dr. Brown, in turn, referred Brian to me as a consult and told me a great deal about Brian and his previous couples' therapy, which had included extensive family-of-origin work. He also told me that Brian had completed a course of individual therapy about 14 years earlier following the breakup of his first marriage, when he recognized the necessity of understanding himself better in order to avoid future relationship mistakes.

Brian was the oldest of three sons of an intact marriage. He grew up in Indiana and married at age 19 when his college girlfriend became pregnant. After graduation they moved to Washington with their young son so Brian could attend law school while his wife pursued doctoral studies in anthropology. Within a short time, their hasty, too-young marriage collapsed, and they divorced. Over time, however, their bitterness softened into an amiable friendship. They had joint custody of their son, whose main domicile was with his mother. After a short stint in the public defender's office, Brian landed an enviable job with a prestigious Washington law firm, and had been working there ever since. It was there that he met and fell in love with Elizabeth, whom he married two years later.

This is not a typical first interview for two reasons, both having to do with the nature of the referral. First, I had much more information about Brian before the interview than is usual, and because Brian was aware of this, he felt he could get to the point quickly. Second, we both knew Dr. Brown's bias that this issue could be resolved in short order, maybe in a single session or perhaps in just a few.

In reading the transcript, it is obvious that Brian was more facile with thinking about questions than most clients, especially in the beginning of therapy. I attribute this to the fact that he had completed so much previous therapy and that he was an attorney, one of the few professions where question theory and practice is routinely taught.

I knew that Brian's difficulties were emotionally complex; and frankly, before the session, I didn't know whether, or how, I might be helpful. When I asked myself, "*What might be the most fruitful beginning strategy?*" my answer was simply to just "be with" him without judgment, and ask questions that might produce fertile openings for interventions.

Question-centered therapy presumes that many of people's conflicts and experiences of being "stuck" develop because they lack new questions that could lead them to fresh perspectives, new resources, and potential resolutions. Therefore, I consider my role, in part, to help clients discover new questions to help shift them out of paradigms where they've been stuck and questions which could lead them to new paradigms where fulfilling resolutions might occur. An individual's own "right" answers often become available once he discovers new questions that are key to opening those perceptual doors. I quickly discovered that Brian was insightful, motivated, articulate, and eager to walk through doors.

ANNOTATED TRANSCRIPT: A CONSULTATION

THERAPIST: So, Brian, you know that Dr. Brown told me a lot about you, and about what's been going on. Tell me, what is it you want to accomplish here?

CLIENT: Let me give you a little more background, OK? I had a fairly long-term affair with another woman, whom I loved very much and still do. I ended that a year ago after my wife and I were in therapy with Dr. Brown. Basically, I agreed not to have any communication with this other woman. I ended that relationship in order to be exclusively with my wife, whom I also love very much. I grieved for months and I still really miss her, even though I haven't seen her at all.

Every day, it's almost like I lead a double life. I have a fantasy life, where she is included, not in any bad way, but whenever I go some place I wish she were there. I can't go to a mall without thinking about what I would buy for her. *(He starts to get teary.)* Geez. I didn't realize I still have this much emotion about it. This situation brought me into therapy last year because of the conflict. Every other aspect of my life is great. My relationship with my wife has continually gotten better and better, but I am in love with this other woman and I continue to be so. I guess I've also been depressed. And I don't know what to do about it.

THERAPIST: It's really gotten to you and it hurts.

CLIENT: Yup.

THERAPIST: What questions are you asking yourself about this?

CLIENT: I've had a lot of questions. I can give you the current ones, even though there have been lots of other questions. Some of them are: "*Well, what do I do about this?*" "*What will make me happy?*" "*What will be the most loving*

*thing for everybody involved?" "Is there a way for me to have the same feelings
about my wife that I do about my ex-girlfriend?" "What would be the best way
to talk with my wife about this, and will that make any difference anyway?"
"Will this go away, and if so, what do I need to do to make it go away or take
some kind of action?"* And part of it is, *"What do I really want?" "What's good
for me?"* That's about it, though there probably are some other questions.

THERAPIST: You're sitting in the middle of a lot of questions.

[I was taken aback by the number of questions he spontaneously offered.
However, I resisted mentioning it, fearing to distract him by having him
think about his process. I wanted him to be *in* the process. So I simply
acknowledged what he said. My internal question: *"What response will
allow him to feel understood and not judged, and least disrupt his flow?"*]

CLIENT: Yeah. I'm sitting in the middle of a lot of questions.

THERAPIST: Do you have anything else to say about her?

CLIENT: Actually, I just miss her a lot, and frankly I don't know what it is I miss.

THERAPIST: Has that feeling changed over time?

CLIENT: I'm not in as much pain as I was. I was plain depressed for a while
about it, and really didn't care about anything. And yet I couldn't leave my
wife, I just couldn't. I asked myself a lot of questions about that, and I never
really successfully came up with an answer that I considered fundamental. I
could say it's because I loved her, or because I was loyal, or because it was
probably the least stressing thing, or it fit my values, or a lot of things. But
really, I just couldn't leave her. Truthfully, I experience a deep connection
with her.
　　Also, I wasn't sure what was going on with me, and I knew that if I didn't
stick it out, I would never be able to get through whatever it was. And I kind
of figured I would never be good for anybody unless I figured myself out,
unless I kind of got right with myself.

THERAPIST: That was a very mature and difficult thing to do.

CLIENT: Yeah, and there is some consolation in that. But you know, I have
looked in every nook and cranny for things to give me consolation, or give
me insight, or get some peace of mind, and I'm still not at peace. I've finally
realized it doesn't have to make sense. I just feel the way I feel about it. But
I'm not willing to sacrifice that part of my life, no matter what.

[One of my personal questions at the beginning of any session, whether
with a returning or new client, is something like: *"What will be the
theme of this session?"* or *"What will be my (and our) goal(s) in this session?"* These go along with: *"What kind of 'going-fishing questions' will
best help me find out?"* At this point, Brian has already given me enough

information to begin answering my questions. He has obviously decided to stay in his marriage and is asking for help in being peaceful and satisfied about that. His goal signals me to examine everything in the session in terms of *"How can this (whatever) be used to help him become more peaceful, satisfied, and happy with his choice to stay with his wife?"* Of course, this also includes *"How can our work contribute to his wife's happiness?"*]

THERAPIST: Which part of your life?

CLIENT: I'm not willing to sacrifice the part of my life that can be in love. I guess on the other side there is also a sexual component. There was a level of passion in the other relationship that was really wonderful. It just always seemed to be there—even though my sexual relationship with my wife is a very good one, and always has been.

THERAPIST: If she had died a year ago, rather than your leaving her, how would that have made things different?

[I have asked myself: *"Is sexuality the main issue here?"* My negative answer is evident in this intervention. Also, I didn't want him to reaccess and reinforce those feelings for his former girlfriend, which would have sabotaged our goals for the session. Anyway, I am guessing that the real issue has more to do with other things, like loss, so I check this out.]

CLIENT: It would have made it easier for me to grieve. But this was my choice. I really felt compelled inwardly to do what I did, even though it didn't feel good. So, knowing she is out there, even though I don't know whether she would be available or not anymore—that gnaws at me.

THERAPIST: So, it would be easier if she were totally unavailable? Does your wife know all this stuff is still going on with you? *(He nodded "Yes.")*

[He brought his wife into the picture, and I want to keep her there.]

CLIENT: Yes, occasionally, particularly if I bring it up in conversation just to kind of keep her apprised of where I am with all this. But it's difficult for me. I don't bring her daily reminders of it, because it's not comfortable for her to experience. I let her know enough so I'm not withholding.

THERAPIST: You're not lying.

[Validating statement. Also implying I value truthfulness in intimate relationships.]

CLIENT: I'm not lying about it.

THERAPIST: But you're also being kind about it.

[Validating again. Also letting him know I understand that honesty should be tempered with compassion, and that I recognize his self-question about his wife as something like: *"How can I be truthful, because I care about her and our relationship—as well as protect her and not be cruel?"*]

CLIENT: Yeah. And I'm always vacillating as to how much to tell her, and how often I should. I mean, if I let her know every time I thought about it, I would say something several times a day. I can't see how that would work or what good that would do. And yet, I look for this woman. Almost wherever I am, a part of me checks out the environment to see if she's there. That's just part of being in love, I guess. *(crying)* There's not much solace from it. *(laughing)* And what makes it harder is that the deeper I get into my relationship with my wife and the closer we get, the more intimate we've become. I wouldn't have the momentum to leave. And I wouldn't know what to do with myself if I did. I mean that wouldn't make sense to me, although I don't know what to do about the other, you know. I actually want them both.

THERAPIST: Yes, I can hear that.

CLIENT: But I can't have them both, because neither one would be happy. It leaves me with an ambivalent question of *"How do I get out of the relationship I'm in?"* Even though I have a fair amount of ability to be committed on an emotional level, unfortunately there is still part of me that says, *"What's the way out here?"* *"Where's the loophole in this?"* And, of course, that's bothersome too.

[His self-questions clearly display the conflict he is experiencing.]

THERAPIST: Sure, because your attention is divided. *(He nods his head, "Yes.")*

[My comment lets him know I'm interested and concerned about his conflict, not about possible morality issues. Also, this is covert training about the function of questions. Questions direct attention, virtually programming the listener (including when the listener is oneself) where to focus. Brian is running simultaneous, conflicting question paths.]

THERAPIST: You've been asking yourself: *"How can I get out of here?"* So you're not asking, *"How can I get closer to my wife?"* Well, maybe you are a little bit.

[I have answered *"Yes"* to my own internal question: *"Are we in enough rapport that I can ask about his wife in a challenging way?"*]

CLIENT: Yeah, I am getting closer to my wife. And yet, well it's weird, but sometimes I think about my girlfriend when I'm sleeping with my wife. So I understand the kind of innate loyalties that being "in love" brings with it. It's like something clashes with an ethic or something inside me, even though this is my wife. *(laughing and shaking his head at the obvious contradiction)*

THERAPIST: And in which your integrity is at stake, no matter what you do.

[Letting him know I appreciate that there's more at stake than "only" choosing between two women—I recognize his integrity is also important for him.]

CLIENT: Right. And where there is a compromise to my integrity whichever way I go.

THERAPIST: And your integrity matters—

CLIENT: More to me. It does matter the most.

THERAPIST: That's very clear. Brian, I've been listening to you, and at the same time asking myself: *"How can I be most helpful to you?"* Obviously, I don't have any answers, and my answers wouldn't fit you anyway. But there may be something I can provide you. I can ask questions that perhaps you haven't asked, or that take you where you haven't been. If you get stretched in any way—either here, or in a dream, or if something liberating occurs to you later as a result of our time together—that could be worth something.

[I'm hoping he'll experience this as a worthwhile offer. If he doesn't accept, I'll have to suggest something else to make the session useful for him. Note that I'm also making a subliminal suggestion that he may get insights in unexpected times and ways *after* the session. This sets him up to anticipate and be open for this. It also takes some pressure off accomplishing anything "major" in this session. Further, I've told him explicitly that new questions are necessary for, and often lead to, new answers.]

CLIENT: Yeah. That would be worth my while, no matter what emotions came out. *(laughing)* I didn't realize how much stuff I had going on about this. *(crying)*

[He accepted. We're in sync now, aligned in our goals for a successful session, whatever it requires emotionally for him to participate in it.]

THERAPIST: The tears—

CLIENT: Well, I'm weary. I really miss her. *(crying)* I'm a little scared, not a lot, but I'm a little scared. It's a little like, like I lost my future or something. *(crying)* So, although I can still create a future intellectually, on an emotional level I don't care much. I don't want to die, but I don't feel like I have much reason to live. I mean it's not reason, it's something else, but that's the only thing I can say. What I am looking forward to feels sort of empty. I still care about helping people through my legal practice and through my volunteer activities. But on the little-kid level, it's like I'm doing the right thing, but it doesn't *feel* very good. I can't be comforted about it—I mean I get comforted to some degree—but it's hard to get deeply comforted about it. I don't think it's going to get better. I'm sure it won't hurt as much, over time, but I don't think that's going to make me feel less empty.

[He's telling me that even though he accepted my offer, he actually feels hopeless about changing his subjective experience of this whole situation.]

THERAPIST: What other experiences have been associated with this situation?

[Here I asked myself: *"Will it serve him best if I follow him into these obviously painful feelings?"* My answer was "No," especially given our time constraint. Instead, I asked a question designed to move him away from those feelings. Actually, I was fishing for what possible, positive aspects there might be to build on, but didn't think it wise to make that obvious yet.]

CLIENT: I know there are parts of my life that are richer, because this situation pushed me in areas of thought and feeling that I hadn't experienced or had to tolerate before. I am able to do that now, and it makes me much more empathetic with other people.

[I noted that he followed my lead away from painful affect fairly easily.]

CLIENT: I certainly have a lot more room to cry, although I was pretty good at that—from all the things I've done in the past. *(crying)*

[He's still close to the pain. My challenge is to give him a different way to frame and recontextualize his distress.]

THERAPIST: These are a different kind of tears.

[Reframe. Making a distinction between tears from past therapy and past experiences and the current situation. The pain of this conflict is different, and since it is, the implication is that these tears could result in new possibilities for him.]

CLIENT: Yeah, but also I've never before been in a situation which was so insoluble for me. *(laughing)*

THERAPIST: What other losses does this bring up for you?

[I'm conceptualizing this whole situation as now dealing with loss—that is, loss of his girlfriend and loss of a piece of his identity as someone who can be "in love." Note the presupposition of loss in my question. If this is not the case, he will tell me.]

CLIENT: It's true. I actually was reminded of other losses I've had over the last year or two. A few years ago my brother died, which was a big loss for me, and I guess I'm still grieving.

[He validates that this issue is more complex than simply getting what he wants romantically. He let me know that there are many more dimensions to this conflict, and perhaps historical antecedents, that contribute to the depth of his present emotional pain.]

THERAPIST: This has been a very teary few years.

CLIENT: It has been. And then, a close friend died in an automobile accident. It wasn't his fault, and he was only 58. *(He begins to get teary again.)*

[This raises a question for me: *"How much of the pain related to the loss of his girlfriend might also be misplaced from, or exacerbated by, other real sources of grieving?"* I then asked myself if this were the best course to follow now. Since the answer was "No," I just continued to gather information.]

THERAPIST: Who was that?

CLIENT: Someone in the law firm, he was like— *(crying)*

THERAPIST: It's OK to make noise here, Brian.

[Giving him further permission to feel. Self-question: *"Will it be helpful to him to experience and express these emotions in the context of relationships other than the one with his ex-girlfriend?"* This was also a case of "riding the horse in the directions it's going."]

CLIENT: I just loved him, too. He was really my best friend.

THERAPIST: My goodness, Brian. You've really had a lot of difficult losses. The sadness you've felt is very understandable.

CLIENT: They were all sensitive and thoughtful people. And each one was a part of my spiritual life, because each knew me in a way I like to be known. I could be myself with each of them, albeit differently. And now, I don't have the same opportunity anymore. Even though I remember what that was like, I don't have those same places just to be myself and know myself. So not only have I lost these people, I also feel like I've lost a little piece of my own self with the loss of each one of them.

THERAPIST: That's one of the most eloquent statements about death and loss I've ever heard. You're describing the experience of not just having lost the person, but having lost the space they provided for you, and you haven't found anybody or any experience to fill that yet.

CLIENT: Thank you.

THERAPIST: Do you think there is a right and wrong way to go about resolving this situation?

[I'm looking for his criteria for resolution. Although this might raise some complex issues, the question must be asked.]

CLIENT: It's funny, that's the first thing I look for—what's the right thing to do or the wrong thing to do. Having come up empty-handed, the current right way is whatever is best for me psychologically. I'm not sure if that makes any damn difference either, but I never found anything. That question "*What should I do?*" was always empty in this situation.

THERAPIST: Because it's too simple. It's actually disrespectful to what you're dealing with. It's disrespectful to the complexity and the fullness of who you are. This is my opinion, even though I know not everybody would say that about what's been going on with you.

[I tell him that I vote for his being respectful to himself, and that includes embracing all of the various feelings, positions, and shadows that are competing for space in his mind and heart. It would be easy to fall into the temptation of addressing the moral considerations of this situation. However, I've asked myself two questions about this: "*Is morality the issue at this point?*" and "*Would this be a useful direction to pursue?*" My answer to both was "No." Brian has already made his choice. And morality is in behavior, not in thought and emotion. If anything, he is craving the experience of congruent morality to finally have his feelings line up with the behavioral choices he has already made.]

CLIENT: There were actually people on either side of the camp. Some told me I should go back with my wife for all those reasons that people say. And there were other people who said I should go with my ex-girlfriend.

THERAPIST: Brian, I just asked myself, "*How have you been expanded as a result of this experience?*"

[I don't see how discussing his friends' opinions about his course of action in the past is going to help him find any resolution in the present or future. My goal is to help him achieve some peace. By asking this question I hope to refocus his attention to possible areas of benefit that have ensued from this experience. Note the presupposition in my question—that he *has* benefited, and now we can discuss in what ways this has been the case. I noted he used the term "ex-girlfriend."]

CLIENT: I know there are parts of my life that are richer, because it pushed me to experiences I hadn't had before. It made me more compassionate with others, like I told you.

THERAPIST: Another benefit I sense comes from the fact that you seem to be conscious of her all the time. (*He looked at me like I had lost my marbles.*)

[Good. I got his attention—this is a major intervention and a major reframe. It's in answer to my internal question: "*Given that he obviously can't forget her, how could he experience the situation in a positive way— one that wouldn't pull him back into the feeling of loss, but open him to being filled, of gaining something in the future?*" I'm also hypothesizing and hoping that this expanded, richer sense of himself could be helpful in his marriage.]

THERAPIST: It seems to me that your consciousness of this new openness in yourself lives moment by moment along with that. That there is a way in which, in addition to being conscious of missing her, you can also appreciate and dedicate to her this new depth that you experience *and* offer to others. It's almost like saying to her internally: "*Thank you, you gave me this particular experience*" or "*Thank you, you gave me that particular experience.*" You could say to yourself, "*Right now I appreciate that she gave me this possibility to be more fully alive.*" (*About halfway through my comment, he began nodding affirmatively.*)

CLIENT: Did you read about who Beatrice was for Dante?

THERAPIST: No, go ahead.

CLIENT: I don't know if this is actually true, but it's a good story. Most of Dante's works were dedicated to, or in response to, this woman, Beatrice. Whoever she was—and she was a real woman—she profoundly affected him to the degree that he wrote these works that have lasted longer than almost any other in Western literature. Certainly he idealized her to whatever degree that he did, and yet there was someplace in him that responded or resonated to her. Not completely analogously, but I can probably resonate. You know, absent my old girlfriend, it becomes more of a memory of things I've wanted.

[He understands what I was suggesting and is running with the ball.]

THERAPIST: She becomes more mythic.

[An important reframe. Also, I believe her power for Brian may lay here more than in any real-time relationship. At any rate, this intervention was an answer to my question, *"How can I direct him to any possible bounty from this relationship in a way that isn't tied to his ex-girlfriend being physically present?"*]

CLIENT: She becomes more mythic, exactly. So in some ways I continue to honor her.

THERAPIST: That's exactly what I mean. And I'm suggesting you do that more consciously. See, you've been living with questions like: *"Which way is better?"* and *"How can I find peace?"* And the answer may be that you can't, or at least, not the way you've been thinking about peace. I think there *are* some other things you can find, and they may be even richer. More of an ongoing appreciation for who you are, thanks to her and the relationship you had.

[Making his internal questions explicit helps him be meta to them—not as imprisoned by them. I'm also telling him that this either/or position can't allow for the richness and diversity of any new, creative possibilities.]

CLIENT: Well, I think the word *generosity* is a word that is important. Each of us is equipped with whatever level of generosity we have at that particular moment.

THERAPIST: It's one of my favorite words.

CLIENT: This is a human being with enormous generosity. And I will say that among women, she is one of the most generous women. Not that she didn't have her own self-interest, but even so, she was enormously generous. I don't know what to attribute that to, but there was that generosity, and that generosity extended to other people, too, not just to me. The relationship really opened up my own generosity.

THERAPIST: And that's another important gift she gave you. You know what, Brian—you just made me think of something. You haven't asked this question exactly, but it seems like your theme for the session has been: *"How am I going to handle this loss?"* (He nodded.) But there's another question that would be much more powerful for you. It would be like asking on a moment-to-moment basis: *"How can I be grateful for this plenty, for this person whom I've become as a result of that relationship?"*

[He certainly hadn't been asking this question in actual words. The way I uncovered his contextual question was to observe his behavior and ask myself: *"What questions might his behavior have been answering?"* and *"Is there a meta question that can encapsulate these experiences and behaviors and confine them to the past?"* Having found that question, I then asked myself: *"What new question could move him forward in the future?"* His comments about generosity reinforced my opinion that he had benefited from this relationship, and that a new focus on being enriched rather than impoverished was possible, desired, and healing for him.

I'm defining paradigms for him by labeling each with the appropriate question. Since a question generally dictates the range of possible answers, I want him to recognize that in the old paradigm he could come up with answers related only to the feeling of loss. Moreover, the old questions would keep him imprisoned with those old, unwanted feelings. I show him where he's been and point to where he could go. With this move, he was freed to go meta to *both* positions, which gave him liberating new perspectives and therefore new choices and possibilities.]

CLIENT: That's true. And it's a good point. But I also don't want to give up the question: *"How can I get what I want?"*

[He demonstrates that he's still in the old paradigm, even though he can see the new possibility as well. His statement carries the presupposition of potential loss within it. Probably, it also stimulated fear on his part; that is, fear of loss.]

THERAPIST: Brian, you could also ask questions such as: *"How can I enlarge what I want?"*

[This is an important intervention. My internal questions were: *"What new position could offer him more than he presently has or can imagine?"* and *"What new choice could be more inclusive and alluring than merely getting what he was already aware of wanting?"* The question I offered him provides a new, unexpected paradigm and set of possibilities.]

CLIENT: Yeah. *Great* question. *"How can I enlarge what I want?"*

[He relaxes and smiles. I could see that he was physically relieved. He also repeats the question verbatim, as if trying it on for size.]

THERAPIST: It *is* a great question for you. It can also lead to other important ones such as: *"How can I find out about things I don't even know are available yet?"* It's like you found a place in yourself that you didn't know was a place, thanks to your girlfriend.

[The shift I sought has occurred. Now I reinforce it by offering him another question that can be answered only from within the *new* paradigm. Also, I sense that he's intrigued by discovery in general, so I built this desirable criterion into the question.]

CLIENT: How will I recognize the potential of a situation, probably a relationship, in which I can experience peace and passion and authenticity? I don't know why I said, "How can I recognize . . . ?" Things don't come with advertisements on them. Maybe it wouldn't be a romantic relationship necessarily, but it might be some new circumstances that will allow for a new experience of myself. There might be opportunities to look—you know, either training or learning, or maybe I should just leave it all open?

[This is a good sign. He followed my lead and begins to articulate his own new paradigm questions. He also demonstrates taking a meta position; he's thinking about his thinking. I'm pleased that he includes the possibility of finding some of these new experiences *outside* of a romantic situation. This really enlarges his possibilities.]

THERAPIST: What you were saying before was, "*How do I handle the loss?*" And now you have this new question: "*How do I fill and extend the new spaces that have been opened?*"

[I'm rephrasing the same basic question. I'm also checking my work by asking him to consider this all on a more obviously conscious level.]

CLIENT: Yeah. Well, it's kind of like: "*How do I put up with being hungry versus how do I get what I need to eat?*" (laughing)

[He's integrating the shift, and even playing with it on a metaphorical level. I've answered "*Yes*" to my question, "*Am I satisfied that enough of a beginning change has occurred?*"]

THERAPIST: I want you to have these questions in writing. Do you want me to write them down or do you want to do it?

[Since I'm satisfied we've accomplished something useful, I'm willing to shift gears. I often write down questions generated in sessions or have clients write them down. I also made a copy for Brian's file; this could help get us back to this track in future sessions, if there are any. Plus, I find that the more I think about questions, and think up new questions, the more facile I become at it. So I incorporate continuous question learning for myself.]

CLIENT: Good. That will be really helpful now.

THERAPIST: Brian, I want to go back to that question you asked a few minutes ago: *"How will I recognize the potential of a situation, probably a relationship, in which I can experience the peace and passion and authenticity that I did before?"* When you asked that, I found myself completing the sentence in my head before you did and this is how it came out: *"How can I keep myself open for more wonderment?"*

[This question had just popped into my mind and I'd asked myself whether it might appeal to him. Obviously, my answer had been *"Yes."*]

CLIENT: That's *good*. When you say *wonderment,* wonderment is like a kind of present future.

THERAPIST: Will you say more about that?

CLIENT: Yeah. Wonderment is outside of linear time. Wonderment is the presence of the future in the present. But not future like an extension of the present, but like a possible future. Like an added dimension to the present, which is not how we think about it; but it is available. And what has been missing for me has been a future.

THERAPIST: A *compelling* future.

[I purposefully suggest another criterion: not just *any* future, but one that can really *motivate* him. This is an important inquiry to open. Without a compelling future to look forward to, any contextual shifts we accomplish in this session could be undermined. The term "compelling future" is often used in NLP, and carries specific criteria and techniques for creating that motivation. (For a detailed discussion on helping clients to create compelling futures, see Cameron-Bandler, Gordon, and Lebeau, *Know How: Guided Programs for Inventing Your Own Best Future,* 1985.)]

CLIENT: I don't have a compelling future. The futures I think about don't have a lot of juice, or they're not all that attractive to me.

THERAPIST: So you haven't got a compelling future right now?

CLIENT: No, I don't, but I sure am interested in one. The way I have compelled myself in the past was probably a function of biology and everything else. Actually, I'm sort of a romantic. And for me, fantasized relationships are as romantic as they are sexual. I think this is a part of my gender which isn't acknowledged a lot of the time. That fantasy was usually enough to compel me into action for certain kinds of things. Like when you've got a woman you're in love with, you can do anything, and will. Lots of other people acknowledge that kind of thing. So part of the relationship with my ex-girlfriend was like that. And I just don't know a way around that yet, because if that isn't there, I guess I'm missing a lot of motivation. Well, I do have a certain kind of juice in helping people.

THERAPIST: You do. It seems very genuine for you, and that *is* some of your juice.

[I decided that pursuing a general conversation about men and women would distract from our goals in this session.]

CLIENT: That will compel me, but it isn't enough to *refill* me. I do love that part of me and it does motivate me, but I am not left with more energy at the end of it. I guess I'm missing some sort of battery charge.

[This is an important distinction he's making, and must be attended to. I am asking myself: *"How can I get more information about this without his getting caught in worrying about loss again?"*]

THERAPIST: And I think energy is an apt metaphor for you.

CLIENT: One of the questions I have is: *"Where is the source of energy that will sustain me, and keep me charged, and keep me happy?"* I'm working on a piece of legislation now that would have been enormously exciting for me a couple of years ago. And the opportunities that would open up for me politically could be huge. I really do think it will get passed, yet my experience is sort of like: *"So what?"* See, I know something is off-kilter when I have a reaction like that.

[Good. He's generating a solution-searching question, rather than problem-focused and past-focused ones.]

THERAPIST: Is it less *"So what?"* than it was before?

[I expected and hoped that he would say *"Yes."* It's a good thing I asked in the spirit of genuine inquiry, because I got an unexpected, and important, answer.]

CLIENT: It's more *"So what?"* than it was before. Two years ago, it wouldn't have been *"So what?"* Two years ago, I was dissipating a whole lot of energy because of all the integrity issues I was dealing with. Now I'm dissipating a lot less energy, but I am putting a lot less energy in. So I guess it really brings other questions like: *"What do I need to explore to have that happen?"* *"What can I ask of my wife?"*

THERAPIST: Here's a question: *"Haven't I opened a place in me where she could fill me more?"*

CLIENT: Here's another one: *"How can I be more available to get the energy she is able to provide me?"*

THERAPIST: I want to refocus us, because we're starting to move into problem solving a little bit about your wife, rather than resolving the internal dilemma you've been in.

[*This intervention was in response to these self-questions: "Is this the most fruitful path for us to follow right now?" "How can I shift us gracefully, so that he sees the shift as beneficial to him?"*]

CLIENT: Okay, that's fine.

THERAPIST: It's not just because of time, it's also because there were some rich places we were exploring, and I suspect we can take them further. Not about your ex-girlfriend the person, but more about your ex-girlfriend as myth and the new depth in yourself. I don't want you to lose that in thinking about your wife. It would be easy to start problem-solving because it's more practical, and all that.

CLIENT: Yeah, it fell into that other set of questions, like: *"What do I need to do?"*

THERAPIST: Right. *"What do I need to do?"* is about *doing*, and the place where we were percolating is more about *being*. This feels more in line with what you said you wanted in the beginning of the session. I would like you to have some closure with that.

[I've concluded that this will probably be a one-session consult. I won't need to give him any setup for the psycho-educational sessions about question asking, since I don't think there will be any. This gives me a little more time for a fulfilling closure that reinforces his changes.]

CLIENT: Well, how do I get back to that place so we can close it?

[Good question. Asking appropriately for guidance.]

THERAPIST: I've been thinking about that, and I have a few thoughts I haven't shared with you yet. One of them relates to the dichotomy you made about the issue between your ex-girlfriend and your wife, and what they represent. Heaven knows I understand; I mean, it's such a big place to be. The problem is that you could get lost there. But more to the point, I think the issue evokes, and maybe even insists on, some areas that are even *bigger*.

CLIENT: Okay, good.

THERAPIST: What I'm experiencing with you is the availability of humility and authenticity. I'm assuming this has been partly a result of the wrestling you've done with yourself over this issue. It's almost like—you will understand that I don't mean this in any negative way—that you have allowed the experience of your girlfriend to be like a Roto-rooter to make you more available as a person. But Brian, I hope you realize this issue is never going to be resolved in some facile, simple-minded way. It is not going to be resolved in the sense of *"Now I've got peace this way or I've got peace that way."* What I'm thinking of is more like a possible *bigger* resolution by your staking a claim for peace with the contradictory-ness of it, with the sheer complexity of it all.

[An important intervention designed to add to his ability to move beyond the either/or thinking that was keeping him stuck.]

CLIENT: Yeah. That's interesting, it's like being able to be with the contradiction.

THERAPIST: Exactly. I'm picturing a rainbow, or different sounds, or different flavors, as if you were saying: *"My life is no longer a single track. I experience my life multitrack and multidimensional, even though I used to be pretty single-tracked. Who I have become out of this is somebody who will forever be multi-tracked and multidimensional. And my life can now be dedicated to exploring who I am now, and expanding that."* Brian, you can do honor to your ex-girlfriend by transforming your experience of the relationship into something that can enrich your *whole* life, including all your other relationships.

[I'm being careful to cover any sensory modality he may be perceiving or experiencing through. I want to make sure this "gets in" (visual = rainbow; auditory = sounds; gustatory = flavors).]

CLIENT: That's great. I mean I actually got a whiff of that.

[He coded the experience as olfactory, which surprised me a bit.]

THERAPIST: Brian, I want you to know something. Even I, someone who is basically just a witness and questioner in this process—this conversation has expanded some possibilities for *me*, too.

[This is true and I'm willing to be personal since he told me that being helpful to others is motivating and gratifying for him. I'm glad to let him know that he succeeded, even though that certainly wasn't his intention in this setting.]

CLIENT: That's great. It really makes me feel good.

THERAPIST: See, Brian, you were understandably looking for how to close down in some way so that you could get closure on the chapter of your ex-girlfriend. But, that was adding to your feelings of loss, so naturally you also resisted that direction. I've been suggesting the questions could go in an opposite and more expansive direction.

[Another important intervention. By refocusing from the old paradigm to the new one, I'm also giving this new possibility some "positive press."]

CLIENT: That's great. I thought I had to *do* something. I see a possibility here because you're suggesting that I *be* someone different and *bigger*. Like having two lives, two tracks in this.

THERAPIST: *Not* just two tracks. You're making yourself smaller when you say that.

[I insist on his expanding, and not limiting, himself to anything that might lock him back into an either-or position. I asked myself, *"Will his statement limit him?"* *"Are these his only options?"* as well as *"Do I need to come on strong about this?"*]

CLIENT: Yeah, that's a good correction. I should say that I have two discernible tracks that I am thinking about now.

[Good. The presupposition of his statement is that he knows his vision can be limited, and there may be other possibilities that just haven't come into view yet.]

THERAPIST: Picture Joseph's coat of many colors. There are *many* colors, and endless possibilities. You have a tendency to keep things too personality bound, too human-bound. You're thinking in terms of personalities rather than possibilities. Wonderment is a question of spirit, not just personalities. Brian, you've had an *experience*. You've been *touched* by something that many people would give their lives to have experienced. Rather than focusing on trying to escape the pain, you can appreciate the wonderment of the *whole* experience, and the gifts it brings you.

[Another important intervention. I want to shift directions so he leaves the session *less* focused on his ex-girlfriend as a person, and much more on the possibility of expanding consciousness that she and their relationship continue to offer him. I really do think it would be a terrible waste if he weren't to appreciate how much he grew and expanded as a result of this relationship. Furthermore, I asked myself: *"How can this experience contribute to Brian in such a way that his wife also benefits?"*]

CLIENT: I can certainly see the validity in that.

THERAPIST: And also, the nobility of not trying to find an easy solution, but living in the complexity and the dilemma, and the courage to stay in the spaces that keep opening up for you.

CLIENT: Yeah. Because I'm experiencing those spaces while we talk. That's right.

THERAPIST: I'm happy you're having that experience. You look more relaxed, like you're breathing deeper. Brian, we really do need to end the session soon. And I would like to make a copy of these questions for you. Would you like to have them?

CLIENT: Great. I would love that. I really appreciate it. I want to say it again. I am appreciating being able to be with the complexity of all of this. This is different from feeling like I have to *do* something. I don't have to solve it, and this is a great respite and relief from having to. I can't say that I won't be interested in solutions or any of that kind of stuff. But I can tell you it feels really good just to accept and appreciate the complexity of all this. I feel how much I've grown from all this. I can respect myself more, too. And that's really important to me. This session has been like a drink of water on a dry day. I appreciate your humanity, too. I mean, I just do.

THERAPIST: Thank you.

Epilogue

This first interview officially became a one-session consult two weeks after it occurred. At that time Brian called to report that he was feeling a sense of resolution for the first time since choosing to stay in his marriage. He said his relationship with his wife had improved significantly, as he was now able to focus on her, rather than obsess about what he might be missing outside his marriage. He also reported that his depression had lifted and he was experiencing moments of happiness for the first time in a year.

Brian also said he felt no need to return for more sessions, but would make further appointments if I thought it were important. I subsequently spoke with Dr. Brown, who had also gotten positive feedback from Brian. Dr. Brown concurred that no further work seemed necessary at this point. In my last conversation with Brian I congratulated him on work well done, and left the door open should he want touch base in the future.

SUMMARY

The case of Brian demonstrated question asking at many different levels. Almost all information-seeking questions were asked with an eye toward how the answers could be used to help him transcend the perceptual corner in which he was stuck. The suggested new questions allowed him a spaciousness of possibilities he had not perceived before and allowed him to feel dignified and enhanced by an experience that brought him so much conflict in the last year. Suggesting new questions representing fresh perceptual possibilities is an important therapeutic strategy in general, especially in a one-session consultation when there will be no opportunity for follow-up.

PART THREE

Question-Centered
Therapy with Couples

12

It Takes Two to Tango

Who's afraid of Virginia Woolf?

— EDWARD ALBEE

This chapter introduces the portion of the book that applies question-centered practices to working with couples. We magnify the model of the Learner Self and the Judger Self into the complex arena of marital relationships, where perhaps it meets its most challenging match. Chapters 13 and 14 examine the four modules of question-centered psycho-educational training in marital therapy. Chapter 15 concludes the couples portion of the book. It presents the case of Julie and Jim Quinn, a couple with a sexual problem who used the psycho-educational training for resolving their difficulties and transforming their win-lose relationship into a win-win marriage.

In previous chapters we explored how internal questions play a significant, though usually undetected role in the thinking process, or internal dialogue, that gives rise to our thoughts, feelings, and behaviors, both alone and in relationship. In the gestalt of those chapters, the individual client was foreground, highlighted against the backdrop of his or her relationships, both past and present.

With this chapter the gestalt shifts, as we change focus to bring the *couple* forward, and broaden our perspective to include the dynamic internal and interpersonal patterns of their verbal interactions and communications. Now the lens expands in breadth *and* depth, driven by the anticipation that new angles will illuminate a couple's foreground dance as it is informed by the background rhythm and actual notes; that is, the affect-ridden internal dialogue by which that dance is choreographed.

Love Is Love

Loving win-win relationships are centered in acceptance, authenticity, thoughtfulness, and respect. They flourish with sex that is satisfying and fun. They are secured with a safety net of forgiveness and compassion. In the home of intimate love reside as well each partner's deepest vulnerabilities, self-doubts, and desires, as well as any unresolved childhood, parental, or traumatic issues. No matter who the partners are, engaging in a committed love relationship takes courage as well as skill (see Gilligan 1997). And Needleman's question, "Who has not been humbled by love, by its joys and sorrows?" probably resonates within us all (Needleman 1996, p. 3).

Not one of the statements in the previous paragraph is limited to heterosexual legal marriages. There are many abiding, joyful, fulfilling relationships that are untraditional because the couple is not legally married, or the partners are the same gender. The perspectives, goals, and processes in these chapters on question-centered therapy with couples are intended for those in both traditional and nontraditional committed love relationships. However, the actual references to relationship are to traditional marriage only. This is out of deference to the complexity and challenge of writing inclusively about the forms of intimate relationship, especially in so short a space. At any rate, the point here is to address the commonalties, not the differences, that love requires for its fulfillment.

We begin in section 1 by focusing on a pervasive marital metaphor, one which frames marriage as inevitably conflicted and warlike. In section 2 we explore some of the linguistic underpinnings that keep this metaphor alive, emphasizing how internal dialogue, especially internal questions, functions as the motor of Judger-dominated, win-lose marriages. In section 3 we examine observe-and-correct thinking in the marital context, focusing on how individual choice requires disengaging from automatic reactions in favor of thoughtful ways of being and relating.

In section 4 we place the marital relationships of the Learner Self and the Judger Self within a theoretical and clinical context. We examine the languaging habits of the Learner and the Judger in light of the work of four psychologists whose focus includes observing skills and internal dialogue: Burns, Seligman, Gottman, and Goleman. We find that each discusses internal dialogue in terms of contrasting categories that are consistent with the model of the Learner Self and the Judger Self. Finally, in section 5 we explore some concepts, methods, and questions that each of these four clinicians prescribe as antidotes to marital conflict and as building blocks of marital happiness.

SECTION ONE:
MARRIAGE AS WAR AND CONFLICT

Edward Albee gave the world a war-torn portrait of marriage in his well-known play, *Who's Afraid of Virginia Woolf?* (Albee 1962). Albee's leading characters, George and Martha, represent the quintessential Judger Self spouses, their horns locked in battle. In order to contextualize their drama we expand from psychological understandings to include social, historical, and even mythic ones.

George and Martha, like most of us, are unknowing prisoners of the paradigm, or metaphor, "marriage as war and conflict." Evidence for this metaphor is omni-present in Greek mythology and modern-day soap operas, in stinging gender jokes, and common phrases like "the war between the sexes." We find the atmo-sphere created by this metaphor contaminates the possibility of peace-based, win-win marriages, regardless of which two unsuspecting humans take up the challenge.

In this light, the tragedy of George and Martha's marriage becomes clearer. The conflict metaphor defined their every thought, feeling, and behavior, both overtly and covertly (see Lakoff and Johnson 1980). It also constrained the out-come of their interactions to be consistent with the paradigm that defined them. War produces a winner and a loser, and behaviors in war are restricted to either attacking or defending. In the case of George and Martha, any interaction could escalate into battle—leaving them imprisoned within the logical impossibility of a happy win-lose marriage. As usual in such arrangements, regardless of which partner wins a particular skirmish, the *marriage itself* is weakened with every vic-tory. Consider the absurdity of the question, "Which *one* of you is winning in your marriage?"

Recognizing George and Martha's pain muffled beneath their battle cries, we might recognize that the answer to the *question,* "Who's afraid of Virginia Woolf?" is probably—all of us. For within us all is the human possibility of becoming ensnared in the reactive, automatic, and fear-filled prison that often characterizes the Judger's interpretations and emotions. However, in response to another ques-tion, "*Is it inevitable to be so hopelessly condemned?*" the answer is a resounding "*No!*" It is in hopes of buttressing this "*No!*" that these chapters on couples ther-apy are devoted. We aim the spotlight most brightly on each spouse's internal questions, and on the transformational possibilities inherent in this focus.

It is the intention of question-centered therapy to mine this perspective, and the therapeutic openings it illuminates, in service of the real goal—helping cou-ples live together in ways that are mutually fulfilling and positively generative for each partner, as well as for the many others whom they touch in their lives. To do this thoroughly is beyond the scope of these few chapters. However, my goal is merely to point to the phenomenon of internal questioning in marital relation-ships in hopes of opening new spheres of inquiry and possibility for researchers, clinicians, and clients alike.

SECTION TWO: INTERNAL QUESTIONS AS A KEY TO MARITAL THERAPY

Because questions are fundamentally more interactive than statements, it is nat-ural that they provide much of the verbal currency of exchange in a couple's communications. While this statement might be intuitively obvious at the level of a couple's *external*, interpersonal question asking, it is probably less so concerning each spouse's respective *internal* question asking. By the same token, it is also unlikely that even psychologically sophisticated couples appreciate how pervasively their daily dance is orchestrated by the actual questions and requests they put to each other, or how these, in turn, are largely generated by their own internal questions.

In this section we discuss the roles that internal questions play in the problems and solutions of couples who seek marital therapy. We note therapeutic advantages in slowing and examining automatic, usually unnoticed internal dialogue. This allows us to study patterns of interactions between spouses in a multidimensional and detailed manner. Lastly, we explore how therapeutic questions that begin with *"How?"* rather than *"Why?"* facilitate this process.

The Influence of Internal Questions on Interpersonal Behavior

Normally, we have little awareness of the complex backstage activities and interactions that give rise to the drama unfolding on center stage. Perhaps this is due to the play's being so riveting that it overshadows any backstage proceedings. Or perhaps, the complex frontstage interactions occur at such lightning-fast speed that it doesn't seem possible, or even profitable, to slow them enough to examine their backstage underpinnings. This last conclusion, however, is inaccurate. In fact, by examining the interactions of a couple's internal dialogues, we gain the opportunity of interrupting automatic, negative communication patterns, revealing a world of possible interventions and solutions.

Examining Marital Interactions, Frontstage and Backstage   The movie of a couple's interactions can be slowed into sequential "freeze-frames," or still shots, a process which makes possible this rich therapeutic harvest. We focus on the dynamic, unfolding nexus as each partner's *internal* behavior—subtle, usually unnoticed self-questions transforming into experienced thoughts and feelings—is expressed in *external* behavior—ways of behaving, relating, and being in the world. The usual speed of a couple's interactions obscures a wealth of information, the observing and understanding of which throws light into the conundrum of marital interactions, and simultaneously onto fresh possibilities for action and changes *in*, and *between*, them both (see Kirschner and Kirschner 1986, and Kirschner, Kirschner, and Rappaport 1993).

Access to this backstage is provided by identifying the crucial influence of one spouse's internal questions on his or her behavior which, in turn, influences the perceptions, internal questions, and finally the behavior of the other spouse. In other words, interpersonal behavior influences and changes each spouse's internal dialogue. Therefore, we widen the spotlight to include not only the couple's external interactions on center stage, but also the backstage internal interactions of their respective internal dialogues. We focus on spouses' internal questions since their external behavior can be understood as answers to their respective internal queries.

This endeavor is analogous to, and about as elusive as physics' attempt to illuminate the nanosecond when a particle becomes a wave, or a wave becomes a particle yet again. Fortunately, therapists have an advantage over physicists in this regard; it is easier to talk to a human being than to an atom. We can explore this phenomenon *with* our clients. Although absolute certainty about such observations is not possible, thankfully, neither is it necessary. Nevertheless, the more distinctions we bring to our observing eyes and listening ears, the more powerful the therapeutic gifts they can render. These gifts appear as answers, suggestions, and intuitions to the marital therapist, immersed as she is in Learner Self questions, such as: *"What opportunities for healing and growth are available in my clients' present interactions?"* *"What can I do to move this couple out of the attack-or-defend paradigm in which they are stuck?"* and/or *"How can I help them experience and express their love with each other?"*

"How?" versus "Why?" in Marital Therapy Gaining access to a frame-by-frame portrayal of their interactions helps free client couples from reactive, automatic ways of relating with each other. It allows them to *observe together*, and in so doing step out of the limiting marital paradigm of attack-or-defend thoughts, feelings, and behaviors. Spouses can ask, "<u>How</u> did we get into such a painful predicament?" This question focuses their mutual attention on their *interactions* and *communications*, rather than on their own, or each other's, individual, objectified "good" or "bad," acceptable or unacceptable personal characteristics. The Judger Self blame-seeking habit of locating fault *in* one person usually eclipses noticing, much less learning, about dysfunctional *patterns between* individuals. This habit also interferes with a spouse taking responsibility for his or her own behavior, as responsibility is quite distinct from blame. In other words, by blaming either ourselves or each other in difficult marital situations, we unknowingly condemn ourselves to the merciless and inescapable prison that Albee depicted so well in *Who's Afraid of Virginia Woolf?*

That prison is often an unintended result of the tyranny that the question "Why?" can impose when spouses attempt to understand the mystery of their marital unhappiness. Not knowing how—or even if it's possible—to answer "Why?" we easily fall into the dead-end conclusion that it must be *somebody's* fault, and if that person would just "get it together," or "get fixed," all would be right once again. On the other hand, questions that begin with "*How?*" focus on *process* rather than personality. Therefore, shifting the question that sets the marital therapeutic frame away from "Why?" and toward "How?" and "What?" allows a corresponding shift in the possibilities the therapy setting can offer to couples. It can become transformed from war zone and emergency room—into peace process and training room.

SECTION THREE: OBSERVE AND CORRECT
IN THE MARITAL CONTEXT

If a war zone is characterized by attacking and defending, the training room and classroom are defined by observing, correcting, learning, and growing. In earlier discussions about cognitive-behavioral therapy we explored the key role of observation with individual clients. These methods require the therapist to engage the nonsymptomatic, observing self of clients in order to train them in the core skill of tracking and monitoring their internal dialogue. However, the marital arena poses daunting challenges to any spouse attempting to maintain the nonreactive, nonjudgmental equanimity of an observing self in the face of the automatic, sometimes primal, emotions that seem to erupt so regularly in marriage. Nevertheless, it is exactly here where live the greatest opportunities, as well as the greatest dangers, of intimate relationship.

The pivotal strength that self-observation and self-awareness bring to the experience of emotion in marriage is the ability to notice what one is experiencing, bypass drowning in an emotional swamp, and choose to go directly into observe-and-correct mode. This feat is accomplished, in part, by asking Learner Self questions such as: *"What is objectively going on?" "Am I overreacting?" "What is she, or he, feeling or wanting right now?" "What is my responsibility in this situation?" "Do I need to cool off before I respond further?"* and/or *"What can we learn from this so we can have a better relationship?"*

Strengthening each spouse's ability to utilize such impulse control in favor of positive short- and long-term consequences is a primary goal of question-centered therapy with couples. One might ask, *"What does thinking clearly have to do with love?"* In fact, thinking clearly and responsibly is one of the finest ways spouses can show respect and caring for themselves, each other, and the wholeness of their marriage. It is worth the time and effort. If there is any doubt, consider the alternative—which is to let impulsive, impetuous emotions and behaviors rule the relationship. Emotional behaving and relating usually lead to continuous crises and stormy relationships. Emotional behaving and relating erode trust, impede effective marital problem solving, and often result in win-lose marriages.

A relationship can be thought of as a house built of bricks. A common misconception is that the big events of married life—the bricks—are what make the relationship.[1] However, it is the everyday interactions that keep it all together—the cement. Observe-and-correct questioning *is* thinking clearly, and is best a part of couples' everyday interactions. Observe-and-correct thinking and relating are the cement of win-win marriages. They are also homeowner's insurance. A spouse who engages in observe-and-correct thinking and relating is taking responsibility for the daily maintenance of the house that shelters love, and keeps it alive.

---

[1] I thank Bill Friedman for this metaphor.

We lay some groundwork here by examining individual choice and responsibility within the marital context. Accordingly, in this section we explore the vital distinction between being on automatic and behaving thoughtfully with one's partner in marriage. Then we discuss personal choice and responsibility, and observe-and-correct questioning in marriage—all attitudes and skills of the Learner Self. The assumption is that when their Learner Selves are aligned and united, spouses can win the battle against individual, automatic, reactive thinking, feeling, and relating that earlier led to conflict and unhappiness. Marital partners can learn to step out of the attack-or-defend paradigm, and create and enjoy win-win marriages.

Being on Automatic versus Being Thoughtful in Marriage

The premise in question-centered therapy is that individuals usually enter into the vows of marriage with experiences of love and respect—and intentions, expectations, and hopes of being partners in win-win marriages. Yet we all know how often these dreams are dashed in the onslaught of daily living, historic emotional baggage, and inevitable marital conflicts. Any of these challenges to marital happiness is likely to trigger automatic emotions, thoughts, and behaviors in either or both of the spouses.

It may well be that this automaticity is the hit-and-run culprit most responsible for marital breakdowns and unhappiness. We all get stuck on automatic from time to time. When that happens, especially in marriage, fears of survival are aroused—whether they are justified—and the ensuing emotional storm often obscures feelings of love and kindness. In other words, fear and anger are mobilized by automaticity, and these feelings are maintained and accentuated by Judger questions such as: *"How could I get hurt?" "How can I protect and defend myself?" "How can I win?"* and *"How can I avoid losing?"* The tunnel vision that results from such questions locks our brains into this survival mode, making it difficult to think from any other perspective. Yet thinking carefully from another perspective—especially that of one's spouse—is precisely what's required for genuine listening, understanding, compassion, and forgiveness. Moreover, willingness and agility in shifting perceptual positions is fundamental to appreciating, respecting, and understanding differences. This skill of "walking in the other person's moccasins" is required for successful negotiating, and ultimately for win-win resolutions.

Because human beings are different, differences in marriage are inevitable. Yet when these inevitable differences show up, they are often experienced as representing conflict. Therapy can help clients learn to think more clearly by drawing this distinction between difference and conflict. Conflict calls for fighting. Differences can call for understanding and negotiating. Negotiations based on appreciating difference can lead to resolutions that "transcend and include" and thus move the relationship as a whole to a higher level (see Wilber 1995). This recognition can transform a marriage into a true partnership, with spouses on the *same* side, fighting *for* their marriage, rather than against each other (see Markman, Stanley, and Blumberg 1994).

The Choice Model and Marital Interactions

Being human, spouses always have a choice about being automatic, reactive, and passive, or thoughtful, responsive, and active. However, without acknowledging this ability they are usually helpless to exercise it. In earlier discussions about the Choice Model, we emphasized how individuals always have a choice, at least in attitude. The crucial distinction drawn by the Choice Model is that the Learner Self recognizes and utilizes the innate human ability to choose. By contrast, the Judger Self—which is all of us at times—either doesn't recognize or denies that choice and hence responsibility are present in every moment.

In marriage, when spouses make automatic, passive choices, or *believe themselves helpless to do otherwise,* they often descend into the experience of marriage as conflict, and reinforce their captivity in the attack-or-defend paradigm. Furthermore, the longer they choose Judger Self and win-lose relating as their marital context, the more dominated they become by their own conflict-producing feelings, beliefs, and behaviors. The goal of explicitly introducing these concepts into couples' therapy is to empower spouses to take active moment-by-moment responsibility for themselves and their relationships, and to equip them with the skills and tools to create win-win marriages.

Observe-and-Correct and the Choice Model

The pilot depicted on the Observe-and-Correct handout must consistently engage in observe-and-correct thinking in order to fly and land her plane safely. The ability to observe requires taming automatic emotional reactions in favor of thoughtful, even strategic responses. In the observe-and-correct mental operation, only objective, descriptive facts are relevant. Anything else—preferences, feelings, distracting thoughts—are not only irrelevant, they are potentially fatal.

A couple locked in a difficult, frustrating marital interaction is rarely in physical danger as might be a pilot and her passengers. But couples are often headed for crash landings nonetheless. It is at just such times that a spouse could choose to make the pivotal difference through a Learner Self rescue operation. He or she could make that cognitive intervention by moving into a purposeful observe-and-correct mode. When a spouse is poised at the crossroads of the Choice Model, choosing to take the first step up into the domain of win-win relating calls for asking a Learner Self question, instead of a reactive, Judger's one. This crucial moment calls for nonjudgmental observation, which occurs in the habit of consistently asking questions such as, "What's this?" "What's going on?" or "What's happening here?"

The interval between such questions (the internal behavior) and what that spouse says or does next (the external behavior) usually takes a second or less. Yet in this tiny, usually unnoticed moment lies a major determinant of the outcome of an interaction, and perhaps ultimately the destiny of the marriage itself. The crucial choice is whether the spouse standing at the crossroads will yield to the pull of the Judger's automatic mindset with its attendant negative, problem-focused thoughts—or consciously take responsibility by shifting into the Learner's mindset with helpful solution-seeking thoughts. With this choice, the potential for therapeutic change is either activated—or abandoned.

Internal Questions and Conflicted Marital Interactions   These behavioral and relational choices will have been driven by internal questions, because they always are. In this case, if spouses abdicate accessing Learner Self mindsets and questions, they are left by default with only Judger Self ones that confine them in the attack-or-defend paradigm. Such questions include: *"What's wrong with me?" "What's wrong with him or her?" "What can I do to hurt (or punish) him or her?" "How can I keep from getting hurt?"* These questions, of course, virtually guarantee that spouses remain triggered, captives of their automatic emotions, as they slide down the trajectory deeper into the domain of the Judger Self and win-lose relating.

Since each is part of a couple, and the upsetting *triggering event was something in their interaction*, each usually attempts to bring the other spouse downward, as well. He or she does this either actively, by projecting blame and judgment externally, and/or passively, by projecting blame and judgment internally. If either spouse succeeds, *both* are likely to end up confined to the Judger Self domain of win-lose relating. And the longer they remain there, the more entrenched they become. The win-lose, conflict-dominated basis of the marriage may come to resemble a cold war, a "hot" one, or many variations in between. Tragically, the more spouses allow themselves to be dominated by the automatic reactions of the Judger Self, especially blaming each other or themselves, the *less* they are able to gaze upon their husbands or wives with the eyes and spirit of love they pledged, in all good faith, on their wedding day.

Blame Automaticity   If blame must be cast, let us blame automaticity. We could each take responsibility for this aspect of our humanness, and then get on with the business of taking care of ourselves, each other, and our relationships. Responsibility and observation are the keys to this level of conscious, caring behavior. Dispassionate, neutral observation is actually a sophisticated cognitive operation, representing an internal decision to step out of an automatic reactive mode into one which is responsive and thoughtful. If spouses were truly able to step back and observe their own behavior in the midst of marital conflict, they would often be appalled. Surely this isn't how they intended to behave toward their beloved, or how they themselves want to be treated. The crucial difference can be made by remembering to ask Learner questions such as: *"What's the kindest possible interpretation of my spouse's behavior?" "How can I take care of myself while supporting and empowering my spouse?" "How can I act most responsibly here?"* and/or *"How can we both win in this situation?"*

These Learner Self questions call to mind the oft-quoted questions of the first century scholar, Hillel: *"If I am not for myself, who will be for me?"* *"If I am for myself only, what am I?"* *"If not now, when?"* Asking these questions frequently and wholeheartedly might remind married friends and lovers to honor themselves, their spouses, and the possibilities and responsibilities of love in marriage and intimate relationship.

The Need for Win-Win Relating, No Matter What   Realistically, some couples who seek therapy will end up divorcing. Others will reconcile, and build and maintain win-win marriages. In either case, learning to operate as one's Learner Self, and utilize the skills of win-win relating, establishes the foundation for maintaining personal dignity and self-respect. It also creates the conditions for effective relating in whatever challenges the relationship may face in the future.

Legacy of Win-Win Relating   Behaving in such a manner also allows couples to model win-win relating for their children. This is imperative whether in divorce or reconciliation, lest the legacy of win-lose relating beget another generation that is oblivious to the spacious world of love, creativity, and wholeness that is always available outside the confines of the attack-or-defend paradigm.

SECTION FOUR:
THEORETICAL AND CLINICAL CONTEXT

In this section we explore the work of four psychologists, Burns, Seligman, Gottman, and Goleman. Their studies of cognitive habits and observing skills provide useful theoretical and clinical dimension to our discussions of the Learner Self and the Judger Self, especially in the marital context. We find that each of the four discusses cognition and internal dialogue in terms of contrasting categories that are generally consistent with the Learner Self and the Judger Self. The section concludes with a diagram which illustrates how these contrasting categories cluster on the Choice Model, either in the domain of the Learner Self and win-win relating, or in that of the Judger Self and win-lose relating. We also revisit each of these four clinicians later when we examine their suggestions for antidotes to marital conflict and creation of marital happiness.

Positive Thoughts versus Negative Thoughts

Individuals naturally bring their usual thinking styles with them when they marry. Someone whose normal tendency is to think positively will likely continue to do. Someone whose tendency is to think negatively will also continue to do so. However, the emotional climate of marriage provides challenges to even the heartiest of positive thinkers. Because most people bring their greatest hopes of love to their marriages, they also bring their deepest fears of not getting it.

These fears keep people on the alert for signs of nonacceptance, rejection, or waning interest—any of which may be imagined even when they're not true.

An avalanche of negative thoughts could follow these negative assumptions. Burns (1989) offered many techniques for challenging and transforming such negative thoughts into positive and helpful ones. Clients might take advantage of these techniques after answering the following useful questions affirmatively: *"Do I want to change my negative feelings . . .?"* and *"Do I really want to feel better?"* (1989, pp. 86–87; my italics). Negative questions, in marriage and elsewhere, are characteristic when the individual's Judger Self dominates. The challenging questions would be typical of a Learner Self after having observed his own emotional state and internal dialogue. The Learner Self spouse might then ask follow-up questions such as: *"Is the way I'm thinking going to help my marriage?" "How could I find out if I'm being unrealistic?"* and *"How can I recover my usual feelings of being loved and appreciated by my spouse?"*

Optimistic and Pessimistic Explanatory Styles

Although Seligman's research (Seligman 1974 and 1991) focused on individual cognitive styles, his findings have considerable implications for working with couples. Recapping briefly, Seligman found that when confronted with difficulty, an individual's explanatory style could be consistently categorized as either optimistic or pessimistic. Each label is predictive of a host of consequences in every domain of that person's life, including learning, health, work, parenting, and emotional stability. Pessimists tend to believe that negative situations will drag on, undermine everything they do, and are their own fault.

On the other hand, optimists confronted with similar circumstances tend to believe that the difficulty is temporary, that its causes are specific to a particular situation, and that it was not their own fault (pp. 4–5). An optimist shares many similarities with the Learner Self, as a pessimist does with the Judger Self. These descriptions would lead a question-centered therapist to ask herself questions such as, *"How might a spouse's customary explanatory style affect how he or she brings himself or herself to the challenges of marriage?* and *"How can we use these insights about optimistic and pessimistic explanatory styles to help clients build and maintain win-win marriages?"*

Self-Soothing and Distress-Maintaining Thoughts

In one of the most intensive studies of couples' interactions ever undertaken, Gottman and his colleagues pinpointed specific and divergent cognitive, emotional, and physiological characteristics and processes that either predictably lead to divorce, or help create sound marriages (Gottman 1994). The discoveries of Gottman's research contribute significantly to understanding the complexity of marriage, including the impact of internal dialogue on marital interactions and outcomes. Gottman told us, "Marital problems easily arise if your thoughts and feelings are distorted—if (they) reinforce a negative view of your partner and your marriage" (pp. 103–104). He characterized such thoughts as distress-maintaining as distinct from those that have the effect of being self-soothing.

The problem lies not only in having the cognitive distortions, but also in the habit of not observing or challenging them by questioning one's assumptions and beliefs. This crucial skill of questioning one's own conclusions, and thereby guarding against righteousness and prejudiced thinking, clearly belongs to the domain of the Learner Self. In this sense, the pivot balancing the emotional see-saw of marriage depends, in large part, on the habitual self-observing focus of the Learner Self. Sophia, whom we met in chapter 10, exemplified such an individual, especially under the pressure of marital interactions.

Effects of Self-Soothing or Distress-Maintaining Thoughts on Marriage

Gottman enjoined readers to take a self-observing stance in order to notice whether their thoughts about their marriages, themselves, and/or their partners fell into the category of self-soothing or distress-maintaining. It is mainly through such cognitive skills that spouses can rescue themselves from a Judger-dominated marriage, a volatile version of which was exemplified by George and Martha. If taking this metaposition does not occur, unnoticed and rampant distress-maintaining thoughts create serious marital problems, and characterize the internal dialogue of spouses in win-lose marriages.

In other words, Gottman recommended that readers take a metaposition to their own thinking process in order to evaluate whether it was working for, or against, themselves and their marriages. Taking a purposeful metaposition is a Learner Self practice, and prerequisite for an enduring win-win marriage. A Judger Self would be likely to just *have* distress-maintaining thoughts, probably not notice this was the case, and therefore be at their emotional sway. Over time, negative assumptions (negative false attributions) about one's spouse come to outweigh positive ones. Gottman explained how this could cause disastrous marital consequences:

> Remember that if your inner script is dominated by thoughts that exacerbate your negative feelings, rather than soothe, you are likely to become flooded. . . . [T]hese negative feelings form a sort of feedback, creating symptoms of flooding like increased heart rate and flow of adrenaline, and the more your body feels flooded, the less able you are to soothe yourself and see the situation calmly. Instead, your thoughts and emotions contribute even more to your sense of being overwhelmed. Over time you become *conditioned* to look for and react to negatives in your spouse and your marriage. This becomes a self-fulfilling prophecy: the more you expect and search for negatives, the more likely you are to find them, and to highlight their significance in your mind (p. 120; his italics).

These cognitive descriptions give spouses a new distinction to add to their self-observing eyes and ears. Now a spouse can ask him- or herself: "*Is this thought self-soothing or distress-maintaining?*" If, in the midst of a marital conflict, he or she discovers the latter to be the case, they are now empowered to ask, *"How can I alter my thoughts so they become self-soothing?"* or *"What am I grateful for in my marriage?"* or *"What kind of thinking would help me understand this situation clearly, and act in a way that was good for us both?"*

High Emotional Intelligence and Low Emotional Intelligence

Goleman coined the term "emotional intelligence," which he defined as including ". . . abilities such as being able to motivate oneself and persist in the face of frustrations; to control impulse and delay gratification; to regulate one's moods and keep distress from swamping the ability to think; to empathize and to hope" (1995, p. 34). When spouses fail to "keep distress from swamping the ability to think," they exhibit low emotional intelligence. When they are able to think clearly and nonreactively, they express high emotional intelligence.

Optimally, for a marriage to grow and mature, both partners actively observe their own internal dialogue, and make effective choices about what to do with what they discover. With this in mind, consider that Goleman called emotional intelligence the "master aptitude" influencing success in life (p. 80). The context of marriage includes the challenges it poses, the complexity of its requirements for stability, and the inherent forces militating against its success. Whether one engages in married life with a highly or poorly developed master aptitude could be *the* variable determining whether it is experienced and regarded as a win-win or win-lose marriage.

In general, the Learner Self exemplifies high emotional intelligence, while the Judger Self demonstrates low emotional intelligence. Of course, these are not permanent states. As the Learner/Judger Chart illustrated, the bridge to the domain of the Learner Self and win-win relating is always available through sincerely asking Learner questions. This would lead to other solution-seeking, self-soothing thoughts characteristic of someone with high emotional intelligence. These might be expressed as, *"He or she probably didn't mean that the way it sounded. Maybe I should ask if he/she had a bad day?"* On the other hand, the problem-focused, distress-maintaining thoughts characteristic of someone exhibiting low emotional intelligence might be expressed thus, *"How dare he/she talk to me like that! What can I do to pay him/her back for such impertinence?!"*

Choosing One's Marital Context

In this section of the chapter we explored the pivotal roles of observation, choice and internal dialogue in leading either to marital happiness or conflict. The categorization of the divergent cognitive habits described by Burns, Seligman, Gottman, and Goleman was consistent with either the Learner Self and win-win marriage, or the Judger Self and win-lose marriage. The diagram in Figure 12.1 transposes the concepts of the Choice Model into the marital context, and illustrates how the cognitive descriptions of these four psychologists cluster naturally

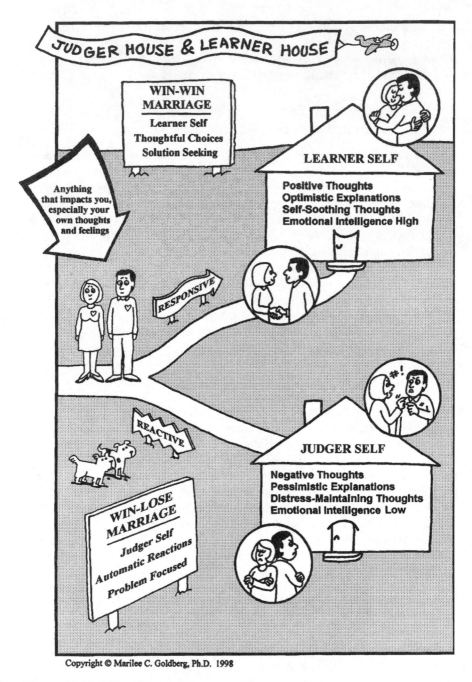

Figure 12.1   Judger House & Learner House.

Copyright © Marilee C. Goldberg, Ph.D. 1998

either in the domain of the Learner Self or that of the Judger Self. Choosing the domain of the Learner Self is depicted as residing in a "Learner home," while choosing the domain of the Judger Self is portrayed as taking up residence in a "Judger home." In this illustration a couple, rather than an individual, stands poised at the ever present crossroads of choice. This diagram also provides theoretical background for a handout for client couples, the Marriage Context Model. It is given to them during their question-centered psycho-educational training, and is presented in chapter 14.

SECTION FIVE: CHOICE IN THE CONTEXT OF MARRIGE

Marriage offers almost unlimited opportunities to ignite conflict. In fact, one of my clients commented wryly: "My marriage is like a tinder box; it's a conflict waiting to happen." Regardless of the etiology of a conflict, the emphasis in couples' therapy must eventually move beyond *why* a triggering event occurred. *In the present*, each individual stands poised at the precipice of the crucial choices of *what to do next*. As we know, thoughtful, active choices move clients upward into the solution-seeking win-win domain of the Learner Self, while passive, reactive choices cast them down into Judger Self, problem-focused win-lose territory.

Of course, the passive choice, the one leading to automatic, reactive conflict, is most common—it is the long-term pattern of such choices that lead to unhappiness, win-lose relationships, and eventually the search for help. The therapeutic goal is for each spouse to become more thoughtful about *how* he or she makes these moment-to-moment choices, and to empower them with the skills to think, feel, and relate in such a way that a win-win marriage becomes a viable possibility.

We find substantial resources for helping clients build and maintain win-win marriages in the work of each of the four psychologists we discussed in the previous section. Here we explore specific therapeutic contributions of each. We also consider ways that question-centered interventions based on the model of the Learner Self and the Judger Self build on and may extend clinical applications suggested by their work.

Positive Questions In Marital Resolutions

Burns devoted a large portion of *The Feeling Good Handbook* (1989) to helping couples improve their communication and their marriages, based on his research on the causes and cures for marital and personal relationship problems. He wrote, "I have discovered that certain attitudes cause people to get stuck in endless cycles of blame, hostility, fear, and loneliness" (p. xv). These damaging attitudes are expressed as negative thoughts, and as an antidote to these problematic thoughts, Burns introduced a list of 15 characteristics of "bad communication" (p. 365). These 15 items represent communication mistakes which could eventually lead to marital crashes. Therefore Burns's list was intended to help readers become more aware of what to do, and *not* do, when attempting to resolve interpersonal conflicts.

Consistent with Burns's emphasis on the potency of internal dialogue, I have rephrased his explanation of each item into an internal question typical of a Learner Self spouse. These are possible questions that could follow a Learner Self spouse's initial inquiry, *"What's this?"* when standing at the crossroads of the Choice Model, choosing which direction to travel in his or her marriage. Such Learner Self questioning is the cognitive intervention that positions a spouse into an observe-and-correct mode—and leverages the couple into a win-win possibility for their marriage. (Adapted from Burns 1989, p. 365.)

- Truth: *Am I insisting that I am "right" and the other person is "wrong"?*
- Blame: *Am I saying that the problem is the other person's fault?*
- Martyrdom: *Am I claiming that I am an innocent victim?*
- Put-down: *Am I implying that the other person is a loser because he or she "always" or "never" does certain things?*
- Hopelessness: *Am I giving up, and insisting there's no point in trying?*
- Demandingness: *Am I saying I'm entitled to better treatment, but am I also refusing to ask for what I want in a direct, straightforward way?*
- Denial: *Am I insisting that I don't feel angry, hurt, or sad when I actually do?*
- Passive Aggression: *Am I pouting, or withdrawing, or saying nothing? Did I exhibit behaviors like storming out of the room or slamming doors?*
- Self-blame: *Am I acting as if I'm an awful, terrible person, instead of dealing with the problem?*
- Helping: *Am I trying to "solve the problem" or "help" him or her, instead of hearing and trying to understand how depressed, hurt, or angry the other person feels?*
- Sarcasm: *Are my words or voice tone conveying tension or hostility which I'm not openly acknowledging?*
- Scapegoating: *Am I suggesting that the other person has "a problem" and that I, of course, am sane, happy, and uninvolved in the conflict?*
- Defensiveness: *Am I refusing to admit any wrongdoing or imperfection?*
- Counterattack: *Am I responding to the other person's criticism by criticizing back instead of acknowledging how he or she is feeling?*
- Diversion: *Am I listing grievances about past injustices instead of dealing with how we both feel right here, right now?*

A Learner Self would naturally ask themselves follow-up questions. For example, if a spouse discovered that he had, in fact, been blaming his wife, he might then ask himself: *"Am I being fair?" "What part am I playing in this?" "If I keep blaming her, where will that lead us?"* and *"Will the way I'm behaving get me what I really want in my marriage?"* Educating clients to ask themselves questions based on Burns's list of cognitive corrections is an empowering therapeutic intervention.

The Optimist and Pessimist in Marriage

An individual's customary explanatory style, as described by Seligman, has far-ranging implications in the challenges of the marital arena. First we explore some ways that the Judger's pessimistic explanations and internal questions might show up in marriage. Then we focus on the cognitive habits of the optimistic spouse and some Learner Self questions he or she might ask themselves.

Pessimism and the Judger Self   A pessimistic spouse tends to bring himself or herself to marriage, as well as to any particular marital interaction, expecting that any difficulty could contaminate the relationship, and would undermine his or her efforts and outcomes in other marital situations. He or she might feel that any fault was personal and feel helpless to do anything about it. He or she is also likely to feel that their intentions were positive. Two distinctly different conclusions could ensue, each representing a disparate version of a Judger Self stance.

In the first case, a pessimistic spouse might expect his or her behaviors to be inept and doomed since he or she is intrinsically flawed, and therefore helpless to change. In the second case, he or she might claim that the *partner* thwarted these intentions, and therefore, he or she was helpless to make things better. In either case, the spouse would conclude that he or she was helpless, basically a victim of circumstances, and without hope of making or enjoying any intentional, positive change. Such beliefs and fears might lead to avoiding conflict, or to becoming emotionally reactive if conflict should occur.

If the spouse judged the problem as his or her own fault, the tendency would be to become depressed, and ask internal questions encoded with negative, limiting presuppositions such as: *"What's wrong with me?" "Why can't I ever do anything right?" "How uncomfortable is this going to be?" "How much will this damage my marriage?" "Why do I always lose, and why would my spouse want to be with such a loser anyway?"* and/or *"Will I ever be able to make it up to (or placate) her?"*

On the other hand, if he or she judged the *spouse* as blameworthy, the tendency would be to become angry and righteous. Subsequent internal questions might include: *"How am I going to win this one?" "How could she/he do that to me?" "Why did I ever marry such an idiot?" "Doesn't she/he realize how lucky she/he is to be married to me?"* and *"How will I make her/him pay for this?"* This last set of queries probably exemplifies the questions that led to George and Martha's heinous behavior, and also qualified them as such frightening marital archetypes.

Optimism and the Learner Self   The profile of the optimistic spouse is quite different. Each brings him- or herself to marriage with the expectation that conflicts are natural, can be confined to any of successive situations, are always resolvable, and that he or she has the skills to fulfill these expectations. Learner Selves, like their Judger Self counterparts, would likely feel that their intentions were positive. At the same time, they would differ by taking responsibility for their own behaviors, including any impact they may have had on a situation, or their spouse's emotional state. Learner Self spouses would make this assumption even if this were distasteful, or felt their image were temporarily tarnished. These assumptions and the self-questions based on them contribute to Learner Self spouses taking active responsibility for creating win-win outcomes in any marital situation, large or small.

The Learner Self and Optimistic Questions   Naturally, the Learner spouse's internal questions are encoded with optimistic presuppositions, and thereby program more positive marital interactions and outcomes. Following are examples of such questions:

- *How soon can we get back to feeling good with each other?*
- *What are my resources to resolve this most successfully?*
- *What are the best questions to get us on a good track?*
- *Is this an optimum time to discuss this?*
- *What can we learn so we do better next time?*
- *What solutions would have us both win?*

Such questions would lead to resolution, fun making up, and maybe good lovemaking. Any of these outcomes would surely add to the overall strength of the marriage. While such scenes would deprive an audience of a fiery spectacle typical of George and Martha, *this* show might capture their hearts, rather than capitalize on their fears.

Gottman: The Study of Marital Conflict and Happiness

We discussed Gottman's categorization of internal dialogue in marriage as either self-soothing or distress-maintaining. Here we explore his findings about marital conflict and happiness in more detail. We include discussions of physiological variables, marital conflict styles, the importance of positivity versus negativity in preserving a satisfying "marital ecology," the four types of marital interactions that spell trouble, and the crucial distinction between complaints and criticisms. We consider each of these in light of the model of Learner Self and the Judger Self. Finally, we focus on converting complaints into win-win requests that strengthen marriages.

The importance of thinking patterns of spouses in troubled marriages shows up vividly in Gottman's discovery that the way a couple fights provides a telling tool with which to diagnose the health and happiness of their marriage—and predict its longevity. Gottman and his colleagues discerned three potentially success-ful marital conflict styles—the validating marriage, the conflict-avoiding mar-riage, and the volatile marriage. As long as partners were able to achieve a crucial balance in a style that fit them both, they could create a successful marital ecol-ogy. Regardless of the couple's choice of conflict style, the success of the marriage would be supported by a preponderance of spouses' self-soothing rather than distress-maintaining thoughts. The significance of this discovery is underscored by Gottman's statement that *"a lasting marriage results from a couple's ability to resolve the conflicts that are inevitable in any relationship"* (p. 28; italics added).

Physiological Variable   However, another influential variable on a spouse's ability to *access* self-soothing thoughts must also be taken into account. Gottman's research revealed an important physiological finding—that men "flood" sooner than women in conflict situations. In other words, their blood pressure, heart rate, and sweating tend to accelerate more quickly, temporarily making it more difficult to think clearly (pp. 115–120). This information has important practical applications for spouses committed to win-win marriages.

For example, a wise wife could assess her husband's stress level in the midst of a difficult interaction. Then she might ask herself: *"Can he hear what I have to say, or is he starting to shut down?"* or *"Would we be better off not talking about this until we're calmer?"* *"Will he feel like he has to withdraw if we try to talk?"* and/or *"If we try to resolve this now, will it make us closer or more distant?"* A savvy husband could ask himself, *"Am I too tense to be able to really hear her right now?"* and say to his wife, "What you're saying is important, but I'll be able to take it in better later. I'd like to talk about this tonight. Is that OK with you?"

The Importance of Reinforcing Positivity over Negativity in Marriage
Another significant contribution of Gottman's research was the remarkable insight that marital success depended on maintaining a ratio of 5 positive experi-ences to 1 negative experience, regardless of whether the marital conflict style were marked by validation, volatility, or avoidance. Learner Self spouses would apply this information by asking themselves and their partners a question such as, *"Have we maintained a robust positive ratio this week?"* If the answer were nega-tive, they might then ask: *"What got in the way?"* *"Is there something between us that needs to be resolved?"* *"What's the best way to go about that?"* and eventually, *"What can we do for fun and relaxation?"* In this way, valuable research data becomes part of the spouses' habitual observe-and-correct thinking pattern.

Gottman was struck by the many ways, large and small, that stable couples showed their positivity. His observations translate into a useful list of ways to rein-force the positive side of the equation for building and maintaining successful marriages. Operationalizing Gottman's suggestions, as we did earlier with Burns's list of communication errors, yields useful questions for the Learner Self spouse. Following are Gottman's points, transposed into Learner Self questions (Adapted from Gottman, pp. 59–61).

- *Am I showing him or her enough interest?*
- *Am I showing my affection?*
- *Am I showing that I care?*
- *Am I being appreciative enough?*
- *Am I demonstrating my concern sufficiently?*
- *Am I being empathetic?*
- *Am I being truly accepting?*
- *Do I initiate playfulness enough in our relationship?*
- *Do we joke around?*
- *Do I let my spouse know when I'm feeling delighted, excited, and even joy-ful in our marriage?*

Complaints versus Criticisms and the Learner and Judger Selves   Gottman's research (pp. 75–76) also revealed four kinds of destructive interactions that tend to proceed like dominoes down the road to George-and-Martha-like scenes, and quite possibly to acrimonious divorces. In order of escalating severity, these destructive interactions were: criticism, contempt, defensiveness, and withdrawal (stonewalling). A critical spouse positions his or her marital domino on the first step of the downhill road to unhappiness, usually without realizing it. This diffi-culty can begin almost invisibly, when complaints turn into criticisms. While a complaint can be a useful communication, this is rarely the case with criticisms. The next few subsections deal with complaints and criticisms, how they relate to behaviors of Learner and Judger spouses, and how this information can be used to develop win-win requests.

Complaints versus Criticisms   It is crucial for couples to understand the dis-tinction between a complaint and a criticism in order to stay off the four-stage highway that leads to such destructive—and avoidable—ends. A complaint is a specific statement of anger, displeasure, distress, or other negativity. A person *complains* when upset about some *specific* action, or lack of action. *Criticism*, on the other hand, is *about the person*, and is much more globally condemning. It is often accompanied by phrases such as, "you always," "you never," and "you should" (pp. 75–76) which is consistent with the Judger's side of the Language and Communicating Section of the Learner/Judger Chart.

Because criticism is likely to be experienced as judgment and blame, it is also experienced as an *attack on the person's worth*, rather than on his or her behavior. To make matters worse, this is not the kind of attack against which one can successfully defend. Such circumstances, therefore, often leave spouses feel-ing defenseless, vulnerable, and damaged. Lacking any perceived alternatives, they often attack back, leading almost inevitably to escalating hostilities, increas-ing pain, and weakening of the marital union. This sequence of interactions is typical of automatic, reactive marital win-lose patterns.

Criticism, if it's mean enough, and often enough, is a love-killer. It is chal-lenging to maintain the experience of being loved, appreciated, and desired by a person who would behave toward one in such a manner. Additionally, criticism is not very sexy. It is difficult to imagine being turned on, feeling intimate, or wanting to make love after being assaulted and barraged with criticisms. This is one of the times when thinking clearly is so important to love. We are responsible for our behavior, even when upset and emotionally aroused—and even when there is a good reason to be. How much better it would be if, at such times, spouses could manage to ask themselves Learner Self questions such as: *"Do I really mean what I'm about to say?"* *"Is it worth it to damage my spouse and my marriage in this way?"* *"How does being criticized make me feel?"* and *"If I keep criticizing him/her, how will that affect our sex life?"*

The Learner Self Complains, the Judger Self Criticizes   This distinction between a complaint and a criticism is a crucial one in question-centered therapy with couples. By considering Gottman's findings in terms of the model of the Learner Self and the Judger Self, we recognize that Judger-dominant spouses typically criticize. In contrast, Learner spouses complain. A Learner spouse might offer a critique, but critiques are meant to be helpful. Criticisms are intended to be hurtful.

By the same token, if the spouse *receiving* a criticism listened through Judger Self ears, he or she might predictably ask questions such as, *"Why is he/she acting like such a jerk?"* or *"How can I retaliate?"* Other Judger responses could include, *"How come I keep screwing up?"* or *"Does this mean I'm really not lovable or sexy?"* None of these questions is likely to lead to an intimate, sexy evening—or contribute to a win-win marriage.

On the other hand, if the spouse on the receiving end of a criticism were listening through Learner Self ears, some predictable self-questions would be: *"I wonder whether he's had a bad day?"* or *"Does she actually realize what she's saying to me?"* or *"How can I stay calm and let him/her know that comment hurt?"* or *"How can I communicate effectively that I expect to be treated respectfully in my marriage?"* If Albee could eavesdrop on the internal questions of such Judger and Learner spouses, he might easily predict where their interactions would lead, and how to logically finish writing the scene.

Complaints Converted to Requests Lead to Resolution   Some of the question-centered therapy psycho-educational information builds on recognizing the necessity of preventing complaints from "sliding into criticism." The ability to transform a complaint into a resolvable situation rests on the recognition that a complaint can be considered an inverted request.[2] Since a request is a question that asks the receiver for something specific and possible, to be done by a certain time, and in a certain way, it also contains within it the possibility of resolution. When an individual makes an effective, well-formed request, there are only three

---

[2] I thank Fernando Flores for this understanding of the connection between questions/requests and complaints.

kinds of responses that allow both speaker and listener to win. For a win-win interaction, these three responses would be to accept, decline, or counteroffer (suggest an alternative plan). In other words, what is wanted is obvious, negotiation and satisfaction are genuinely possible, and the relationship as a whole can be strengthened by the interaction. The importance of this realization lies in the possibility that complaints can serve as the beginning of *resolving* a dissatisfaction, and so contribute to the strength of the marriage.

By contrast, criticism tends to poison the marital atmosphere by setting a negative process in motion. Because the Judger Self's win-lose requests provided no specific way for the person criticized to ameliorate the situation, the interaction is uncomfortable and negative (at least for the spouse criticized), and the marriage as a whole is eroded, if only slightly. Nobody is perfect, and all of us are likely to be critical in our intimate relationships from time to time. However, when these interactions become excessive and cumulative, an atmosphere of criticism and negativity becomes established in the marriage, opening the door for contempt, the next negative emotion in the sequential downward highway that Gottman and his colleagues identified.

Here are a few examples of how Learner Self spouses can use this understanding about criticisms and complaints to enrich their marriages. A Learner spouse might ask observing and correcting questions such as, *"Did I sound like I was whining and criticizing?"* and *"How could I turn that criticism into a complaint?"* and *"How can I convert my complaint into a win-win request?"* Or the other Learner spouse might say, in as neutral a tone as possible: "I couldn't tell whether that was a complaint or a criticism. Is there something specific you're asking me to do about that situation?" They both might be thinking, *"How can we keep this situation confined to a complaint, and keep criticism out of it?"* Such interactions would also represent their shared contextual question for the relationship, *"How can we both win?"* With these examples both spouses made conscious choices about communicating thoughtfully and responsibly, rather than reacting automatically. Both contributed to the quality, durability, and loving experience of their marriage.

Win-Win versus Win-Lose Requests

Converting a complaint into a request is a crucial move for getting off the four-lane highway to unhappiness and divorce that Gottman described. It is also an imperative step for getting and staying on the road to marital happiness. But it is not enough. *The request must be one in which both partners can truly win.* The bottom line of a win-win request is that the person making it is responsible for his or her own satisfaction—by asking for what they want, and in a way that the other person can succeed, will want to, and will be pleased afterward to have done so. Of course, in win-win requesting, the other person can counteroffer and a satisfying negotiation can follow. The other person can also decline, and trust that the relationship will remain whole. In this way, a win-win request, once accepted, is one in which what is wanted is sufficiently specified—including a timeline—and it is truly possible to fulfill the request. What would be the point of asking for something in such a vague way that the other person wouldn't know what it would take to make you happy and satisfied?

But that's what often happens. People are regularly careless with their communications and requests, assume the other person can mind read, or are embarrassed to ask for anything at all—much less specify what they really need or want. Sometimes they haven't figured it out themselves, so it would be impossible to communicate it to anyone one else anyway. Maybe they confuse being declined with being rejected, and are therefore afraid of being turned down.

The situation may be mundane, as in asking one's spouse to pick up cereal, but not specifying what kind or when it was needed. Maybe they never asked, either hoping the other would notice the cereal box was empty and buy some, or perhaps a spouse was concerned about having already asked for too many things that day. If there weren't any cereal for breakfast, annoyance or just good-natured shrugging of shoulders might follow. However, transpose the same kind of careless, losing behavior into the tender setting of the bedroom, and the possibilities for feeling hurt, angry, and rejected magnify exponentially—and can cut to the very heart of the marriage.

This kind of tragic scenario was vividly brought home to me when a client in individual therapy commented, "When my husband comes home, if he hasn't done what I want, I'm going to be so mad I won't want to have sex for a week." Though I was a bit taken aback, I naturally asked if she had told him what she wanted and expected. She answered, "Well, sort of. I mentioned something about it a few days ago. He should be able to figure it out on his own. If he really loves me, he'll just know." Maybe she just didn't consider her husband's untenable position, or anticipate the consequences of how he might feel and act toward her during that week. However, it's not hard to predict that some form of marital wreckage would result, and resemble the damaging emotional tangle so unhappily exemplified by George and Martha.

Gender Differences in Marriage

In the previous section we explored Goleman's concepts of high and low emotional intelligence, especially in the marital context. Here we add the issue of gender to the complicated mix required for marital happiness. Goleman opened the topic of gender and emotional intelligence by pointing to some of the significant, current research of gender theorists (1995, pp. 130–135). Collectively, their work called attention to major differences in the typical emotional training of boys and girls in our culture, profoundly affecting the perceptions, capacities, and expectations, as well as the needs and fears, which men and women bring to marriage. The inevitable conflicts of marriage exacerbate and highlight these differences even further. Goleman concluded that ". . . *there are, in effect, two emotional realities in a couple, his and hers*" (p. 130; my italics).

Two emotional realities in this most vulnerable and volatile arena of human relationships geometrically increases the possibilities for miscommunication, mistrust, and painful rather than loving unions. Therefore, no conversation about win-win marriages would be complete without taking into account the findings of this important new field of gender research. As in any new area of inquiry, the first task is to cast the broadest net possible, in hopes of catching glimmers and hints to hurl us beyond the limitations of our usual paradigms. In this case, we urgently need ways to move us beyond the attack-or-defend paradigm that has wreaked such havoc with our ability to experience and express love.

New questions call forth that which is not yet invented, allowing doors to open which were invisible until attention was focused in those directions. In the complex arena of relationships between men and women, we need uncharted seas where treasures can be discovered to help heal the chasm between the genders, and the extraordinary, practically unfathomable damage this has brought. In this spirit, the questions posed below are meant to percolate and stimulate; we would best "dwell" in them, and add even more, least we foreclose new possibilities for love, intimacy, and marriage by prematurely grasping at easy or obvious answers. Some of these questions include:

- *What is the nature of these disparate gender-based realities, and how is this reflected in men's and women's internal dialogues—especially their self-questions?*
- *How are men's and women's answers to these differing internal questions expressed emotionally and behaviorally in their marriages?*
- *How can we understand, appreciate, and value the richness of the differences of our genders, rather than react to them as sources of conflict?*
- *How might different gender-based realities influence a spouse's choice to react automatically as a Judger Self, or respond thoughtfully as a Learner Self?*
- *What are some of the implications of this important gender research for therapy, education, and other disciplines?*
- *How can we neutralize the damage caused by the paradigm of the "war between the sexes"?*
- *How can we empower win-win marriage as a cultural norm and a personal possibility?*
- *How can we prevent negative stereotypical Judger Self attitudes toward both men and women from undermining basic research into these essential questions?*

Rilke enjoined us to ". . . love the questions themselves (so that we could) live along some distant day into the answer(s)" (1984, p. 34). Perhaps our loving questions could help neutralize the anxiety of not knowing, and move us beyond the terrified pretension that it is possible to absolutely and enduringly know what is "right" (and thereby be anointed as judge and jury for what is "wrong"). Thus unmasked, we might garner the patience and humility to live into answers that help us identify with our common humanity rather than with any differences or limited perspectives of our respective genders. What else could make a more profound impact on the day-to-day experiences of those couples who can't understand why "happily ever after" hadn't ever happened to them?

SUMMARY

The chapter opened by shining a spotlight on the omnipresent theme of conflict in marriage. The metaphor of marriage as war was personalized through the brutally archetypal win-lose marriage of George and Martha in Albee's *Who's Afraid of Virginia Woolf?* We then explored the internal linguistic underpinnings that contribute to such difficult, Judger-dominated marriages. We pinpointed automatic reactions as a primary culprit in win-lose marriages, and promoted thoughtfulness as a necessary antidote for impetuous marital behaving and relating. Being thoughtful, in contrast with being on automatic, was also discussed as the foundation for individuals to exercise choice and responsibility in their marriages.

The chapter also examined some of the theoretical background of question-centered therapy with couples through the work of four psychologists: Burns, Seligman, Gottman, and Goleman. A diagram illustrated how their work fits the model of the Learner Self and the Judger Self, as well as how these concepts cluster on the Choice Model. In addition, we explored how a question-centered therapeutic focus could blend with, and perhaps extend, the healing and growth possibilities in the work of each of these four writers.

Now, perhaps with a sigh of relief, we end this act and darken the stage on George and Martha. We move on to chapter 13, throwing a floodlight on an alternative marital metaphor: *marriage as a peace process.* Specifically, we next examine the first part of a question-centered model for psycho-educational training to help make win-win marriages a realistic possibility for our client couples.

13

All's Fair in Love and War—Or Is It?

*The solution, like all solutions to apparent contradictions,
lies in moving away from the opposition and changing the
nature of the question, to embrace a broader context.*
— HUMBERTO R. MATURANA AND
FRANCISCO J. VARELA

S uggesting that the context of marriage could shift from conflict to a peace
process might seem as absurd as awakening in the finale of some fluffy
happy-ending musical. And well it should. Win-lose relating between the sexes
has been the norm for so long we've come to assume that it *is* the way it is. Breaking out of the marriage as war metaphor requires transforming the fundamental
questions we answer through the ways we relate to members of the "opposite sex,"
especially those others with whom we're most intimate. In marriage, our Judger
Selves ask only, "*How can I win?*" while our Learner Selves expand to inquire,
"*How can we both win?*"

The question this chapter asks—and attempts to answer—is: "*How can we
empower our client couples to alter the basis of their marital relationships from win-
lose to win-win?*" However, this question is incomplete without including: "*How
can we engender our clients with the ability to relate from their Learner Selves, and
subdue their Judger Selves, especially in the midst of marital conflict?*"

The purpose of this chapter and the next, therefore, is to respond to these
questions by providing an overview and format for presenting the four psycho-
educational modules of question-centered therapy with couples. Section 1 of this
chapter offers a brief summary of the literature assessing the efficacy of psycho-
education and of cognitive-behavioral therapy in working with couples. The section also covers practical considerations of such training undertaken from a
question-centered perspective. Sections 2 and 3 present the first two modules of
this psycho-educational training for couples. The exposition of each module
includes its goals, handouts, examples of therapist's explanatory narrative with

clients, and background information about the teaching points. Some modules also include case examples. Chapter 14 presents modules 3 and 4.

SECTION ONE: PSYCHO-EDUCATION— PRACTICAL CONSIDERATIONS

In this section we first discuss the efficacy of psycho-educational approaches in working with couples. Then we explore practical considerations of this approach, including the advantages of conjoint training, how to introduce the psycho-educational aspects of therapy to clients, and the timing of this training within the course of treatment. The organization of the four modules is also addressed.

Efficacy

Psycho-educational approaches to both family and marital problems have been shown to be very effective (Shadish et al. 1993). A meta-analysis of 15 studies conducted by Shadish and his colleagues, each of which used control groups, showed that the psycho-educational method had a treatment effect size of between .36 and .41, which is highly significant ($p < .05$). In this study, Shadish et al. also found that cognitive-behavioral therapies had the highest effect size of all methods tested in their meta-analysis (.83). When working with marital problems, it would therefore appear clinically promising to combine these two highly effective strategies, cognitive-behavioral therapy and psycho-educational training. Question-centered therapy integrates cognitive-behavioral therapy along with a psycho-educational orientation in treating couples.

Introducing the Psycho-Educational Aspects of Therapy to Clients

The therapist usually tells the couple in the initial interview that their therapy process will include educational training designed to strengthen their chances for therapeutic success. She stresses that this will also increase their ability to *maintain* that success. In these introductory comments, the therapist also tells her clients that they will receive printed, illustrated materials to keep for study and reference. Further, she notes that these lessons will be organized into three modules (not counting the initial interviews), consisting of approximately one to three sessions each. However, the therapist also recognizes that the number of sessions required for each module will depend upon the severity and complexity of the presenting problem, and the level of maturity of each spouse, especially with regard to issues of responsibility and blame.

Timing of Training within Course of Treatment   The closer the teaching sessions are positioned to the beginning of therapy, the more therapeutic advantages they can yield. The psycho-educational material gives couples important, practical tools which immediately empower their ability to make use of therapy. Moreover, the actual delivery of the question-centered material is a therapeutic intervention in itself. It can interrupt dysfunctional, automatic interactive patterns, and give clients a much needed metaposition to their individual, as well as their interpersonal patterns.

Clients are naturally more open and less defensive in explicit educational sessions than later when the spotlight is aimed on them more personally. For this reason, another benefit of delivering the psycho-educational training early in treatment is that it can help the therapist build rapport with her clients' Learner Selves. Early on, her clients' receptivity and ability to listen to the material is more likely to be focused by the Learner question, *"What's of value for me here?"* Since the Judger Self lives within the tight constraints of a "blame-others, blame-self" paradigm, the only questions available to listen through are those such as: *"What's wrong with this information?"* or, *"What's wrong with this therapist?"* or, *"What does this therapist think is wrong with me that she hopes this information will fix?"* The point is to avoid rousing such Judger questions as much as possible by developing rapport with each spouse's Learner Self.

Conjoint Training

Under ideal circumstances, the question-centered psycho-educational material is taught to couples conjointly. It may also be delivered in a time-limited educational couples' group. If circumstances make conjoint training impractical, this training can be given to partners individually. However, conjoint training offers definite therapeutic advantages over individual training.

Since partners learn together, they start on a level playing field. Neither has learned something before the other, and this may preclude either from feeling excluded, or "one-down." By the same token, neither spouse can realistically claim superiority or dominance in relation to this new material. More important, the couple can begin practicing these methods in their interactions right away, while receiving immediate feedback from the therapist. The initial purpose is for partners to learn to use strategic, Learner Self internal-questioning techniques to interrupt negative, automatic conflict patterns. This enables them to build new, successful problem-solving patterns into their experience and resources as a couple. Additionally, this experience helps set the foundation for the therapeutic work to follow.

Conjoint training also facilitates practice with the new skills at home, so the spouses' learning curve can be relatively simultaneous and mutually reinforcing. They have the advantage of in vivo practice working out difficulties, making plans, or simply engaging in everyday life. As practicing Learner Selves, spouses learn to ask themselves questions such as: *"Am I overreacting to this situation?"* *"What questions could I ask myself (or my spouse) to get us out of this reactive rut?"* *"What is my goal in this conversation, and what questions could help get us there?"* and *"Have we set this up so we both can win?"*

Andrea, whom we met in chapter 6, provided an example of a successful therapeutic outcome based on learning to observe her own *internal* questions and altering them in accordance with the positive experiences she wanted in her marriage. However, Andrea was in individual, not couples' therapy. The benefits of learning this material are much greater with both partners participating and cooperating toward a shared goal of a win-win marriage.

Psycho-Educational Training with Couples Rather Than Individuals   There is an important therapeutic advantage in focusing on spouses' *individual* internal dialogues in the beginning of therapy. This focus promotes a "research-and-learn" emphasis which can be cooperative, in contrast to the blaming and accusing behavior typical of the attack-or-defend paradigm and win-lose marriages. It sets the frame for the couple to behave in an observe-and-correct, win-win manner from the beginning of treatment. However, in presenting this material to couples, there may be a temptation to skip over some of the training in individual internal dialogue in order to move ahead quickly to self-questions about the marriage. This, however, would be a mistake; in fact, it could undermine the effectiveness of the psycho-educational contribution to therapy.

It is essential for spouses to learn to track their *own* internal dialogue to increase self-awareness in their lives *in general*, not only in the marital context. Without this base of self-awareness, spouses do not have the best foundation for taking responsibility for their *own* thoughts, feelings, and behaviors within the marriage. Nor will they have the best chance for developing the thinking skills required for avoiding projecting blame and judgment onto their spouse, and/or onto themselves. For these reasons, this chapter includes examples of internal dialogue which are focused on individual, as well as marital concerns.

A Different Kind of Communication Training   This is a different kind of communication training than the couple may have ever encountered previously. Most communication training naturally focuses on interpersonal speaking and listening. However, there is rarely an emphasis on internal dialogue, much less the internal questions which exert such a profound influence on the interpersonal domain. Therefore, a prime purpose of this question-centered psycho-education training is to provide a sturdy foundation for the communication skill building which takes place later in couples' therapy.

Presentation of the Modules in These Chapters   The presentation of the four modules in this chapter and the next presumes that they occur sequentially without interruption, beginning with the initial interview(s). However, depending on circumstances, the modules may not be taught in sequence, or some of the training may not be given at all. This material has also been used with creativity and flexibility in the middle and even ending phases of treatment to good benefit.

Organization of the Modules   Each of the four modules follows a similar organization. Each begins with introductory comments about the purpose of the module followed by a list of the goals which help fulfill that purpose. Some of the goals are self-explanatory; others require elaboration. This is presented following the statement of the goal, which appears in italics. Following the statement and commentary of each goal, any handouts for that module are presented and discussed. Question-centered therapy with couples utilizes the same handouts as those presented in chapters 4 and 9 for individuals. There are five additional handouts specific to marital and relationship issues, which will be discussed in the appropriate modules.

SECTION TWO: MODULE 1

The first psycho-educational module is subsumed into the initial interview(s). It utilizes one handout, the Marriage Barometer (see Figure 13.1). The purpose of this module is informational for both therapist and clients. The module is designed to accomplish five basic goals. The explicit nature of the first three goals of the initial interview is information-gathering. While this is intended primarily for the therapist, it may also be useful for clients. They may never have thought about the questions asked, and they can learn something new about their spouses, as well as about themselves. The informational nature of the last two goals of the module is to introduce the psycho-educational nature of treatment and set a foundation for therapy for the couple. The five goals of this module are to:

1. *Learn about each spouse's interpersonal perceptiveness, basic communication skills, awareness of internal dialogue, and the level of responsibility each assumes for the current state of the marriage.*
2. *Discover each spouse's questions about the marriage, as well as his or her reasons and goals in seeking, or agreeing to, couples' therapy.*

The emphasis is on specifying, as much as possible early in treatment, what each spouse wants to stop or diminish (if this is the case), and what each spouse wants to start or increase (if this is the case) in the relationship. A simple assessment instrument, the Marriage Barometer, helps the therapist understand each spouse's individual and marital goals in relation to the severity of the experienced win-lose parameters of their marriage. Moreover, the therapist specifically asks what questions each partner has about the marriage, even though she is aware that either or both spouses may not be certain, or may not be ready to disclose their real questions this early in treatment.

3. *Gain a sense of the general "atmosphere" in the couple's relationship for asking questions and making requests.*

Either in couples' sessions or in individual sessions related to marital therapy, questions such as the following can reveal helpful information: "In general, how do you feel about the way your spouse asks you questions, or makes requests of you?" "In general, what is your level of comfort and success in asking questions or making requests of your spouse?" "Is there anything you're afraid to ask your spouse (say, about his/her family, his/her previous marriage, his/her financial situation, etc.)?" "Is there something you would like to ask your spouse to do, or *not* do (for example, sexually or emotionally), that you're afraid to ask for?" and "Does your spouse make requests of you in a way that you feel you both can win?"

Additionally, the therapist is interested in each spouse's question-related experiences in his or her family of origin. Early restrictions on question asking could point to an authoritarian upbringing, a cloaking of family secrets, or denial about some aspects of family life. Goleman made this point in saying that, "Questions that can't—or won't—be asked are a sure sign of a lacuna . . . (since) . . . [t]he creation of blind spots is a key tool of repressive regimes, allowing them to obliterate information that threatens their official line" (Goleman 1985, p. 128). While he wrote of lacunae in culture and society at large, he also illustrated how this same process takes place in families. Consider these questions of a young woman to her father, a former Nazi: "*Daughter*: What was the war about? *Father*: I don't want to talk about it. *Daughter*: Did you gas any Jews? *Father*: If you care to leave my house, forever, right now, you need only repeat what you just said" (p. 128).

"Repressive regimes" of client families are rarely so blatant in ordering silence. Yet such rules, whether explicit or implicit, and the threat of punishment that accompanies them, contaminate the atmosphere of family and marital life, and exact a damaging toll on individual family members. For these reasons, inquiries about question asking in spouses' families of origin can reveal important information. Here are examples of such questions: "Do you remember any time somebody got angry, or acted funny, when you asked what you thought was an innocent question?" "While you were growing up, was there anything you *weren't* allowed to ask questions about?" and "Was there anything you *just knew* you should *never* ask about?"

4. *Set the stage for the psycho-educational nature of question-centered therapy.*

This includes discussing the general purpose and character of the question-centered educational focus, as well as addressing practical considerations such as the approximate timing and the conjoint nature of the training, and the materials used. This explicit focus on question asking also forecasts the therapeutic emphasis on questions and questioning throughout treatment.

5. *Boost each spouse's hopefulness for positive change through the implied promise that a win-win relationship is possible and deserved, that skill*

training facilitates this accomplishment, and that each spouse already possesses the ability to learn, change, and take advantage of the possibilities of the therapeutic setting.

The Marriage Barometer Handout

The Marriage Barometer is an assessment tool which is typically used in the initial interview, or in an early therapy session. It serves two main purposes: to acquaint the couple with the concept of win-win and win-lose marriage, and to help each spouse define his or her marriage (and self) from this perspective. The Marriage Barometer helps spouses move beyond the usual general comments about what does and doesn't work in their marriage. It may also stimulate some spirited and revealing conversation about the win-lose experiences of their marriage which caused them to seek therapy.

Presenting and Using the Marriage Barometer   Before introducing the Marriage Barometer, the therapist opens the conversation about the concept of win-win and win-lose marriage by asking the spouses to define what these terms suggest to them. She listens for similarities and differences in their definitions, and for the congruency of their expectations for marriage. Even though the term *win-win marriage* may be new to the couple, the therapist assumes that at the time they wed, each spouse experienced the relationship as win-win, and expected it would remain that way. Therefore, the therapist listens for when this balance shifted, and for what events in the life cycle of the marriage contributed to destabilizing the experience of at least one spouse into win-lose. Of course, the therapist recognizes that any particular response from either spouse on this topic is likely to be affect laden, and therefore may elicit emotional reactions, opinions, and interactions.

After this warm-up conversation about win-win and win-lose marriages, the therapist tells the couple that she has something called the Marriage Barometer that will help each indicate his or her feelings about the present state of the marriage. She then hands each a copy, and further explains how to fill it out, pointing to the three columns on the right side. Reading across, left to right, the first column asks for the spouse's assessment of him- or herself within the marriage. The second column asks each to assess him- or herself relative to the other spouse. The third column calls for a guess about how the marriage appears to the "outside world." Therapeutic conversations address each spouse's opinions in each of the three categories.

Naturally, the instrument is meant to be used in any creative way the therapist finds supportive of her diagnostic or therapeutic work with a particular couple. For example, she could ask each spouse to guess where the other might rate him- or herself. She could ask each to indicate a general level of hopefulness about the marriage, or note the level of the best and worst it's ever been, and what specific behaviors, events, and feelings account for these differences. She might

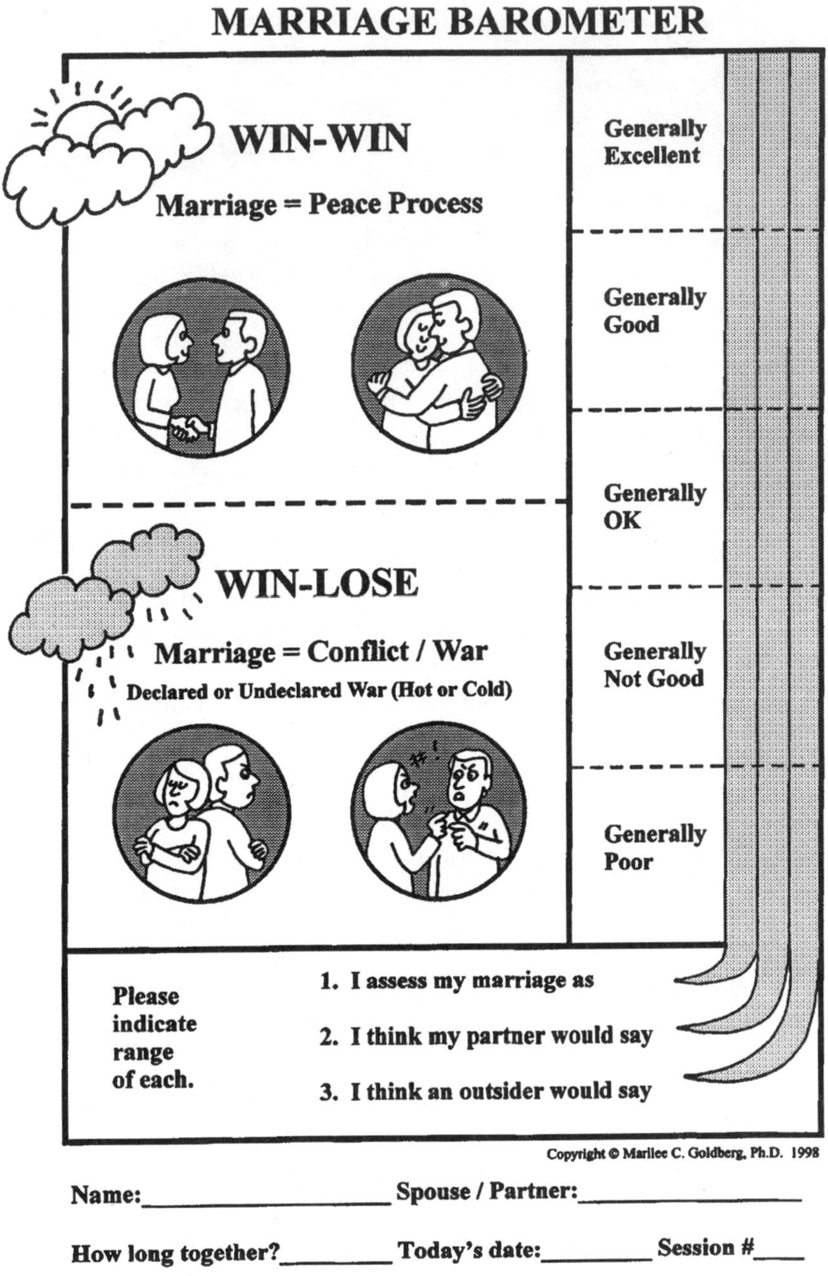

MARRIAGE BAROMETER

WIN-WIN Marriage = Peace Process		Generally Excellent
		Generally Good
		Generally OK
WIN-LOSE Marriage = Conflict / War Declared or Undeclared War (Hot or Cold)		Generally Not Good
		Generally Poor

Please indicate range of each.

1. I assess my marriage as

2. I think my partner would say

3. I think an outsider would say

Copyright © Marilee C. Goldberg, Ph.D. 1998

Name:_____ Spouse / Partner:_____

How long together?_____ Today's date:_____ Session #____

Figure 13.1   The Marriage Barometer.

also draw a few extra vertical lines on the far right and mark them for appropriate time periods. For example, if the couple had been married for 15 years, they could draw three columns, each representing five years of the marriage, and mark their assessment of the marriage in each of the three columns.

Using the Marriage Barometer throughout Therapy   The Marriage Barometer can also be used to focus conversation at later points during the course of treatment. For example. when it comes time for more specific goal setting, this instrument helps the therapist direct her clients to be more detailed about their individual versions of a win-win marriage. Furthermore, the Marriage Barometer is used throughout therapy to assess progress, helping answer the spouses' question *"How are we doing?"* as well as the therapist's internal questions such as, *"What else do they need to change and/or learn in order to be successful?"* and *"What are the best ways to help them with this?"* Finally, the instrument is used to help focus assessment conversations about readiness for termination of treatment.

SECTION THREE: MODULE 2

The purpose of module 2 is to introduce the couple to the importance of internal dialogue in marital conflict and marital happiness. Module 2 has five goals, which can usually be accomplished in the two standard sessions allotted for it. The second session of the module is necessary in order to complete the homework assignment from the first. The second session also gives the therapist an opportunity to assess whether she needs to reinforce specific teaching points about internal dialogue, and especially about internal questions, before moving on to module 3.

In general, the presentation of the question-centered psycho-educational material in therapy with couples is similar to that given to individuals. This is especially true in module 2 where the emphasis is on each spouse's individual internal dialogue. The reader is referred to chapter 4 which reviews this presentation with individuals extensively in section 4. With couples, as with individuals, the therapist need not worry about her clients being "perfect" students, nor herself being a perfect teacher, since this material will be reinforced and utilized many times during the course of treatment. At this point, the therapist need only make certain that each spouse achieves a general understanding and beginning acceptance of the material. It is more important for spouses to experience a positive, affirming learning experience than to memorize any of the data or concepts.

Couples may understandably question the emphasis on *individual* internal dialogue in couples' therapy since their goal is to interact with each other more successfully. The point, of course, is to increase individual awareness and skills as a foundation for more successful marital communication. Presumably, if the couple had been communicating effectively, they would not have developed the problems that prompted their seeking therapy. Interpersonal questioning is covered in module 3, especially with reference to win-win requests.

The therapist introduces two handouts in this module, both of which she also uses with individual clients: Observe-and-Correct (see Figure 4.2) and Switching Questions (see Figure 4.3). The homework assignment between the two sessions is for each spouse to monitor his or her internal dialogue, especially self-questions, including those related to the marriage. Homework for strengthening the ability to observe is essential—for many clients the education in this module marks the formal beginning of intentional learning in being an observing self. In effect, this training in self-observation represents stepping onto a rung of a ladder they will climb, in one form or another, for the rest of their lives. The five goals of this module are to:

1. *Establish, or reinforce, a nonjudgmental awareness of internal dialogue.*

This, of course, is a fundamental skill of an observing self. The emphasis is on recognizing the importance of internal questioning as the basis for problem solving and decision making, and ultimately for its influence on the general shape, content, and experience of our lives. It is important for spouses to recognize that internal dialogue is comprised of statements *and* questions. As we have emphasized, question-centered therapy assumes that behaviors are generally answers to questions that preceded them, even if these questions were implicit, and therefore not obvious. The point is for spouses to recognize that what happens in their relationships is strongly influenced by the questions they ask *themselves*. In fact, these unrecognized internal questions are often at the source of couples' automatic, reactive conflicted interactions. By the same token, clients' marriages are also shaped by questions *not* asked, either because they're afraid to ask, or simply because they don't understand the importance of questions.

These theoretical points make practical sense to couples when their specific problems are examined from these perspectives. For example, Helen and Fred came for marital therapy, referred by Fred's individual therapist. From the beginning, their sessions were characterized by Helen's incessant complaining about her husband. Toward the end of the psycho-educational training, I turned to Helen, and inquired, "When you talk about your husband like that, are you answering the question, '*What did he do right?*' or '*What did he do wrong?*' " She looked startled, and then answered, "Well, I guess it would be '*What did he do wrong?*' but then, he usually *is* wrong." "Do you mean to tell me," I responded, in a lightly teasing way, "that in *all* the time you've known him, he's hardly *ever* done *anything* right?" Helen smiled sheepishly and said, "Well, I guess he's done some things OK." "Good," I replied. "Then, will you tell me about something Fred did that was quite fine?" The rest of the session followed her impressive positive answer.

At the end of the session, Fred left to go back to his office, and I asked Helen to remain for a moment. I said I had an important question for her, but didn't know if she were ready to hear it. She assured me she was. Having secured her permission to deliver my intervention, I said, "OK, I'll tell it to you under one condition. After I say it, will you promise to leave the office without saying a word, and not speak to *anyone* for half an hour?" She agreed, although she looked puzzled. My question to her was, "In the *long* run, will *you* be happier in your marriage if you spend the rest of your life answering the question, 'What did Fred do *right*?' or 'What did Fred do <u>wrong</u>?' "

Another clinical example illustrates how sometimes the questions our clients *don't* ask underlie their marital difficulties. Melissa, fresh out of college, met Matthew at the company picnic at her first "serious" job. Popular and good-looking, Matthew had just been selected as Salesman of the Year and his star seemed to be on the ascendancy. Melissa was dazzled that someone like him could be interested in her, and after a whirlwind romance, they wed. She knew he had been married twice before, but it just didn't seem all that important because he was so smart and attentive to her.

Melissa never asked Matthew, *or* herself, why his first two marriages ended. Moreover, she never asked herself, "*Do I know enough about this man to commit myself to him for the rest of my life?*" After only a few months of marriage, Melissa recognized that her husband was a closet drinker, and that his engaging sociability was often alcohol-stimulated. What brought Melissa into therapy was an incident in which Matthew had drunk too much and slapped her.

2. *Take responsibility and ownership of his or her own internal dialogue.*

This point about ownership and responsibility is pivotal for optimum utilization of the question-centered material. If each spouse can catch even a glimmer of comprehension about personal responsibility, the stage is set for Learner Self development, and participation in a win-win marriage. The goal is for each spouse to recognize that we human beings have the ability to choose and direct much of our thinking, but much less power or control without being able to identify what is *already* "passing through." When spouses accept and own what is actually present, they have more ability to choose where to go from there. Otherwise, there would be no starting place from which to move forward. Clients usually grasp this point if the therapist asks them to imagine calling a friend for directions, but without being able to give a fix on the present location.

If either spouse expresses confusion, denial, or outright hostility about ownership and responsibility, the therapeutic task ahead will have quite a different complexion. At one extreme of the continuum, refusal to take self-responsibility and externally projecting blame might manifest as controlling, abusive, or violent behavior. At the other end of the continuum, internally *or* externally projected judgment and blame reinforce the belief that one is helpless, vulnerable, unprotected, and out of control—or potentially so—at any moment, which is sometimes called "victim thinking" or a "victim mentality." Refusal to assume even the possibility of personal responsibility for one's own thinking, feeling, and behaving is precisely what permits and reinforces the paradigm of projection and blame that characterizes the Judger Self and its concomitant sentence to win-lose, attack-or-defend marriages.

3. *Recognize the power of internal questions.*

As we have seen, questions virtually program thoughts, feelings, and behaviors. There are identifiable features to questions that lead to optimistic moods and effectiveness in general. These questions contrast with others that lead to limitation, pessimism, depressed feelings, and even failure. Once spouses are able to identify self-questions already present in their internal dialogue, they can develop the skill to habitually question their questions (internal and interpersonal); or rather, analyze them for their degree of potential effectiveness. Upon discovering a limiting question, the same skill can be used to reword the query in order to increase the probability of its leading to success.

The distinctive impact of different kinds of questions is a startling and useful realization for spouses. Naturally, it is also instructive for spouses to recognize that negative questions about their mates and their marriages contributed to the difficulties that impelled them to seek therapy. For example, those treacherous questions, *"What did he/she do wrong?"* and *"What's wrong with him/her?"* lie at the source of countless painful, no-win marital conflicts. Sometimes a simple change in such basic questions can transform the experience and expectation of their relationship, and even begin to release both spouses from the linguistic traps that contributed to their win-lose perceptions, feelings, behaviors—and relationships.

The skills of self-observation and identifying internal dialogue, especially self-questions, fortify mature, responsible problem-solving behavior. This may be particularly confronting in marriage, where ideally spouses habitually ask themselves questions which require unflinching personal honesty, such as: *"Did I make that sarcastic remark about her mother's driving because I was really mad at her for not inviting my mother to dinner last week? or "Did I turn down his advances for sex last night because I was too tired, or was it really because I was angry at him for making fun of my driving?"* The origin of such responsible questions would have been a metaquestion (probably a nonlinguistic one) such as, *"Did I contribute to this problem?"* or *"What's my responsibility in resolving this?"*

Personal Guiding Questions in Marriage   In addition to the kinds of questions which predispose the listener to different moods and behaviors, there are other kinds of internal questions that pervasively influence the individual who asks them. These personal guiding or operating questions silently embody and impose the rules by which we lead our lives as individuals and in relationships of all kinds. An individual discovering a previously unconscious question that programmed his perception, experience, and limitations gains the metaposition essential for making new and better choices for guiding his life.

Helen and Richard were in marital therapy. Helen, who had been abused by her father as a young child, discovered that one of her main guiding questions was, "*How can I get men to be nice and pay attention to me?*" She also recognized that a long string of destructive relationships represented her inevitably disappointing answers. Asking instead, "*How can I get men to respect and support me?*" "*How can I develop a win-win relationship with my husband?*" as well as "*How can I develop appreciation and respect for myself first?*" opened a different vista of potential answers and a far more satisfying relationship with her husband.

Richard was an army brat, the son of an authoritarian colonel, who died when Richard was 17. His mother died when he was 12. Richard realized he had unknowingly programmed his life through several operating questions. The first such question was, "*How can I prove myself to my father?*" This client put his foot on the road to freedom when he asked for the first time, "*Is this actually possible?*" His realization that it was not allowed him to ask follow-up questions that opened many new possibilities for him. These new questions included, "*In my job, what men might be appropriate mentors for me?*" and "*By what criteria, and with what expectations, will I choose whom to approach with that request?*"

Richard's second overriding guiding question was, "*How can I find a woman who will approve of me and take care of me?*" Like Helen, he needed to begin asking, "*How can I develop appreciation and respect for myself first?*" He also realized that different questions would predict a far more positive and enjoyable marriage than either of them had seen as children. Some of the questions he created included: "*What do we bring to each other that's special?*" "*How can we help each other be better marital partners without making anybody wrong?*" and "*How can we develop a marriage that is truly satisfying and supportive to us both?*"

4. *Establish at least an intuitive grasp of the concept of retrospective analysis, which is the method of discovering background questions.*

Retrospective analysis is the process of identifying a behavior (or statement), and then backtracking to speculate about what earlier, implicit questions could logically have led to, or culminated in, that behavior (or statement). Again, everyday, ordinary examples work best. For instance, I often pick up a glass of water and ask spouses what internal questions could have led to my decision to pick up the glass. They easily guess, "*Am I thirsty?*" or "*Is this a good time to take a quick sip?*" or "*Will this water satisfy my thirst?*" If I ask them to imagine opening the refrigerator, then picking up a milk carton and shaking it, they consistently guess that this behavior answered questions such as: "*How much milk is left?*" or "*Do I need to buy milk?*" or "*Did I remember to ask my husband to pick up milk?*" Similarly, if I ask them to speculate about implicit questions leading to an internal statement such as, "*I have to make a doctor's appointment*" they easily offer background questions such as "*Am I sick enough that I have to go to the doctor?*" or "*Can I put this off any longer?*" or "*What's going to happen if I don't go?*"

5. *Become acquainted with observe-and-correct thinking, including switching questions.*

The Observe-and-Correct Handout

We have discussed observe and correct, the cognitive strategy for staying on track and moving effectively toward a goal, in clinical examples throughout the book. To recap briefly, observe-and-correct thinking occurs in alternating sequences, and each of these segments is driven by self-questions. An example of an observing self-question is, *"What's this?"* An example of a correcting self-question is, *"What is the simplest, easiest, and/or best correction for getting us back on course?"*

The Importance of Observe-and-Correct Thinking in Marital Happiness
This mental discipline of observe-and-correct thinking is challenging enough when there is only one goal, when this goal is objective and well-defined, and when its accomplishment depends on only one individual. The complexity and difficulty of achieving a goal expands exponentially when its accomplishment depends on two individuals who may have different definitions of the goal, different styles of moving toward it, and different, perhaps conflicting means of communicating and coordinating about the goal they have chosen to share. Furthermore, when these two individuals are in the emotionally laden context of marriage, and their goal is mutual happiness, the opportunities for misinterpreting, miscommunicating, and automatic, negative Judger Self reactivity are far greater.

In marriage, emotion often overwhelms and undermines reason and the ability to be thoughtful. Yet mutually satisfying, win-win marital resolutions *require* "cool heads," thoughtfulness, and conflict resolution skills. As part of learning to resolve differences and build win-win marriages, a prime purpose of question-centered therapy is for spouses to develop the Learner Self attitudes and skills that provide protection from Judger Self "hotheaded" behavior that characterizes win-lose interactions. If, as Gottman and his colleagues discovered, effective conflict resolution skills is the major predictor of marital longevity and happiness, then surely spouses' ability to successfully observe and correct should contribute substantially to win-win marriages.

Multiple Goals
Especially in the marital context, some astute clients may remark that they seem to have multiple, simultaneous, and sometimes incompatible goals, and ask the therapist about this. For example, a wife may lament: "At any one time, I may have a goal of getting my son to soccer practice, a goal of getting ready for a special weekend with my husband, a goal of finishing up a long-term project for work—*and* a goal of being graceful under pressure!" Of course, this client's experience of being overwhelmed is justified. In fact, our consciousness is virtually always divided with different "parts" focused by different goals, each of which is directed by internal questions which are probably silent and implicit.

The therapist would acknowledge this client for her perceptiveness, and then explain that because of all this possible complexity, the observe-and-correct handout is necessarily modest. Its purpose is simply to help spouses learn to identify the mental mechanism of tracking *one* goal, whether this goal be an individual or marital one. In order to do this, clients must learn to identify their own potentially distracting Judger Self internal dialogue, and also how to communicate appropriately and effectively with a mate whom they think may also have gotten stuck in Judger Self thinking.

Presenting and Using the Handout   Observe-and-correct thinking is the strategy taught to couples to use for interrupting automatic, reactive conflict patterns. Therefore, the therapist encourages discussion about observing and correcting, for example, by reviewing spouses' past conflicts and how these might have worked out differently if even one of them had been able to observe and correct in the heat of the fray. Usually with couples, as with individuals, before the therapist presents the actual handout, she illustrates the concept of this goal-directed thinking process with the teaching story in chapter 4 about the pilot who flies from New York by consistently observing and correcting toward her goal of the San Francisco airport.

The opportunities for straying off the course of a win-win marriage, especially in conflict situations, are ubiquitous. It is usually Judger thoughts of blaming either self or other that distract couples away from a win-win resolution of a particular difficulty. The therapist's goal is to encourage spouses to practice observe-and-correct thinking and behaving in such situations, just as the pilot lines up the readings on her flight instruments in relation to her goal of reaching San Francisco, and asks herself questions such as: *"How close are we?" "How much of a correction do we need at* this *moment?"* and *"How can I best accomplish this?"*

Switching Questions Handout

Observing interrupts automaticity; switching questions help spouses choose positive alternative directions. Some clients have called switching questions the secret weapon in transforming their win-lose marriages into win-win ones. Taking advantage of switching questions is especially vital in resolving marital conflict—when an individual or couple recognizes that a current track (cognitive, affective, behavioral, or interactive) could lead to trouble—and that it is imperative to *switch* tracks in order to avoid a dangerous conflict. Because switching questions help avoid danger, some clients also call them "rescue questions."

Switching Questions and Feeling in Control   The first goal in teaching switching questions to couples is to demonstrate that the reactive thoughts and feelings they consider automatic, and therefore out of their control, are usually *not*, if properly understood. In other words, they have a choice when they thought they had none—since feeling out of control is related to the experience of having no choices other than the current dominating thought, feeling, or behavior. That "proper" understanding occurs when an individual is able to survey his or her instantaneous, streamlined internal process in slow motion, so the frame-by-frame elements can be discerned. Asking switching questions rescues spouses from feeling helpless and unable to control the runaway train of many difficult marital situations. Couples learn to locate the point where their interaction derailed, and figure out different ways to resolve the situation. They can choose a different, positive direction, and thereby share control over their future.

The second goal of emphasizing the importance of switching questions is to *make it compelling to remember to ask these questions*, especially in the midst of marital conflict. Ideally, learning to instinctively ask a switching question comes to replace the old automatic reaction of Judger Self questions that kept them captive in the attack-or-defend paradigm. The third goal addresses the ways in which myopic short-term thinking exacerbates couples' difficulties. Therefore, the third goal is to provide an *experience* of shifting from short-term problem solving—which is usually impulsive, seeking either anxiety reduction or gratification of some sort—into long-term problem solving—which is usually in their better interests.

Presenting the Handout   Placing couples in the structure of studying the handout (i.e., looking at the picture of the train cab and railroad tracks, and playing out various moves as one would in a chess game) forces spouses to "try on" long-term thinking, and experience both the strategic escape from danger and the positive expansion of alternatives and possibilities. As with individuals, I ask spouses to imagine being the train engineer on the handout, responsible for getting the train safely to its destination. Looking ahead at the tracks, the engineer suddenly realizes that the bridge over the river is *out*—and that continuing down that same track spells certain disaster.

I then ask, "What could *stop* this hurtling train, and have it switch to another, *safe* track?" Spouses are usually stymied by this inquiry. The answer, of course, is an internal question, a *switching* question that directs them to *respond* to the crisis as their Learner Selves by *thinking about alternatives*. The old behavior would have been to allow their Judger Selves to react to the situation, engage in attacking or defending behavior, and cause an "accident." Sometimes I ask them to draw a bold line *across* the tracks so they can *see* and *experience* slowing and stopping the train, and redirecting it to an alternative, safe track.

After this, we construct the sequence of self-questions that resulted in the successful switch away from danger. It is important to actually walk couples through this internal dialogue since it provides practice for when it is needed in "real life." The sequence goes something like this: After observing that the railroad bridge is out, one instantly goes into Learner Self problem-solving mode (having asked, "*Do I want to keep going this way?*" and gotten an emphatic "*No!*"). Next one asks, "*What can I do?*" or "*How can I save us?*" That would lead to the question: "*Are there other tracks to take?*" A "*Yes*" answer would be followed by, "*Should I take the track to the right, or the one to the left?*" The engineer's behavioral answer represents his choice (say, the track to the right). Then I ask spouses to imagine actually *physically pulling on* the lever that switches the tracks, and then looking ahead for reassurance that they're now okay by asking, "*Is this new track safe?*" A "*Yes*" answer allows them to finally say, "*Whew! We made it! I can finally relax!*"

This exegesis illustrates for couples the importance of interrupting automatic reactions and slowing a moment in the movie of a difficult marital interaction into the still-shots that make a frame-by-frame analysis possible. This format allows them to "catch" many of the subtleties and distinctive cognitive moves of which a choice is comprised. It also gives them the opportunity to observe—and thereby potentially gain control over—the internal questions by which they always make choices, but perhaps had never recognized the process by which this takes place.

Case Examples

After this discussion in a couple's session, Sandra asked: "You mean, it's like, 'When life hands you lemons, make lemonade?' " I chuckled because her annoyed expression read, "*This is what I came to therapy to learn!?*" "You're right, Sandra," I replied. "Sometimes those sayings actually have some truth in them. Think of it this way: When life hands you lemons, you have a *choice* about what you do with them. You could just have an automatic knee-jerk reaction like a Judger Self, and cry or get angry because you don't like lemons. *Or* you could ask yourself a switching question like, '*How else could I deal with this?*' Then you might ask a Learner Self question like, '*What could I do with these lemons that I would enjoy?*' Then you might make lemonade—or a lemon meringue pie." Her husband, David, an artist, added, "How about asking, '*How would that lemon look in the still life I've been painting?*' " Sandra laughed, then looked perplexed, and finally exclaimed, "You mean once you realize you *always* have a choice, there's *no limit* to the questions you can ask, and the things you can do!"

A Switching Question Victory   Larry and Vivian, married for 11 years, came to therapy after incessant quarreling about visiting their respective in-laws, especially Larry's parents who lived far away. It soon became apparent that one of the variables in this case was Vivian's mild case of agoraphobia and panic attacks. She had experienced these prior to marriage, but they had started getting worse in the past year. Even after the couple's dynamic issues were basically resolved in therapy, Vivian's anxiety, though lessened, remained intrusive.

With Larry sitting in, I taught Vivian how to use switching questions to stop her "runaway anxiety thinking." She recognized that once those anxiety-inducing thoughts got going, they accelerated faster and faster, which she said felt like a runaway train. Of course, her heartbeat kept pace, and she experienced increasing panic. She said, "Those thoughts just take over, and I'm completely helpless." It had never occurred to her that it was possible to *stop* her thoughts, and *switch her thinking to a better track,* just by asking the right kind of question. The three of us looked at the Switching Questions handout with its picture of the train and the railroad tracks. We practiced different switching questions that could stop Vivian's runaway thoughts and rescue her by switching her thinking to a track where she felt safer and in control. Larry even contributed a few questions.

A few weeks later Vivian proudly reported a victory she had had over a panic attack while driving with their two young children. She used observe-and-correct questions to keep driving, avoid giving in to the anxiety, and get home safely. We debriefed her successful internal dialogue like this: "*Is this a heart attack, or am I just panicked?*" She told herself, "*I'm feeling panicked,*" and then asked, "*What will happen if I give in to it?*" Her answer was, "*an accident, hurt the kids, make Larry mad.*" Then she asked herself, "*Do I want that to happen?*" Of course, the answer was "*NO!*"

After that, Vivian rescued herself with the switching question, "*What else can I do?*" She told herself to take deep breaths, and that it was going to be okay. Then she complimented herself and said, "*Good, now what else can I do?*" Remembering she had a tape of cheerful children's music, she played it loud, and cajoled her children into singing along with her until they reached home. Later in the session, Vivian told Larry and me:

> I think it was the first time in years that I didn't feel like a victim to whatever it was that was going on. I realized there was something *I could do to* make things better. It also helped that it was something simple, and that I could do it *right away*. This incident made me realize I've been acting like a victim a lot with Larry. Like all the times we've visited his parents, it never occurred to me that I could say "No," or that there were any options other than just going along and feeling awful. I blamed him for "forcing" me on those long trips. I do think he could be more thoughtful, but it's also true that I was the one who never spoke up for myself. I've been a "go-along" person for years, sort of like a helpless passenger in the back seat along for the ride. But the other day, I realized I *like* being the driver. Even though I was a little shaky, it was OK because I also felt like I was in control.

SUMMARY

This chapter presented the first two modules of a model for teaching the question-centered psycho-educational material to couples. The purpose of module 1 is for information gathering in the most general sense, including informing the couple about the psycho-educational aspects of therapy. Module 2 begins the couples' training in internal dialogue, especially internal questions. The chapter introduced three handouts, the Marriage Barometer in module 1, and Observe-and-Correct and Switching Questions in module 2. Each of the handouts is part of a unified approach to teaching self-awareness and conflict resolution skills to couples, in support of their accomplishing *enduring* therapeutic success in the form of win-win marriages.

14

"If I am for myself only, what am I?"

If I am not for myself, who will be for me?
If I am for myself only, what am I?
If not now, when?

— HILLEL

This chapter completes the presentation of the structured psycho-educational training for couples in question-centered therapy. Here we focus directly on win-win marriages and conflict resolution. We have already discussed one of the primary findings of Gottman's landmark research on marital success and failure—that the outstanding predictor of the health and longevity of a marriage was the couple's effectiveness at conflict resolution. Casting this finding in light of the distinctions and terminology of the present book, we can presume that the more highly each spouse develops his or her Learner Self, the more consistently the couple can resolve conflict in a way that supports the win-win basis of the marriage.

In other words, the fundamental requirement for altering the context of marriage from win-lose to win-win calls for spouses to behave thoughtfully instead of automatically, and to utilize their Learner Selves for resolving marital conflict. Section 1 presents module 3, which addresses choice and responsibility in the marital context, handling conflict as a Learner Self, and training spouses to ask effective questions of each other, including making win-win requests. In module 4 the couple's presenting problems and desired outcomes are addressed directly, although of course a focus on their personal and interpersonal issues has been woven throughout the first three modules. Section 2 comprises module 4, which may also be thought of as the application module.

SECTION ONE: MODULE 3

The purpose of module 3 is to empower the couple's ability to resolve conflict by introducing the concept of the Learner Self and the Judger Self, personal choice and responsibility in marriage, and the skills of interpersonal question asking and win-win requesting. It is usually possible to fulfill the 10 basic goals of module 3 in three sessions. A suggested format for presenting this material is to introduce the Choice Model and the Marriage Context Model in the first session of the module, the Learner/Judger Chart in the second session, and to practice interpersonal questioning and making win-win requests in the third. Four handouts are used in module 3: the Choice Model (see Figure 4.1, p. 80), the Judger House & Learner House (see Figure 12.1, p. 260), the Marriage Context Model (see Figure 14.1, p. 298) and the Learner/Judger Chart (see Figure 9.1, pp. 161–178).

The Marriage Context Model, which is an elaboration of the Choice Model, illustrates the relationship of the Learner Self to win-win marriage and the metaphor of marriage as a peace process. The Judger Self is associated with win-lose marriage, and the metaphor of marriage as war and conflict. The Marriage Context Model demonstrates how each spouse continuously *chooses* the peace or conflict marital context through the internal questions he or she asks, consciously or not, especially during conflict situations. The Learner/Judger Chart used with couples is the same as the one presented to individual clients. The goals of module 3 are for each spouse to:

1. *Strengthen their observing self and Learner Self.*
2. *Recognize that everyone has a Learner Self and Judger Self, and accept these as normal expressions of being human.*

These perspectives empower each spouse to become more thoughtful and understanding as well as less automatic in their interactions with their partners. "Having" or "being" a Judger Self does not imply that oneself or one's spouse is bad, wrong, or pathological. Nor does "having" or "being" a Learner Self make one right, good, healthy, or superior. Furthermore, the point is not what one is, so much as *who one chooses to be*, and in which mode one chooses to think, feel, and behave *at any moment*.

When working with the Learner/Judger Chart, the therapist can help spouses *own* these recognitions by asking each partner to point to some of his or her own Learner Self *and* Judger Self qualities and tendencies. It's also useful to have clients identify Learner Self questions that might be helpful in their marriages, as well as a few of their own Judger Self questions they recognize as having already caused difficulties. Of course, the therapist cautions the couple about any possible temptation to label, or "name call" each other as "a Judger." As with individual clients, the therapist might indicate several of her *own* Learner *and* Judger characteristics, or how she used Learner strategies in a particular relationship situation.

3. *Recognize the relationship of the Learner Self to win-win marriage and the metaphor of marriage as a peace process, and the Judger Self to win-lose marriage and the metaphor of marriage as war and conflict.*

4. *Recognize and acknowledge personal choice and responsibility in the marital context.*

5. *Establish that seemingly unresolvable marital conflicts usually occur when one or both partners become triggered—and thus captors—of reactive, automatic negative Judger Self thoughts and feelings.*

6. *Realize that the consequences of being dominated and controlled by one's Judger Self are negative and undesirable.*

7. *Develop a desire to identify with and strengthen one's Learner Self, as well as detach from and manage the Judger Self.*

8. *Promise to behave as a Learner Self in resolving conflicts—and to recognize that this is a fundamental aspect of committing to a win-win marriage.*

9. *Be more effective in asking questions of their spouse.*

Spouses asking questions of each other is such a normal everyday occurrence that few even notice how often they do it. Life occurs around such everyday exchanges as: "What time are you coming home?" "When can we invite the Smith's for dinner?" and "What should we do about Johnny's report card?" The experience of these necessary daily interactions is the mortar that holds together the house of marriage—when the bricks are thought of as the major events, such as births, anniversaries, graduations, and the like. However, a poorly asked question in any area can touch off conflict, or prevent the necessary information, opinion, or sentiment from being conveyed, received, or acted upon.

In fact, even a question that is set up, worded, and delivered well may result in an uncomfortable communication tangle. This is to be expected. Any question or communication in marriage occurs in the context of the relationship as a whole, including any current unresolved issues. In addition, the other spouse may be listening through personal operating questions such as: *"Does he/she still love me?" Does he/she really find me attractive?"* or *"Does he/she really accept me for who I am?"* The inherent communication sensitivities in marriage are compounded by the fact that many people don't like to be asked questions in the first place. It is common to feel put on the spot when asked a question, and people often get defensive, even when there's no need to be.

There is no guaranteed way to guard against all such potential communication pitfalls in marriage. Life happens too fast, we can never know all the variables, and none of us is perfect anyway. However, there are some general principles to keep in mind when facilitating question-centered communication skill training with client couples. The points in the following section are meant to act as a guide in coaching couples in the communication skills of effective question asking. Of course, it's reassuring to clients to point out that *no one* fulfills the criteria of these guidelines all the time.

Question-Centered
Communication Training With Couples

- *The general goal is to ask a question effectively.*   This means to acquire or convey the information necessary, or initiate some specific action, *while maintaining respect and rapport.* Effective questions are more often asked by one's Learner Self, not one's Judger Self.
- *Observe the Golden Rule in asking questions.*   Ask questions of your spouse as you would like to be asked questions.
- *Make sure you have your spouse's attention.*   If your spouse doesn't realize they're being asked a question, there's little chance they'll answer it, or that you will get what you're asking for.
- *Know what you want before you ask.*   For example, is this a question for getting information, to get some action started, or for bringing up a subject to think about?
- *Recognize that questions can convey information or feelings.*   For example, "Did you know that Johnny's soccer practice was changed to Tuesday?" or "Have I told you recently that I love you?"
- *Timing is everything.*   This concerns *when* a question is asked, as well as the potential *length* of the interaction. If the question interaction isn't likely to be brief, say to your spouse, for example: "I have something to ask you. Is this a good time?" or "Do you have a minute?" Also, consider the circumstances and use common sense; for instance:
  - Don't ask a complicated or emotional question when your mate is late for work.
  - Don't ask about an expensive vacation after your spouse just lost a job.
  - When sex is in the picture, keep distracting, complex, or potentially upsetting questions out of it.
- *When is the answer needed?*   Let your spouse know if this is something for which you need an immediate answer, or if it's simply something you want them to think about so you can talk about it later.
- *Be careful about how the question is delivered.*   To neutralize "defensive listening," deliver questions in a neutral tone, or even an accepting, light-hearted one—with congruent facial expressions and body language. (Remember, even on the phone you can tell if someone is smiling.)
- *Set the question up properly.*   For example, "This is about that problem with Johnny's report card" or "Dear, I just had a tough conversation with my mother, and I want to ask you about it."
- *Consider who else might be listening.*   Never ask questions that could make your mate feel uncomfortable or look bad in front of anyone else.
- *Keep questions simple.*   Also, ask only one question at time, as much as possible.
- *Be certain your spouse understands the question*—or the implications of the question—and clarify or elaborate if necessary.
- *Give your partner enough time to think and respond.*

- *Listen carefully to the response.*   Observe and be sensitive to your spouse. Ask yourself questions such as: *"Did I get what I was looking for?" "Did this work for him or her?" "Are we still in rapport?" Is this complete?"* and *"Is there anything else I need to do here?"*
- *Complete any question-answer interaction* with a simple "Thanks" or an acknowledgment such as, "Good. That's just what I needed. That helps a lot."
- *Here are some questions to ask yourself before asking questions of your partner:*
  - *What do I want my question to accomplish?*
  - *What do I need to take into account when asking it?*
  - *Are my intentions positive?*
  - *What's the best way to ask this question?*
  - *Is this a good time to ask it?*
  - *Is there anything I should tell my spouse before I ask this question?*
  - *Can we both win with this question?*
- *If a questioning interchange doesn't work, the first thing to do is acknowledge that this is the case.*   Learner Selves would then ask themselves questions such as: *"What interfered; how come this didn't work?" "How would I feel if I were asked that question, that way, in this setting, at this time?" "Would I feel respected if my spouse asked me a question like that?" "What is <u>my</u> responsibility here?" "<u>Could</u> we both win the way I asked that question?" "What could I have done differently?"* and *"What is there to learn from this?"* A clincher question for correcting one's questioning style in marriage is, *"Would I feel like making love after being asked a question like that by my spouse?"*

Receiving the Question   Of course, the spouse *receiving* the question also has responsibility for the interaction working out in a win-win way. When discussing this with client couples, it's helpful to have them revisit the Choice Model and the Marriage Context Model. The large arrow on the left of both handouts notes that it represents "Anything that happens to a person," and of course that includes any questions asked of them. No matter *what* question was asked, or *how* it was asked, the receiving spouse has a choice about whether to respond as a Learner, or react as a Judger.

Moreover, being asked a question does not automatically mean the question must be answered, although it's usually important to acknowledge and respond to it in some way. Spouses are not "victims" of their mate's questions, even if they feel offended or put on the spot by one. Clients can also be counseled to give their spouses the benefit of the doubt if a question has been asked poorly. It takes time to learn to ask effective, graceful questions, especially after a lifetime of asking questions with no training or coaching at all. Spouses on the receiving end of an ineffective question can ask themselves questions such as: *"What's the kindest interpretation here?" "Did my spouse have a hard day?" "How might I have contributed to this?" "What question was I listening through that made me react like that?"* and *"What can I do to turn this into a win-win?"*

For example, if the timing wasn't appropriate, the receiving spouse can say something like: "I can tell that's an important question to you. However, there isn't time to give you as complete an answer as you deserve right now" or "I need to think about this. Can we talk about it tonight?" or "That question threw me off guard" or "I'm not ready to answer that yet. Can we talk about it over the weekend?" If the receiving spouse doesn't understand the question, he or she can say, "I'm not sure I understand your question. Can you ask it another way?" or perhaps, "Is there a question behind your question that I'm not getting?"

10. *Make win-win requests, and avoid making win-lose requests.*

Although most questions can be considered requests, here we use the term in a more formal sense. A request is a speech act, and the interaction is usually considered complete when the listener responds by accepting, declining, or making a counteroffer. However, the spirit of a request is a more subtle matter. The same request, or rather, the same words, can leave the listener feeling valued and respected—or about as significant as a squashed bug. In marriage, win-win requests contribute substantially to each spouse's happiness, as well as to the couple's ability to *prevent* conflict. Win-lose requests, on the other hand, either add fuel to the flame of conflict, or ignite it altogether.

The purpose of a request is to ask someone to do something we want them to do. A win-win request is designed *so the other person can be successful* in giving us *what* we want, in the *way* we want it, and *when* we want it. A spouse makes win-win requests intending that respect and rapport be sustained in the relationship, even if his or her partner declines. Naturally, all the guidelines for asking effective questions also apply in making win-win requests. Moreover, it is especially important to be careful with requesting in the inevitably tender context of marriage. As Bruner wrote, "Of all forms of language use, requesting is bound to be the one most deeply enmeshed in context" (1983, p. 91).

Despite all these important reasons to make win-win requesting a priority in marriage, spouses are often careless with their communications, including their questions and requests. Perhaps they don't recognize the relevance of effective requesting to their marital happiness. Or perhaps they don't know the necessary elements of a request—that what is wanted must be specified, including the timeline, that the listener must be capable of fulfilling the request, and that he or she has the right to say "No."

Nevertheless, the final requirement for a win-win request may be as important as all the rest put together. It is generally so that in our dealings with people we implicitly train them in how to treat us. Nowhere is this more true than in marriage. A request may be constructed perfectly, offered in a spirit of cooperation, and the requester may get what he or she asked for. But without an appropriate acknowledgment or thank you, the interaction is incomplete. Certainly, it will not be a source of pleasure, or reinforce a spouse's desire to fulfill the next request. After all, the success of any marital interaction, including requesting, becomes part of the history of the marriage, and part of the context in which the next requests are made. This is true in all aspects of marriage. A thank you in the bedroom may sound different from a thank you at the dinner table, but in any case it signals one's spouse that they were successful, are appreciated, and that it matters to let them know that.

The Choice Model

The goal of presenting the Choice Model to couples is to establish the concept of *individual* moment-by-moment choice in life. The therapist introduces and discusses the Choice Model with couples just as she does with individuals. It's useful to direct this first conversation about choice and responsibility with them to *individual* concerns such as career or health. Thus, the point about individual responsibility is already established and part of the background conversation before moving on to explore choice as depicted on the Marriage Context Model.

The Judger House & The Learner House

This illustration is optional; however clients relate to it easily. It graphically depicts home life that is dominated either by Judger Self thoughts, which correlate with a win-lose marriage, or by Learner Self thoughts, which correlate with a win-win marriage. In addition, the handout may be useful in discussing sexual issues, focusing on the couples pictured in the "bedroom."

The Marriage Context Model

Of course, the Judger Self and Learner Self do not make choices in a vacuum — their context is inextricably social, including the recognition that in marriage virtually any personal choice may affect the spouse, and even the shape and future of the marriage itself. The Marriage Context Model, which is a logical visual elaboration of the Choice Model, illustrates the phenomenon and consequences of personal choice in the marital context. This handout shows how every moment brings a fresh opportunity to choose which mindset to "put forward" in one's marriage. This handout also functions as preparation and background for the more extensive Learner/Judger Chart that will be introduced soon after it, probably in the following session.

The Marriage Context Model illustrates how the typical thoughtful choices of the Learner Self reinforce the possibilities of a win-win marriage, while the habitual automatic, passive choices of the Judger Self reinforce the parameters of a win-lose marriage. The addition of the metaphor of marriage as war, in contrast to that of marriage as a peace process, makes the implications of individual spousal choices more poignant and imaginable, as well as therapeutically applicable. The model depicts this graphically so spouses can visually trace and predict the impact and implications of their individual choices on the marriage — especially those inevitable affect-laden, moment-by-moment choices that occur in the midst of any conflicted marital interaction.

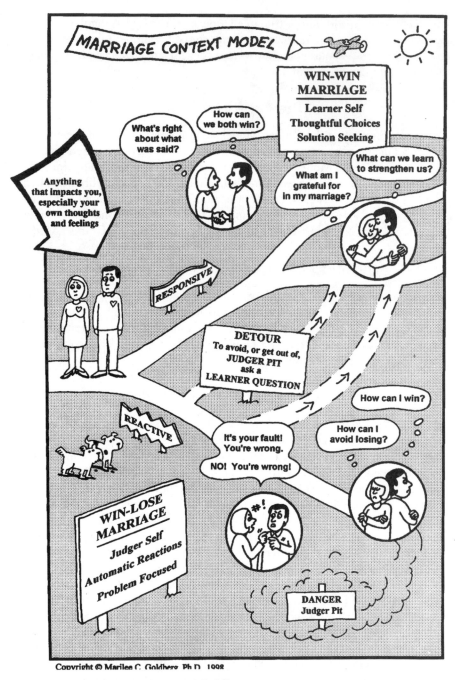

Copyright © Marilee C. Goldberg, Ph.D. 1998

Figure 14.1   Marriage Context Model

Choice and Responsibility in Marriage   The therapist uses the Marriage Context Model to underscore this very point, that each individual spouse is responsible for his or her choices at each moment, including during heated marital conflicts, no matter how difficult or emotional these may become. One of the therapist's main goals is to deter blaming and avoidance of personal responsibility evidenced in comments such as: "He made me so mad, it was *his* fault I threw the ashtray" or "She did it on purpose to get me upset. I just couldn't help it, I *had* to (take a drink, kick the dog, get into a fight)."

The explicit point—which the therapist will return to and emphasize in as many ways as necessary—is that blaming someone else for one's own emotional state and behavioral choices is almost always inaccurate. Nor is blaming someone else acceptable as an excuse for one's own choices, behavioral or otherwise. Furthermore, the very act of blaming undermines the *blamer's* ability to do anything proactive and positive for the relationship. As one of my clients put it, "This reminds me of that old saying—that when you point your finger at someone else, you're actually pointing three fingers *back at yourself.*"

The point is that the *cost* of projecting blame is unacceptably high, for it is nothing less than the equivalent diminution of one's own personal power, as well as the prevention of win-win relating. The habit of the Judger Self to blame and shame self and other (and not to take responsibility for his or her own choices and behaviors) is tantamount to locating power over him or herself *externally*, rather than owning it personally. Blaming and shaming are defining behaviors of couples caught in the all too typical dance of Judger Self lockstep. Unfortunately, the longer the spouses dance to this tune—that is, the more they diminish their personal power by denying responsibility for their choices—the less optimism is warranted for their ability to resolve marital conflicts. Sadly, another cost of being so externally oriented is that such individuals, married or not, usually find it difficult to experience themselves as authentic—or to feel worthy of being loved.

In actuality, assuming responsibility for one's own emotional state and behavioral choices, especially during marital conflict, is the most assured way of untangling the real issues concealed behind the volley of internal and external blaming that fuels the Judger Self and the attack-or-defend paradigm of win-lose relating. It is for these compelling reasons that the therapist uses the Marriage Context Model to help each spouse recognize and own the consequences of his or her own internal and interactional choices in each moment.

Reason for Marital Hope:
Observe-and-Correct and Switching Questions

The therapist takes care to point out the detour roads located on the Judger Self road of the Marriage Context Model. *The point is that detours out of conflict are always available*, the instant either spouse remembers to ask a Learner Self question. The first choice is to wake up and observe what is occurring—either within oneself or in a situation. The second choice is to notice whether a correction is called for, and then to ask a switching question if something different is desired. The therapist emphasizes that these detour roads represent the opportunity to rescue any situation by moving to Learner Self territory. The therapist may also let the couple know that in a few sessions they will receive a handout with switching questions designed specifically for conflict resolution and win-win marriages.

Discussing the Marriage Context Model   The therapist gives the couple sufficient time to muse on the implications of the model, think about past events in this new light, ask questions, and register feelings and concerns. Naturally, she encourages their taking a Learner attitude toward the material. Here are examples of questions to help guide their conversation.

- What were your first responses to this material? How come?
- How does this fit with your understanding of choice and responsibility, especially in marriage?
- What can you learn from this about some of your past successes and difficulties as a couple?
- Can you think of a situation between the two of you that this illustrates or makes more understandable?
- Can you think of a time when one of you was able to shift from Judger Self to Learner Self and turn a conflict into a successful resolution? How would you explain this in light of the Marriage Context Model?
- How could this material be helpful to you in the midst of a fight, especially one of those old repetitive ones?
- How could using the Marriage Context Model contribute to your ability to create, experience, and *maintain* a successful, loving relationship?

The Learner/Judger Chart

The construct of the Learner Self and the Judger Self has already been introduced to couples via the Choice Model and the Marriage Context Model. The purpose of presenting the Learner/Judger Chart is to deepen their understanding of the Learner Self and the Judger Self, and to make these concepts more practical and useful in their marriages. Because the Learner/Judger Chart is an elaborate description of the Choice Model and the Marriage Context Model, it adds new distinctions to help spouses to observe and understand themselves and each other better. The chart empowers their ability to think more clearly, and to have better control over their affective and behavioral choices.

Presenting the Learner/Judger Chart to Couples   In introducing the actual chart to the couple, the therapist may comment that some people feel a bit overwhelmed at first glance, but within a short time find that the chart easily makes sense. She shows the couple the six sections of the chart: Orientation, Thinking, Feeling, Behaving, Relating, and Language and Communicating, as well as the list of self-questions typical of the Learner Self and the Judger Self related to each section.

The Relating Section of the Chart   Marital difficulties fall most naturally under the Relating section of the Learner/Judger Chart. Therefore, the therapist first asks the couple to read through the Relating section, and usually the Orientation section as well. Then she asks for general impressions and comments, and focuses the conversation so spouses connect the information on the chart to their own relationship difficulties, as well as to their strengths and resources as individuals and as a couple. Following is a list of sample inquiries therapists can use to help spouses discover, identify with, and learn about their Learner and Judger Selves:

- In what ways (and in what areas of your life) are you generally able to think and behave as your Learner Self?
- In what ways (and in what areas of your life) do you sometimes act like a Judger Self?
- In general, what situations "bring out" your Judger Self tendencies? How can you tell when your Judger Self has taken over?
- So far, what are the best ways you've learned to deal with yourself when your Judger Self takes over?
- In what ways were your parents like Learners and Judgers while you were growing up?
- What are the biggest Judger triggers in your marriage?
- What signals you that your spouse's Judger Self has shown up?
- So far, what are the best ways you've learned to deal with your spouse when his/her Judger Self takes over?
- How do the two of you typically recover from a Judger Self skirmish?
- Ideally, how would your Learner Selves work together to handle conflict?

SECTION TWO: MODULE 4

Module 4 is the application module, as the processes and handouts most directly address the couple's presenting problems and desired outcomes. The purpose of this final psycho-educational module is simple—to make win-win marriages a more *attainable* reality by providing specific, practical, easily usable tools to help couples resolve issues and conflicts in a win-win way, beginning in therapy and continuing for the rest of their lives.

Ideally, three conditions should be fulfilled before the couple embarks on this module:

1. Each spouse has developed a minimally sufficient operating level of Learner Self to use the question-centered material in addressing problems and issues.

2. The spouses have practiced, and are at least minimally competent, in asking effective questions and in making win-win requests of each other.
3. The partners share an intention of shifting the basis of their marriage
   from win-lose to win-win.

Two new handouts are introduced in this last module: Clearing the Way (see Figure 14.2) and the Peace Process Guidelines (see Figure 14.3).

The first handout, the Clearing the Way exercise, is a self-assessment proce-
dure to help couples discover concerns and fears that could undermine their
therapeutic success. Acknowledging and addressing these is prerequisite to each
spouse's ability to *choose* and *own* a therapy goal of a win-win marriage. The second handout, the Peace Process Guidelines, is designed as an intervention for the
couple to use themselves, when and how they choose. The Peace Process Guidelines is a resource for couples to use when they are mired in automatic, reactive
Judger Self conflicts, and need access to Learner Self resources to resolve and
move beyond a current difficulty.

In addition to these two new handouts, any of the previous ones may be used
to support the therapeutic process. The most specific homework in module 4 is
to practice the steps of the Peace Process Guidelines. Sometimes supportive reading materials are also suggested. Some examples are: *Why Marriages Succeed or
Fail: and How You Can Make Yours Last* (Gottman 1994), *Fighting for Your Marriage: Positive Steps for Preventing Divorce and Preserving a Lasting Love* (Stanley,
Markham, and Blumberg 1994), and *Getting to "Yes": Negotiating Agreement
Without Giving In* (Ury, Fisher, and Patton 1991). The psycho-educational portion of module 4 is estimated to be completed in two to three sessions. It is also
intended to transition naturally into the remaining course of treatment.

Clearing the Way Handout

The purpose of this exercise is to facilitate each spouse choosing and owning the
goal of a win-win marriage. This requires eliciting and addressing specific individual and/or couple's issues, as well as fears and concerns about change itself.
During therapy, the more that spouses can be aware of their own issues and concerns, the more they can understand and cooperate with the therapist's interventions. During and after therapy, married life will continue to present ample
opportunities for problem solving. At those crucial times, the better prepared
spouses are to manage conflict on their own, the more successful they will be at
maintaining the win-win status of their marriages.

The exercise is presented as a self-assessment handout for spouses to complete in session. Of course, therapists use this process creatively; for example,
rather than give the handout to clients, the therapist might choose to read these
questions to the couple, and then have them write and discuss their respective
answers. She might also add questions of her own, or simply use the exercise as
background for a conversation with the couple about what could get in the way
of their success in therapy.

CLEARING THE WAY

FOR A WIN-WIN MARRIAGE

The purpose of this exercise is to help partners resolve obstacles to a win-win marriage. Here are some suggestions for ways to use this exercise:

(a) On a blank sheet of paper, each partner answers questions 1 through 12 in the sequence presented. If there's more than one answer to the first question, do the entire exercise for *each* of these answers.

(b) Each partner completes all questions separately, then discuss answers together.

(c) Partners write and discuss responses to each question one by one.

(d) During a conflict this exercise can help discover what's needed for resolution.

(e) The exercise can also be used as a regular "check-up" (e.g., every six months), to help the relationship stay on track for win-win. To use it this way, just change question # 1 to read, "What would change if we had *more* of a win-win marriage?"

1. What would change if we had a win-win marriage?

2. How would that affect me personally?

3. What would be different in our relationship?

4. How would that difference affect our relationship?

5. What would I like about that?

6. What would I *not* like about that?

7. What would I *gain* as a result of having a win-win marriage?

8. What concerns might that bring up?

9. What might I *lose* as a result of having a win-win marriage?

10. What concerns might that bring? Why might it be worth facing them?

11. What do I love and appreciate about my partner and my marriage?

12. What am I willing to do so we can enjoy a win-win marriage?

Copyright © Marilee C. Goldberg, Ph.D. 1998

Figure 14.2   Clearing the Way

PEACE PROCESS GUIDELINES

STOP...WAIT!

Is this what I want to be feeling?
Is this how I want to be behaving?
Is this what I want to be saying?
Can this work as a win-win?

↓

**COOL DOWN,
GET DISTANCE**

How can I really listen to my partner?
What feeling state or mood would help?
Do I need some deep breaths, a walk, etc.?

↓

**TAKE STOCK OF
THE SITUATION**

Am I coming from win-win or win-lose?
Am I being self-righteous or judgmental?
Am I contributing to this problem?
Is there something I should apologize for?
What are my concerns or fears?
What do I want in this situation?
What questions should I ask myself?
Is my partner's reaction personal to me?
Is either of us in attack-or-defend mode?
Is either of us on automatic?

↓

**WALK A MILE IN
HIS/HER MOCCASINS**

What is my partner feeling and wanting?
What pressures is my partner dealing with?
Do I have enough information?
What questions might help my partner?
How can my partner access Learner Self?

↓

NEGOTIATE A WIN-WIN

What am I grateful for in my relationship?
Am I being my Learner Self right now?
Can I like and respect myself here & now?
Will my requests have us both win?
Do our solutions have objective criteria?
What promises are appropriate from each?

↓

GET TOGETHER AGAIN

What makes us each *feel* loved & wanted?
How can I *show* my partner my love?
What can I *acknowledge* each of us for?
What can we *learn* to strengthen us?
What can we *do* differently next time?

Copyright © Marilee C. Goldberg, Ph.D. 1998

Figure 14.3   Peace Process Guidelines

If the exercise is used as a handout, there is a therapeutic advantage in having each spouse write responses to *all* the questions before discussing their answers together. Their respective responses will be more truthful and revealing, and less contaminated by fears of the other spouse's interpretation of what was written. Of course, the therapist is aware that her clients' emotional reactions to their own and each other's answers could well necessitate addressing these specifically. The time required to do this could easily add to the number of sessions required for this module, and therefore for therapy as a whole.

Using Clearing the Way   The Clearing the Way exercise can also be used advantageously throughout the course of therapy. When an impediment to progress occurs, the therapist can have spouses fill out the handout again, *this time from their current perspectives*. Therapists can also recommend that couples use the structure provided by the handout as a self-help tool *after* therapy, in order to understand and resolve issues and conflicts as they occur. It is exactly at those times when a Judger Self entanglement needs the calming, thoughtful presence of Learner Self perspectives, strategies, and questions for resolution.

The Peace Process Guidelines Handout

The Peace Process Guidelines is a step-by-step method for couples to use in resolving conflicts and differences, and sometimes simply in negotiating plans and everyday life. When difficulties between husband and wife occur against a shared background of conversation and agreement about managing conflict, some of the potential difficulty is already neutralized. With this context established, conflicts become less of an emergency, and more of a normal occurrence with familiar and proven procedures for resolution. These are exactly the points the therapist makes to her clients in introducing the concept of the *peace promise*. This contextual conversation usually precedes the introduction of the handout of the Peace Process Guidelines.

Peace Promise   The peace promise in marriage, as used in question-centered therapy, is that each spouse promises to be responsible for bringing his or her Learner Self to the "peace table" when conflicts occur. Using the term *peace promise* makes this conversation more powerful simply because it gives the intention and behavior a *label* by which it can be remembered. The peace process is operationalized through Learner Self questions such as, "*Am I operating as my Learner Self right now?*" and "*Am I keeping my peace promise right now?*" If the answer is "No," then the obvious next questions are, "*What do I need to do so I can?*" and "*What's in the way?*" Additionally, spouses are encouraged to ask Learner Self relationship questions such as, "*Am I doing anything that's triggering my partner's Judger Self?*" "*How can I help my spouse bring out his/her Learner Self?*" "*In all honesty, can this conversation lead to peace, or just to more conflict?*" and "*Am I (or we) operating in an attack-or-defend mode right now?*"

It is important to use the phrase, *peace process*. The more conventional term, peace, objectifies the process by implying there is a "place" to get to, and once "there," nothing further need be done. This is as distant from the truth as telling a dieter that after reaching his weight goal he need do nothing more to maintain success. This magical thinking, exemplified by the fairy tale promise of ". . . and they lived happily ever after," is as destructive to marriage as it is sabotaging to one's health. Such unrealistic, unquestioned assumptions predictably undermine peaceful marital conditions by lulling spouses into believing they need not be vigilant and protective of their marriages, especially with regard to Judger Self ambushes.

The therapist can initiate the discussion about making the peace promise with questions such as: "Now that we've covered all this educational material, what would you say is the key to resolving conflict in a win-win way?" or "Are you more effective in resolving conflict with your Learner Self or your Judger Self?" or "Would you rather fight with your spouse when he/she is coming from Learner Self or Judger Self?" After sufficient conversation, the therapist might ask the spouses if they're willing to make the peace promise to each other in session. It is a powerful intervention when they choose to do so. If they do not, this can also become the basis for productive therapeutic conversations.

Case Example   Belinda and Chuck, married for 12 years, worked with the Peace Process Guidelines on their own for about a month. After a particularly gratifying resolution Belinda commented: "What could be more obvious than learning how to fight fair so we can *both* win? We even went through premarital counseling, and we never learned any of this. The question that's most useful for me is: '*Are we operating in attack-or-defend mode right now?*' If we are, then I realize that if we keep going, *nothing* good can happen. I admit that it's hard to stop acting like that, especially since that's all we did for so long. But you can't make peace if you're still acting like you're at war. You have to *declare* peace before you have a chance at peace. And I have to *act* that way, or Chuck won't believe me, and join me at the peace table."

Presenting the Peace Process Guidelines Handout   The Peace Process Guidelines is presented as a "first aid" resource for couples finding themselves in Judger Self automatic, reactive conflict situations. It can be thought of as a sequence of switching questions for transforming a marital situation from win-lose to win-win. These guidelines are based on the premise that when people are very emotional (upset, anxious, angry, scared, etc.) they need help that is concrete, practical, simple, and *immediate*. This format of Learner Self questions takes advantage of the observe-and-correct thinking strategy by focusing spouses in a proactive, win-win, solution-seeking manner.

It is important to include each of the six steps, and each of these is operationalized by self-questions most appropriate for it. It is not necessary to ask each question listed, but it is important to preserve the spirit of each step. In general, the exercise works best if the steps are followed in the sequence presented. It is recommended that the therapist conduct several behavioral rehearsals of the Peace Process Guidelines in session. She could ask the couple to practice first with relatively current situations, or even "make-believe" ones.

The more that partners practice the Peace Process Guidelines in therapy, the more natural it will be for them to take advantage of this process during an actual conflict at home. Either spouse can call a "time-out," and consult the handout after having answered "No" to a question such as, "*Is there any way for this situation, as is, to work out as a win-win?*" A spouse may also use the process after having answered "*Yes*" to the question, "*Are we in that attack-or-defend mode right now?*" The point is for couples to become comfortable with the process and make it a habit, so that utilizing these guidelines at home will be natural—*and so they will remember to use them.*

The Peace Process Guidelines are meant to be personalized for any particular couple. Spouses can make up customized uses of the material, including adding more questions. They will almost certainly streamline the process through the years. However, the therapist should emphasize that each of the six steps remains important. The six steps of the Peace Process are:

1. *Stop.*   Step 1 is *the* critical step. Referring back to the Marriage Context Model, we see that step 1 occurs symbolically at exactly the point where a spouse stands at the crossroads under the arrow representing whatever triggered the current conflict. Spouses may actively and thoughtfully choose to engage as their Learner Selves, *or* take the alternative possibility and passively and automatically slide down the trajectory into Judger Self territory. Arriving in either Learner Self or Judger Self territory is neither random nor accidental; spouses have choice and control over their location on the Marriage Context Model, as they do in their lives.

This control may be invoked when either partner calls a halt to an interaction, simply by saying "Stop. This isn't working. I don't see how we can get to win-win from here." With this observation the spouse already engages his or her Learner Self, and simultaneously creates the foundation for a potential win-win resolution to the conflict. Of course, there is no guarantee that they will be able to maintain this position until resolution occurs. However, we *can* predict that unless at least one partner is able to activate and remain Learner Self–dominant until the conflict is resolved, the interaction is likely to end up as some version of a Judger Self standoff.

2. *Calm Down/Get Distance.*   Because high affect is associated with similar high physiological arousal, it can be difficult to access the calm reasoning of the Learner Self during a conflict. Therefore, it's important to take enough time to get distance from the situation affectively, and perhaps physically as well. This could be as simple as deep breathing, getting a glass of water, or taking a walk. This stage of the peace process is essential. Some physiological shift is usually required for a corresponding shift in affect and mood, and these changes, in turn, facilitate effective Learner Self interactions.

3. *Taking Stock.*   This stage requires focusing on what's going on with *oneself*, on how one has been behaving and on what one is feeling, thinking, and wanting. Taking stock calls for skill and honesty in noticing personal Judger Self

thoughts, feelings, and behaviors, which generally take the form of blaming or attacking either oneself or one's spouse.

4. *Walk a Mile in His/Her Moccasins.*   Win-win means that any resolution must work for *both* partners. It is therefore essential to *consider what one's partner may be feeling, thinking, and wanting.* It is also important to *ask*—one can easily misinterpret another's communications or intentions, especially during a conflict. This purposeful shifting of perceptual position is akin to "walking a mile in his or her moccasins."

5. *Peace Table and Win-Win Negotiations.*   This is the beginning of the negotiation process, which is symbolically the move to the "peace table." The couple decides how to use the Peace Process Guidelines, or whether to pursue another strategy for negotiating a win-win resolution.

At the same time, it is important to remember that many marital conflicts are *not* about the apparent content, whether the argument is over something major, like what house to buy, or something minor, like what movie to attend. Rather, most marital conflicts are *emotional* negotiations, rooted in assessments of being respected and loved sufficiently, or in the "right way." For this reason, by the time a couple has proceeded successfully through the peace process to this point, the emotional negotiation may already have dissolved the "problem." Sometimes all it takes is a wink. The couple may therefore be ready to move on to "making up" that occurs in step 6.

6. *Together Again.*   Some reconnection signals the end of the conflict, representing the success of the partnership of the spouses' Learner Selves. With this alliance, they have triumphed over their individual Judger Self counterparts. The spouses' experience of reconnection is loving, and probably even physical. A hug, an apology, good sex, some flowers—any of these could be a "peace offering" that is mutually recognized and appreciated as reaffirming the win-win basis of the marriage.

SUMMARY

This chapter presented modules 3 and 4 of a model of working with couples that integrates psycho-educational and cognitive-behavioral approaches. The purpose of module 3 is to facilitate conflict resolution by focusing on choice and responsibility in marriage, teaching the model of the Learner Self and the Judger Self, and training spouses to ask effective questions of each other, including making win-win requests. The purpose of module 4 is to resolve presenting problems and empower the couple to enjoy a lasting win-win marriage. The handouts for these two modules include the Choice Model, the Marriage Context Model, the Learner/Judger Chart, Clearing the Way, and the Peace Process Guidelines. In the next chapter we meet Julie and Jim Quinn, a couple whose sexual difficulties were resolved using these four psycho-educational modules of question-centered therapy with couples.

15

The Case of
Julie and Jim Quinn

In the end these things matter most: How well did you love?
How fully did you live? How deeply did you learn to let go?
—JACK KORNFIELD

This chapter presents the case of a couple with a sexual problem who went through the standard psycho-educational modules of question-centered therapy as they were outlined in the last two chapters. The focus of this chapter is on the practical applications of the concepts and materials discussed previously, and on how these were utilized therapeutically to bring the case of Julie and Jim to a successful conclusion. Section 1 introduces the Quinns. Section 2 focuses on therapy strategies for this couple. Section 3 highlights the Judger Self aspects of their problems. Finally, section 4 presents important points of Julie and Jim's progress through question-centered therapy.

SECTION ONE: INTRODUCING THE QUINNS

Julie and Jim Quinn, married 23 years, with twin sons in college, presented in therapy with an issue about sexuality, which they described as a difference in sex drive. They agreed that their sexual experiences were "basically fine"; however, these happened, on average, only once a month. The Quinns were referred to therapy by their family doctor, Dr. Taylor, after Jim went for his annual physical and expressed concern about his prostate. In the conversation that ensued, Jim expressed his disappointment, anger, and confusion about his sexual relationship with Julie in the last few years.

In our first interview, the Quinns were pleasantly engaging, and seemed to have a comfortable and caring relationship. However, there was a noticeable difference in how this couple described their marriage, which they both evaluated as win-win, and their sexual relationship, which was obviously win-lose. Jim, an engineer, age 46, said he loved his wife very much; however, he thought his pain in "that region" resulted from the infrequency of their sexual contacts. Julie, a high school art teacher, age 43, affirmed her love for her husband and the importance of their marriage, but commented, "I wish I felt sexually like I did in the beginning." Her voice trailed off when she said, "But it's been so many years. . . ."

The Quinns met in college and were immediately attracted to each other. However, Julie, raised in a fundamentalist religious family that "expected perfection in all things" succeeded in remaining a virgin until their wedding night. The sexual permission bestowed by marriage allowed Julie to begin her erotic awakening, even though I sensed she silently resented Jim's impatience with her "slow learning curve." Jim, the son of an alcoholic doctor and "suffocating" nurse mother, did have a short fuse. Julie and Jim both admitted that sometimes he "blew up" for no apparent reason at all.

Eventually, Julie and Jim developed a satisfying sexual relationship, including mutual masturbation, and even oral sex, which Julie would occasionally perform for Jim. Julie became orgasmic, although she still usually preferred sex in the dark. In the last few years, however, the frequency of their sexual contacts had dwindled to about once a month, coinciding approximately with the twins departure for college and when Jim got downsized to a job he found "embarrassing." Jim commented regretfully, and not without an edge in his voice, "I can't remember the last time she was willing to do 'that' for me." Julie and Jim agreed that the problem was really hers, because she didn't "want it" that much anymore, even though she also said their frequency of intercourse was fine for her. It became an issue only because Jim wasn't satisfied, and also because he was worried about his prostate. Julie summarized her feelings about beginning therapy by saying, "I'm glad to be here if it will make Jim happier."

SECTION TWO: THERAPY STRATEGIES

As is often the case, it seemed that the Quinns were channeling other marital issues into the sexual arena. However, since they specified sex as the presenting problem, I felt it was important, especially for Jim, to honor their own way of thinking about these issues. Actually, it was a moot point. Individual and relationship issues would be addressed naturally through the doorway provided by the sexual problem for which they had sought help. Moreover, the cognitive strengthening and communication skill building they would develop through the training in the psycho-educational modules would empower them to deal more successfully with the dynamic and sexual issues.

Therapist's Self-Questions

The Quinns' progress through the first three psycho-educational modules went well, as evidenced by their active engagement with the material and their growing ability and interest in tracking internal dialogue, especially self-questions. However, now in the sixth session, and beginning Module 4, my major questions about them were still not fully satisfied. These were:

- *What specifically stands in the way of their enjoying a win-win sexual relationship?*
- *What will it take for Julie and Jim to get back in touch with their love for each other?*
- *What issues are priority for each partner, and how do these contribute to their problematic communication and interaction patterns?*
- *How could this information—about each spouse <u>and</u> their interactions—be understood in terms of Learner Self and Judger Self, automaticity, choice, and responsibility, as well as about internal questions and behavioral answers?*
- *How can I translate my responses to these questions into therapeutic strategies to help them reinforce a win-win marriage—while developing a win-win sexual relationship?*

Clearing the Way to Win-Win

To help me answer these questions, I gave Julie and Jim the Clearing the Way exercise (see Figure 14.2) and customized it to their needs by altering the focal question to: *"What would change if we had a win-win <u>sexual</u> relationship?"* The process revealed significant issues for both spouses, and their Judger Selves figured predominantly in most of them. These issues could be traced to fear and automatic negative reactivity, which took the usual forms of either defending or attacking (self and/or other).

SECTION THREE: JUDGER SELF COMBAT ZONE

In fact, as I listened to Julie and Jim discuss their answers to the Clearing the Way exercise, I couldn't help thinking about their similarity to Albee's George and Martha. Fortunately, there were also *major* differences between the two couples. The Quinns loved each other, had a basically good marriage, and had confined explicit combat to one area of their lives. Furthermore, they both wanted their relationship to work and were confused and upset at not being able to do it on their own. While there was definite Judger Self damage present, I believed it could be untangled and healed, and the Quinns could be taught how to neutralize, if not prevent, future Judger Self ambushes.

George and Martha, on the other hand, were over the brink. The rampage of their Judger Selves had reached epic levels; one could easily imagine them on a Greek urn, eternally frozen in battle. Certainly, any romantic dream of marital happiness had been an early casualty of their relationship. With such a pair, how many couples therapists would have the temerity to take them on, the naiveté to expect cooperation, or the "starry-eyed optimism" to expect therapeutic success in the form of a loving reconciliation?

Thankfully, the therapeutic challenge posed by Julie and Jim was far different, and I looked forward to working with them. Their Judger Self combat zone saw mostly hand-to-hand skirmishes when compared to the action of George and Martha's missiles and tanks. Nevertheless, by looking beyond the smoke, chaos, pain, and noise, a startling similarity between the two couples was also apparent: Julie and Jim's fights, as well as George and Martha's full-out pitched battle, could be understood as elaborate behavioral, cognitive, and emotional answers to internal questions whose themes fell within the imprisoning confines of the defend-or-attack paradigm of the Judger Self.

For Julie and Jim, as I suppose for George and Martha, these Judger Self internal questions included:

- *How can I protect and defend myself?*
- *How can I keep from getting hurt even more?*
- *What's wrong with him/her that justifies how I'm behaving?*
- *How can I get even?*
- *What's the most cutting/damaging thing to say or do?*
- *How can I hurt him/her for hurting or rejecting me?*
- *How can I get what I want, regardless of how it affects my spouse?*
- *In what ways is he/she more (or less) important, worthy, or valuable than me?*
- *What might he/she find unworthy, inadequate, or lacking about me?*
- *In order to save myself, how can I win/triumph over my spouse?*

Instead of these kinds of questions, I suggested to Julie and Jim that they ask Learner Self questions which included:

- *What does he/she want, or need right now?*
- *Is this conflict connected to something in the past* (in our relationship, or in a family of origin)?
- *What's really going on here?*
- *Should I take this personally?*
- *What's the kindest possible interpretation of his/her behavior right now?*
- *In what way might I be contributing to the problem?*
- *What do I need to forgive my spouse and/or myself for?*
- *What can we learn from this to strengthen our marriage?*
- *What am I grateful for in our marriage?*

- *What do I appreciate about my mate?*
- *What is my long-term goal in my marriage?*
- *Is the way I'm behaving likely to help me achieve that?*
- *Am I behaving in a way that can help my spouse access his/her Learner Self?*
- *How can I make sure we both win?*

As an exercise, sometimes I ask couples to read over the questions listed under the Relating section of the Judger/Learner Chart, and then I ask them: "Would you rather spend your life asking and answering Learner questions or Judger questions?" "Which set of questions would be more fun?" "Which set of questions would help you be more resourceful, and feel better about yourself, and more hopeful about your relationship?" "Which set of questions will bring you love as you deserve and want it?" "Which set of questions would you rather wake up to every morning for the rest of your life?"

Julie and Her Judger Self   In responding to the question, "*What would you not like about the difference in your relationship (if you had a win-win sexual relationship)?*" Julie revealed a fear that ". . . if we had a great sexual relationship, he would want it all the time." She also realized she was more uncomfortable with her body, and her "40-year-old spread" than she had been willing to admit to herself. In fact, Julie commented musingly, "This plays right into the self-esteem problems I had when I was lots younger. I'm amazed they're related to my feelings about Jim today. Maybe that's part of the problem. Maybe I've been taking out some of my old bad feelings about myself on him." Since we had already spent so much time studying Learner and Judger internal questions, it was relatively easy for Julie to see that the same negative, self-doubting, self-punishing questions that defined her teenage years were back in full force. Some of these were: "*Why can't I get anything right?*" "*Will I ever get the approval I want?*" "*Why can't I be perfect?*" and "*What's wrong with me that everybody treats me so badly?*"

Jim and His Judger Self   Jim, or rather, his Judger Self, appeared to be a culprit in their marital woes, despite his opinion that everything was Julie's fault. Jim truly believed himself "innocent," and that their sexual difficulties rested with Julie. However, the self-righteous, almost smug nature of his anger was a tip-off. Self-righteousness usually signals that an individual, by virtue of the "authority" of his "superiority," has judged another person as morally deficient, often because he secretly feels deficient in some way. Deikman underscores this point: "One of the symptoms of projection is an attitude of righteousness coloring persons' statements of their beliefs and views of others . . . through projection we reassure ourselves that we are good (as in the child's world) by pointing out that someone else is bad. The covert 'I am good' is signaled by self-righteousness, which requires the devaluation of someone else" (1994, p. 105). Jim was able to maintain his self-righteousness because Julie bought in to the devaluation, which was evident in, and reinforced by, the Judger Self questions she habitually asked herself of late. In this way, the couple maintained the homeostatic balance of the relationship— and unwittingly held in place the problem for which they sought help.

The Quinns agreed that the marital problem was Julie's fault, and that it was she who needed to be "fixed." Nevertheless, self-righteousness in one or both spouses blocks a primary requirement for resolution of marital unhappiness— *joint* ownership of the problem. Whenever a spouse considers the *entire* problem the *other* spouse's fault, I'm fascinated that he or she hasn't asked, "*Is it possible that I contributed to this in any little way, even if I don't know it, and didn't do anything bad on purpose?*" At any rate, I was certain that Jim didn't realize that the more he blamed Julie for their difficulties, the more he enfeebled his *own* ability to do anything about them.

The Clearing the Way exercise led to Jim's first breakthrough. To his surprise and consternation, Jim discovered that his resentment toward Julie for resisting his sexual advances currently served a useful purpose for him. The question, "*What would you lose as a result of having a win-win sexual relationship?*" led to his chagrined recognition that blaming his wife for his prostate pain diverted his attention from fears of failing health, lagging sexual powers, and aging. Jim's willingness to acknowledge this uncomfortable insight was a good prognostic sign. It probably meant that, on some unconscious level, he had asked himself, "*What do I want more—to maintain my 'perfect' image of myself—or enjoy a better sexual relationship with my wife?*" He might also have been asking, "*Am I being fair to Julie?*"

SECTION FOUR: JULIE AND JIM'S THERAPY

Taming the Judger

I congratulated Jim for his insight about the prostate concerns. "You handled that well. It takes courage to recognize you're part of the problem when you never even suspected it." In response, Jim made a sound best translated as "Yuk." Then he said: "I can't say I'm enjoying this, but at least it moves us off of dead center. And maybe it will be helpful—nothing else has been." Following the opening he handed me, I replied: "Well, I'm glad that's your attitude. It gives me the confidence to tell you that I suspect you've got even more Judger Self mischief going on here. But I don't know how much bravery you've got left for today. May I keep going?"

[I often ask clients for permission to tell them what I know needs to be said. This strategy gives clients the experience that they're listening to what *they* asked for, which transforms my message into an affirmative response to *their* request. Anyway, people generally *really* listen only to what they want to, or to what they expect can be helpful to them. In other words, the basic questions that people listen through are: *"What could be useful/valuable/important for me here?"* and *"Will I find out something necessary in order to take care of (or protect/defend) myself, someone else, or something I care about?"*

In particular, if I have a difficult message to deliver, or must push into some well-guarded denial, I may ask at intervals with "Shall I continue?" or "Have you had enough for today?" This allows clients to feel respected and have the experience of keeping the conversation *within their control.* Then they listen with less defensiveness and more receptivity. My purpose is to leave them with more "attention units" to deal with the *real* issues. They may not like what I say, but can't justifiably be as defensive or angry with me for having said it.

Of course, this works only if I make good on my implied promise of respecting their boundaries. Therefore, if a client says, "No, I've had enough today" I must accede to that. At the same time, it is my job as therapist to manage the process, including whatever content I assess must be part of it. So I might respond to such a comment with something like: "That's fine. Thanks for being honest, and saying so. However, we will need to get to this in the next few sessions. Would you rather that I give you some homework to help you start thinking about it, or should I just bring it up next week?" This way, clients maintain control because they maintain choice.]

It was more Jim's attitude than his words that led me to believe it was OK to continue. He laughed at my remark, and flexing a Popeye bicep, said, "I'm a strong guy. I can take it. Go ahead."

Win-Lose Requests

I told the Quinns, "When a couple has sexual difficulties, often one of the problems is how one spouse asks his or her partner for sex. I'm sure that makes sense to you since we've already gone over the differences between win-win requests and win-lose requests. So I want to check this out. Julie, will you describe how sex gets initiated with you two?" It turned out that many of Jim's advances were under such win-lose terms that they were bound to fail. For example, Jim often made his requests at times that were inconvenient for Julie; say, as she was dressing to go to an important meeting. This, of course, put her in no-win position. If she said "*Yes,*" she would be late, probably resentful, and unable to focus on pleasing him, much less enjoying herself. If she said "*No*" he would get angry, pout, and complain that she was rejecting him "again." Julie interjected, "It's gotten to the point that when he gets that look on his face, and I know what he wants, I automatically get tense, and just feel like getting away from him."

This was too much for Jim, even though he had given me permission to continue the conversation about his Judger Self. He turned to Julie and commented in an acid tone, "Well, my dear, if you initiated more, like you *used* to, we wouldn't have these problems in the first place." I let them go back and forth a bit, and then interrupted with, "Jim, I understand your feelings, and I predict that *will* start to happen again at some point. But in the meantime, shouldn't the person who wants something *more* be *more* responsible for making it happen?"

As I watched Jim's shocked expression, I was glad I finally learned how to "drop" a question, and just let it be there, without rushing on too quickly to something else in order to preempt my client's anxiety—or my own. Jim did look completely taken aback—it was obvious this point had never occurred to him. For a moment he wouldn't look at me, and just shook his head from side to side, as if in amazement. When he did make eye contact, he smiled ruefully as he admitted, "Well, I guess you got me there."

> [A direct hit. A pivotal building block for the Quinn's therapeutic success was moving into place. At least one of the Quinns was beginning to take responsibility for the couple's problems. My intervention with Jim was an answer to my internal question: *"How can I get Jim to take responsibility for his part in this problem?"* I had been biding my time, waiting for a promising place to drop in an appropriate comment.
>
> At this point I appreciated the therapeutic advantage of the construct of the Judger Self which allowed me to maintain rapport with Jim, the human being, while we discussed what to do about the behavior of his Judger Self. Functionally, this is similar to saying to a client: "I want you to imagine you're now a consulting master therapist, and we're discussing the case of John Doe. What do you think is going on and what would you advise me to do next?"
>
> My therapeutic task with Jim was to directly describe his problematic *behavior* without simultaneously conveying any condemnation about *him*. We would be able to "blame" Jim's behavior on his Judger Self, allowing him some distance so he could be less defensive, and not feel personally attacked—by Julie, me, or himself. Pinning Jim's difficulties on his Judger Self also helped maintain our therapeutic partnership, and kept him from feeling "one-down," obviously a weak, compromised position from which to make important personal changes.
>
> I set the context for this move earlier in therapy, when we went over the Learner/Judger Chart. I pointed out that everyone has a Judger Self, myself included, and emphasized that it is *not* the Judger Self that causes problems. It just does what it does. *The focus needs to be on the Learner Self, and how well it relates to, and handles, its Judger Self counterpart.* While it is often useful and necessary to focus therapeutic attention on a client's Judger Self, ultimately, it is the empowerment of the Learner Self that promotes healing, resolution, and growth.
>
> This point underscores why it is so vital for clinicians to maintain their own Learner Self mode in therapy. Operating through her Learner

Self, the clinician has maximum therapeutic maneuverability, and of course, continues to serve as a subliminal model for the client. As we will see shortly, my neutral, accepting Learner position made an important difference as things heated up between the Quinns.]

We continued to explore Jim's Judger Self behavior. For example, any time Julie declined a sexual request, Jim's Judger Self would take over, internally and externally. His Judger Self would sneer at him for getting rejected "again," and tell him something like: *"You obviously aren't sexy enough for her anymore."* In reaction to this internal statement, "Jim the Judger," would spew something nasty at Julie, perhaps for not responding to him as she used to, or for her slight weight gain, or her lack of professional advancement.

As the three of us discussed Jim's Judger Self, Julie commented, "You can imagine how much I feel like being around him when he makes comments like that." Jim abruptly turned toward her and growled, "Listen you bitch," and then gasped as he realized what he'd done. "Honey, I'm so sorry," he said, looking genuinely upset. But it was too late; Julie was already in tears. Jim dropped his head into his hands, and said, more to himself than anyone else: "I *hate* it when I do that. It's like I lose myself for a second, and boom, I'm out of control and I've done something stupid like this," gesturing toward Julie who was still crying slightly. "Can't I just get a lobotomy or something and get *rid* of that part of me?"

This was a delicate moment, and it was vital that I demonstrate a Learner's stance regarding the interactions that had just occurred. "Listen you two," I said softly, ignoring Jim's question for the moment, "let's change the scene so we can talk about what just happened. It's going to be very useful to both of you, and I want to show you how." Their surprised look seemed to register cautious hope. "Julie," I said, touching her arm lightly, "will you forgive Jim?" Her reply seemed to come easily. "Sure, I know he doesn't mean it, but I still have a hard time controlling my feelings when he snaps out at me like that." Jim looked surprised. "I thought you both were going to jump down my throat for that little stunt," he said, still looking embarrassed. "You know, I wasn't kidding before. I really would like to cut out that part of me. You call it my Judger Self. Well, it doesn't do me any good, and it *sure* doesn't do Julie any good." He continued, with obvious disgust in his voice, "The Judger Self doesn't do anything but make trouble. It's my enemy. It's been getting me in trouble practically my whole life. Now it's becoming obvious that it's even responsible for a lot of the problems in my marriage."

A Practical Test

The Clearing the Way exercise obviously worked. With these insights about their Judger proclivities, life for Julie and Jim, sexually and otherwise, was considerably more comfortable and relaxed. I decided to give them homework—to have a fulfilling, romantic, sexy evening together. This was a diagnostic assignment; I wanted to find out what would happen.

When they returned for their next visit, it was obvious that something was wrong. They sat apart on the sofa, and began that, "You start" "No, you start" routine with which marital therapists are so familiar. After learning that their discomfort was related to the homework assignment, I commented: "Well, you two sure ran into a roadblock. You might be surprised to hear that I thought that might happen, and in a way I'm glad it did." Julie's mouth dropped open, and Jim commented dryly, "I'm not surprised, I'm shocked. I thought you were on *our* side."

I laughed. "Come on you two, lighten up. You came here because something wasn't working in your marriage, and because you both deserve a fulfilling sexual relationship. We've cleared out some of the emotional barriers. You're developing a good understanding of your Judger Selves and you're both strengthening your Learner Selves. You've made some practical changes. Next, we needed a real live conflict so we could study and correct what's been going wrong. If everything worked, how would we know what's been in the way? It was time for a test of what you're getting in therapy. You have to be able to *use* what you learn. Otherwise, this isn't *real*. At the end of the day, if therapy isn't practical and you haven't learned how to make and *keep* your relationship in good shape—what's the point?"

They both appeared to relax and nodded in agreement. After a moment I added, "Now, what question was I asking myself that had me say all that to you?" There was a longish silence. Then Jim grinned, and said: "You were probably asking yourself something like: '*What can I find valuable in the mess they made of that evening?*' " and we all laughed. Then Julie jumped in with another question: "I'm sure you also want *us* to ask ourselves, '*What can we learn from what happened?*' " I was pleased, and said so. "Great. You've been doing your Learner Self homework, and it shows."

I continued with, "Now, let's find out how well you're learning to think the way researchers and reporters do. By the way, how *do* they think? What are their main questions?" Julie responded first by recalling that researchers and reporters have to act like video recorders and tape recorders; they just pick up what's actually there and describe it. Jim added, "Their main questions are: "*What's going on here?*" and "*What's this?*" as he made a gesture like a detective looking through a magnifying glass. I responded with, "Good. Now please tell me what happened on your 'date.' "

Judger's Night Out, or A Romantic Evening Gone Awry   Julie and Jim had a pleasurable time at dinner and Jim was looking forward to his "reward" when they got home. However, they'd gotten back later than expected, as Jim had been delayed at the office, and they had gotten a late start for their date. It was well after what Julie called "my bewitching hour. I'm a 'goner' after that, and Jim knows it." Even so, he was disappointed, and had pouted, "Can't you just do me a quick little favor?" Julie retorted, "That's not *my* idea of romance," and they'd slept on opposite sides of the bed.

After they replayed the details, Jim remarked, "I'm amazed we explained something that was so emotional as calmly and objectively as that. Maybe we *are* learning something. If we'd tried to describe that night even a month ago, I probably would have ended up mad and yelling and Julie would have been in tears." She agreed, adding, "Our Judger Selves would have been out in vengeance." I commented, "This is useful; we're making good progress. Now, will you tell me more about what happens when your Judger Selves take over? You know what I mean, when you've gone on automatic." It was Jim who replied: "Well, I gave you a good display of that a few weeks ago. *That* kind of automatic is sort of like automatically out of control. There are other times when my Judger Self jumps on Julie, like when I feel really righteous for some reason, and say stuff to myself like *'What's <u>wrong</u> with <u>her</u>?' 'Why can't she just get it together like me?'* "

At this, Julie turned to Jim, started to speak, stopped, and finally said almost woefully, "That's when you start telling me everything that's wrong with me, especially sexually, or with my body, which I know isn't perfect. Then I feel like a failure, like I'll never be able to make you happy like I used to, so why should I bother trying, anyway? After that happens between us, that's when I'll only have sex in the dark. I ask myself: *'How come I can't ever measure up?'* or *'What's wrong with me?'* I start feeling hopeless, like it'll never be better for us, like I don't have any control, just like I felt around my parents, especially my father." She concluded with, "When we get into that vicious cycle I usually stay depressed for days."

I asked Julie if she recognized how much she was judging *herself*. She said she did, and also denied having any negative feelings toward Jim. I turned to him and asked: "Jim, do you know what gets you started being so judgmental toward your wife?" His expression turned to one of puzzlement, as he replied: "I haven't thought much about it. It's just that sometimes I snap out, like I've done ever since I was a kid, and then I get disgusted with myself." I asked if he remembered what happened just before his outburst at Julie in that earlier session. After a long silence, Jim's eyes opened wide, and he exclaimed: "Julie said something that felt like a put-down, so I got upset and wanted to retaliate."

Julie seemed miffed. "Jim, I have a right to feel hurt when you say mean things to me." Jim, looking annoyed, responded, "But Julie, *you* get mad at *me*, too, and put me down. *You* also act out your Judger Self on *me*." She was shaking her head from side to side, as if saying, "*I do <u>not</u>.*" I decided to step in.

[It was vital for the well-being of the marriage that they *both* take responsibility for their relationship *and* their own feelings. The time had come to challenge Julie. She would never be a fully *satisfied* partner if she were in therapy only "to make Jim happy," as she said in the first interview.]

"Julie, I can understand that Jim's comment might have surprised you a little. But you've learned enough here to realize that *everybody* has a Judger Self, and you've already talked about yours before. You know that the Judger part of us goes two ways—that Jim judges himself *and* you, and you judge yourself *and* him. And when you two get into a tangle, or a 'vicious cycle' as you put it, what's really happened is that it's like Judger's night out with you two, and *neither* of you remembers to call on your Learner Self for help. My question is: 'Who's going to be in charge, *you*—or your Judger Self?' Julie, if you're not aware that your Judger Self is operating, or even willing to acknowledge it, *guess* who's going to be in the driver's seat?"

Jim interrupted. "Julie, I can't believe this. I thought you were past your goody-two-shoes preacher's daughter routine. You get pissy and snippy with me, and you know it. I can feel it when you're judging me, like telling yourself I'm stupid or insensitive. Sometimes you get on your high horse and tell me: 'Oh, there you go again, acting just like a man.' I hate it when you do that. I'd rather you just tell me straight out what you're mad or upset about." Then Jim turned to me, and said: "This is one of the problems in our marriage, but I never realized it before. Julie won't tell me when she's mad, but I still get the cold shoulder for days, and lots of times I don't even know what I've done. . . ." Julie muttered under her breath, "I hate it when we get like this." Then she turned directly toward me, and demanded: "Who's fault is it, anyway? Who's *really* to blame?"

The Attack-or-Defend Battlefield   Seizing the opportunity, I commented: "Julie, you've just asked the *classic* Judger Self question, and I'm pretty sure you don't even realize it. Jim asks it, too. It's one that practically *guarantees* that you two will stay stuck on the Judger's battlefield." I looked at them both, and asked: "Does either one of you know what I'm talking about?" Jim started to defend his wife, though he looked a little confused as he commented, "It's *got* to be some-body's fault. Well, *doesn't* it?"

I replied, "Jim, that's exactly the point. As long as you're looking for fault, that's mostly what you'll find. Not only that, when you're only looking for fault, you'll hardly ever get beyond it. You'll stay stuck in the past, and reinforce prob-lems instead of finding solutions. Looking for someone to blame is like an extreme case of myopia."

Jim commented: "I read over the chart last night. You have blame all over the place on the Judger side, but the Learner seems pretty accepting and opti-mistic. The Learner just seems to stay focused on what's useful in anything." "That's on target, Jim," I replied. "The Learner also knows that letting the Judger be in control means *blaming* yourself or someone else all the time. It's like a prison you can't escape from. The key to freedom is a Learner question that basi-cally programs you to look for *solutions* instead of complaining about the situa-tion. Here's the deal: If all the power is with whatever's *outside* you, then you don't have any way to change things the way *you* want. You'll always be in danger of feeling like a victim, with no ability to make life any different. Let me put it to you this way: 'Would you rather have excuses and reasons for not being happy, or the power to have your life work, and the *real* chance to *be* happy?' "

Jim and Julie looked at each other, and Jim chuckled. "That's some choice you just gave us." I replied, "Jim, I know you're half kidding, and that's OK, but I *promise* that *knowing* you have that choice—it's like having the keys to the kingdom. That's what this is all about—turning you on to your own real power to be in control of your life." Julie said wistfully, "I've hardly ever felt in control. This is all new. The way I grew up, *everything* was judgment and blame—and I was *never* good enough. But if I *really* have a *choice*, I'd sign up for the Learner side of things." She sighed, and finished up, saying: "That chart's so *long*, though. I'll never remember it all." I touched her arm reassuringly, "You absolutely do have a choice, Julie. Lots of choices. And you always will. Don't worry about the chart. Just concentrate on asking Learner Self questions and you'll be just fine."

From the Battlefield to the Peace Table

Refocusing the session, I said, "Let's finish straightening out what didn't work about your date, especially how you handled your feelings that night, Julie. Before you can leave the battlefield, you have to admit you've been on it. I'm *sure* you can think of a time when you've been mad at Jim, and taken it out *on* him instead talking *with* him, and dealing with it. I don't know *anyone* in a long-term intimate relationship who hasn't ever done that, especially if you consider not doing it on purpose. Me included. Julie looked thoughtful, and finally commented slowly: "Now that you mention it, the night of our fiasco date I *was* upset with Jim for getting home late from the office. And then he didn't apologize or *anything*. That was the evening I was supposed to feel *special*. Ha! I just stuffed my feelings inside, as usual. But we did have a good time at dinner, so I didn't think about it any more. And it really was too late for sex when we got home." Then, seeming embarrassed, she looked down and said quietly, "And I guess I didn't want to either. I guess I was still mad."

Many therapists have experienced those rare, but precious occasions, when the therapy office seems filled with grace, and everyone senses a healing shift has occurred. This was one of those times. Jim looked at me as if to ask: "Was *that as good as I think it was?*" I nodded to him and smiled at them both. "Good work, Julie. It really took something to admit that, to yourself *and* to us." Julie smiled shyly, giggled suddenly, and remarked: "In his sermons my father used to tell us that 'the truth shall set you free.' But I'll bet he never intended it to improve my sex life!" The three of us shared a hearty laugh at the thought. Then I continued, "OK, Julie, let's make sure we use this well. Let's figure out how you could have handled the evening differently if you had put your Learner Self in charge. Looking back to that evening, at what point did you know you were angry at Jim?"

Julie replied easily, "As soon as he came in late and didn't apologize, or say anything about it. I didn't want to mess up the rest of the night by mentioning anything about his being late—I didn't want him to get mad at me for getting mad at him. And I thought if I stayed cool, I'd be more likely to be 'in the mood' later, because I was really looking forward to feeling close." She hesitated, and added, "Even though things *are* better between us, I've missed that feeling of closeness so much. I guess I've missed feeling sexual, too, I just didn't want to admit that either. And, well, the truth is, when I was mad I really didn't know what else to do except be nice, and smile, as usual." Julie paused, and commented, "I guess I wasn't as nice as I thought."

I said, "Julie, it's good to hear you claim your own sexuality. It's a precious birthright, and so important to your experience as a whole woman and as an adult. Now, I'm curious about those feelings of anger. What happens to them when you're upset with Jim?" She replied musingly, "The only way I know how to stop being angry and cool off is to get distant. But when I feel distant, I obviously can't feel close." Turning to Jim she said, "I need to feel close to you *before* I can feel sexual. And *certainly* before I feel like doing 'you know what.' " I glanced at Jim and almost laughed out loud at the expression on his face. He obviously had just made the connection between *his* behavior and his sex life. He practically sputtered, "I'm a pretty basic guy. Let me get this straight. You're telling me that when I do something dumb and make you mad and we don't deal with it, that eventually *the cost is that you don't want to have sex??!*" Julie replied, looking sheepish, "Well, it sounds awful when you put it so bluntly. But, yeah, I guess that's about it."

Peace Promise Review

"The peace promise makes sense to me now," Jim said, "although it seemed pretty dumb when you first told us about it. But now I can see that just that one move—calling up my Learner Self to be in charge—changes *everything*. It all depends on my Learner Self getting stronger than my Judger Self when I need it to, which is probably most of the time. If I'd been able to get out of my Judger stupor that night and wake up my Learner, I would have just apologized for being late and I wouldn't have been such a dumbo when we got home after dinner. If I'd done that, I'll bet we wouldn't have ended up hugging opposite sides of the bed instead of each other." After a pause, he continued, "You know, I think most people are on automatic most of the time. I think *I'm* usually on auto pilot, myself." I smiled, and said, "That might have been so, Jim, but it was your *Learner Self* who just made that comment," and I noted that he looked pleased with himself.

[My use of the past tense with Jim was a purposeful linguistic move. If he didn't notice, and just "bought" it, it would imply that he had unconsciously accepted the presupposition of my statement—that he *used* to be on automatic all the time, the implication being, "*That was then, this is now.*"]

I continued: "Life is very different once you *really realize* that you always have a choice about putting on your Learner mindset or your Judger mindset.

However, for this to make a *real* difference in your life, you have to *keep* remembering. But don't worry. You'll have plenty of opportunities, since things happen every moment that give you the choice to react *or* respond. The essence—and the challenge—of being human is to *rise above* just reacting to everything, to purposefully put on your Learner Self hat, and make that *active choice* about who you'll be and how you'll behave. This is definitely *not* something you get just once and then you've got it forever. I smiled at Julie, and said sympathetically, "That would be like saying that when you diet to your goal weight, you never have to do anything to maintain it. And we know from experience that that's not true. Don't we, Julie?" She made a face, and nodded her head in agreement.

"Remembering to keep putting on our Learner mindset, and to observe and correct is a *daily* practice, and will be for the rest of our lives. And I said 'our' because it's *my* practice, too. Every day. All the time. That's what it takes to be awake and aware. This isn't just for people who want to handle problems. It's for *anybody* who wants to be more human, more effective, and more secure and loving with themselves, and everybody else, too."

Revisiting the Marriage Context Model

At the end of this conversation, Jim said thoughtfully, "This is all coming together now. We've given you lots of demonstrations of that handout, the one that shows the territory of the Learner Self and the Judger Self, and what happens when the Judger Self screws up." I reminded Jim that the handout was called the Marriage Context Model, and gave him an extra copy. I also handed him a Learner/Judger Chart, opened to the Relating section.

I commented, "Jim, let's go back to how you ask Julie to have sex." I asked him to read over the questions on the Learner/Judger Chart in terms of win-win versus win-lose marriages. He realized he had only been asking questions like: "How can I win?" and "How can I get what I want?" By not having asked, "How can we both win?" and "How can I help Julie get what she wants?" they had both suffered—and lost. Shaking his head, Jim said ruefully, "What I should have been asking myself was, 'How can I approach my wife for sex in a way that turns her on?' This is really ironic. By not going for win-win, I ended up not winning at all." Following this long conversation, I wasn't surprised that their mood was quite different when they showed up for their next appointment, which for logistical reasons was nearly a month later. Despite a near blow-up on Jim's part, they had what Jim called "a breakthrough."

Transforming Conflict into a Peace Process—and Sexual Success   Julie and Jim decided to have another date. Again they had a lovely dinner out together. To avoid the troubles of last time, they had wisely gotten an early start. But just as they got home, the telephone rang. Jim pleaded with Julie not to answer, but she said, "You *know* I have to, Mother's been so sick." Jim reported: "I started a slow burn right then, and went upstairs because I couldn't stand it. She was on the phone with her mother for *over 20 minutes*. At first, all I could do was pace, and punch one hand into the other, and think things like, *'How could she do this to me?'* My mind was just racing. And then I noticed it was like a Learner/Judger battle going on in there. My Judger Self said things like, *'She cares more about her mother than she does about you. Why are you putting up with this?'* and then my Learner Self would say: *'What would she want you to do if the tables were turned?'* Then my Judger Self said: *'Shouldn't her husband be the most important person in her life?'* Then my Learner Self said: *'Maybe you shouldn't take this so personally'* and finally it asked, *'Is this really as big a deal as you're making it?'* "

[The fact that Jim could identify this internal Learner/Judger debate *while it was happening* meant that he had taken an observing stance toward his own mental process. This represents the establishment of a new cognitive skill that grants him the freedom to discern and choose attitudinal and behavioral alternatives that were previously invisible, and therefore hadn't been available to him.]

"Suddenly, the whole thing started to seem funny. The two of us were acting like a puppet show that was on automatic control—especially *me*. *(He rolled his eyes at this last comment.)* We've had different versions of this fight hundreds of times. I even imagined you watching the two of us. That was pretty embarrassing because I was acting like a child, not an adult. So I decided to do something different this time. I *made* myself walk slower and take deep, slow breaths. I admit I even used that cheat sheet on fighting you gave us. Anyway," Jim finished, grinning widely, "My Learner Self won. I was actually calm and in a pretty tame mood when Julie came upstairs."

Julie picked up the story from there. "I was dreading going to the bedroom. I expected Jim to look hurt and pouty, and say something sarcastic like how much he *hates* being right that I always have excuses to avoid sex. I was prepared for the worst, which was really sad because the *truth* was that I had been looking forward to coming home. I *wanted* to make love. It was the first time in a good while that I felt sexual. I was so upset about answering the phone and I *wouldn't* have, if mother weren't so ill. I felt like no matter what I did, I was going to hurt somebody, especially me. So you can imagine how shocked I was when I walked in the bedroom, and Jim smiled, and said, 'Hi Sweetheart, how's your mother?' like he really meant it."

Julie's eyes got a little misty, then she composed herself, smiled at Jim, and continued. "I was so relieved—and grateful—that I almost started crying. I really *was* upset; Mother had been to the doctor's that afternoon and he wanted to do some emergency exploratory surgery. I just needed for Jim to understand and not take the whole thing so personally. So when he held out his arms to give me a hug, I felt *wonderful*. Then we got under the covers and talked and kissed a little, and snuggled like we haven't in ages. I told him how much I appreciated him and how glad I am I married him. And we fell asleep like that."

Jim's eyes fairly twinkled as he took up where his wife left off. "Julie's too shy to tell you what happened in the morning. But *I'm* not. She woke me up with a wonderful surprise. *Guess* what she was doing! And then she actually gave me a *choice.* She said, 'Do you want me to keep going, or should we just have regular sex?' Now, *there's* a question that's music to my ears." I must have looked at Julie quizzically, because she explained, "Well, I was feeling so good, and so well taken care of, that it just seemed natural. It really didn't matter what we did. He was so wonderful that night that I felt like giving him anything he wanted, and I knew that if I did '*that*' he would love it."

Julie paused, and looked thoughtful. "You know, when we started here, it seemed like the problem was all with me. We both thought so. But we've accomplished a lot. Jim's done something I wouldn't ever have believed. He's really thought about himself and about us. He realized some things he didn't like about himself, and he apologized, and he's worked really hard to change. I know I have, too. This is still new for me, but I make a point now of telling him more what's going on with me, the hard stuff *and* the good stuff. So that morning I wanted to make sure he heard what was good, to know how much I appreciated what he's accomplished. And besides," she said, smiling at me, "That morning in bed, my question was: '*Since I feel so good, how can I make sure Jim does, too?*' " It was easy for me to reply by saying: "Julie, you get an A+!" Jim added, "From *me,* too!"

Pleased, I redirected my attention to Jim. I wanted to make sure we reviewed what had worked. And I was also curious about something. "Jim," I began, "Congratulations to you, too. You did a great job. You actually changed your emotional state on purpose when you realized it was going to hurt both of you. You did something to change how you were reacting physiologically. I can also tell you kept your peace promise, since you obviously called up your Learner Self to take over. You looked at the situation from Julie's point of view, and not just your own. From how you behaved with Julie, I can tell that you asked yourself win-win questions. You even remembered to consult the first aid handout, the Peace Process Guidelines, on handling conflict when you were upset and pacing around." Jim nodded in agreement at each point. "But here's what I can't resist asking you, Jim. Was there a special question, a personal one that made the difference, that turned it all around?"

Even I was surprised at how flushed Jim got and by his long, embarrassed silence. Finally a funny smile crossed his face, and he conceded, "I guess there's no way out of this. The answer is '*Yes.*' " He glanced at Julie, and said, almost pleading, "Julie, you know I love your mother." She nodded. "And you also know how self-righteous I can get." She nodded vigorously this time, rolled her eyes, smiled at him, and said, "That's for sure, but what was the *question,* dear?" He replied, only half teasing, "Well, I hope you still love me after this." He paused for another moment, and then said, "The question that did it for me was, '*Do I want to be right or do I want to get laid?*' " Julie did, indeed, look a little startled. But after a moment, she patted her husband on the knee, and said with a smile, "Jim, if that's what it takes to shut up your Judger Self and keep it away from me, I'm all for it!"

With this last interchange, I thought the session was done. But I was wrong. Julie interrupted our laughter and said, with more assertiveness than I had ever seen in her, "There's one more thing. And I *have* to say it." Jim and I both turned in our chairs to face her, and she paused, as if gathering her thoughts. "What made that night special was *more* than how good I felt. That night was also *important*. For the first time since we started having these problems, we got *beyond* the kind of fight that always made me feel so bad and made me doubt our marriage. That night I started to feel like I could trust *us* again. And the *real* star was Jim. What he used to do was get mad and *stay* that way, and then I never knew what was going to happen next. But this time, he knew he could be in control. He knew it was his choice if he wanted to *stop* that feeling and get his mind going in a different direction. And it worked!" Turning to him, she continued: "Like I said before, the fact that you were willing to change showed me that you care about our marriage—and about *me*. *That's* what made me feel so loved. And that's what made *me* want to act different, too."

Follow-Up

At a six-month follow-up, Julie and Jim appeared relaxed. There was a sense of lightheartedness, and they made a few warm, kidding comments to each other. I gave them each the Marriage Barometer, and asked them to mark it in two ways—for the marriage as a whole and for their current sexual relationship. They both gave the marriage and their sexual relationship a solid score of win-win. In discussing their therapy, Jim commented, "When we started, I thought this was really just a sexual issue. I didn't realize how much it affected our *whole* marriage. I had no idea about the Judger Self or how much it had taken over my life and Julie's, and was hurting us both. Just changing the question from '*What's wrong with her?*' to '*What's wonderful about her?*' makes a big difference because it makes me think about the good stuff." Of course, I asked Jim if he were still using his favorite question and he assured me that it worked like a charm almost every time.

Julie was pleased to tell me that they were having sex about once a week now, sometimes with intercourse and sometimes in "other ways." She added, "Now that there's hardly any tension around sex, it's much more fun. There's nothing to dread, no fight that's going to hurt for days. Even if we get into a little one, we can change it pretty quickly. I guess what I'm trying to say is that now that it's easier, and I feel more appreciated by my husband, and more connected to him—well, the truth is, I like to have sex more often, too."

SUMMARY

This chapter presented the case of Julie and Jim Quinn who came to therapy to resolve a sexual problem. The Quinn's therapeutic process was facilitated with use of several psycho-educational handouts. The therapist concentrated on helping both become accepting of their Judger Selves, strengthen their Learner Selves, and take responsibility for their individual contributions to the problem. Julie and Jim learned to recognize the power of their internal questions and use this information to help them bring honesty, appreciation, respect, and love back to their marriage—as well as resolve their sexual issues successfully.

PART FOUR

Conclusion

16

With Our Questions We Make the World

It is not the answer that enlightens, but the question.

—IONESCO

Chapter 1 asks "What Makes Questions Important?" and Chapters 2 and 3 explore the roles of questions in human functioning and in therapy. The rest of the book provides various theoretical and practical answers to these initial questions. Now, in this final chapter, we summarize those answers with an assertion that may seem hyperbolic: With our questions we make the world. The Buddha himself was the inspiration for this assertion. In a statement with which most cognitive-behavioral therapists would agree, he is reputed to have said, "With our thoughts we make the world." In that light, this book can be understood as inquiring of therapists: "Are you asking the right questions to help your clients make the worlds they want?" And that, of course, has been the whole point.

In section 1 we consider what it means to "make a world." In section 2 we explore further applications of the model of the Learner Self and the Judger Self by examining its utility in the context of organizations. In section 3 we turn our attention to what it takes to live as a skillful Learner Self. Finally, in section 4 we open an inquiry about win-win relating in the world at large.

SECTION ONE: WORLD MAKING

Fundamentally, this book is about how people create and inhabit their worlds through their questions, especially the internal ones, and how they can choose different worlds by choosing different questions with which to guide their lives. However, it seems that the less aware we are of our questions, the more power they have to influence, and often even control us. The premise argues for questions being more seminal than statements in directing our lives, since the moment of questioning is also the moment of choice which usually holds the greatest leverage for effective action and positive change. This leads to the conclusion that helping clients discover and alter limiting automatic questions, as well as learn to ask proficient questions in general, makes a significant contribution to the effectiveness and efficiency of their therapy, as well as to their personal and professional happiness.

These choices of how and what we think may represent each individual's greatest ongoing challenge. Recognizing that we choose much of what colors our cognitive landscapes is the prerequisite first step in taking charge of that very ability. Nonetheless, in the face of recognizing the reality of personal choice, life sometimes throws curve balls, situations which test the veracity of beliefs such as, ". . . there are always some alternative constructions available to choose among in dealing with the world. No one needs to paint himself into a corner; no one needs to be completely hemmed in by circumstances, no one needs to be the victim of his biography" (Kelly 1963, p. 15). Sometimes circumstances conspire to put ultimate challenges to our capacity to retain our humanness, our ability to exercise ". . . the last of human freedoms—the ability to choose one's attitude in a given set of circumstances" (Frankl 1963, p. 104). Loss, suffering, illness, and tragedies of all sorts belong in this category. Viktor Frankl was the Viennese psychiatrist who met his personal test incarcerated in a Nazi concentration camp, and after the war founded the existential school of psychiatry known as logotherapy.

In *Man's Search for Meaning: An Introduction to Logotherapy*, Frankl wrote, "Man does not simply exist, but *always decides what his existence will be*, what he will become in the next moment" (p. 206; italics added). He called the concentration camps "this living laboratory and . . . testing ground" (p. 213), and wrote: ". . . in the final analysis it becomes clear that *the sort of person the prisoner became was the result of an inner decision*, and not the result of camp influences alone. Fundamentally, therefore, any man can, even under such circumstances, decide what shall become of him—mentally and spiritually. He may retain his human dignity even in a concentration camp" (p. 105; italics added). This inner decision ". . . was an opportunity and a challenge. One could make a victory of those experiences, turning life into an inner triumph, or one could ignore the challenge . . ." (p. 115). Frankl clearly let us know that even in a concentration camp an individual makes choices about the "world" that he inhibits.

Furthermore, Frankl was aware of the decisive power of his internal questions. He wrote about a time in the camps when he thought death was near: "In this critical situation, however, my concern was different from that of most of my comrades. Their question was '*Will we survive the camp?*' The question which beset me was '*Has all this suffering, this dying round us, a meaning?*' " (p. 183; italics added). I speculate that Frankl answered "*Yes*" to this question, and went on to ask himself others such as: "*What is that meaning?*" "*What is that meaning for me?*" and "*How shall I find the courage to fulfill that meaning?*" Moreover, such questions would have been nested within a more global, context-setting one, such as, *"What attitude shall I choose, even here, and with what behaviors will I live it?"* Living in an unspeakable and dehumanizing reality, Frankl managed, in part through his questions, to distinguish a world that held meaning, and even worthy possibility.

Fortunately, few of us will ever have to bear a testing ground as severe as a concentration camp. But that does not diminish the lesson; in fact it is underscored. For if, even under those circumstances, Frankl and others were able to *choose* to turn "life into an inner triumph," does that not put the lie to any comforting presumptions that we are not responsible for the choices *we* make, or the worlds that *we* inhabit? The point is that a question has the potential to alter any circumstance, if we include in the definition of circumstance one's choice of attitude toward it. And what could be more "world making" than that? This premise leaves in its wake an important query for therapists, *"How can we impart a working knowledge of the power of questions to our clients, especially as this endows them with choice, freedom, and possibility?"* Another way to state this question would be, *"How can we help our clients strengthen their Learner Selves, and thus empower them to be more skillful, effective, and responsible in building the worlds they want?"*

Short-Term Question-Centered Therapy

Question-centered therapy utilizes the phenomenon of questions, both internal and interpersonal, to develop strategies that extend the range and types of therapeutic interventions which can be helpful with individuals, couples, and families, as well as with groups and organizations. It positions questions as the cornerstone of therapeutic interventions, as well as the basic linguistic tool for gathering information. The theoretical and practical aspects of question-centered therapy are organized around the metaphorical construct of the Learner Self and the Judger Self. Problems are associated with attitudes, behaviors, and ways of being and relating located in the Judger's domain. By contrast, the attitudes, skills, and personal resources required for resolving problems, as well as growing beyond them, are consistently located in the domain of the Learner. The basic goal of therapy, along with ameliorating presenting problems, is to facilitate clients' moving from a Judger-based life to a Learner-centered one. By extension, the same therapeutic intentions help couples develop win-win marriages.

The primary organizing strategy of question-centered therapy is based on a psycho-educational therapy model that empowers clients to think more clearly, and become more responsible, resourceful, skillful, and successful in living their lives. In large part, these abilities are based on becoming increasingly proficient self-observers, including noticing internal dialogue, especially self-questions. Clients are taught how to question their questions, that is, how to notice, analyze, and revise their internal and interpersonal questions in accordance with specific criteria and in support of particular goals. This method of choosing and using helpful questions is taught in the context of the model of the Learner Self and the Judger Self, which makes the concepts and tools relatively simple to learn and practical to implement.

Question-centered therapy trains and supports clients in developing specific cognitive, affective, and behavioral skills which underlie any mature individual's ability to make effective choices, experience personal freedom, and take responsibility for his or her own thoughts, feelings, and behaviors—both in terms of self-management and in relationships of all kinds. This therapy approach assumes that under optimal conditions, clients discover their own answers and sources of wisdom, and the questioning methodology provides specific tools for facilitating this process.

Question-centered therapy generally makes treatment more efficient since the right questions tend to go directly to the heart of the matter, while "wrong" questions often result in useless answers, needless detours, and often not reaching one's destination. Finally, question-centered therapy is sufficiently atheoretical that it can be integrated into any system of therapy, and adapted usefully with most clients, regardless of diagnosis or presenting problem.

SECTION TWO: THE LEARNER AND JUDGER IN ORGANIZATIONS

At the heart of the model of the Learner Self and the Judger Self is the construct that while language structures reality, questions help structure language. The utility of this construct and the model which builds upon it extend into the larger world beyond therapy. Organizations and businesses are an essential part of that larger world. While therapy and organizational consulting occur in different arenas and are driven by disparate goals, they share an intention of enhancing personal effectiveness. This is also the purpose of the model of the Learner Self and the Judger Self. Therefore, in this section, we consider some implications that the constructs, principles, and practices presented in this book hold in the world of organizations and businesses.

Personal Effectiveness and Organizational Life

Personal effectiveness is a bottom-line concern for organizations and businesses. From the highest level of leadership to the most basic levels of implementation, the ability of the individual to self-manage and think effectively and efficiently is of central—and increasing—importance. It should be second nature to thoughtfully ask oneself questions such as: *"Is my time best spent writing that report or planning for the meeting on Tuesday?"* or *"How can I make sure every member of our team is prepared for the interview with the new marketing director?"* or *"Am I thinking from the point of view of my department, or from the perspective of the organization as a whole?"*

Personal effectiveness is a more crucial variable in today's business and organizational world than ever before in history. At the same time, the challenges to mental and behavioral agility required for such effectiveness have never been greater. Consider the demands that today's business climate thrusts upon the individual. "Without doubt, today's ever-quickening cycle of (business) change is unprecedented . . . change that is marked by chaos in markets, businesses struggling to redefine themselves, organizational forms that no longer work, and management thinking that is quickly outdated. . . . A collision of technological, competitive, and cultural pressures is forming the vortex of what we have begun to call the 'information age' " (Campy and Nohria 1996, p. xiii).

This brave new technology-driven world, along with the dizzying complexity of globalization and the omnipresent bottom line, conspire to keep organizations on an impassioned search for new models and ideas of empowerment. As it turns out, some of the most forward-thinking and successful conclusions are consistent with the premises and practices presented in this book.

We will take a brief look at two of these, which share a recognition of the importance of questions with W. E. Deming, the originator of the Total Quality Management (TQM) movement, which is practiced by a majority of large companies worldwide. All three understand that progress in this rapidly changing world requires thinking, and that thinking *requires* asking questions. The gist of Deming's remarks in a speech in the late 1980s was: "The question is more important than the answer. The answer will always change, but the question shows that you are thinking. And thinking is what's important."

Learning Organizations

The term "learning organization," coined by Peter Senge (1990), has come to represent the ideal of organizational effectiveness for the 90s and beyond. In fact, a 1995 National HRD Executive Survey, conducted by the American Society for Training and Development, said that 94 percent of respondents felt it was important to build a learning organization (Gephart et al. 1996, p. 36). Further, a 1996 survey of almost 200 German companies found that, ". . . 90% consider themselves to be a learning organization, or are in the process of becoming one" (p. 36).

A learning organization is one ". . . that is continually expanding its capacity to create its future" (Senge 1990, p. 14). Such organizations are noted for learning that goes beyond that needed for merely surviving and adapting; they encourage "generative learning," that is, learning that potentiates creative and positive growth processes. The five learning disciplines of the learning organization are "personal disciplines," and do not refer to what might be considered traditional management practices. Each of the five is centered around how people think, what they most deeply value and want, and how they interact and learn with one another. Senge wrote, "Each provides a vital dimension in building organizations that can truly 'learn,' that can continually enhance their capacity to realize their highest aspirations" (p. 6). These five disciplines are: systems thinking, personal mastery, mental models, building shared vision, and team learning. Of course, question asking, both internal and interpersonal, plays a vital, irreducible role in each of these five disciplines. However, here we comment on just two of these.

Personal Mastery   We focus first on the discipline of personal mastery, the term Senge and his colleagues used to refer to intentional personal learning and growth, and which he described as ". . . an essential cornerstone of the learning organization" (p. 7). Developing employees with high levels of personal mastery is important to organizations because such people are more committed, take more initiative, have a deeper and broader sense of responsibility in their work, and generally learn faster (p. 143). For these reasons, learning organizations invest in improving employees' quality of thinking and empowering their capacity for reflection and inquiry (p. 289).

Many of the attitudes Senge noted as conducive to developing personal mastery are consistent with those valued, pursued, and exhibited by the skillful Learner Self. These include having a creative, responsive way of being as contrasted with a reactive one; being deeply inquisitive, seeing current reality as an ally, not an enemy; working with forces of change rather than resisting those forces; and viewing failure as an opportunity to learn and grow, rather than as a comment on one's unworthiness or powerlessness (pp. 141–143). Senge noted, "People with high levels of personal mastery are not just acquiring new information, they are continually expanding their ability to create the results in life they truly seek. From their quest for continual learning comes the spirit of the learning organization" (p. 141).

Team Learning and Dialogue   The second personal discipline we explore, team learning, provides a potent example of the construct that questions help structure the language that structures reality. Effective team learning depends on making a fundamental distinction between two primary types of discourse—dialogue and discussion. In his explication of these, Senge relied extensively on the thinking of physicist David Bohm (*The Special Theory of Relativity*, 1963). Senge wrote, ". . . Bohm's most distinctive contribution, one which leads to unique insights into team learning, stems from seeing thought as 'largely as collective phenomenon' " (Senge, p. 240).

Bohm pointed out that the word "discussion" suggests conversation resembling Ping-Pong, a game which is played by hitting the ball back and forth between players. Since the purpose of a game is to win, the individual's goal in a Ping-Pong-like discussion is have his views accepted by the group. By contrast, the goal of dialogue is to go *beyond* any one individual's point of view. Here, winning does not occur by an individual asserting, defending, or even dominating with his views. Rather, the *team* wins by developing collective insights that could not be achieved individually. Each participant in such a dialogue wins by virtue of the whole team winning. Senge wrote: "In dialogue, a group explores complex issues from many points of view. Individuals suspend their assumptions but they communicate their assumptions freely. The result is a free exploration that brings to the surface the full depth of people's experience and thought, and yet can move beyond their individual views" (p. 241).

Senge also noted that for dialogue to succeed, "Fear and judgment must give way. Dialogue is 'playful'; it requires the willingness to play with new ideas, to examine and test them" (pp. 245–246). Not surprisingly, the mental operation which permits and encourages dialogue occurs in the domain of the Learner. Recalling that self-observation is the primary ability undergirding the Learner's effectiveness, we find the Learner's propensity toward dialogue to be consistent with Senge's views. He wrote, "*In dialogue people become observers of their own thinking*" (p. 242; his italics).

Dialogue and the Learner   Dialogue shows up as open, creative, free-spirited, and generative. It is a product of the Learner's beginner's mindset, rooted in the recognition that not knowing represents an opportunity for learning and inventing. In fact, in dialogue one appreciates that not knowing is a *precondition* for learning and inventing. Discussion, however, is often a product of the Judger's knows-it-already mindset. It often appears to be closed, inflexible, defensive, and as "protecting one's turf." Since question asking is the primary linguistic move through which both Learner and Judger think and then express themselves, the distinction between dialogue and discussion naturally shows up through typical questions found in each type of conversation.

By example, in dialogue a Learner would typically inquire of self and others: "*What's of merit in this?*" "*What commonalities and patterns exist among our points of view that might point to a greater understanding?*" and "*What's missing in our thinking, the thinking of which could catapult us to previously unimaginable possibilities?*" On the other hand, in discussion the Judger might ask: "*How can I prove I'm right?*" "*How can I demonstrate my point?*" and "*What arguments would help me win?*"

It's as if the deep-structure question generating dialogue were something like, "*What questions would be future-focused, creative, solution-seeking, assume that helpful clues could be anywhere, and remain open to all possibilities?*" By contrast, the deep-structure question generating discussion would be a past-focused one such as, "*How can I protect myself* (the same as one's idea or project) *against all 'comers'?*" The self of dialogue is "I/We." It has permeable boundaries, and depending on circumstances, could be virtually boundless. On the other hand, the self of discussion is "I." It has discrete borders, and for whatever reasons, refuses to examine or relinquish them.

Naturally, the interactions, conversations, and realities generated by Learner questions and Judger ones would be distinct, a prediction we make based on the formulation that behavior largely represents answers to preceding questions, whether implicit or explicit. It becomes apparent that the Learner and the Judger, whether functioning as aspects of individuals, teams, or organizations, function in distinctive paradigms, and that the attitudes, behaviors, and outcomes generated by these disparate contexts would inevitably be quite different. Nonetheless, it is also the case that both kinds of discourse have their utility.

Managing Conversations   Particularly in a business environment, dialogue could only result in "all talk, no action," while discussion could produce decisions, action plans, and completed projects. Therefore, a Learner team or organization which understands the importance of strategically managing conversations would ask, *"What are our goals in this instance, and would dialogue or discussion most likely serve those goals?"* Increased efficiency and effectiveness would naturally result from managing conversations with such Learner consciousness. In fact, one might conclude that the most successful and generative learning organizations would be those peopled by the greatest critical mass of skillful Learner Selves.

Organizations of "Continuous Renewal"

The learning organization's focus on personal growth, including learning new attitudes and practices, is akin to that of organizations which Oakley and Krug (1991) designated as devoted to "continuous renewal." These authors describe revitalizing scores of companies and organizations based on their assumption that ". . . the way to create real and lasting change . . . is to *deal with the issue of attitude/mindset first,* or at least concurrently with . . . system changes" (p. 18; italics added). Asserting that a company's most valuable employees were those most open to change, Oakley and Krug found that these 20 percent were usually responsible for providing 80 percent of the effective work. This reinforces a general premise of the model of the Learner Self and the Judger Self—that attitude, or mindset, has a profound effect on behavior. Furthermore, the model of the Learner Self and the Judger Self emphasizes that attitudes are focused and operationalized by internal questions, a point with which Oakley and Krug strongly agree.

In a schema reminiscent of the Learner Self, Oakley and Krug subsumed the qualities and characteristics of the productive 20 percent of employees under the rubric "creative," while the foot-dragging 80 percent, who they characterized as "reactive," were relatively consistent with the Judger Self. Furthermore, Oakley and Krug asserted that the required paradigm shift—that is, moving people from the "disempowered state of reactive thinking to the empowered state of creative thinking" (p. 138)—depended on how attention and energy were focused. They described effective questions as the *"ultimate empowerment tool"* for doing this (p. 138; italics added). They wrote, "In simple terms, the human mind . . . works by continually looking for answers to questions. . . . Just as a car runs differently depending upon what type of fuel it uses, *the mind runs differently depending upon the kind of questions it is asked to answer"* (p. 139; italics added).

SECTION THREE: THE SKILLFUL LEARNER SELF

This book has been all about questions, especially internal questions, those unassuming directives that so quietly—and forcefully—shape our lives. However, a question has power only if someone *asks* it; and, as we have seen, a question asked by the Learner Self leads to quite a different world than the "same" question posed by the Judger Self. As we have said, in the model of the Learner Self and the Judger Self, symptoms, problems, and dissatisfaction are most associated with the Judger Self, and the goal of therapy is to activate or reinforce Learner Self aptitudes, attitudes, and skills, enabling clients to resolve their presenting problems, as well as lead their lives with more happiness and effectiveness. Therefore, we come to recognize that this book has fundamentally been about empowering the Learner Self, that part of each of us where lives the possibility of realizing the fullest and best expressions of our humanity.

In the preface I wrote that the major question guiding my clinical and theoretical work is *"What makes for real and <u>enduring</u> therapeutic success?"* The criterion of "real" depends on inquiring about deeply held values and developing goals and behaviors consistent with these. The criterion of "enduring" requires taking into account the passage of time and the human tendency toward what could be called "the New Year's Resolution effect," wherein we naturally become less proactive in our commitments as time rolls along. To counter such expected entropy, therapeutic methods that can be reliably and enduringly successful must be simple, natural, powerful, and repeatable. Yet such methods must also be flexible enough to change to accommodate new information, circumstances, and intentions.

The method of asking Learner Self questions fits all these criteria. It is simple to ask: *"Am I asking the right, or most effective, questions here?"* It is natural: We've been asking questions all our lives. It is powerful: This book has been filled with examples of the transformative power of questions. And effective questions definitely can, and should, be asked repeatedly. In addition, this method is flexible; at any moment one can ask: *"Is this question the best one to ask <u>right now</u>?"* *"What criteria should I (we) use in considering this?"* *"What do I (we) want this question to accomplish?"* and/or *"What questions could successfully take me, or us, in our direction of choice?"* Moreover, the model of the Learner Self and the Judger Self is a seaworthy cognitive lifeboat capable of supporting numerous and generative applications. For example, this last list of questions could accrue as much benefit for an organization or team as for an individual or couple.

Observe-and-Correct:
Life Discipline of the Skillful Learner Self

My answers to the question about real and enduring therapeutic success began with developing a model of being human that could encompass necessary healing as well as desired growth. A model may be thought of as describing a way of being. However, a model, no matter how well-conceived, is static; it requires a "doing mode" to activate its "being mode." As Senge told us, "Learning always involves new understandings and new behaviors, 'thinking,' *and* 'doing' " (p. 37; italics added). For a model to come *alive*, people need a method to render it practical and useful on a regular basis. Without a method of practice, the enduring success of psycho-educational change work is left too much to chance. Only through intentional practice can such new learning become integrated as a dependable empowered foundation for living.

The method of asking the *right question*, in the *right way*, at the *right time*, to the *right person* (especially to oneself) is the activation mode of the skillful Learner Self. Successful activation depends on consistent use of the strategic thinking method of observe and correct, including switching questions, which prescribes specific cognitive behaviors (i.e., Learner Self questions), and sequenced formats for asking these questions in relation to particular goals. To observe and correct consistently and successfully requires repetition and practice. Learning and integrating an intentional habit is best served through the discipline of regular, even daily, practice. This is the case, for example, in learning any sport, the martial arts, or meditation.

Moreover, the by-product of such practice is more than the sum of its parts. Ultimately, committed practice of a discipline such as observe-and-correct transforms the practitioner himself or herself in fundamental ways. Sophia, my client who we met in Chapter 10, illustrated this point when she commented, "Nowadays, if I fall into my Judger Self, I take my Learner eyes with me. I am not who I was before."

It takes practice to build one's strength as a skillful Learner Self, and operate one's personal and professional life in such a manner. This book has aimed at describing a method that is specific and practical enough that it *can* be practiced, a discipline of meeting each moment with the skillful Learner's beginner's mindset, rather than the Judger's knows-it-already mindset. As Senge observed: "To practice a discipline is to be a lifelong learner. You 'never arrive,' you spend your life mastering disciplines. You can never say, 'We *are* a learning organization,' any more than you can say, 'I *am* an enlightened person' " (pp. 10–11; italics added). Claiming to *be* a learning organization, or to *be* an enlightened person, would imply having *reached* one's destination, which is often the signal to stop.

But *life* goes on, and if we would go *with* it, rather than being overcome *by* it, we would best *choose to respond*, rather than merely react, to whatever comes our way—moment by moment by moment. In my opinion, Viktor Frankl exemplified the fulfillment of this evolved human capacity. It would have been easier for him simply to succumb to the tyranny of the camps, as any others understandably might when starved, terrified, or in pain. What made Frankl stand apart was his developed consciousness, an ever present realization that it was up to him to choose how to be in any moment, as well as what thoughts and behaviors would support and reflect that choice.

After all, in life it is our thoughts that come at us more than anything else, framed by whatever habits of thinking we have developed or cultivated. For this reason, observing and managing our thinking, especially our internal questions, should command a good deal of our respect and committed attention. If "by our questions we make the world," we had best be certain we ask effective ones, develop a well-trained habit of asking many of them, and make lavish use of a system for evaluating the questions we ask, as well as those that are asked of us—at least if we choose to have any control over the directions, experiences, substance, and legacies of our lives.

Skillful Learner Consciousness

Every one of us learned about life by asking questions. There is no substitute method. We are all Learners. In fact, Kelly wrote that: ". . . learning is not a special class of psychological processes; it is synonymous with any and all psychological processes. It is not something that happens to a person on occasion; it is what makes him a person in the first place" (1963, p. 75). However, there is a major distinction between asking questions to learn about life, in contrast with *choosing* questions to create the worlds in which we live. While we are all Learners, with the potential inherent in that state of being, not everyone chooses the consciousness required for raising himself or herself to the position of a skillful Learner Self.

While we are all human beings, not all of us step into the class of a Viktor Frankl. But we could. For Frankl, representing countless others throughout history, is simply an example. He was not a saint, and he let us know he had his fears and shadows like the rest of us. However, he shared an essential characteristic with others who've survived similar kinds of horrific circumstances. People as diverse as ". . . diplomats captured by terrorists, to elderly ladies imprisoned by Chinese communists" (Csikszentmihalyi 1990, p. 91) maintained their sanity, their dignity, and even their lives through some purposeful mental activity, by choosing to structure their consciousness around some goal, as Frankl did in wanting to learn about the meaning of "all this suffering we see around us."

The Structure of Choice   There is a pivotal, though subtle, learning here. It takes us beyond the particular ways these heroic individuals enabled themselves to prevail, rather than be prevailed upon. *The point is that they made the choice to do this in the first place.* It is this capacity to make a "choice of being" that separates a human being from any other kind of animal. It is seizing the opportunity to do so, against any reasonable odds, that separates persons like Viktor Frankl from others in similar circumstances. For the rest of us, the knowledge of such exemplary models might guide us in our everyday lives, and even inspire us to take on similar mantles should it ever become unfortunately necessary. The point is that understanding the structure of choosing—that is, of its essential question-driven nature—can contribute to making the empowering difference.

By birthright, the capacity to choose is part of what grants us the designation "human being." However, it takes the Learner-centered *behavior* of active and intentional choice to *earn* the status of *evolved* human being: one who often naturally and consistently observes and corrects in a thoughtful, positive, and solution-seeking manner. In some situations, the only possible solutions have to do with choice of attitude and frame of mind. It is probable that Frankl and countless others sustained themselves through implicit skillful Learner Self questions such as: *"Will I make an active choice to prevail, or a passive, default choice, and allow myself to be prevailed upon?"* and *"Regardless of the circumstances, who do I choose to be, and with what behaviors will I live that choice?"*

The Choice Model Revisited   Think of each moment of our lives as a clear choice point, as concrete as that depicted for the individual standing at the crossroads on the Choice Model. That figure represents every one of us. The arrow represents the whole range of things that might happen, from a flat tire to inhumane imprisonment. In each instance, the moment of impact will be followed by the inevitable decisions about what to do next. Choices that are reactive and passive place one on the downward trajectory leading to the Judger pit, from which it gets harder to recover with each successive landing. In sharp contrast, choices that are responsive and active position us on the high road, headed toward creating and inhabiting the world of the Learner Self. In truth, each moment of our lives *is* a crossroads, a time and place requiring at least an implicit decision about who we will be, and how we will act to fulfill our choices of being. Such moments are not always obvious, or dramatic, but such moments are always there, or rather, here.

Nonetheless, the concept of choice is abstract, as are the notions of responsibility and self-control. While each is an important, even noble sentiment, it is difficult to behaviorally fulfill such abstractions. *On the other hand, asking a question is not abstract; it is concrete and specific.* And knowing that Learner Self questions predictably lead to resolutions and win-win relationships gives clients an invaluable foothold, a "how to" that helps them place that all-important step on the ladder to experiencing, accomplishing, and having what they want.

The ability to choose, along with the capability to create options to choose among, is core to positive self-esteem and a sturdy sense of self-efficacy. Question-centered therapy positions the empowered capacity of personal choice as central to healing and growth, as well as fulfilling the possibility of living a life of evolved humanness. The more we therapists make this pivotal concept of personal choice behaviorally specific, simple, and practical, the more we support our clients in strengthening their Learner Selves. Question-centered therapy offers explicit methods for empowering people to walk that path. In working with its precepts and practices, we can help our clients understand and fulfill the enlivening possibilities inherent in the assertion: "With our questions we make the world."

SECTION FOUR:
THE LEARNER IN A WIN-WIN WORLD

Therapists are in the business of helping people solve their personal problems. We spend our careers intimately involved in helping people grapple with how to make their lives work. Yet we have a privileged opportunity and responsibility beyond that, granted by our status and training, as well as the trust accorded us by our clients and society at large. As a community of therapists, we can illuminate human possibilities beyond simply solving problems and getting along in life. We can also point to inspiring models of evolved humanness, empower our clients with reliable methods for growing in those directions, and call forth their desire to fulfill and pass along these important legacies to future generations.

Challenge, Opportunity, and Responsibility

Imagine any dark day in a concentration camp. Probably no one in those dire circumstances could focus on much more than living through the next few moments. Not in the wildest fiction could Viktor Frankl have imagined that his life, and his choices of mind, would someday restore hope to many in a world disillusioned by the cataclysm of the Holocaust. Frankl was just doing his best to live his life where he found himself, probably not thinking about the big picture of history, or the ripples that any life might cast into the future, much less his own. Along the same theme, my great grandmother, whom I mentioned in the preface, could hardly have imagined that a single spontaneous question to her young daughter would someday contribute to a great-granddaughter's love of books, and eventually to her writing one about the importance of questions.

Considered in this light, how can we therapists know the effect of our moment-to-moment interactions with our clients, and how could we predict ultimate outcomes of any of those moments, much less therapy as a whole? Furthermore, how can we know whether any particular client might be destined to evolve into a Frankl, or turn out to be a tyrant, either local or global? What we *can* say with confidence is that for some short time, in our sanctioned role as therapists, we influence the life directions our clients pursue. The point is that therapy, while aimed at helping people resolve personal problems, can also make a positive difference in the world at large. After all, many clients fill responsible social roles, most are explicit or implicit models for others, many work in organizations, and all are citizens in the larger worlds of their communities or beyond. What we provide them as therapists accompanies them into that larger world.

A Judger World or a Learner World?   If the world we inhabit at the end of the twentieth century represents our collective answers to our human questions, it's not much of a stretch to posit that automatic, reactive Judger questions and answers have dominated the scene. The customary, usually fearful, Judger questions, *"How can I avoid losing?"* and *"How can I win?"* inevitably restrict one's base of operations to the attack-or-defend paradigm. These questions, whether asked by individuals, couples, organizations, or countries, lead inevitably to win-lose relating, as well as to the win-lose Judger "reality" that characterizes our world, poised as we are at the end of the century as well as the end of the millennium.

Since this is the world we've inherited, it's natural to assume that its conditions represent the only possible reality. Nevertheless, in this book we explored an alternative perspective, one that is essential for therapeutic change. That perspective asserts that what is familiar is only one *version* of reality, and that others are possible. As Langer wrote, "When faced with something that hasn't been done before, people frequently express the belief that it can't be done. All progress, of course, depends on questioning this belief" (Langer 1997, p. 5). Change and progress, whatever the context, depend on asking questions. And change and progress are virtually the whole point of therapy.

Change and progress are also needed in this world we share, a world beset with problems, both large and small. We characterized our troubled human history as having been dominated by Judger thinking, expressed through automatic Judger questions and answers. Yet Einstein told us: "Our thinking creates problems that the same type of thinking will not solve" (Dilts 1994, p. 29). A win-lose world, created through Judger perceptions, fears, and questions, cannot evolve naturally into a win-win world. An altogether different, shared consciousness is required to lift us out of the Judger's win-lose paradigm and allow us the possibility of stepping into a win-win one. This recognition could lead us to speculate on an interesting question: *"If the Learner Self win-win mindset provides a foundation for individuals, couples, and organizations to resolve problems, as well as enjoy effectiveness and satisfaction, might the same be valid in society, in politics, and even for our planet as a whole?"*

Questioning Our Paradigms   In an earlier chapter, I wrote that one way to describe—or initiate—a paradigm shift is by asking questions from within the current paradigm that can be answered only from *outside* it. Soon we will live our questions in the information and computer-worshipping world of the twenty-first century. While the wonders of computers are truly awesome, this unprecedented historical phenomenon also calls for great collective caution. Information isn't necessarily knowledge; and it certainly isn't wisdom. Information is generated by questions, be they thoughtful, thoughtless, or foolish. In other words, information can only be as valuable as the questions that generate it—*and* the questions with which one responds to it.

We have explored the construct that language creates our worlds, and how pervasively, though usually implicitly, questions help structure language. The Choice Model and the Marriage Context Model graphically illustrated the consequences of choosing to ask questions either in the Learner's paradigm or that of the Judger. Learner questions position us to face the future in ways that are solution-seeking, committed to win-win relationships, and centered in taking responsibility for our choices. The questions generated by the Learner's beginner's mindset bring with them possibilities, creativity, and freedom. Learner questions open us to dialogue, where we can appreciate and learn from our differences, making it possible to include as well as transcend them in the spirit of evolution and the possibility of inventing new worlds together.

The Judger's problem-focused questions, on the other hand, dispose one to a future shackled to the past. The Judger's reactive, automatic emotionalism and knows-it-already mindset preempt clear-sighted, long-term thinking. Moreover, the win-lose goal of Judger questions forever imprisons one in its attack-or-defend paradigm. These crucial distinctions between the world created by the Learner and that created by the Judger illustrate how Learner questions have the power to catalyze new paradigms, while Judger questions do not, and cannot.

Let Us Inquire Together   In a world increasingly overwhelmed with information, we can ask Learner-centered, solution-seeking questions about what to do with all we know. As Learners we can join in creating an age of inquiry, rather than merely living in an age of information. Among our first questions would be: *"What will it take to step together out of the win-lose paradigm and into a win-win one?" "How can we accept and manage our individual and collective Judger tendencies?" "How can we be both loving and practical in creating a win-win world?"* and *"How can we remember to keep asking questions such as these?"*

Learner answers would be rooted in sensing the webs of connections that have always existed among individuals, families, society, and our physical world. I believe we share an intuitive knowing that any viable—even desirable—future, must pay homage to this knowledge and build upon it. As Learners we can join as participants in a living dialogue about a win-win future. This inquiry positions us outside the limitations of the Judger's paradigm, and creates a spaciousness where these question-centered methodologies can make the empowering difference. Taking advantage of the question-driven nature of choice and responsibility, we can dedicate ourselves to speak, listen, and act together in enlivening the spirit and expression of genuine community.

Bibliography

Albee, E. *Who's Afraid of Virginia Woolf?* New York: Pocket Books, Inc., 1963.

Andreas, S. *Virginia Satir: The Patterns of Her Magic.* Palo Alto, Calif.: Science and Behavior Books, Inc., 1991.

Andrews, F. *The Art and Practice of Loving.* Los Angeles: Jeremy P. Tarcher, 1991.

Bandler, R. and J. Grinder. *Structure of Magic: A Book about Language and Therapy, vol. I.* Palo Alto, Calif.: Science and Behavior Books, 1975.

Bandler, R. and J. Grinder. *Structure of Magic: A Book about Language and Therapy, vol. II.* Palo Alto, Calif.: Science and Behavior Books, 1975.

Bateson, G. *Steps to an Ecology of Mind.* New York: Ballantine, 1972.

Beck, A. T. *Cognitive Therapy and the Emotional Disorders.* New York: Penguin, 1979.

Beck, A. T. and G. Emery. *Anxiety Disorders and Phobias: A Cognitive Perspective.* New York: Basic Books, HarperCollins, 1985.

Binswanger, L. "The Case of Ellen West; An Anthropological Case Study," translated by Werner M. Mendel and Joseph Lyons from the original "Der Fall Ellen West," *Schweizer Archiv Für Neurologie & Psychiatric,* 1944, vol. 53, pp. 255–277, vol. 54, pp. 69–117, vol. 55, pp. 16–40. In May, R., E. Angel, and H. Ellenberger, eds. *Existence.* New York: Simon and Schuster, 1958.

Bloom, P. "The Creative Process in Hypnotherapy," Fass, M. L. and D. Brown, eds. *Creative Mastery in Hypnosis and Hypnoanalysis: A Festshrift for Erika Fromm.* Hillsdale, N.J.: Lawrence Earlbaum, 1990.

Bruner, J. *Child's Talk: Learning to Use Language.* New York: W.W. Norton, 1983.

Burns, D. D. *Feeling Good: The New Mood Therapy.* New York: Morrow, 1980.

Burns, D. D. *The Feeling Good Handbook.* New York: Penguin, 1989.

Cameron-Bandler, L., D. Gordon, and M. Lebeau. *Know How: Guided Programs for Inventing Your Own Best Future.* San Rafael, Calif.: FuturePace, 1985.

Cameron-Bandler, L., D. Gordon, and M. Lebeau. *The Emprint Method: A Guide to Reproducing Competence.* San Rafael, Calif.: FuturePace, 1985.

Cameron-Bandler, L. and Singleton, M. *Unpublished workshop materials.* San Rafael, Calif.: FuturePace, Inc., 1988.

Champy, J. and N. Nohria, eds. *Fast Forward: The Best Ideas on Managing Business Change.* Boston: Harvard Business Review, 1996.

Crystal, D. *The Cambridge Encyclopedia of Language.* Cambridge, England: Cambridge University Press, 1987.

Csikszentmihalyi, M. *Flow: The Psychology of Optimal Experience.* New York: Harper & Row, 1990.

Csikszentmihalyi, M. *The Evolving Self: A Psychology of the Third Millennium.* New York: HarperPerennial, 1993.

de Bono, E. *de Bono's Thinking Course.* New York: Facts on File, 1994.

de Shazer, S. *Putting Difference to Work.* New York: W.W. Norton & Company, 1991.

de Shazer, S. *Words Were Originally Magic.* New York: W.W. Norton, 1994.

de Torres, C. and D. Sauber. *Unpublished workshop materials.* Philadelphia, Pa., 1985.

Deikman, A. J. *The Observing Self: Mysticism and Psychotherapy.* Boston: Beacon, 1982.

Deikman, A. J. *The Wrong Way Home: Uncovering the Patterns of Cult Behavior in American Society.* Boston: Beacon, 1994.

Dilts, R. B. and T. Epstein. *Dynamic Learning.* Capitola, Calif.: Meta Publications, 1995a.

Dilts, R. B. *Strategies of Genius, vol. I.* Capitola, Calif.: Meta Publications, 1994a.

Dilts, R. B. *Strategies of Genius, vol. II.* Capitola, Calif.: Meta Publications, 1994b.

Dilts, R. B. *Strategies of Genius, vol. III.* Capitola, Calif.: Meta Publications, 1995b.

Efran, J., S. Lukens, and R. J. Lukens. *Language, Structure and Change: Frameworks of Meaning in Psychotherapy.* New York: Norton, 1990.

Ellis, A. *Reason and Emotion in Psycho-Therapy.* Secaucus, N.J.: Citadel, 1979.

Fisher, R., W. Ury, and B. Patton. *Getting to YES: Negotiating Agreement Without Giving In.* 2d ed. New York: Penguin, 1991.

Flores, F. "The Leaders of the Future." In Denning, P. J. and R. M. Metcalfe, eds. *Beyond Calculation: The Next Fifty Years of Computing.* New York: Springer-Verlag, 1997.

Frankl, V. *Man's Search for Meaning: An Introduction to Logotherapy.* New York: Washington Square Press, 1963.

Friedman, M. *The Healing Dialogue in Psychotherapy.* Northvale, N.J.: Jason Aronson, Inc., 1985.

Gallagher, J. M. and W. L. Wansart. "An Assimilative Base Model of Strategy: Knowledge Interactions." *RASE—Remedial and Special Education,* 12(3), 1991: 36–37.

Gelb, M. J. *Thinking for a Change: Discovering the Power to Create, Communicate, and Lead.* New York: Harmony, 1995.

Gephart, M. A., V. J. Marsick, M. E. Van Buren, and M. S. Spiro. "Learning organizations come alive." *Training and Development.* December, 1996: 35–45.

Gilligan, S. *The Courage to Love: Principles and Practices of Self-Relations Psychotherapy.* New York: W.W. Norton, 1997.

Goldberg, M. *Out of Control: The Subjective Experience Associated with Binge Eating Among Obese Females.* (Doctoral dissertation: The Fielding Institute.) *Dissertation Abstracts International,* 1986.

Goleman, D. *Vital Lies, Simple Truths: The Psychology of Self-Deception.* New York: Simon & Schuster, 1985.

Goleman, D. *Emotional Intelligence: Why It Can Matter More Than IQ.* New York: Bantam, 1995.

Gordon, D. "Modeling," *Anchor Point Magazine,* Sept. 1989, p. 1.

Gottman, J. *Why Marriages Succeed or Fail: And How You Can Make Yours Last.* New York: Simon & Schuster, 1994.

Grinder, J. and R. Bandler. *The Structure of Magic: A Book about Communication and Change, vol. 2.* Palo Alto, Calif.: Science and Behavior Books, Inc., 1976.

Grinder, J., J. DeLozier, and R. Bandler. *Patterns of the Hypnotic Techniques of Milton H. Erickson, M.D. vol. 2.* Cupertino, Calif.: Meta Publications, 1977.

Gross, R. *Peak Learning: A Master Course in Learning How to Learn.* New York: Putnam, 1991.

Guignon, C. *Heidegger and the Problem of Knowledge.* Indianapolis: Hackett, 1983.

Haley, J. *Uncommon Therapy: The Psychiatric Techniques of Milton H. Erickson, M.D.* New York: W.W. Norton, 1973.

Haley, J. *Problem-Solving Therapy.* San Francisco: Jossey-Bass, 1977.

Heidegger, M. *On the Way to Language.* San Francisco: Harper and Row, 1971.

Heschel, A. J. *I Asked for Wonder: A Spiritual Anthology.* New York: Crossroad, 1990.

James, T. and W. Woodsmall. *Time Line Therapy and the Basis of Personality.* Capitola, Calif.: Meta Publications, 1988.

Keeley, S. M. *Asking the Right Questions in Abnormal Psychology.* Upper Saddle River, N.J.: Prentice Hall, 1995.

Keeney, B. P. *Aesthetics of Change.* New York: The Guilford Press, 1983.

Keeney, B. P. *Everyday Soul: Awakening the Spirit in Daily Life.* New York: Riverhead Books, 1996.

Kelly, G. A. *A Theory of Personality: The Psychology of Personal Constructs.* New York: Norton, 1963.

Kirschner, D. A. and S. Kirschner. *Comprehensive Family Therapy: An Integration of Systemic and Psychodynamic Treatment Models.* New York: Brunner/Mazel, 1986.

Kirschner, S., D. A. Kirschner, and R. L. Rappaport. *Working with Adult Incest Survivors: The Healing Journey.* New York: Brunner/Mazel, 1993.

Kornfield, J. *Buddha's Little Instruction Book.* New York: Bantam Books, 1994.

Lakoff, G. and M. Johnson. *Metaphors We Live By.* Chicago: University of Chicago, 1980.

Langer, E. J. *The Power of Mindful Learning.* New York: Addison-Wesley, 1997.

Langer, S. K. *Philosophy in a New Key: A Study in the Symbolism of Reason, Rite, and Art.* Cambridge, Mass.: Harvard University, 1993.

Lazarus, A. A. *The Practice of Multimodal Therapy: Systemic, Comprehensive, and Effective Psychotherapy.* Baltimore: Johns Hopkins University, 1989.

Maher, J. M and D. Briggs, eds. *An Open Life: Joseph Campbell in Conversation with Michael Toms.* New York: Harper & Row, 1989.

Manning, M. *Undercurrents: A Life Beneath the Surface.* New York: HarperCollins, 1994.

Markman, H., S. Stanley, and S. L. Blumberg. *Fighting for your Marriage: Positive Steps for Preventing Divorce and Preserving a Lasting Love.* San Francisco: Jossey-Bass, 1994.

Maturana, H. R. and F. J. Varela. *The Tree of Knowledge: The Biological Roots of Understanding.* Boston: Shambala, 1987.

May, R. *The Courage to Create.* New York: W.W. Norton, 1975.

Middelton-Moz, J. and L. Dwinell. *After the Tears: Reclaiming the Personal Losses of Childhood.* Deerfield Beach, Fla.: Health Communications, 1986.

Milgram, S. *Obedience to Authority.* New York: Harper and Row, 1974.

Minuchin, S. *Families and Family Therapy.* Cambridge, Mass.: Harvard University Press, 1974.

Needleman, J. *A Little Book on Love.* New York: Doubleday/Currency, 1996.

Oakley, E. and D. Krug. *Enlightened Leadership: Getting to the Heart of Change.* New York: Fireside Book, Simon and Schuster, 1991.

O'Hanlon, B. and J. Wilk. *Shifting Contexts: The Generation of Effective Psychotherapy.* New York: Guilford, 1987.

Penzias, A. "Questions That Illuminate," *Benchmark Magazine,* Fall 1991.

Postman, N. *Crazy Talk, Stupid Talk.* New York: Delacorte, 1976.

Postman, N. *The End of Education: Redefining the Value of School.* New York: Knopf, 1996.

Rilke, R. M. *Letters to a Young Poet.* New York: Vintage Books, 1984.

Schank, R. C. and C. Cleary. *Engines for Education.* Hillsdale, N.J.: Lawrence Erlbaum Associates, 1995.

Seligman, M. E. P. "Depression and learned helplessness." In *The Psychology of Depression: Contemporary Theory and Research.* R. J. Friedman and M. M. Katz, eds. Washington: Winston-Wiley, 1974, pp. 83–113.

Seligman, M. E. P. *Learned Optimism.* New York: Knopf, 1991.

Senge, P. *The Fifth Discipline: The Art and Practice of the Learning Organization.* New York: Doubleday/Currency, 1990.

Shadish, W. R., L. M. Montgomery, P. Wilson, M. R. Wilson, I. Bright, and T. Okwumadua. "Effects of family and marital psychotherapies: A meta analysis." *Journal of Consulting and Clinical Psychology,* vol. 61, 1993: 992–1002.

Shapiro, D. H. Jr., C. E. Schwartz, and J. A. Astin. "Controlling ourselves, controlling our world: Psychology's role in understanding positive and negative consequences of seeking and gaining control." *American Psychologist,* 51(12), 1996: 1213–1230.

Singleton, M. *Rapporter.* Cottonwood, Arizona. 1986, p. 3.

Tomm, K. "One perspective on the Milan systemic approach: Part I. Overview of development, theory and practice." *Journal of Marital and Family Therapy,* 10, no. 2, April 1984a: 113–125.

Tomm, K. "One perspective on the Milan systemic approach: Part II. Description of session format, interviewing style and interventions." *Journal of Marital and Family Therapy,* 10, no. 3, July 1984b: 253–271.

Tomm, K. "Interventive interviewing: Part III. Intending to ask lineal, circular, strategic, or reflexive questions?" *Family Process,* 27, March 1988: 1–15.

Welwood, J. "Reflection and Presence: The Dialectic of Self-Knowledge." *The Journal of Transpersonal Psychology,* 28(2), 1996.

Wilber, K. *Sex, Ecology, Spirituality: The Spirit of Evolution.* Boston: Shambhala, 1995.

Wilen, W. W. *Questioning Skills for Teachers.* Washington, D.C.: National Education Association, 1982.

Winnicott, D. W. "Transitional Objects and Transitional Phenomena." In *Collected Papers.* New York: Basic Books, 1958.

Winograd, T. and F. Flores. *Understanding Computers and Cognition.* Reading, Mass.: Addison-Wesley, 1986.

Winter, D. *Ecological Psychology: Healing the Split Between Planet and Self.* New York: HarperCollins Text, 1996.

Index

LTSS Lineberger Memorial Library

3 5898 00116 1195

RC 489 .N47 G65 1998
Goldberg, Marilee C.
The art of the question

F98319

LINEBERGER
MEMORIAL LIBRARY
LUTHERAN THEOLOGICAL
SOUTHERN SEMINARY
COLUMBIA, SOUTH CAROLINA 29203

DEMCO